THE BOOK OF
MOVIE
PHOTOGRAPHY

DAVID CHESHIRE
THE BOOK OF
MOVIE
PHOTOGRAPHY

The complete guide to better moviemaking

Alfred A. Knopf New York, 1987

Project editor Alan Buckingham	**Art editor** Ron Pickless
Editors Fiona MacIntyre Jonathan Hilton **Picture researcher** Angela Murphy	**Designers** Pauline Faulks Mark Richards Michele Walker
Managing editor Amy Carroll	**Art director** Stuart Jackman

For Catherine

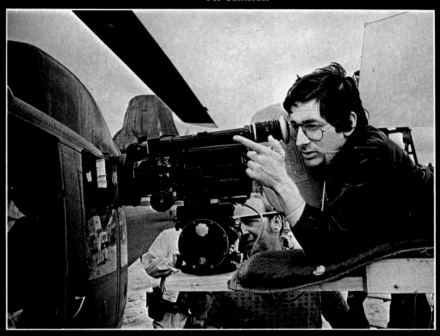

This is a Borzoi Book published by Alfred A. Knopf, Inc.

The Book of Movie Photography was conceived, edited and designed by
Dorling Kindersley Limited, 9 Henrietta Street, London WC2

Copyright © 1979 by Dorling Kindersley Limited, London
Text copyright © 1979 by David Cheshire

Published in the United States by Alfred A. Knopf, Inc.,
New York, and simultaneously in Canada by Random House of
Canada Limited, Toronto

Distributed by Random House, Inc., New York

Library of Congress Cataloging in Publication Data
Cheshire, David F 1944 –
  The book of movie photography.
  Includes index.
  1. Cinematography. 2. Amateur moving-pictures.
I. Title.
TR851.C44 1979   778.5'3   79–2128
ISBN 0–394–50787–8

Printed in Italy by A. Mondadori, Verona

First published October 30, 1979

Reprinted twice

Fourth Printing July 1987

Contents

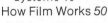

Introduction

It has been estimated that over a quarter of a million movies have been made since the invention of the Cinématographe in 1895. This represents about five million miles of film, or fifty years of continuous viewing, day and night: clearly, even in these crude numerical terms, filmmaking is by far the most dynamic art form of the twentieth century. What is more, no other form of creative self-expression except still photography is so widely practiced by amateurs. Home movies, in sound and color, can achieve, even on the simplest equipment, a sophistication that it took the feature film industry decades to attain. The amateur can now call on a whole battery of conventions and traditions that were painfully invented – or perhaps one should say discovered – by the pioneer filmmakers: the cutaway, the close-up, the pan, the track, the flashback and the dissolve are now all accepted without question as narrative signposts in the language of film.

Narrative, indeed, is at the heart of film. Unlike still photography, film is a sequence, a procession of sounds and images from which we naturally draw conclusions. From just two shots, say of a gravestone and a weeping woman, it is inevitable that we build a story. And the same applies with equal force to the simplest form of home movie: the job of any filmmaker is to manipulate the materials at his command so that the story he is trying to tell is lucidly and powerfully expressed.

This book proceeds on the premise that certain broad, fundamental principles apply to all moviemaking, both amateur and professional. For the aspiring amateur, there is no faster way of learning how to make a film than to go to the movies – except perhaps watching television. Once you have developed a habit of watching movies with an eye for pace, cutting and framing, your own films will benefit enormously. For that reason, this book includes a number of extracts from great movies of the past. These are shown as *sequences*, for no shot in a film exists in isolation. Like a note in music, or a word on a page, it has meaning only in relation to its neighbors. It is the filmmaker's job to guarantee that the notes are in the same key and that they are singing the same tune.

As a means of communication, only television is more complex than film, and as your moviemaking becomes more and more ambitious, your imagination will make increasing demands upon your technical knowledge. This book is designed so that if you wish you can progress from the simplest "aim and fire", unedited home movie, to sophisticated, dramatized films with all the refinements of double system editing, stereo sound and widescreen projection. Choosing the equipment, planning, shooting, editing and projection lie in an unchanging sequence which you can follow through the book.

In the process of offering advice, it may often seem that we are prescribing a "right" or "wrong" way of doing things. In fact, of course, all such rules are made to be confidently discarded once you have learned enough to know what it is that you are throwing away. It is fair to say that there is not a single rule in any book that cannot be broken if your skill is great enough. On the other hand, you cannot expect to blunder into excellence: there is no substitute for experiment and experience.

Film and the image
Bernardo Bertolucci used the flag to express political attitudes in his film, *1900*.

Film and dramatic effect
Ken Russell began his movie on the life of Gustav Mahler with this sequence of house consumed by fire an example of images used to convey abstract ideas.

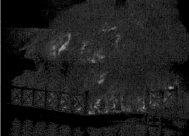

Film and composition (right)
David Lean set the night-time procession on converging railroad tracks in the frozen Russian countryside to produce a provocative image in his film, *Dr Zhivago*.

Film and the Single Shot

Film expresses itself not only by cutting between separate images but also by varying the image-content of one continuous shot. The most satisfactory and complex way of achieving this is through the moving camera. The single shot illustrated on this page, which Orson Welles filmed in 1941 for *Citizen Kane*, is one of the most flamboyant single shots ever filmed. He described the set of RKO Studios, where he was given a free hand in his first picture, as "the best train-set any boy could have". Here the "toy" is used to the full. As Gregg Toland, the cameraman on the film, put it: "Welles was insistent that the story be told most effectively, letting the Hollywood conventions of moviemaking

go hang if need be". This "exterior" shot was filmed indoors.

In this single crane shot, Welles encompasses the pathos of Susan Alexander Kane's whole career: her husband, the newspaper magnate and the "Citizen" Kane of the film's title, has forced her to become a singer – a task for which she is grotesquely unsuited. The camera soars upwards, through the driving rain, through the very middle of the neon sign pronouncing her fame, through the glass of the skylight and down into the night-club where she is crying. The shot is both eloquent and astonishing. Here, the camera is not mimicking the eye; it is an entirely new way of seeing.

Opening shot
The single camera shot, which lasts for 25 seconds, begins with a white screen – a lightning flash – which passes to reveal a hoarding on which there is a poster of Susan Alexander Kane. The bill poster gives no sense of scale. The one-frame lightning flash and the rain driving across the screen are all studio effects.

1a ⏱ 25 sec Lightning flash

1b The poster of Kane's wife

1c A second lightning flash

Crane shot
After further lightning flashes, the camera cranes slowly upwards above the poster to reveal the brick wall on which the hoarding is mounted.

1d The camera cranes upwards

1e The view over the roof

Crane shot continues
Still in the course of the single shot, the camera cranes further upwards. The poster disappears from the frame and we see the view over the top of the wall and across the wet roofs to a neon sign flashing in the distance.

Track forward
At this moment the camera begins to track forward, rising clean over the roof of the building and moving relentlessly toward the neon sign. We see Susan Alexander Kane's name up in lights.

1f The neon sign appears

1g Tracking forward

Tracking shot continues
As the camera approaches nearer to the sign, it tilts upwards and we discover that Susan is singing in a cabaret show at a night-club called "El Rancho". We can now also see the light from inside the club shining through the glass skylight.

Track up to the sign

The rain still teems down onto the set and there is another vivid flash of lightning. Meanwhile, the camera continues its steady track towards the sign. The neon letters which spell out Susan's name gradually fill the frame.

1h A further lightning flash

1i The track continues

1j The sign grows larger

1k The camera reaches the sign

1l The sign parts

1m The camera passes through

Track through the sign

In one continuous movement the camera tracks into the middle of the neon sign. Unbelievably, the sign itself parts, allowing the camera to pass effortlessly through. This was done by dismantling the sign in the studio during the filming of the shot.

Track and tilt

Having passed through the night-club sign, the camera tracks and tilts down to the skylight in the roof. There is rain drumming on the glass but, as the camera moves closer and closer, we can just see the slumped figure of Susan Alexander Kane at one of the tables in the empty club.

1n The skylight appears

1o Tilt down to the skylight

1p The view through the skylight

Dissolve

The view of Susan blurs, and an extreme close-up of the rain on the skylight dissolves into a new shot. Even Orson Welles was not able to track straight through a pane of glass. However, the dissolve is quite difficult to spot -- the effect is of a continuous shot.

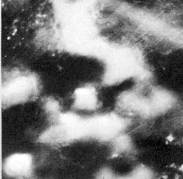

1q Dissolve

2 The interior of the night-club

New interior shot

This new shot of the inside of the night-club opens from the same camera position as the last shot -- high up in the corner of the room, looking down on Kane's wife. Thus, the camera's progress over the roof, in between the words of the sign, through the glass skylight and into the room appears smooth and uninterrupted.

Film and the Creative Use of Color

Color can be manipulated to reflect not only mood but also very subtle aspects of personality. One of the most adventurous modern attempts to manipulate color came with Michelangelo Antonioni's first color film, *Red Desert* (1964). This is essentially the study of a woman (Guiliana), played by Monica Vitti, who is neurotically isolated from her environment. The hideous factories, canals and docks near her home on the east coast of Italy are filmed in relentless grays and pastels, with misty soft-focus that emphasizes her own detachment. Antonioni even went so far as to paint fruit gray, and on another occasion he re-painted her bedroom pink after Guiliana,

on the verge of insanity, had made love to Corrado. In the scene illustrated, Guiliana is telling a story to her son Valerio. The story, which is of course a fantasy, vividly expresses her desperate longing for freedom, childhood and natural beauty.

Antonioni conceived this unreal and magical vision in dazzling primary colors, over which there is nevertheless a faint, but deliberate, tinge of pink. The symbolism of the unattainable sailing boat, as of other-worldly singing which the girl hears, is reinforced by the grim return to reality at the end of the story; as if only the world of the imagination is natural.

Boy: "Tell me a story"

Guiliana's story
As Guiliana begins her story we cut to a de-focused shot of the beach which pans down to the little girl in the sea. The translucent beauty of the water is an astonishing contrast to the filthy canals that we have seen near Guiliana's home. The cormorants, seagulls and wild rabbits further reinforce the imagery of natural paradise.

Mother: "Once a little girl lived on an island. Grown-ups bored and frightened her, so did the children who played at being grown up"

1 ⏱ 11.5 sec The mother turns to the boy

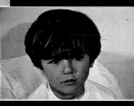

2 ⏱ 3 sec Close-up of her young child

3 ⏱ 18.5 sec The mother and child on the bed

4a ⏱ 6 sec Cut to unfocused shot of beach

4b ⏱ Pan to young girl swimming

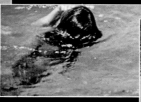

5 ⏱ 2 sec Girl swims underwater

"She was always alone . . ."

6 ⏱ 3.5 sec She surfaces

7 ⏱ 4 sec A cormorant swimming

"With the cormorants . . ."

8 ⏱ 3 sec A seagull on the rocks

"The seagulls . . ."

9 ⏱ 6 sec A rabbit on the water's edge

"And the wild rabbits . . ."

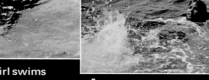

10a ⏱ 14 sec Beginning of tilt from rocks

10b ⏱ Tilt ends on long shot of girl swimming

The beach
The transparency of the sea and the pink sand are almost gloated on by the camera: "The colors were so beautiful and there was no real noise at all".

"She had discovered a little beach far from the crowds where the sea was transparent and the sand was pink"

11 ⏱ 11.5 sec End of pan from the sea

12a ⏱ 17 sec Beginning of pan from beach

12b ⏱ End of pan in deeper water

13 ⏱ 12.5 sec The girl comes out of water

14 ⏱10.5 sec She hides behind some bushes

15 ⏱4.5 sec White sail on the horizon

16 ⏱3.5 sec Aerial view of sailboat

17 ⏱4.5 sec Aerial view of two boats

"One morning she saw a sail on the horizon. The boat was different. It was a red sailing ship . . ."

She is alone

There is a further sequence of shots (left and below) used to extend the sequence and to convey the fact that the girl has often visited the beach and that she is alone.

She sees the ship

As the boat approaches, two other boats are seen with brilliant blue and red sails. The boat seen in the distance also has strong primary colors. It represents the approach of vigorous, romantic possibilities. It has "weathered the seas and storms of the world and, maybe, beyond the world . . .". The girl leaps in to the sea and swims towards it.

18 ⏱16.5 sec The white-sailed boat approaches

19 ⏱5 sec It gets closer

20 ⏱6 sec The girl jumps into the sea

"From afar it was a splendid sight. Close to, it had a look of mystery. Was there anyone on board? It stayed motionless for a few minutes, then it veered off and sailed away as silently as it had come."

21 ⏱9 sec She swims towards the boat

22 ⏱4.5. sec They get closer

23 ⏱1.2 sec Close-up of the girl

⌒24 ⏱6 sec Boat approaches

The ship disappears

The boat at first seems to be swinging towards her, but at the last minute it veers away and disappears over the horizon. No-one is ever seen on board.

25 ⏱4 sec Side view of the boat

26 ⏱3.5 sec Boat sailing in middle distance

27 ⏱3 sec Boat sailing far away

Reality

After the disappearance of the boat there follows a sequence in which the girl hears a mysterious and haunting voice singing. Indeed, "everything was singing", says Guiliana, to whom Antoniono cuts abruptly as though to interrupt her dream. The brutal awakening is further hardened by a cut to a ship steaming down the canal outside the window. This is the ship that was glimpsed in shot 1

28 ⏱7 sec Cut to mother's face

29 ⏱4.5 sec Oil tanker sailing from harbor

11

Film and the Power of the Cut

The so-called New Wave of the early sixties was essentially a highly sophisticated way of throwing traditional "rules" out of the window. In particular, one of the best-known of the new French directors, Jean-Luc Godard, brought a vivid spontaneity to the big screen that had in the past been associated with smaller gauges and experimental films. The storm of controversy which the movement provoked broke with *A Bout de Souffle* ("Breathless", 1959), which, according to Godard, was intended partly as a tribute to American gangster movies of the thirties and forties such as *Scarface*. Godard's use of natural lighting, unpredictable narrative, wayward moods, jump cuts and reverse cuts is both disconcerting and exciting. The film's narrative is still there – but it is reduced to a kind of shorthand and is told in a quite original way. In this kind of anti-editing, the passage of time is reduced to a straight cut, reverse angles and jump cuts are accepted and, in the more extreme forms of the genre, relished. Whereas the function of smooth, classical editing is to be invisible, *anti-editing* (as it might be thought of) is designed to draw attention to the process of filmmaking itself. In this scene where Michel (Jean-Paul Belmondo) shoots a policeman, the disjointed jump cuts and reverse cuts convey a powerful impression of a man on the run.

The opening shot
Michel, having stolen a car, is being chased by two policemen on motor cycles. His car engine has broken down, he has turned off the road and, although still clearly visible, he has pulled up on a dirt track. He leans out of the car window and looks back in the direction of the road.

1 ⏱ 5.5 sec Michel in the car

2 ⏱ 1 sec The first policeman passes

The first policeman
Godard cuts to a brief shot of the first policeman riding past the end of the dirt track – although why he cannot see Michel's car is not explained. Michel, in a voice-over, claims to have trapped the policeman – although the nature of the trap is not explained either.

Michel: "The fools have fallen into the trap"

Michel fixes the car
In these three shots, Michel opens the front of the car and begins to repair his engine. There is a cut to what we assume to be the second policeman – who also rides past the end of the track – although up until now the two policemen have been riding side by side. We cut back to Michel again as he hears the motor cycle return.

3 ⏱ 5 sec Michel looks at the car engine

4 ⏱ 1 sec The second policeman passes

5 ⏱ 5 sec Michel looks up

The policeman approaches
In this shot, one of the policemen rides back in the opposite direction – we assume that he has turned around, although we do not know why. He comes down the track and rides towards Michel. This shot breaks the alternating pace previously established and is the longest shot of the policeman so far. There is nothing as yet to suggest that he is shortly to become the victim.

6 ⏱ 3.5 sec The second policeman returns

7 ⏱ 3.5 sec Michel reaches inside the car

Mid shot of Michel
We cut back to the car. Michel runs around from the front and leans inside, reaching through the open window. There is no dialogue, and, although we have no idea what he is looking for, the abruptness and unpredictability of the sequence builds up an atmosphere of suspense and unease in its own right.

8a ⏱ 2 sec Tilt down

8b Tilt continues

8c Tilt continues

8d Tilt continues

Michel: "Don't move or I'll shoot"

Tilt downwards
From the shot of Michel leaning into the car, there is a reverse cut to a shot which begins on his hat and then tilts down over his face to his shoulder. His lips do not move, but we hear his voice.

Jump cut
The movement of the camera down over Michel's hat and face is interrupted by a jump cut to his elbow. In terms of editing, the jolt is not strictly necessary, of course, but it serves to exaggerate the sense of unease with which the sequence progresses – and also to "interrupt" the illusion of reality which any film tends to create.

 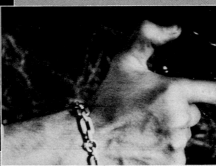

9a ⏱ 2 sec Pan left to right

9b Pan continues

Pan along arm
The shot continues with the camera panning from left to right along Michel's arm – thus executing a ninety-degree camera movement. It is here, at this crucial point in the building of suspense, that Godard makes his audience most aware of the filming process. The concentration on minute detail is contrived, self-conscious and disconcerting. It is impossible *not* to be aware of the camera, so intrusive is the technique.

Big close-up of gun
There is another jump cut here. We hear the loud click of a gun being cocked, and the pan along Michel's arm jumps to a giant close-up of the gun in his hand. The chamber spins and the pan continues along the gun to the end of the barrel. No further words are spoken, and we have no idea where the policeman is or whether or not he has moved.

10a ⏱ 2 sec Pan left to right

10b Pan continues

10c Pan continues

11a ⏱ 2.5 sec The bullet hits the policeman

11b He falls back

The gun fires (left)
There is a loud explosion and we cut to a brief shot – merely a glimpse – of the policeman falling back into the undergrowth. The sense of shock is heightened by the brutality and suddenness of Michel's act – for which no motive is offered.

The final shot (right)
The sequence closes with a jump in time to a lengthy shot of Michel running across a field, away from the scene of the shooting.

12 ⏱ 16 sec Michel runs across fields

Film and the Subjective Camera

It is one of the paradoxes of film that the image presented to us by the lens is not necessarily "seen", or supposed to be seen, by an actual person. Thus, you can convincingly film someone in solitary confinement: we see their solitude, though in reality only they would experience it. At other times, through a subjective point-of-view shot, the camera is presumed to be inside a person's head – it represents their eye. It is curious how easily we accept this radical change in the status of the lens itself. Within a single sequence we can move from external observation, through to one subjective shot, then to a different person's subjective shot, across to a subjective dream and back to external observation, all without strain or

confusion. However, as will be seen in this sequence from Nicholas Roeg's film, *Walkabout* (1970), the transition to a subjective shot is almost invariably preceded by a shot containing that person's face so we know whose point-of-view is being explored.

Nicholas Roeg's films, including *Performance* and *Don't Look Now* all share a brilliantly imaginative visual style. In *Walkabout* the girl and her brother, abandoned by their father in the Australian outback, have been walking for days and are at the end of their tether. Here, subjective and objective shots merge with hallucinations of thirst and exhaustion as they finally come across a waterhole.

The vultures
The camera begins with a close-up of the little boy's face. He is hanging over his sister's shoulder, asleep. The camera then tracks out, via a pan onto the girl, to a mid shot. There follows a shot of a vulture flying above them. After a moment it is joined by another. The voice-over of the girl makes it clear that the vultures are not a subjective shot.

⏱ **6.5 sec M.S. of girl carrying boy**

2 ⏱ **5 sec One vulture**

Girl: "If you're awake you should try and walk"

2a Two vultures

They see the oasis
Shot 4 is a hand-held subjective shot of the girl's feet, looking down from where her head would be. The scorpion, which is a static shot, is not subjective. After cutting back to a mid shot to establish the fact that the boy is upside down, Roeg cuts to the boy's upside down view of the oasis, but shot 9 is again the girl's

3 ⏱ **10.5 sec M.S. of children**

4 ⏱ **5 sec Subjective shot of girl's foot**

5 ⏱ **6.5 sec C.U. of scorpion**

6 sec Boy starts to slide

7 ⏱ **4.5 sec Boy's view of oasis**

8 ⏱ **4 sec M.S. of children**

9 ⏱ **3.5 sec Girl's view of oasis**

Boy: "Look, what's that?" Girl: "What?" Boy: "That"

10 ⏱10 sec M.C.U. of girl

10a Boy hangs upside down

10b He reaches sand

10c He disengages himself

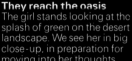

10d He sits up

10e He starts to stand

11 ⏱ 5 sec He walks towards oasis

The boy runs off

This sequence of shots is relatively straightforward objective shooting. The boy, having seen the oasis, slips down and stands up. He walks off towards the tree. Shot 11 could possibly be a subjective shot, since the camera is at-eye height and the girl has stopped at this point.

They reach the oasis

The girl stands looking at the splash of green on the desert landscape. We see her in big close-up, in preparation for moving into her thoughts. This takes the form of a superimposition of green leaves over her face. It appears in shot 12a, then fades again. Finally, in a high long shot, the boy is found drinking at the pool. The girl joins him.

How has Roeg managed to make this complexity so clear? First, he has matched the movement and angle of all subjective shots. Thus, shot 4 is walking and hand-held, 7 is inverted, 9 is stationary. Second, we see each person just before we enter their eyes, although in shots 11 and 12 it could be argued that the identification comes in retrospect. With care, even these complex manipulations can be crystal clear.

12 ⏱ 8 sec C.U. of girl

12a Superimposition

12b Superimposition fades

12c C.U. of girl

13 ⏱ 2.5 sec C.U. of berries

14 ⏱ 2 sec C.U. of berries

15 ⏱13.5 sec Boy at oasis.

The Role of the Director

Directors
Sam Peckinpah (below) and Woody Allen (right) view the action from the camera postion.

Communication
Franco Zeffirelli (above), Peter Bogdanovich (right) and Jean-Luc Godard (above right).

On location
Michael Cimino (above), writer-director of *The Deer Hunter*. Director Ridley Scott (right) between scenes of *The Duellists*. François Truffaut (above right) directs *Anne and Muriel*.

The Book of Movie Photography reflects the great difference between making a movie and other creative endeavors: filmmaking is not an act in itself, but rather it is a *sequence* of acts. Before shooting the film, you need to plan the sequence of events, which may involve writing a script. You must also be sure that the equipment you have at your disposal is suitable for the job. And the shooting itself requires a clear idea of how the next stage – editing the footage – will proceed. In its turn, the editing of the film will to an extent be governed by the techniques of dubbing and projection you have in mind for the final screening of the movie.

While it may be true that a professional film such as *Ben Hur* and an amateur effort like *Baby on the Lawn* share a common language, there are clearly pretty fundamental differences in approach. These include money, collaboration and technique, and they are interrelated. For, unlike a novelist, for instance, the moviemaker's imagination is physically constrained. He cannot scribble down a battle scene involving a cast of thousands. For it is true to say that in the otherwise unbroken chain that runs from the amateur's backyard to the battlefields of Hollywood, movies become progressively more and more expensive. Also, as your movies become more ambitious and sophisticated the more collaboration with others is required. In Hollywood, it is estimated that no fewer than 246 separate *trades* are involved in a major motion-picture production! At a slightly less exalted, more down-to-earth level, a modest local film club may well have ten people at most working on one movie – actors, camera operator, sound recordist, editor,

lighting assistant and, of course, director. The director must learn to work with all these people, get the best possible effort out of them, and yet leave the production with his or her own individual stamp.

In a strictly one-person film, of course, the problem does not really exist. For better or for worse, you are at the helm. But if you are working with others, you will find that the process of collaboration, sharing your ideas and thoughts, can be extremely rewarding, as well as potentially enriching the film you are all making together.

The primary importance of the director in making any film was recognized rather late in the development of the movies, but it is now firmly established. The French avante-garde of the sixties, with their very personal *films d'auteur*, did a great deal to assert the primacy of the dirctor. They also proved that the big-timers had a great deal to learn from the hand-held spontaneity of the smaller film gauges. "Anyone can become a director or an actor", said François Truffaut. Claude Chabrol went even further: "All you need to know to become a director can be learned in four hours." To that he perhaps forgot to add "... and thirty years in a movie theater". He also omitted the other great limitation to instant moviemaking – technical expertise.

If all this sounds too much like hard work, it should be added that moviemaking is enormously rewarding to those involved in the process. It is astonishing to think that people are actually paid to do it. Even though you, perhaps, are the one paying, you cannot but have fun in the process of creation.

THE
HISTORY
OF
MOVIEMAKING

"Now that we can photograph our loved ones, not only in stillness, but as they move, as they act, as they make familiar gestures, as they speak – death ceases to be absolute" *La Poste de Paris* (1896), on seeing Lumière's Cinématographe

Making Pictures Move

Although it is generally accepted that the technique of modern moviemaking was invented by Edison and perfected by Lumière in the 1890s, their work crowned a century of intensive effort by others. The methods of these earlier 19th century inventors varied wildly; their devices were often bizarre, even cranky, but they all shared one aim: to create a lifelike image of *movement*.

The years after the turmoil of the French and American Revolutions were intensely dynamic. The Industrial Revolution gradually transformed the face of society, and produced several crucial breakthroughs in chemistry and physiology which were important for the development of movies. These included the discovery by Peter Mark Roget (who also wrote the famous *Thesaurus*) that the eye retains an image for a fraction of a second after it has actually disappeared. His paper "The Persistence of Vision with Regard to Moving Objects" (1824) generated a wave of scientific inventions. The *thaumotrope*, Stampfer's *stroboscope*, *Faraday's Wheel*, among others, were all designed to simulate a moving image. They were serious scientific instruments that looked like toys, which, surprisingly they soon became. Along with complex animated magic lantern shows, flip books, spinning disks and twirling coins, they soon familiarized everyone with the truth of Roget's observation that the eye can "see" movement where in truth there is really only a succession of still images.

What was now needed was to combine this work with the new science of photography. Louis Daguerre's invention of the *diorama*, in 1822, was in some ways a painted, moving version of a pageant: the spectator sat in a theater as realistically-painted screens were moved around him. Daguerre was straining at the limits of realism that painting could achieve.

In that same year (1922) Joseph Nicephore Niepce produced a crude but permanent photograph. Soon Daguerre and Niepce began to collaborate, and in 1839 Daguerre unveiled the *daguerrotype* in Paris, just as Henry Fox Talbot developed his *calotype* process in London. Still photography was born, and by 1847 half a million photographic plates a year were being sold in Paris. Baudelaire was soon able to pronounce, "From today, painting is dead". The first person to combine scientific toys with photography, was the Belgian J. A. F. Plateau. In the course of his experiments Plateau blinded himself by gazing at the sun. He was only 28. Nevertheless, he combined photographic images with the simulated motion of his own *phenakistoscope*, and even succeeded in projecting some crude moving images onto a screen. Other comparable machines, such as the *Kinematoscope* and *Phantasmatrope*, used painted images.

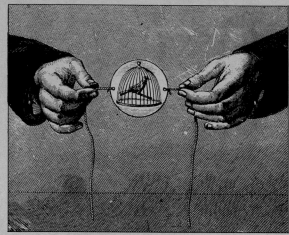

The Thaumotrope
To produce a caged bird, a disk with a bird on one side and cage on the other was spun very rapidly by a cord on either side.

Early moving picture machines
The *Mutascope* and *Kinematoscope* worked on the same principle. By rapidly rotating a selection of pictures on a wheel, they would appear in motion when viewed from above. The *Phenakistoscope*, or rotating disk, allowed successive representations of different positions of a certain action to be seen through slits in the outer wheel.

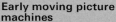

Mutascope

Kinematoscope

Phenakistoscope

Flip book
When the even-numbered pages of the history are rapidly flicked, Muybridge's horse and buggy will be seen in motion. This illustrates the phenomenon known as "persistence of vision".

Zootrope

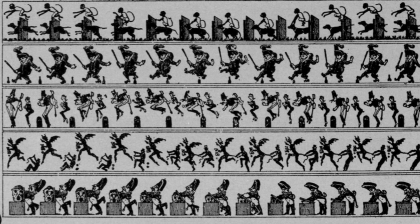

The Praxinoscope
This was a more complicated optical instrument which employed mirrors to exhibit a continuously seen but incessantly changing image.

The Zootrope
The *Zootrope* (top left) was a perfected model of the Phenakistoscope. Designs (such as the ones above) were placed inside the cylinder and rotated. When viewed through the slits they could be seen as continuous movement.

Eadweard Muybridge

The next spurt of innovation was indirectly generated by a controversy over the depiction of horses in early hunting prints where they frequently appeared to be suspended by faith rather than physics. In 1877, in the USA, an argument arose over whether a trotting horse ever lifted all four feet off the ground. A wager was struck. Eadweard Muybridge, an English photographer in America at the time, was commissioned to resolve the matter. With his assistant John Isaacs, he rigged up twenty-four cameras, each triggered by a trip-wire, to record a 24-frame sequence of the trotting horse. The horse was declared undeniably airborne, and Muybridge was then free to develop his technique (see below).

The Zoopraxinoscope and Muybridge
The *Zoopraxinoscope* was developed by a French horse painter Meissonier. It consisted of a lamphouse and lens from a normal projector with a revolving disk in the place of the usual slide mechanism. It enabled Muybridge's photographs to be projected onto a screen in rapid sequence. In effect it was the forerunner of the modern projector.

Muybridge continued making his studies of animals and people in motion using a bank of cameras until by 1887, when Marey brought out the photographic revolver, he could shoot up to 100 frames a second.

The First Movies

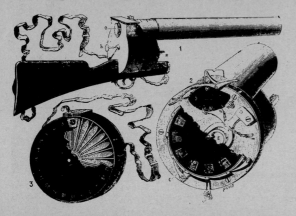

Marey's photographic revolver

Edison and the movies
The development of the Kinetoscope by his assistant W. L. Dickson, enabled Edison to create a chain of "peep shows". Dickson invented the celluloid film strips and a shutter and transport mechanism which allowed the film to pass through the camera and projector. In his studios (below right) Edison re-created historical dramas for the edification but not "mere entertainment" of thousands.

The first self-contained camera able to take all the frames in rapid sequence was invented by a French physiologist, E. T. Marey, and it took the form of a "photographic revolver" in which the "barrel" was a lens, and the rotating "chamber" contained strips of film. By 1887, this first of all portable sequence cameras could shoot up to 100 frames per second on the new celluloid film. But the results of this "chromo-photography" were still not projectable as a coherent sequence. For that, the world had to wait one or two more years, for George Eastman, Thomas Edison and Louis Lumière.

In the eight years between George Eastman's patent on celluloid film, in 1887, to Louis Lumière's first public showing of his *Cinématographe*, on December 28th 1895, inventors and scientists in Europe and the USA worked on moving pictures at astonishing speed, and with astonishing unanimity. Thomas Edison had already invented the phonograph in 1888, and his first idea was to incorporate sound and vision onto the same wax cylinder: "Everything should come out of one hole" he said. He handed the project over to his English assistant W. K. L. Dickson, who devised the idea of sprocket holes to hold George Eastman's film in register. An aspect ratio of 1.33:1, the same as today's 16 mm and super 8, was decided on for Edison's film, and a width of 35 mm.

In 1889 Dickson's development, the *Kinetoscope*, was demonstrated to Edison, with syncronous sound! The first true movie was also, therefore, the first talkie. Over the next few years Edison produced a large number of silent films for his chain of giant one-man peep-shows. They were shot in the "Black Maria" the world's first and most improbable studio, and consisted of short (1 minute) static single-shot dramas such as *The Execution of Mary Queen of Scots*.

The Bioscope
Germany's Skladanowski was only one of the many who developed machines abroad based on Edison's unprotected patents.

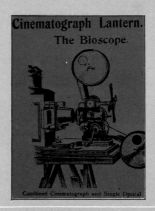

Lumières Cinématographe (left and center)

In 1895, the French scientist Louis Lumière demonstrated his *Cinématographe* to an audience of 33. It was both a projector and a camera, and it had a claw film-transport movement. "My brother invented the cinema in a single night" said Auguste Lumière. From then on there was a three year boom in single one-shot movies in every civilized capital in the world. In Europe, unlike America, the emphasis was not on static narrative, but on events and, above all, on movement. Lumière's dynamic shot of a train rushing past the camera and apparently through the screen towards the audience caused panic wherever shown. The Lumiéres built a fortune on Edison's ideas. They filmed waves, processions, funerals, horses, dancing. The images were unruly and vigorous. Maxim Gorky said in 1896 of Lumière's waves, "You think the spray is going to hit you and you instinctively shrink back". But in truth, these single shots from a static camera were only faint glimmerings of the possibilities of the new art-form which even Lumière did not grasp.

Right: Lumières famous moving train

Early Filmmakers

While Edison and Lumière regarded moving pictures as merely a scientific curiosity, a professional magician, Georges Méliès appreciated the artistic value of the medium. He became in a few years the first true imaginative artist of the cinema. For him, it was a branch of magic. He created longer films composed of several linked shots, fades, dissolves, jump-cuts, super-impositions, double exposures, fast and slow motion, and hand-tinted color film. The camera itself was still firmly fastened to its spot, however, and he did not attempt to manipulate time or space, but in such films as *Journey to the Moon*, *The Eruption of Mt Pelée*, or *The Coronation of Edward VII* (all filmed in a tiny Paris studio) Méliès demonstrated for good that film is limited only by the maker's imagination.

At the beginning of the century, the most important developments took place in America. Edwin S. Porter made two films, *The Life of An American Fireman* and *The Great Train Robbery*, in which the power of the cut was really explored for the first time. Consecutive scenes were brutally cut together without either fades or dissolves, and he introduced the beginnings of parallel editing – two simultaneous actions running alternatively. He even panned and tilted the camera. This was an enormous advance, and his audience accepted the new conventions at once. In these early years, movie goers were unsophisticated, often poor and often, in the United States, recent immigrants. For many of these, whose grasp of spoken, let alone written English, may have been shaky, the silent film was a very popular entertainment.

David W. Griffith

But at least one person was unhappy with the restriction of the one-reeler. This was David W. Griffith, the son of a Kentucky colonel. He began as an actor, then turned to directing movies in 1908. In the years 1909–13 he made over 400 short films for the Biograph company in New York, and in the process revolutionized the entire medium. He changed camera positions for purely dramatic reasons; introduced big close-ups of both characters and objects; used split-screen and matte effects to expand action; compressed time and space by removing unnecessary linking elements; varied the pace of shots to create tension; developed compositions and dramatized lighting; used landscape and extreme long shots; and left us with an "invention" that now has all the glow of a discovery: the language of film.

In 1913, after having seen the more ambitious Italian epics and "Films d'Art" imports from Europe, including the first four reel feature shown in the USA, with Sarah

"The Merry Frolics of Satan"
One of the early films directed by Georges Méliès in 1906. He first discovered the imaginative and magical uses of film, but died a pauper in Paris.

Bernhardt, distributed by Adolph Zukor, he joined Mack Sennett and Thomas H. Ince to form the Triangle Company. In 1915 Griffith made *The Birth of a Nation*. It was all of twelve reels, and ran for three hours, but Woodrow Wilson said it was "like writing history in lightning". That film, and *Intolerance* (1916), gave the movies their first true classics.

In 1915 the first comfortable 3,000 seat theater opened on Broadway and catered for a new middle-class public. Mack Sennett had founded the Keystone Studios in Los Angeles in 1915 and produced 140 comedies in his first year. In time, he employed, apart from lesser Keystone Kops, Harold Lloyd, Buster Keaton, Gloria Swanson, Carole Lombard, W. C. Fields, Bing Crosby and Charles Chaplin. The Studios moved to California and by 1919, Hollywood accounted for 80 per cent of the world's film production. Hollywood held another phenomenon: the star. Charlie Chaplin moved to Hollywood in 1913, and by 1915 he was earning $1,250 a week, a figure exceeded at that time only by Mary Pickford. She went on to play Queen of Hollywood to Douglas Fairbanks' King, while Chaplin developed his own tramp into the best known single character in dramatic history.

Early twentieth century equipment
A mahogany and brass Moy and Bastie camera of 1905 (above), which was used by the English Hepworth Company.

The Cinéclair projector (right) was manufactured in 1903 for the Pathé company. It was used both as a viewer and as an editor.

D. W. Griffith
Although Griffith did not think a great deal of the state of the art when he began directing in 1908, in the next four years he was responsible for inventing the language of film. He and others finally freed the movies from the irrelevant theatrical and literary traditions.

Keystone Film Company
One of the first big Hollywood studios founded by Mack Sennett.

KEYSTONE FILM CO.

Moviemaking in the Twenties

In Europe, there was none of the continuity enjoyed by the Americans. In the aftermath of the First World War the film industry was forced to make a fresh start, and nowhere was it fresher than in post-revolutionary Russia. "Of all the arts", Lenin had declared, "the cinema is for us the most important", and the Russian school of filmmakers, building on Griffith's pioneering work, revolutionized the possibilities of the silent film.

Intolerance had reached Russia in 1919, where Lenin himself arranged for its distribution. The young science graduate V. I. Pudovkin was turned towards movie-making by his experience of seeing this one film, and others, too, who were to become great Russian directors came under Griffith's influence. These included Vertov, Kuleshov, Eisenstein and Dovzhenko. In particular, they began to explore the significance of editing – a development partially attributable to the desperate shortage of film. Vertov, in *The Man With a Movie Camera* (1929), analyzed the filmmaking process itself as a sort of Futurist machine, while Eisenstein evolved his theories of editing as a series of collisions. In *Strike* (1924) and *Battleship Potemkin* (1925) the symbolic value of each new shot is dramatically charged by each cutting point so that the total effect is greater than the sum of its parts. Eisenstein was less interested in narrative flow than in the cumulative intellectual effect of his visual imagery. He wanted to "[liberate] the whole action from the definitions of time and space", and his explorations of political and social symbolism frequently became over-loaded and obscure. Pudovkin, on the other hand, kept the dramatic narrative to the fore, though he too relied on the accumulation of telling details. In *Mother* (1925), for instance, the hero thinks of the outside world as he awaits release from jail. We see his hands; his smile; a spring stream; and finally a laughing child.

A comparable poetic symbolism is found in Dovzhenko's *Earth* (1930), which is filled with powerful, static images of the rhythms of nature, life and death. Although their content is often crudely propagandist, the works of these great Soviet directors carried the silent film to perhaps its greatest pitch of intensity.

In Germany, there was also an astonishing explosion of creativity for a brief period between 1919–25. They had the best-equipped and largest studios in the world at Neubabelberg – U.F.A. The Neubabelberg studios could produce the most lavish of epics, and directors such as Ernst Lubisch, G. W. Pabst, Paul Leni and Fritz Lang made opulent, if somewhat overstuffed, historical dramas. Their revivals of Germany's golden past, real or imagined, were understandable reactions to the grim realities of the Weimar Republic, which, however, found

"United Artists"
Douglas Fairbanks, Mary Pickford and Charlie Chaplin, the founders of the company.

Sergei Eisenstein
The director of *Ivan the Terrible* shooting on location in Alma-Ata, Russia.

"The Cabinet of Dr Caligari"
The servant slave in Robert Wiene's famous film.

"The Blue Angel" (right)
Marlene Dietrich as she appeared in the 1930s film by Josef von Sternberg.

more direct expression in the "street films" of contemporary urban life. Their most remarkable feature was the mobility and agility of the camera work, which reached its apogee in F. W. Murnau's *The Last Laugh*. Here, the camera *becomes* the eyes of a hotel doorman, yet at the same time, it permits us to see the man from the outside as well. The "subjective camera", as it is now known, was also used with outstanding freedom by Wiene in *The Cabinet of Dr Caligari* (1919). Here, the camera's eye relates a story told by a madman; its distortions and those of the scenery, give a nightmarish intensity to what was effectively the first psychoanalytic film. It was followed by many other Expressionist works, such as *Dr. Mabuse* (1922) and *The Secrets of a Soul* (1926). These somber and searching studies of the inner life owed a good deal to Scandinavian films of the time, but their macabre quality was peculiarly German. After 1925, however, Hollywood began literally to buy out the German talent, and the industry declined.

In France, after the collapse of the Pathé empire which had distributed Lumières films, it was essentially the critic and director Luis Deluc who first crystallized the aspirations of a new generation of filmmakers. Under his influence came Abel Gance, whose multi-screen and flash-frame techniques remain revolutionary till this day; the young René Clair, whose comedies of Parisian low life were already inventive and assured; Jean Renoir, who was tentatively developing a style of his own and Jacques Feyder, with his acute eye for social nuance. At the end of the decade, Buñuel was to produce the surrealist *Chien Andalou* with Salvador Dali, and the Danish director Carl Dreyer was to direct France's last, and perhaps greatest, silent classic, *La Passion de Jeanne d'Arc* (1929). Its crushingly tight close-ups both crown the achievement and emphasize the limits of the silent film. And indeed, while it was being made, the Talkies were invented.

In Hollywood, the twenties were a decade of consolidation that ended with the twin upheavals of the Talkies and the Slump. In those ten years, production costs soared, and the studios, run by such names as Zukor, Fox and Mayer, tightened their grasp on the star-system. Three stars alone – Chaplin, Fairbanks and his wife Mary Pickford – managed to extricate themselves from the tyranny of the studios by founding United Artists. Most other actors and directors were to a greater or lesser degree the prisoners of an increasingly onerous and commercial system. As Hollywood rose, so the European film industries were ransacked for talent. Directors such as Murnau, actors such as Emil Jannings, and scriptwriters such as Somerset Maugham, were simply purchased and shipped West. Very often they found that the requirements of American commerce or puritanism made their work impossible. There was at this time an extraordinary gulf between the "morals of Port Said", as Mencken described Hollywood, and the projected piety of Hollywood's actual output.

Two great American traditions remained unchanged, however: the Western, and the comedy film. In films such as *The Covered Wagon* (James Cruze, 1923) and *The Iron Horse* (John Ford, 1924) the Western hit a new

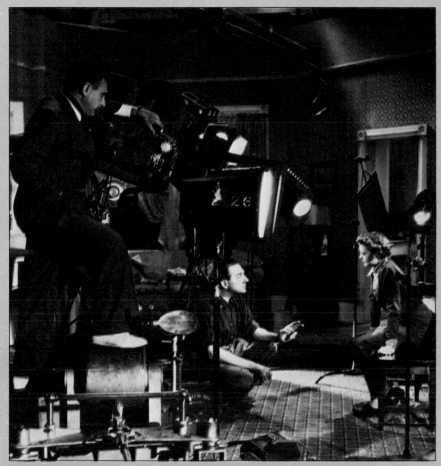

stride – the cowboy was now an idealized knight of the plains, and the Western became a branch of mythology.

In comedy, Buster Keaton, Harold Lloyd, and Charles Chaplin did most of their finest work. Keaton, perhaps the most delicate and brilliant of the three, was eventually forced out of directing by the studios, in the shape of Irving Thalberg at M.G.M. Thalberg, widely regarded as a youthful genius, was also responsible for the brutal editing of Erich von Stroheim's masterpiece *Greed*.

In the technical field, evolution had continued. Daylight was no longer relied upon for lighting, and the glass roofs of the early studios were replaced by "klieg" arc lamps, diffusers, gauzes and barndoors of the twenties: these were refined into a sophisticated tradition of lighting that was in no way naturalistic. Panchromatic black and white safety film, which was sensitive to all colors of the spectrum, had replaced orthochromatic film, which was insensitive to red, and a wide variety of color film was demonstrated between 1913 and 1930. The frame-rates used when shooting silent films had wavered between 15 and 25 fps. They would finally be standardized at 24 fps by the introduction of sound, on which a number of experiments were already being made. This was the revolution that Hollywood needed, and it was ironically provided by a company on the verge of bankruptcy.

In 1927 Warner Brothers pinned all their hopes and cash on the *Vitaphone*, a disk based recording system. This system was only one of many that offered synchronous sound and vision, and in fact was soon abandoned in favor of the sound-on-film arrangement that has continued in a modified form to this day.

Fritz Lang on the set with Sylvia Sidney

Ufa studios
Shooting in the rain for *Looping the Loop*. Ufa Studios were the only film organization to compete with Hollywood for foreign markets.

A Hollywood cowboy set

The Early Talkies

By 1929, the year of the Crash, every studio in the world had begun conversion to sound as an urgent matter of survival. The silent film was finished, carrying with it pit-orchestras, pianists, lipreading, subtitles, and, at first, subtlety, too.

The first Talkies after *The Jazz Singer* tended to emphasize sound to a disproportionate extent. The passion for dialogue and music, at all costs, further paralyzed a camera that was already, in the early years, imprisoned in a huge soundproof box along with the operator. Barely-modified stage plays were simply performed in front of this static lens. The hard-fought artistry of the silent film was effectively junked. Only Walt Disney (*Steamboat Willie* appeared in 1930) kept a fluid camera, but then he had no silencing problems.

However, the novelty of sound was short-lived, and a new generation of directors such as Ernst Lubitsch, King Vidor, Frank Capra and Rouben Mamoulian began to use sound as a way of confronting the realities of modern America, by now in the depths of the Depression. Gangsters, bootlegging, unemployment, the Dust Bowl and the "heroic little man" were soon familiar images of the thirties. Paradoxically, the thirties also saw the rise of the singing–dancing musical, possibly as an escape from the harsh realities of the economy. Busby Berkeley was to transform this genre into a particularly abstract art form of his own.

Color, too, had made an abortive appearance in *On With the Show* (1928), with *Technicolor*. This two-color process was not at first widely accepted, and the three-color Technicolor that was used from 1934 to 1953 required a complex camera with three separate strips of film. The first three-color tripack film, Kodachrome, was introduced for amateur use (16 mm and 8 mm) in 1935, though it, too, was not perfected until 1951. Black and white films were therefore the norm until the early fifties, in both professional and amateur work.

The sophisticated web of diffused light that directors such as Josef von Sternberg had woven around the screen-goddesses persisted into the era of the Talkies. Now Garbo and Dietrich could be heard as well as glimpsed through the glimmer of gauzed lenses. The visual gags of the silent movies were supplanted by the verbal humor of the thirties. Flowery lines were stripped and clipped to a semblance of natural speech. By the time of *Citizen Kane* (1941), Orson Welles could introduce into film (among many visual innovations) complex overlapping dialogue and sound-montage. Adapting a technique from his radio experience, Welles compiled a many-layered sound track which blended dozens of different voices.

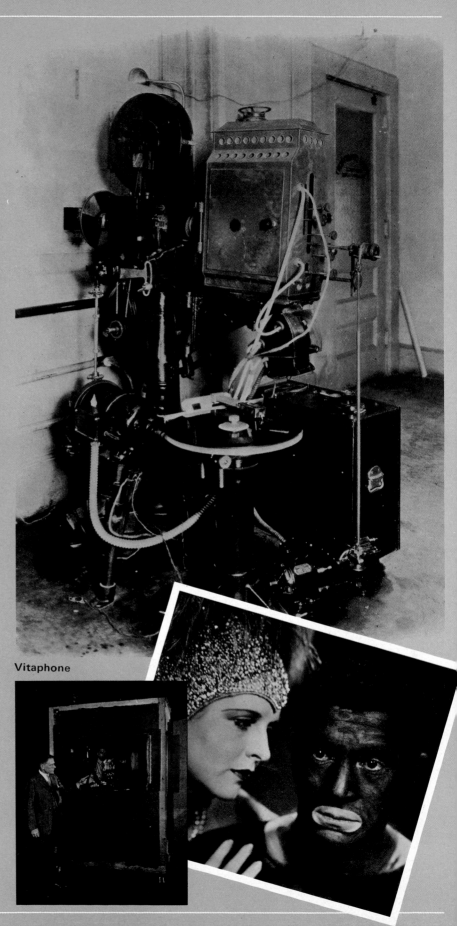

Vitaphone

"The Jazz Singer"
When Al Jolson appeared as the Jazz singer in 1929 the movies became the "Talkies" (far right). However, it was necessary to muffle the camera in a huge soundproof box during filming (right).

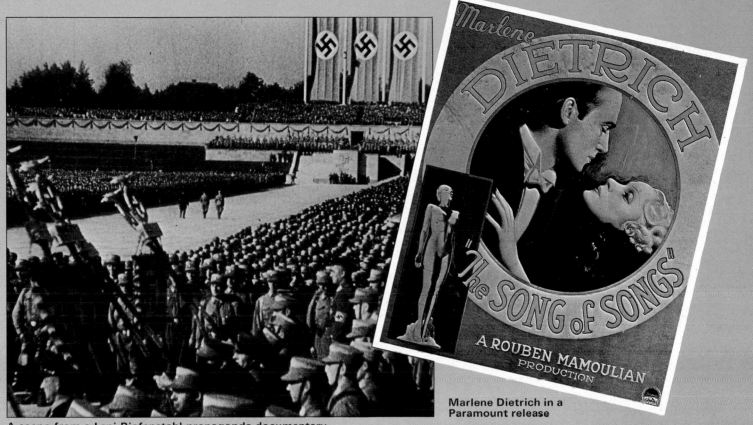

A scene from a Leni Riefenstahl propaganda documentary

Marlene Dietrich in a Paramount release

In France, René Clair had early mastered the possibility of sound. In his sound comedies *Sous les Toits de Paris* (1929) and *Le Million* (1931), he kept dialogue to a minimum, concentrating on a mosaic of music and effects. He discovered that if you heard a window breaking you needn't see it as well. In fact, he discovered that a sound track could be used for atmospheric rather than mechanical purposes.

Many of the films of this period were shot through with melancholic despair (the so-called *films noirs*), and the figure of the doomed proletarian hero – combined romanticism with a realistic appreciation of a depressed decade. The most profound summary of the vanished social order was found in Jean Renoir's masterly *La Grande Illusion* (1937) and *La Règle du Jeu* (1939). Renoir's subtle vision of the futility of war and the permanently changed rules of peace, is perfectly matched by his gliding, insidious camera and deep-focus photography.

The early documentaries

In the field of documentary, John Grierson's G.P.O. Film Unit had fostered some remarkable talents. The Russian influence was initially very strong on Grierson (particularly in editing technique), as it was on the American, Robert Flaherty. In documentaries such as *Nanook of the North* (1922), *Moana* (1926) and *Man of Aran* (1934), Flaherty's Eskimos, South Sea Islanders and Irish crofters gave him performances of unfor-

Logo of one of the great studios

Nanook of the North
A shot from the documentary film of the same name by Robert Flaherty.

gettable power. Documentaries thus pioneered the use of the non-professional actor.

In Germany, Leni Riefenstahl had already foreshadowed the propaganda documentaries of the coming war in *The Triumph of the Will* (1936) and *Olympia* (1938). Indeed it was the war that most changed the nature of documentary filmmaking throughout the world. In Britain, Grierson's G.P.O. Film Unit became the Crown Film Unit in 1940, and documentary filmmakers joined forces with fictional directors, to their mutual benefit. The lines between newsreel, documentary and fiction became blurred by the requirements of propaganda. The newsreels, which began in the early thirties, had emerged as a powerfully realistic source of biased information, and they were now to strengthen the documentary. They were of course filmed on 35 mm, and it is worth remembering that almost all footage was then shot on 35 mm, even during battle, though 16 mm had been available since 1923. If 16 mm was used (to save weight), it was always subsequently blown up to 35 mm for editing. 8 mm, which had been released to the amateur market in 1932, was not even considered for documentary use. However, the use of 16 mm for release prints during wartime was to open up its eventual use by a whole new generation of avant-garde filmmakers after the war. Only with the progressive refinement of film-stocks in the fifties and sixties could there be any cross-pollination between the smaller, "amateur" gauges of 16 mm and 8 mm, and the professional 35 mm world.

Postwar and the New Wave

The effect of the war on the American feature industry was complex and far-reaching. There was a strong tendency for the twin drives of the thirties – towards realism and towards escapist romance – to drift even further apart. On one hand, in John Ford's *Grapes of Wrath* (1941) or *The Battle of Midway* (1942) the influence of documentary is clearly evident in the bleakness of the images. There is a new toughness and violence, too, in the numerous Raymond Chandler adaptations and the gangster movies of the later war years. More explicit action was needed by an audience that had watched their relatives star in the newsreels of Okinawa and Normandy.

In England, too, the movies were more popular than ever. Movie theaters were packed even during the Blitz. Michael Balcon's Ealing Studios, in particular, specialized in fictional films with a powerful admixture of documentary footage. The cross-fertilization between fictional and documentary film was eventually to prove the greatest strength of Britain's revitalized post-war film industry.

In every country, the Second World War created a shockwave that tended to produce either a more desperate flight from reality (as in the American epics of the early fifties) or else a deepened sense of the importance of realism. In Italy, the neo-realist movement may be said to have begun with Visconti's *Ossessione* (1942), which liberated the camera from the studio and unobtrusively placed its actors among peasants. This process was carried much further by Roberto Rossellini in *Romma, citte aperta* (1945), which was revolutionary in its use of raw documentary footage amid staged scenes: much of it was shot even as German troops were evacuating Rome.

Hollywood responds to television

In Hollywood the advent of television caused panic by 1949 ("the year of the television jitters"). Hollywood plunged into a series of technological solutions to artistic failure. Using Kodak's new Eastman Color integral tripack film (see p. 51), a whole series of widescreen processes were launched. *Cinerama* (1952) used three overlapping projected images from three synchronized films; *CinemaScope* (1953) squeezed a wide image onto 35 mm by use of an anamorphic lens, giving an aspect ratio of 2.55:1; *Todd AO* (1955) used 70 mm film projected onto a large curved screen; *Vistavision* (1954) ran 35 mm film through the camera *sideways* (and therefore unsqueezed); and finally *3-D* projected stereoscopic pictures onto a flat screen. The studios used such ponderous vehicles as *The Robe* (1952) to carry this ever increasing weight of technical innovation.

Throughout the middle fifties, the American and European movie industry was in a phase of shocked self-appraisal: not until the reinvigorating influence of the New Wave in 1959 was there a clear direction. But both Japan and India produced outstanding work at this time. Kurosawa's *Rashomon* (1951) and Satyajit Ray's *Pather Panchali* (1956) won major prizes at Venice and Cannes. Kurosawa's dynamic yet intimate use of history, and Ray's incomparably delicate feeling for the Indian countryside and its people, were a revelation to the new art-cinema audience in the West. Though Ray's achievement was, and is, unparalleled in Indian cinema, Kurosawa sprang from a rich Japanese film-culture that included Ichikawa, Mizoguchi and Ozu. The Japanese revaluation of their past, coupled with an austere visual purity, had considerable effect in Western Europe and Scandinavia. For the cinema was now becoming internationalized.

The New Wave

The New Wave, as it was soon christened, broke in 1959. For several years, a group of young French film-critics had grouped themselves around the influential writer André Bazin, whose journal *Cahiers du Cinema* was to be the Bible of a radically new cinematic religion. Among their names were Claude Chabrol, Louis Malle, François Truffaut, Alain Resnais, Eric Rohmer and Jean-Luc Godard. What they shared was a rejection of traditionally accepted commercial values; a distrust of conventional montage-techniques; an enthusiasm for composition-in-depth, as pioneered by Murnau, von Stronheim, Welles and Renoir; and, above all, a belief in the director as *auteur*, the sole author of his film. Their differences were buried in these clear points of similarity. In the next four years no less than 170 French

Fifties innovations
Among the various widescreen formats used by Hollywood to lure television audiences back to the movie theaters was Todd-AO and 3-D. Todd-AO used 70 mm film, projected on a large curved screen (right); 3-D movies required special polaroid glasses to view the stereoscopic picture projected on a flat screen (below).

The cult of the director
The fifties and early sixties saw the rise of the director as star. European, Indian and Japanese directors controlled their films in a way that most Hollywood directors could not. Truffaut, Ray, Kurosawa, Resnais and Godard, among others became household names.

directors made their first feature films, and in the process radically revised the world's ideas about the cinema. Narrative could now proceed by jump cuts, improvisations, interpolations and diversions. The genres of comedy, tragedy, politics, documentary and black farce were mixed without regard for conventional wisdom. At an even more experimental level, documentarists such as Chris Marker exploited the portability of the 16 mm camera to give us *cinéma-vérité* in a raw, unpolished, and perhaps uncut, slice of life. This was, if anything, the moment when the conventional separation between the "amateur" and "professional" worlds of moviemaking began to be eroded.

In the USA, too, the early sixties saw the rise of the "independent" filmmaker, working largely in 16 mm at that stage. But with the introduction of the super 8 and single 8 formats in 1965, many experimental films were made in the new filmstock, with considerable savings both in weight and expense. Over the next ten years many ideas that had been explored in independent, small-format movies later found their way onto the commercial 35 mm screen. All this can be traced to the liberating influence of the New Wave in the early sixties. The first phase of the French New Wave subsided in 1963 (when there was a world slump in the cinema), although many of the most talented directors went on to create their finest work in the seventies.

Italy was responsible for two of the most original and stylish of all modern directors in the late sixties – Bernardo Bertolucci and Michelangelo Antonioni. Indeed, it has been observed that the modern Italian film lies at the end of a *painterly* tradition, in which the great image has always counted for more than the word. This is certainly true of the late, opulent work of Visconti.

The internationalized cinema
Clockwise from top left: *Last Year in Marienbad* (1961) directed by Alain Resnais; *Distant Thunder* (1971) by Satyajit Ray; *Shoot the Piano Player* (1960) by François Truffaut; and *The Seven Samurai* by Akira Kurosawa (1954).

The Present and Future

During the last ten years Hollywood has enjoyed a Renaissance. A series of blockbusters, running from *Bonnie and Clyde* (1967) to *The Godfather* (1971), *Jaws* (1975), and *Star Wars* (1977) have transformed the studios' financial outlook. (*Star Wars* earned more than half a billion dollars.) The special effects departments came up with ever-more-brilliant tricks, giving a new lease of life to the science-fiction movie. Stanley Kubrick's *2001* (1968) and Stephen Spielberg's *Close Encounters of the Third Kind* (1978) owed more, however, to a kind of mystical revival among the young than to their models and matte effects. The young had in fact come to dominate the cinema-going public. Peter Fonda's *Easy Rider* (1969) cost $40,000 and grossed $30 million: the studios became interested in low-budget pictures aimed at a youthful market. Robert Altman's *Woodstock* (1970), and the rock-revivals *Saturday Night Fever* (1977) and *Grease* (1978) were the result. At the same time there was a dramatic rise in "permissiveness" towards both sex and violence.

One last genre that cannot be omitted is the disaster movie. Many of the numerous movies in which jumbo-jets, ocean liners and civilizations meet their doom may be thought of as collective fantasy on the part of an over-mechanized society. The most recent, *The China Syndrome* (1979), on a nuclear reactor "melt-down", has turned out not to be fantasy after all.

Worldwide, there are comparable signs of energetic life in an astonishing number of countries. Particularly distinguished are Japan, Germany, South America, Australia, Spain and, as ever, France and Italy. By far the largest film-producing country in the world is India, and a handful of original films each year are made by her own New Wave directors.

Big time commercial moviemaking is in fact enjoying a success that was unimaginable in the early days of television. This is only partly a matter of the special effects, widescreen, Dolby stereo and all-star casts. It has more to do with the enduring magic of *going* to the movies, which remains a communal experience that television cannot match. At the same time, film schools, film buffs, and filmmaking have never before been so widely popular in all the gauges.

There is a New Wave of quite another kind among the independents, both in America and in the rest of the world. With the cheaper small-gauge films (16 mm and super 8) you can make a film for purely personal reasons, without worrying about the size of your audience. The "underground" movie was begun by figures such as Kenneth Anger, Stan Brakhage and Andy Warhol, but it was soon enormously active

"2001: A Space Odyssey"
The big budget science fiction movie with its vast array of special technical effects started with Kubrick's film in 1968 and continues right up to the present day.

"The China Syndrome"
This contemporary thriller, which stars Jane Fonda, Jack Lemmon and Michael Douglas, is based on the controversial issues surrounding the cover-up of an accident in a nuclear reactor.

worldwide, in film schools, film clubs, cooperatives and communes. The range of material is as wide, and as variable in quality, as you might expect. Many of these movies, in the anxiety to establish their independence of commercial considerations, go to some lengths to avoid a smooth finish. Soft focus, wobbly camera, jump cuts and very lengthy silences are all part of the message of the film experience in many cases.

Other films, such as *Sebastiane* (1978), have been shot on 16 mm and blown up to 35 mm for commercial distribution. Bypassing the film industry's expensive structure, low-budget films have managed to combine the freedom of an "experimental" movie with the straightforward commercial appeal of conventional movies. But the most significant developments in 16 mm over the last few years are undoubtedly among the films made for television. In Britain, for instance, directors have produced much of their finest work for TV, and they have all exploited the flexibility of 16 mm to the full. In particular, one can trace the emergence of a new kind of realism which exploits fast film, fast lenses, low light, improvized acting and natural settings, to give a drama that is closely allied to documentary. John Cassavetes pioneered similar work in the USA. For the amateurs, however, the most significant change over the past decade is undoubtedly the advent of the sound super 8 camera, closely followed by the 200 ft (61 m) magazine. Now that super 8 can offer single or double system sound, with fullcoat editing on magnetic film and a magazine with a 13-minute running time, it is a strong contender for use on television. It was in fact used, in remote control, by Claire Francis for filming her solo round-the-world voyage in 1978. Only a tiny proportion of the TV audience spotted the difference between super 8 and the usual 16 mm footage.

However, at the very moment that super 8 threatened 16 mm and came of age, the video revolution occurred. In the past few years, there has been an explosive growth of home video-cassette recording units. The material cost of recording one hour on tape is now the same as filming for about three minutes on single system sound super 8 film. The cost of video equipment is certain to fall. However, editing remains beyond the home-user's reach, and at the moment video and super 8 are not in direct competition. Indeed, in one area, they work in tandem – it is now possible to transfer home movies onto cassette via a "videoplayer" for showing on home TV. The other technological advances, such as "laserscan" transfer of video to film, large-screen video displays and moving holography, are unlikely to have much impact for five or ten years. For the moment, it remains true that super 8 and 16 mm are without question the medium for the amateur, the aspiring moviemaker and the true professional. What is more, it is easier than ever before to achieve professional results with comparatively simple equipment. There is less distance now between the inspired amateur and the professional multi-million dollar spectacular than at any time since the first days of the silents.

THE
CAMERA
AND THE
FILM

"Film is reality at twenty-four frames per second"   *Jean-Luc Godard*

The Mechanics of Film

All movie cameras have the same fundamental purpose: to record a moving subject as a large number of successive images on a roll of light-sensitive film. When these images are developed, and projected onto a white screen at the same speed as they were filmed, they will appear once more as continuous, uninterrupted motion. This is because, at a speed of anything more than sixteen frames per second, the eye cannot separate one image from the next. Neither can it see the brief split seconds of darkness between frames. The principle is known as "persistence of vision" and was discovered by Peter Mark Roget in 1824.

What it means is that we believe we are seeing movement when all we're really seeing is a succession of still images. All movie cameras work on the principle of intermittent movement in order to capture a rapid succession of stills, and whatever its design the film movement mechanism allows each frame to be caught for the moment of exposure and then moved on. In fact, the exposure is normally 1/50th or 1/60th of a second at the camera's usual speed. Moreover, the projector shutter is designed so that each frame is shown three times. This reduces flicker still further, and the illusion of motion is complete. You have moving pictures.

The design of the camera and the projector is in many ways very similar. In both cases, the film moves from a feed spool to a take-up spool, passing through a "gate" on its way. It is while the film is in the camera gate that it is exposed and a latent image of the subject is recorded; while in the projector gate the image is projected.

How the image is recorded

The simple camera
Light reflected from the subject is collected by the camera lens and focused onto the film, where it forms an inverted image.

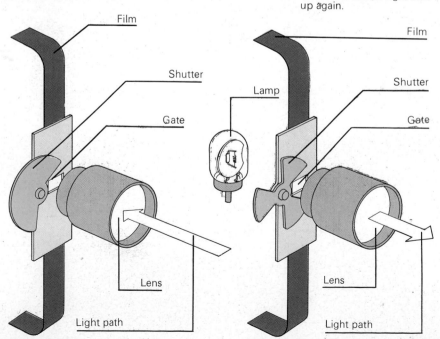

Film

Shutter

Gate

Lens

Light path

The simple projector
Concentrated light from an incandescent lamp passes through the film projecting the image through the lens where it is turned right side up again.

Film

Lamp

Shutter

Gate

Lens

Light path

What is film

Film is the basis of movies. It is a thin, flexible strip made up of an acetate or polyester base coated with a layer of emulsion. The emulsion is composed of silver salts which are sensitive to light. It is these salts which record the image focused onto the film by the lens (see *How Film Works*, p. 51).

Movie film comes in magazines, on metal spools or in cartridges. It is perforated either along one or along both sides with small *sprocket holes*. These enable it to be alternately held still for exposure or projection and then moved on by a claw inside the camera or projector. The distance between one hole and the next is known as the *pitch*. The area occupied by each separate image is the *frame*.

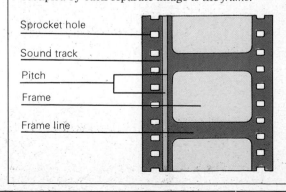

Sprocket hole

Sound track

Pitch

Frame

Frame line

The Formats

The invention of movie film in 1889 was the result of a remarkable collaboration between George Eastman and Thomas Edison. Eastman provided the film and Edison designed the format. The film they came up with was *35 mm* wide and was produced on a cellulose nitrate base. The format was well-suited to commercial film-making and has been the norm in the movie industry ever since that time.

In 1923 Eastman Kodak introduced film that was *16 mm* wide. It was cheaper, safer (since it used a new, less flammable cellulose acetate base), and gave acceptable quality. It is the format used by both amateur and professional filmmakers. It is the only economical way for an amateur to make a commercial film, and it is the only way that many professionals can afford the films they most want to make. For television companies, 16 mm is now the almost universal film gauge.

However, in 1932 Eastman introduced another new format. Known as *standard 8* or *double 8*, it was basically 16 mm film with twice the number of perforations and a picture area about a quarter the size. It was designed specifically for the amateur market and reduced the cost of moviemaking still further, but its curious "double-run" system (see p. 41) still deterred some people.

In 1965, Kodak brought out their new *super 8* equipment and opened up the home-moviemaking market still further. Super 8 film was packaged in simple plastic cartridges and gave a fifty per cent larger picture area than standard 8. It was a cheap, easy-to-use format capable of producing good results.

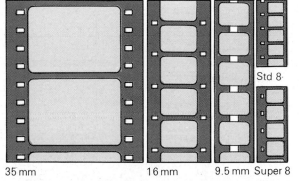

35 mm   16 mm   9.5 mm   Super 8   Std 8

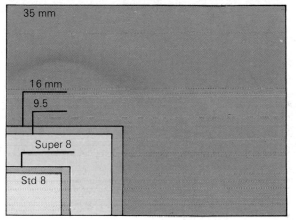

35 mm / 16 mm / 9.5 / Super 8 / Std 8

Comparison of film sizes
The small strips of film are shown here actual size. As new formats were introduced, the width of the film decreased from 35 mm to 8 mm, and camera manufacturers were able to make their equipment smaller, simpler and, above all, cheaper. Super 8 (and its Japanese version, single 8) is now the leading format for amateur moviemakers.

Comparison of frame sizes
One frame of 35 mm film gives a picture area nearly four times that of 16 mm film and twenty times that of super 8. The size of the frame is standard for each gauge; it is determined by the dimensions of the aperture in the camera. However, the projector aperture is very slightly smaller – and so the frame is cropped a little on all four sides. This does not alter the aspect ratio.

Aspect ratio

When Edison first conceived the idea of movie film, he envisaged his 35 mm frame as having an *aspect ratio* of 4:3 or 1.33:1. Indeed, the early 35 mm silent pictures used this ratio. It was called "full frame" or "full screen aperture". When sound movies were introduced, the size of the picture was reduced to leave room for the sound track, but the aspect ratio was unchanged. The new size was known as "Academy aperture". Super 8, standard 8, 16 mm and television videotape have all retained the original 1.33:1 shape as well.

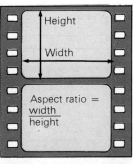

Height / Width

Aspect ratio = width / height

Definition of aspect ratio
The term "aspect ratio" is used to express the shape of the frame rather than its size. It is obtained by dividing the width of the frame by its height. As shown below, both the silent and sound versions of 35 mm film have the same aspect ratio – 1.33:1.

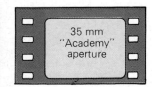

35 mm "full frame"

35 mm "Academy" aperture

Altering the aspect ratio

The movie industry has used wide screens to attract audiences back into the movie theaters by altering the aspect ratio in two ways.

Mattes
The simplest way of making the picture fill a bigger screen is to enlarge it when it is projected. However, if you only want it to be wider, not taller as well, then the top and bottom of the picture must be masked off using *mattes*. This technique gives aspect ratios of 1.66:1, 1.75:1 or 1.85:1.

Anamorphic lenses
An *anamorphic lens* can be fitted to the camera to "squeeze" a wide horizontal angle-of-view into the normal 35 mm frame. When the film is screened, a similar lens is fitted to the projector so that the image can be "unsqueezed" back to its original proportions (see p. 256). According to the lens, this will give an aspect ratio of 2:1, 2.35:1 (CinemaScope), 2.55:1 (early CinemaScope) or even 2.66:1.

Mattes
When filming for wide-screen projection, mask the picture as shown.

Anamorphic lenses
Below left is the image as it appears, after being unsqueezed. Below right is the image as it appears on the film.

Super 8

The super 8 format was first introduced by Kodak in 1965 as a way of improving on the existing standard 8 mm film. It was immediately successful since it gave a larger picture on the same width of film, and it came in virtually foolproof cartridges which were easy to load.

Super 8 has smaller sprocket holes and a larger frame than standard 8. On projection, the picture has a fifty per cent greater area for the same degree of magnification. This means that the image produced when the film is projected onto the screen is of high quality.

Super 8 film is packaged in "single-run", light-tight plastic cartridges which can be slotted easily into the camera. The system is fast and effective. On the front of the cartridge are a series of notches. One locates the cartridge accurately in the camera; one "tells" the camera what film speed to set on its automatic light meter mechanism; one "tells" it whether or not to engage the built-in Type A or "85" filter needed for outdoor filming (see p. 92); and another indicates how the film should be processed. Loading the cartridge into the camera is as easy as loading a ballpoint pen. As long as it is facing the right way and is not upside down, nothing can go wrong. The film itself is never touched.

In 1973 Kodak introduced the super 8 sound cartridge. It is designed to carry film which has been "striped" with a thin band of magnetic iron oxide so that a sound track can be recorded onto it as the film is shot (see *Single System Sound*, p. 112). The sound cartridge is about $\frac{1}{2}$ in. (13 mm) taller than the silent one and has a cut-out at the base so that a recording head inside the camera can engage the magnetic stripe on the film.

How the super 8 cartridge works

The cartridge uses a "co-axial" design. This means that the film travels from the feed spool on one side of the cartridge, past an opening at the front (where a built-in pressure plate holds it firmly against the camera aperture during the exposure), and then onto a take-up spool on the other side of the cartridge. Regular cartridges take 50 ft (15 m) of film, which lasts for 3 minutes and 20 seconds at 18 fps. However, 200 ft (61 m) cartridges which last 13 minutes are also available.

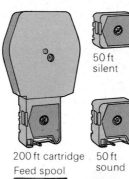

Film speed notch

Cartridge-locating notch

Processing notch

Film aperture

Filter notch

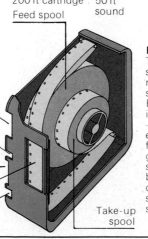

Feed spool

Take-up spool

Super 8 film
All super 8 film is 8 mm wide, whether it is silent or sound. The aspect ratio of the frame is 1.33:1.

Bell & Howell 2123XL
This "XL" or "existing light" camera is designed for filming in conditions where there is not very much light. It has a specially wide 225° shutter and a very "fast" f1.2 lens which has a high light-gathering capability. It represents a fairly typical lower-priced super 8 camera.

50 ft silent

200 ft cartridge   50 ft sound

Sankyo XL61-200
This camera is designed for sound filming. It will take both 50 ft and 200 ft super 8 sound cartridges: the sound can either be recorded on the striped film in the camera (single system) or on a tape recorder linked to the camera via a built-in "sync output" socket (double system).

Beaulieu 5008S
This camera is regarded by some to be the top of the range. Because of its mirror shutter mechanism, the Beaulieu is capable of taking interchangeable lenses – a rarity in super 8 cameras. It has a reflex viewfinder system with a ground glass focusing screen. The camera accepts both silent and sound film cartridges and will record single or double system sound.

Super 8 cameras

There are more than 130 different super 8 cameras currently on the market; they are all compact, lightweight and easy to use. They range from the simplest "aim and shoot" variety to highly sophisticated, sound-on-film "microcomputer" models. The quality you get will naturally depend largely on the price you pay – although there is no point in buying elaborate equipment that will never be used (see *Camera Specifications*, p. 266). There have been many rapid advances in the design of super 8 cameras since their introduction in 1965. Power zooms, XL cameras for low-light shooting, built-in intervalometers for time-lapse and animation, sound lap-dissolve features, and even autofocus are now all common. As a result some super 8 models now have more features than 16 mm cameras.

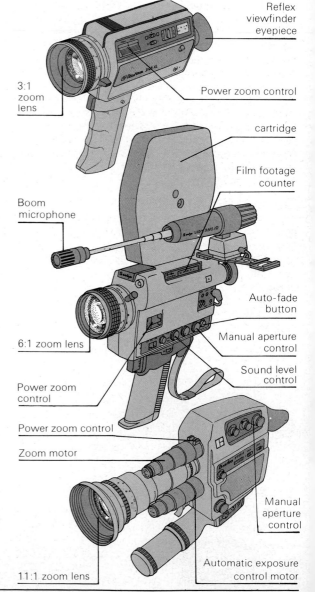

Reflex viewfinder eyepiece

Power zoom control

cartridge

3:1 zoom lens

Film footage counter

Boom microphone

6:1 zoom lens

Auto-fade button

Manual aperture control

Sound level control

Power zoom control

Power zoom control

Zoom motor

Manual aperture control

11:1 zoom lens

Automatic exposure control motor

Flexibility with super 8

Super 8 has now effectively replaced standard 8 as the popular 8 mm format. The equipment is portable, versatile and largely foolproof. It is also far cheaper than any other gauge, apart from standard 8, and has therefore brought moviemaking within the range of almost everyone. It is the ideal format for the amateur. Moreover, because of the mobility and unobtrusiveness which super 8 allows the cameraman and because of the constant improvements in the technology, it is increasingly used by professional filmmakers.

Super 8 filmstocks

The range of super 8 filmstocks is continually being expanded. The film actually inserted into the camera is called "raw stock" or "camera original", and there are now over forty kinds available in super 8. They offer color or black and white, silent or sound-striped, "fast" or "slow" film speeds, and several different color-balances. They also come in 50 ft (15 m) or 200 ft (61 m) cartridges. There are four major manufacturers of film – Kodak, Agfa, GAF and Fuji (single 8 only). The films they produce all vary enormously in terms of color rendition, contrast, grain size, etc. Different situations will require different types of film, and the best way of selecting the most suitable filmstock is to assess the shot and to decide on your priorities: do you need a fast film speed, or is fine grain more important? Finally, experiment with various types and compare the different results to decide which you like best (see *Choosing a Filmstock* p. 52, and *Filmstock Specifications*, p. 272).

Double super 8

Super 8 film is also available in a double-run form. The film is 16 mm wide, but has super 8 sprocket holes on both edges, and comes on 100 ft (30 m) spools which give a running time of 6 minutes 40 seconds at 18 fps. Like standard 8, it is run through the camera twice, exposing one half of the film each time. Double super 8 cameras (e.g., the Canon DS8 or the Pathé Duolight) are sophisticated and expensive, making this a semi-professional gauge, used chiefly for newsreel work.

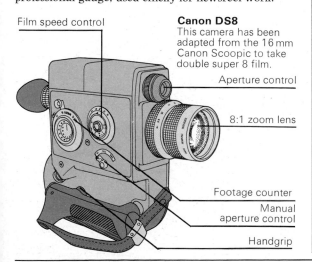

Film speed control

Canon DS8
This camera has been adapted from the 16 mm Canon Scoopic to take double super 8 film.

Aperture control

8:1 zoom lens

Footage counter

Manual aperture control

Handgrip

Single 8

Single 8 film, and the cameras designed for it, are made exclusively by Fuji of Japan. The film is the same width and has exactly the same format as super 8, but it differs in two important ways: the cartridge is a different shape, and the film emulsion is on a polyester base. Polyester is stronger and thinner than the standard acetate base used for super 8 film. However, when single 8 is edited, the film usually has to be tape-spliced; an ordinary cement splice will not work, because normal film cement has no effect on polyester (see p. 212). Single 8 film can be run through super 8 projectors, but it is inadvisable to intercut it with super 8 film. The difference in thickness shows up as a difference in focus when the spliced sequences are projected.

The Fuji cartridge is similar to a tape cassette, with the feed spool vertically above the take-up spool. It is smaller and thinner than the coaxial super 8 version. Another advantage of the Fuji cartridge is that, unlike super 8, there is no limit to the amount of film that you can backwind when making double-exposure effects such as dissolves or multiple super-impositions (see p. 186).

Fuji cameras are varied, versatile and well-made. Because the cartridge is smaller, they tend to be slimmer and more compact than super 8 cameras. At the top of the range, they are comparable to anything on the super 8 market.

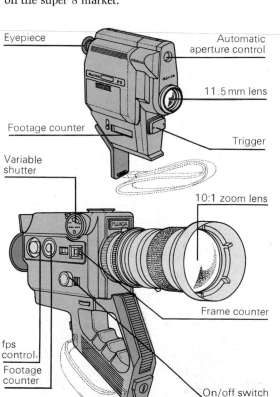

Eyepiece

Automatic aperture control

11.5 mm lens

Footage counter

Trigger

Variable shutter

10:1 zoom lens

Frame counter

fps control

Footage counter

On/off switch

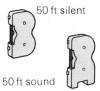

50 ft silent

50 ft sound

Single 8 cartridges
Fuji cartridges carry 50 ft (15 m) of film. They are available in silent or sound-striped versions.

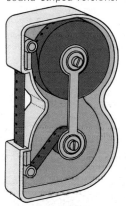

How the single 8 cartridge works
The feed spool is at the top and the take-up spool is at the bottom.

Fujica P2
This single 8 camera is one of the smallest and simplest 8 mm models available. It has a reflex viewfinder and a non-reflex automatic exposure control (see p. 48–49).
The f1.8 lens has a fixed focal length of 11.5 mm and does not zoom. Focusing is fixed so that all subjects further than about 5 ft (1.5 m) will be in sharp focus.

Fujica ZC1000
This is Fuji's top-of-the-line camera. Like the Beaulieu, it has a mirror shutter and will therefore take interchangeable lenses. It is shown here with an f1.8 7.5 to 75 mm macro zoom lens, but both 16 mm "C" mount lenses and 35 mm still photography lenses can be used on it. It offers all the features included on the best super 8 cameras, including double system sound.

How the Super 8 Camera Works

Like the human eye, the camera depends on a *lens* to gather light and to focus it onto the unexposed film. As the light enters the camera, the curved glass elements within the lens concentrate it to form an inverted image of the subject which is recorded on the film. Like the human eye, also, the lens is able to focus on subjects at various different ranges.

In order for the image to be transferred onto the film properly, the amount of light let into the camera must match exactly the sensitivity or "speed" of the film chosen. The intensity of the light is controlled by a variable *aperture* or *diaphragm* which is usually incorporated into the lens. In very bright conditions the diaphragm is closed, or "stopped down", to reduce the amount of light passing through it; in darker conditions it is opened up to increase the film's exposure to light.

Today, in most cameras the aperture is operated automatically by a built-in *light meter*.

The length of exposure which each frame of film receives is determined by the camera *shutter*. This is a rotating circular disk from which a segment has been cut out and which blocks out all the light while an unexposed frame is moved into position. It opens for a precise fraction of a second to expose the film, and then closes as the next frame is advanced. At the instant of exposure, the film must be perfectly flat and stationary. At this moment it is said to be in the "gate". The focused light falls on it through a hole in the *aperture plate*.

The intermittent motion of the film through the gate is controlled by a *claw* which is synchronized to the shutter. The claw engages a *sprocket hole*, one of the succession of small perforations down the edge of the

Technical annotation
1 Zoom motor
2 Pulldown claw
3 Viewfinder optics
4 Film gate
5 Printed circuitry
6 Drive to film cartridge
7 165° shutter
8 Shutter motor gearing
9 Beamsplitter prism
10 Image-forming elements
11 Shutter motor
12 Aperture blades
13 Beamsplitter prism
14 Focusing lens elements
15 Zooming lens elements
16 Power zoom ring
17 45° mirror

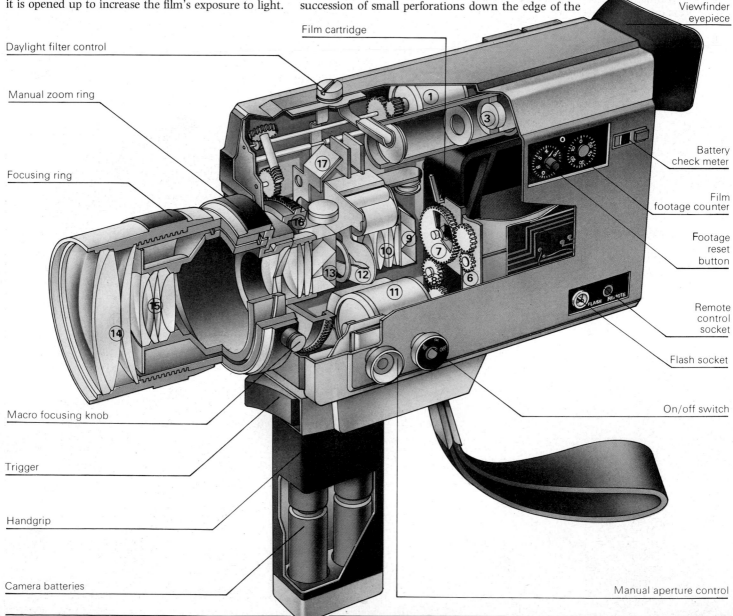

Daylight filter control

Manual zoom ring

Focusing ring

Macro focusing knob

Trigger

Handgrip

Camera batteries

Film cartridge

Viewfinder eyepiece

Battery check meter

Film footage counter

Footage reset button

Remote control socket

Flash socket

On/off switch

Manual aperture control

film, and pushes the film into place, one frame at a time. The *camera motor* drives both the intermittent movement of the claw and the smooth movement of the film transport mechanism. A loop of film within the cartridge absorbs the discrepancy between the two.

In order to see what you are filming, the camera has a *viewfinder* which frames the image to correspond to what the camera "sees". It may be either the "direct" or the through-the-lens "reflex" type (see p. 48).

Super 8 film is contained in plastic cartridges which simply slot into the camera, either from the back or from the right-hand side. The *feed spool* (which holds the dwindling roll of unexposed film) and the *take-up spool* (which holds the growing roll of exposed film) are placed beside one another. The film passes through the gate on its way from one to the other.

Reflex viewfinder system

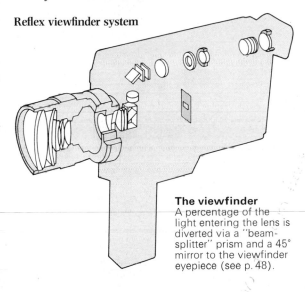

The viewfinder
A percentage of the light entering the lens is diverted via a "beam-splitter" prism and a 45° mirror to the viewfinder eyepiece (see p. 48).

Reflex metering system

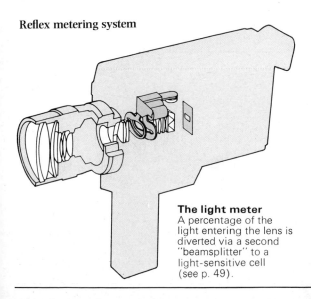

The light meter
A percentage of the light entering the lens is diverted via a second "beamsplitter" to a light-sensitive cell (see p. 49).

The "microcomputer" camera

Super 8 manufacturers are now beginning to take advantage of the revolution in the micro-electronics industry. The newest super 8 cameras incorporate microcircuits on tiny silicon chips. These allow the cameras to be rather smaller, lighter, more versatile and easier to operate. The Bauer S715 XL, for example, contains a programmable "microcomputer" which controls most of the camera's functions – variable running speeds (of 9, 18, 24 and 40 fps), single-frame intervalometer (at 1, 10, 60 or 240 frames per minute), automatic titling or animation (allowing the exposure of 1, 2, 3 or 4 single frames at a time), a self-timer giving a delay before the camera starts (so that you can be in the shot yourself), and a scene-length control (which stops the camera after 6, 8 or 10 seconds). The microcomputer also performs automatic sound-and-picture fades and dissolves. The lens is a remarkable f1.4 15:1 zoom which has two speeds and ranges from 6 to 90 mm.

Bauer S715 XL
This sound camera is one of the most sophisticated super 8 cameras on the market. It contains a microchip "computer" which allows you to program all the camera's functions – from variable frame-rate to pre-selected time lapse. The camera has four motors: one for the zoom, one for pressing the film against the sound drive spindle, one to bring the sound drive spindle up to speed, and one for the film transport.

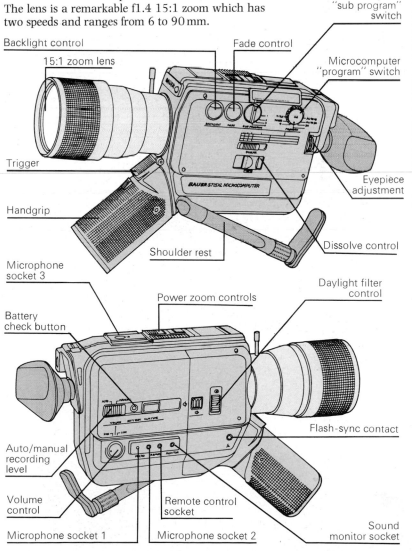

Backlight control
15:1 zoom lens
Fade control
Microcomputer "sub program" switch
Microcomputer "program" switch
Trigger
Handgrip
Eyepiece adjustment
Shoulder rest
Dissolve control
Microphone socket 3
Power zoom controls
Daylight filter control
Battery check button
Auto/manual recording level
Flash-sync contact
Volume control
Remote control socket
Sound monitor socket
Microphone socket 1
Microphone socket 2

16 mm

Film measuring 16 mm in width was first introduced in 1923 by Eastman Kodak. The cost of making movies in 35 mm had proved too expensive for amateurs, and it was this market which Kodak hoped to attract with its new format. Attempts had already been made to make film available to amateurs – in the form of 35 mm stock slit down the middle to give a 17.5 mm gauge, for example – but until 16 mm none had really caught on. Kodak followed up their success by introducing 16 mm sound film in 1939.

The 16 mm format is now the gauge where professionals and amateurs come together. For the professional, 16 mm is the ideal medium for educational films, newsreels and documentaries. The quality is high, the equipment is portable and versatile, and, in fact, almost all TV films are now shot on 16 mm.

For the amateur, 16 mm offers an image area about three-and-a-half times that of super 8. This means that when the film is projected there is a corresponding improvement in the grain and sharpness of the picture. Moreover, 16 mm is the smallest gauge you can easily inspect by eye while editing; it is the smallest gauge to have latent "edge numbers" (see p. 209) on the original filmstock; and, lastly, it is the smallest gauge on which you can make movies for commercial distribution.

16 mm cameras

Most 16 mm cameras are heavier, bulkier, more expensive and, surprisingly, less sophisticated in some ways than their super 8 grandchildren. At the lower end of the scale, a small outlay will buy you a second-hand, clockwork-driven camera with 50 ft or 100 ft daylight-loading spools; in the mid-range there are several electric-driven cameras such as those made by Beaulieu, Bolex or Canon; and at the top of the line a great deal of money will buy lightweight, silent-running, super-system cameras such as the Arriflex SR or the Aaton. However, if most of your shooting is without sound, there is no reason why the cheapest camera, used with skill and a decent lens, should not give fully professional results. For more demanding work, it is probably worth renting the camera you need. Remember, though, that the cost of the filmstock, processing, dubbing and editing equipment will remain pretty formidable.

16 mm filmstocks

16 mm film is available in various lengths, the most common being 50 ft, 100 ft, 200 ft and 400 ft. It is manufactured either with perforations down one side or down both sides (see top right). Double "perf" is now rarely used, being reserved primarily for high-speed cameras. It has been largely superseded by single "perf" film which allows space on one side for an optical or magnetic sound track.

Both color and black-and-white film is available in a "negative" and a "reversal" form (see p. 52). Reversal is the most often used since a positive print does not have to be made before the film can be viewed. However, negative film (designed primarily for making prints) is much more flexible since it allows for exposure compensation and color correction during processing.

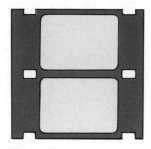

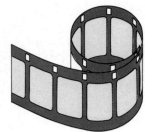

16 mm film
The film is 16 mm wide, and it has 40 frames per foot. The aspect ratio of the frame is 1.33:1.

Double "perf" film
This was the original form of all 16 mm film. It has sprocket holes on both sides of the frame.

Single "perf" film
This 16 mm film has sprocket holes down one side and a magnetic or optical sound track on the other.

Bolex H16 RX–5
This Swiss-made 16 mm camera is driven by a powerful spring motor, wound up with a handle at the side. It has a turret which holds three "C" mount lenses and is rotated by a lever. Film is loaded into the camera on 100 ft spools, but a 400 ft magazine is also available.

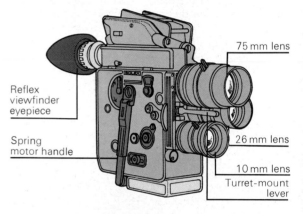

Reflex viewfinder eyepiece

Spring motor handle

75 mm lens

26 mm lens

10 mm lens

Turret-mount lever

Beaulieu R16
This French 16 mm camera is compact, lightweight and reliable. It has an electric motor, reflex viewfinder, automatic metering with manual override and variable speeds, from 2 to 64 fps. It takes interchangeable lenses and comes in either a single-lens or a turret form. A 200 ft magazine is available.

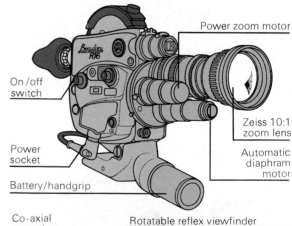

On/off switch

Power socket

Battery/handgrip

Power zoom motor

Zeiss 10:1 zoom lens

Automatic diaphram motor

Arriflex 16SR
This is the newest model in the range of German-made Arriflex cameras. It is fairly light, but extremely robust, and is designed to be supported easily on the shoulder. The position of the viewfinder can be adjusted in any direction. Lenses are completely interchangeable, and have the standard Arri bayonet mount. The camera is very quiet and is equipped for synchronous sound filming. It has a 400 ft quick-change magazine.

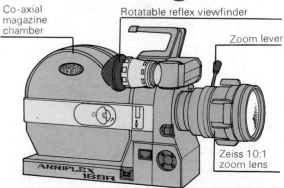

Co-axial magazine chamber

Rotatable reflex viewfinder

Zoom lever

Zeiss 10:1 zoom lens

General rules on loading film

16 mm film comes either on spools or in reels. The spools can be loaded in daylight and usually carry 50 ft or 100 ft of film. The reels are for the longer lengths: the film is coiled around plastic cores and is for magazine loading in darkness.

Daylight-loading spools

Many 16 mm cameras (such as the Beaulieu or Canon Scoopic) will take 100 ft spools. These are designed to be loaded in daylight, but it is still important to avoid bright light where possible. The threading path for the film will vary from camera to camera, and it is vital that you follow the manufacturers' instructions carefully. Above all, check that the loop of film on either side of the gate is adequate, and that the inside of the camera is cleaned between each fresh spool of film. A sequence can easily be ruined if there is any dirt at all in the camera gate.

Magazine loading in darkness

If your camera will only accept roll film, the magazine must be loaded in complete darkness – either in a changing bag or in a darkroom. It is a good idea to practice loading the camera, using exposed film, with your eyes closed, *outside* the changing bag, until the procedure becomes second nature.

When you peel off the bit of adhesive tape on the front of the new roll of film, stick it on the outside of the empty can. This will avoid its gumming up the inside of the camera, and after shooting will remind you that the can contains exposed film.

Accessories for 16 mm cameras

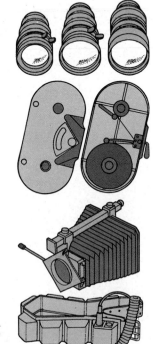

Lenses

Many 16 mm cameras have interchangeable lenses. Most 16 mm lenses have a screw-in "C" mount or a bayonet "A" mount. Adapters are available.

200 ft and 400 ft magazines

Many cameras will take either of these magazines. They allow for longer periods of uninterrupted shooting, and are therefore often used for newsreel filming.

Matte box and filters

The matte box fits onto the front of the camera and doubles as a sunshade. It holds filters and masks called "mattes" (see p.192).

Battery belt

16 mm cameras are usually powered by nickel cadmium (ni cad) batteries. If they are not built into the camera, they can be carried on the shoulder or in a belt worn around the waist.

Different film winds

Single "perf" 16 mm film comes in two forms: "A wind" and "B wind". In its A wind form, the film has the sprocket holes on the right of the gate as seen from the front of the camera; in B wind they are on the left. The emulsion faces inwards on both. B wind film is more common.

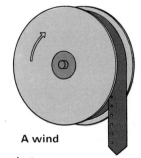

A wind   **B wind**

How the 16 mm camera works

This standard Arriflex 16S camera has a turret mount for three interchangeable lenses. It contains a 170° mirror shutter set at an angle of 45° to the film plane. A claw moves the film into position and a registration pin holds it steady while the frame is exposed.

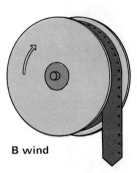

Feed spool

Take-up spool

Pressure roller

Eye-piece

Film

Aperture plate

Mirror shutter

Pulldown claw

Registration pin

Viewfinder optics

45° prism

Turret-mount lever

Third lens mount

Second lens mount

Lens cap

10 mm to 150 mm Angénieux zoom lens

Manual zoom lever

Super 16

Super 16 is a variation on the ordinary 16 mm format. By shooting 16 mm single perf film in cameras that have been modified to give a slightly larger film gate, the picture area can be made to extend over into the space on the edge of the film – the space normally used for a soundtrack. This increases the frame area by as much as 24 per cent and alters the aspect ratio from the standard 1.33:1 to 1.66:1. Super 16 is most often used for 16 mm film which will later be blown up to "widescreen" 35 mm.

Super 16 mm film
The film is the same as 16 mm single perf, but has a larger frame area.

35 mm

Ever since Edison invented the format, 35 mm film has been the cornerstone of the movie industry. It was the gauge on which the first feature films were made and, although there are now more and more films being shot by film groups and independent filmmakers in 16 mm, 35 mm is still regarded as the norm for commercial movies, though not for TV.

The area of the 35 mm frame is almost four times that of 16 mm film and twenty times as large as super 8. This means that the quality is very good. Even after countless prints have been made from the original master copy, the "grain" of the film is extremely fine and the "resolution" is high. Moreover, when projected onto a screen, 35 mm film provides a very steady image. There are two reasons for this: firstly, the degree of enlargement of the frame is smaller than for other formats; and secondly, 35 mm cameras use a greater number of sprocket holes to hold the film perfectly still during exposure of each frame.

It must be stressed that this is the professional format. The cost of the equipment and of the film processing are prohibitively high. Amateurs would only be likely to use 35 mm for optical printing effects or, in some cases, for animation work.

35 mm film
35 mm film has 8 sprocket holes per frame – 4 on each side. Commercial films are invariably shot on "negative" film, which is usually Eastmancolor.

35 mm cameras

The wide range of cameras used for filming in 35 mm falls into two broad categories: hand-held and studio. Hand-held 35 mm cameras, although larger and heavier than 16 mm ones, are smaller and lighter than the massive 35 mm studio cameras. They are generally designed so that they balance well, fit easily onto the cameraman's shoulder, and can be held steady fairly easily. The big studio cameras such as the Mitchell or the Panavision PSR, however, are enormously heavy, very expensive and highly sophisticated. They offer the filmmaker every conceivable feature – from variable shutters and viewfinder filters to 1,000 ft magazines and interchangeable focusing screens. In many cases, the professional cameras can now be fitted with video viewfinder units so that both the director and the camera operator can see what the shot will look like.

Perhaps the biggest problem with 35 mm cameras is that of sound. The noise made by the camera motor is often so loud that it can be heard on the sound track if recording is being done at the same time as filming. To overcome this, bigger cameras are often sound-proofed or "blimped". This unfortunately increases their weight and size quite considerably.

Arriflex 11C

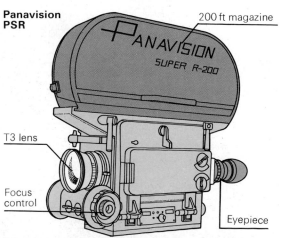

400 ft magazine

Matte box

Eyepiece

Filter holder

Handgrip

Panavision PSR

200 ft magazine

T3 lens

Focus control

Eyepiece

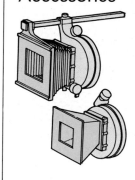

Hand-held camera
The weight of the camera is designed to be supported on the shoulder. The position of the eyepiece can usually be adjusted for easier viewing.

Studio camera
The larger 35 mm cameras are mounted on a firm studio base. These may be of the friction, fluid or geared head type. The last is the best for commercial studio work.

Accessories

Matte box
The matte box is a rigid or flexible bellows-like device which is attached to the front of the camera. It serves as a sunshade to protect the film from lens flare and as a holder for lens filters or specially-shaped masks called "mattes".

Geared head
Most professional tripod heads are of the heavy duty "geared" type (see p. 57). With skilful operation of the hand controls, the geared head can produce smooth pans and tilts at varying speeds.

Anamorphic lens
Some movies are shot using an anamorphic lens on the camera. It "squeezes" a wide horizontal angle-of-view into the 35 mm frame so that, when "unsqueezed" again on the projector, the image fills a wider screen (see p. 253).

Other Formats

Standard 8

Standard 8 mm film (sometimes known as "double" or "regular 8") was introduced in the 1930s and was specially designed for the amateur market. It has now been virtually replaced by super 8 which offers a larger frame size on the same width film. However, standard 8 film is still available – both in color or black and white and in a silent or a sound version. It is in fact 16 mm film which has been perforated with twice the number of sprocket holes. It generally comes in 25 ft spools which can be loaded, with care, in daylight. The film is run through the camera twice – once in one direction and once the opposite way – each time exposing half the width of the film. In between the two runs the spool must be removed, turned over and rethreaded. In the processing laboratory the film is then split down the middle and the two pieces are joined together to give a 50 ft single length of 8 mm film which has the sprocket holes all down one side. At 16 fps, originally the normal silent standard 8 shooting speed, this gives just over four minutes of footage; at 24 fps, the normal sound speed, it gives two minutes and forty-six seconds.

The loading system of standard 8 mm cameras is perhaps their most unsatisfactory feature (see right). It is a fiddly process and, when the reel of film is changed around at the end of its first run, it is easy to make a mistake. The most important points are: do not load in bright light, and hold the film so that it cannot unwind – both can lead to fogging.

The standard 8 frame area is about one third smaller than super 8 and as a result, when projected, the quality of the picture is not so high. The frame has to be enlarged to a greater extent if the picture is to fill the same area on the screen. Moreover, the sprocket holes, which take up more space than on super 8 film, lie directly opposite the frame bars. This means that when you are making a splice in the film, your cut crosses through the sprocket hole. The join will not therefore be as strong as on a piece of super 8 film. However, the standard 8 format still offers the cheapest of all ways of making movie films, and both cameras and film are still widely used.

Double standard 8 film

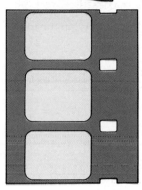

How to load the film

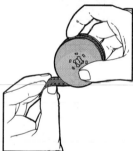

1 Load film in subdued light. Hold spool so film cannot unwind – this would cause fogging.

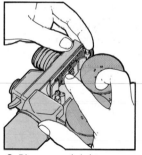

2 Place spool right way up on feed spindle. Thread film behind gate and over sprocket wheels.

3 Check film loops and attach film to take-up spool. Close camera and run for a few seconds.

Standard 8 cameras

Although standard 8 cameras are not made any longer, there are still many thousands in existence – still being used and still giving excellent results. Unlike super 8 cameras, which are all motorized, they may be either hand-wound or electric. Some of them became extremely refined before they were superseded by super 8. The cameras are very lightweight, and may have a single fixed lens, a group of turret lenses or a zoom lens.

Variable shutter control

Automatic aperture control

f1.9 4:1 zoom lens

Manual aperture control

Spring-motor winder

Trigger

Bolex K2
This standard 8 camera is equipped with reflex viewing, automatic metering and a built-in zoom lens.

9.5 mm

This decidedly odd gauge was developed by Pathé in 1923 as France's *riposte* to Kodak's 16 mm format. The film is now hard to find in Europe, and impossible in the USA. Despite this, 9.5 mm's surviving European friends, few but boisterous, are convinced that there is a life after death. On 9.5 mm film the sprocket holes are between the frames so that this gauge wastes less image area than any other. Indeed, the frame size is almost as big as 16 mm, although the film itself is much narrower and the cameras lighter and more compact. The film is loaded into the camera in special cassettes or "chargers", which are rather like single 8 cartridges but which are made of metal and are reloaded by the manufacturer after the film has been returned for processing. Because the film and equipment are so rare, it is difficult to resist the view that this engaging and ingenious format is a doomed one.

9.5 mm film

Reflex viewfinder eyepiece

f2.2 4:1 zoom lens

Power socket

Trigger

Handgrip

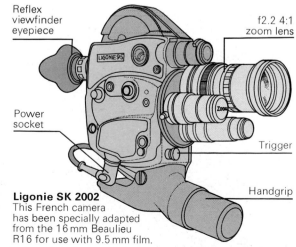

Ligonie SK 2002
This French camera has been specially adapted from the 16 mm Beaulieu R16 for use with 9.5 mm film.

The Film Transport and the Shutter

In any camera, the unexposed film must be transported frame by frame from the feed spool through the camera gate and then onto the take-up spool. As it passes through the gate the film halts for a fraction of a second, the shutter opens to expose one frame and then, in darkness again, the film is moved on ready for the next frame to be exposed. This is a fast, complex operation requiring great accuracy, especially in the smaller gauges. The slightest variation between the position of one frame and the next will produce a jiggle, weave or blur when the film is projected; if this happens the camera is said to have poor *registration*.

Film transport

The film is moved into position in the camera gate by a *claw*, operated by the motor, and in some cases it is then held in place by a *registration pin*. In super 8 cameras the claw pushes the film into place; in all other cameras the claws pull the film downwards. This movement is synchronized with the shutter so that the film is perfectly still for the moment of exposure. Moreover, except in cartridge cameras, the film is also threaded through sprocket wheels. Their continuous rotary movement is isolated from the intermittent movement of the film through the gate by a loop of film which absorbs the discrepancy.

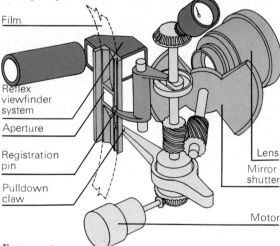

Film

Reflex viewfinder system

Aperture

Registration pin

Pulldown claw

Lens

Mirror shutter

Motor

Frame-rate

The *frame-rate* or *shooting speed* is the speed at which the film is moved through the gate; it is expressed in terms of the number of frames which are exposed per second (fps). Because the shutter is coordinated with the film transport, the exposure of the film will depend on the frame-rate that you choose: a slow frame-rate clearly gives a longer exposure to each frame. Many cameras offer a wide variety of speeds (from 9 fps to 54 fps, for example), but the most commonly available are 18 fps and 24 fps. For professional filming 24 fps is normally used since it has the advantages of better sound quality and some marginal improvement in image quality because more "information" per second is passing through the shot. However, if you shoot at 18 fps you will use less film, the camera motor will be quieter, and the batteries will last longer.

How the film is exposed

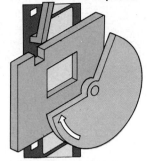

1 With the shutter open, the film is stationary. The claw engages the film.

2 The shutter closes, and the claw pushes the film downwards.

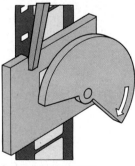

3 The film is now in position one frame lower. The claw retracts.

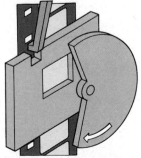

4 The shutter opens and the film is exposed. The claw moves up again.

The shutter

The camera shutter is simply an on/off switch for light positioned between the film and the lens. While the film is held still in the gate, the shutter allows light in; while the film is moving from one frame to the next, it blocks light out. Almost all movie shutters are disks from which a segment has been cut out. The disk rotates once per frame, alternately admitting and cutting out light as shown below. The amount of the disk which has been cut away determines the length of the exposure for each frame: the larger the cut-away, the longer the exposure. A typical shutter might have a 165° segment removed. At a shooting speed of 18 fps this would give each frame an exposure of about 1/40th second; at 24 fps it would be only 1/52nd. However, many cameras in all gauges are now equipped with *variable shutters* (see below).

In Arriflex 16mm cameras the circular shutter is positioned at an angle of 45° to the light path (see left). The shutter has a mirrored surface and as it rotates it alternately reflects the light into the viewfinder (where the image can be seen by the camera operator) and allows it onto the film (where the frame is exposed).

Instead of a rotating disk, some sophisticated cameras (the Beaulieu super 8 and 16mm, for example) have a "guillotine" mirror shutter which rises and falls vertically across the gate (see p. 48).

Variable shutter

Quite a few cameras in all gauges are now equipped with "variable shutters". This means that the size of the open segment can be adjusted to lengthen or shorten the exposure which each frame receives. Some cameras can do this while running. The technique can be used to produce a fade-in or fade-out (see p. 186), to change the exposure independently of the aperture, and to reduce flicker from certain types of lighting or to reduce strobing. Halving the angle of the shutter opening is equivalent to closing the lens aperture by one stop.

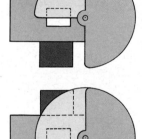

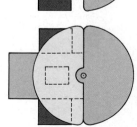

XL shutter

XL or "existing light" shutters have cut-away segments of up to 230°. This allows perhaps thirty per cent more exposure and therefore better low-light filming capability.

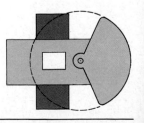

The Camera Lens

The lens is the device which allows light into the camera and onto the unexposed film. It is composed of a number of curved glass elements of varying thickness arranged one in front of the other within a tube or "barrel". The purpose of the lens is to collect the scattered light reflected by the subject you are filming, and to concentrate it into a form which will produce a recognizable image when focused on the film. As the beams of light from the subject enter the lens and pass through the glass elements they are bent or "refracted" in such a way that they converge to a point behind the lens. It is at this point that they form an image of the subject, and it is here that the film must be placed for the exposure. The point where this occurs is known as the *film plane*. The image recorded on the film must be inverted, since the light rays are turned upside down in the lens.

The subject may of course be at differing distances from the camera. To compensate for this it must be brought into *focus* on the film plane (see p. 44). This is done by moving the lens backwards and forwards in relation to the camera body – away from the film to accommodate a close subject, and towards the film for a distant object. Beyond a certain point, a distant object is said to be at infinity, and when the lens brings this object into focus, the distance between the film plane and the optical center of the lens is known as the *focal length*.

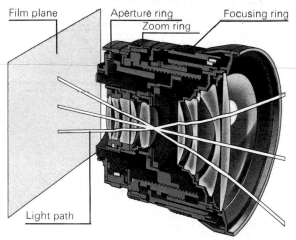

Focal length
The size of the image on the film depends on the focal length of the lens: the longer the focal length, the larger the image, and vice versa. But because each film-gauge has a certain fixed size, and because all lenses can effectively cover only a certain area, the focal length is directly related to the *angle-of-view*. In other words, the amount of the subject contained in the picture varies according to the focal length of the lens. The angle-of-view is widest at short focal lengths and narrowest at long focal lengths (on a telephoto lens, for example). A "normal" lens is a convenient compromise between the two extremes. 50 mm is conventionally supposed to be a "normal" lens for 35 mm film; 25 mm for 16 mm film; and 13 mm for super 8. These all have an angle-of-view of about 25°, which gives a pleasing close-up of a face, but is not "normal" if the subject is a small room.

Prime lens
Wide-angle prime lens on a turret 16 mm camera

Zoom lens
11:1 power zoom lens on a super 8 camera

How the lens works
The light reflected by the subject is represented in the illustration by three white lines (see left). The beams of light pass through the curved glass lens elements and are inverted at the optical center of the lens. An upside-down image of the subject is then focused on the film plane. The size of the image in relation to the subject will depend on the focal length of the lens.

Focal length and angle-of-view
The four shots shown here illustrate how a change in the focal length of the lens alters the angle-of-view. In each case, the distance between the subject and the camera was unchanged. The 40° (a), 25° (b), 15° (c) and 5° (d) angles-of-view are obtained by using 7, 13, 20 and 60 mm focal-length lenses on a super 8 camera and 12, 25, 35 and 100 mm lenses on a 16 mm camera.

Prime lenses
Prime lenses, or fixed focal-length lenses, were until fairly recently the only lenses at a filmmaker's disposal. They are still used as the fixed lenses on simple cameras, and they still provide the highest quality for any given focal length. Sometimes two or three interchangeable prime lenses are mounted on a turret which can be rotated quickly to select the appropriate lens for a shot. At "normal" and telephoto focal lengths, prime lenses may contain only a few glass elements. But, as the focal length decreases, so the lens becomes more complex.

Zoom lenses
A zoom lens is simply a lens with a variable focal length. It contains about a dozen elements which fall into three groups: the prime lens at the rear, which does not normally move; the zooming group, which racks in and out internally to vary the focal length, and the focusing group, which is twisted in and out to adjust the focus. The zoom lenses on most modern super 8 cameras are motor-driven, enabling you to go from telephoto to wide angle and back by simply pressing a button. Many modern zoom lenses also have a "macro" setting in which the prime lens itself is moved slightly away from the film, making it possible to focus as close as the surface of the lens itself (see *Macrophotography*, p. 178).

Choosing a zoom lens
The largest zooming range currently available in super 8 is from 6 to 90 mm. This lens is said to have a 15:1 zooming ratio (the longest, divided by the shortest, focal length). Its angle-of-view will vary from 55° to 3.7°. More typical for super 8, however, is a range such as 9 to 25 mm, and for 16 mm filming, 10 to 100 mm.

When choosing a zoom lens, consider whether the wide-angle or the telephoto end is more important to you. If you intend to hand-hold the camera, remember that a wide-angle lens reduces the effect of camera wobble and that telephoto shots should be filmed from a tripod. Almost all super 8 zooms are fixed permanently to the camera, so when making your choice go for the widest-angle zoom you can afford. Worry about the telephoto end only if you will really need it.

Focus and Focusing

Once the light from your subject has passed through the camera lens it converges to form an inverted image at what is called the *focal point*. The purpose of *focusing* is to make sure that this focal point falls on the film plane and that the image produced is in sharp focus on the film. If the lens is either too near or too far from the film plane, the image will be out of focus. Its distance from the film can be altered by turning the focusing ring.

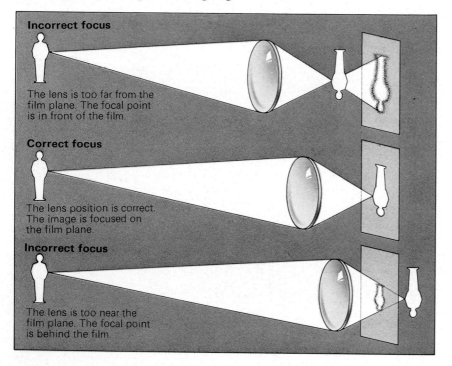

Incorrect focus

The lens is too far from the film plane. The focal point is in front of the film.

Correct focus

The lens position is correct. The image is focused on the film plane.

Incorrect focus

The lens is too near the film plane. The focal point is behind the film.

How to focus

When focusing, always try to begin by zooming in to the telephoto end of the lens. The "depth of field" (see p. 47) is narrower here and it is easier to focus accurately. Afterwards, zoom out again ready to shoot. This pre-focusing is most important if you intend to zoom in during the shot. Nothing is more irritating than a long zoom-in to a face which becomes increasingly blurred.

How to focus with a zoom lens

If your camera does not have a built-in rangefinder, you will either have to estimate the distance between the subject and the camera, or measure it out. The correct figure can then be set on the focusing ring of the lens. If your camera does have a rangefinder, the image in the viewfinder will show you whether or not your subject is in focus (see opposite page).

Point the camera
Set up the camera at the required distance and frame your subject in the viewfinder.

Zoom in
Zoom to the telephoto end of the lens. It is a good idea to zoom manually while focusing as this will help to conserve the batteries.

Focus on the subject
In the case of a person, focus on the subject's eyes. For more complex shots, choose a point one third of the way into the range which you wish to be in focus.

Zoom out
When sharply focused, zoom back out to the required focal length for the shot. The increased depth of field will guarantee accurate focus throughout the shot and during a subsequent zoom-in.

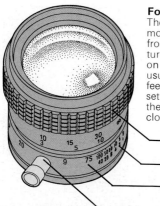

Focusing ring
The camera lens can be moved towards or away from the film plane by turning the focusing ring on the barrel. This ring is usually calibrated in both feet and meters. When it is set at infinity (indicated by the sign ∞) the lens is at its closest to the film plane.

Focusing ring

Macro focusing scale

Zoom ring

Manual zoom lever

Eyepiece adjustment control
Adjustable eyepieces are calibrated in "diopters". On most cameras, they vary from plus or minus two to three diopters.

Adjustable viewfinder eyepiece

Almost all movie cameras nowadays have adjustable eyepieces for the viewfinder. This means that near- and farsighted people are able to use the viewfinder without wearing glasses. A nearsighted person will need a negative adjustment; a farsighted person, positive. In the case of all cameras that offer this feature, the very first thing to do is to adjust the eyepiece so that it is set for your own eyesight. This is done by defocusing the lens, pointing the camera at a blank wall, and then twisting the eyepiece until the focusing screen (or in the case of an aerial image, the cross) is perfectly sharp. At this point, lock off the eyepiece; it is now calibrated for your eyesight.

Focusing systems

All the methods of focusing illustrated below are "reflex" systems. This is to say that some of the light entering the lens is deflected to the viewfinder and an image of the subject is viewed through the eyepiece. You can therefore *see* the actual image which will be received by the film. The lens is then adjusted until the image is in sharp focus as an aerial image or on some form of glass screen.

Aerial image
The image is formed in space, not on a screen. A cross in the viewfinder focuses your eye on the right plane for viewing the image.

Split-image rangefinder
In the center of the frame a small prismatic structure splits the image into two halves. When the halves line up exactly, the subject is in sharp focus.

Central microprism
A circle of tiny prisms shimmer and fracture the image when the subject is out of focus. When in focus, the shimmering disappears.

Ground glass screen
The image falls on a very fine ground glass screen. If the subject is out of focus, the image will look unclear and hazy.

Ground glass spot
The ground glass screen is restricted to a circle in the center of the frame. The image is therefore brighter than with a full screen.

Dichroic rangefinder
If the subject is not in focus, it will appear in the viewfinder to have a colored "ghost" image on either side. The images coincide when the subject is in focus.

Sankyo ES-44XL VAF

Auto focus

Some cameras now have automatic focusing systems. They work well for a subject in the center of the frame but can be fooled by such complex subjects as a figure glimpsed through leaves. However, manual override is possible, and the inherent flaws are no worse than those of automatic metering. For snapshot-style movie photography, auto focus seems likely to become the norm.

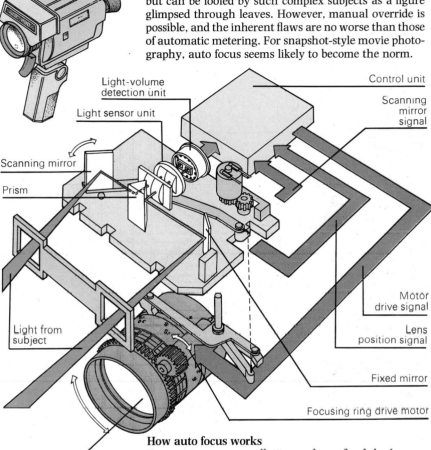

How auto focus works
Two mirrors, one oscillating and one fixed, both compare the intensity of light reflected by a subject in the center of the frame. A control unit then assesses the difference between the two signals and instructs a servo-controlled motor to adjust the focusing ring on the lens until the brightness on both mirrors is equal. At this point the subject will be sharply in focus.

Information in the viewfinder
In addition to the focusing screen, other information may be visible in the viewfinder. The ideal viewfinder is one which displays all the information you need but which leaves the image itself uncluttered.

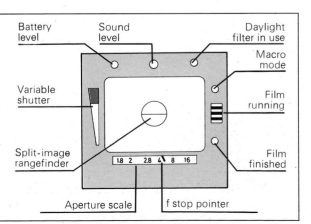

Aperture and Depth of Field

The amount of light which falls on the film is critical. Too much light will over-expose the film; too little light will under-expose it. To compensate for this, the lens controls the amount of light that passes through it by means of a variable *aperture*. This works in exactly the same way as the human eye. Just as, in bright conditions, the pupil contracts to prevent too much light entering the eye, so a *diaphragm* in the lens closes and cuts down the amount of light that reaches the film. In conditions of low light, however, the pupil will dilate so that as much light as possible is taken into the eye; accordingly, the diaphragm in the camera opens right up to set the light-gathering area of the lens at its widest. On super 8 cameras there is a built-in metering system which makes this adjustment to the aperture automatically (see p. 49). Most cameras that take interchangeable lenses have to be adjusted manually.

f stops

The setting of the diaphragm – whether it is open or closed – is usually indicated on the lens barrel, and sometimes in the viewfinder, by *f stops* or *f numbers*. These numbers are a mathematical expression of the relationship between the aperture and the focal length of the lens. The wider the aperture, the lower the f number; the narrower the aperture, the higher the f number. The progression is logarithmic and runs as follows:

Full stops f 1 1.4 2 2.8 4 5.6 8 11 16 22 32 45

Half stops f 1.2 1.8 2.2 3.5 4.5 6.3 9 12 18 25 36

If the diaphragm is progressively closed (or "stopped down"), then each stop on the scale will represent a halving of the amount of light reaching the film. These are known as "full stops"; there are also "half stops" in between. The f number registered when the diaphragm is wide open is known as the *speed* of the lens – thus an f1.4 lens has a maximum aperture of f1.4. An average super 8 camera might have an f1.6 lens, although XL cameras have lenses as fast as f1.2 or f1.1.

Depth of field

Depth of field is the range of distances from the camera within which your subject will be in adequate focus. If your lens is focused at one particular distance, you will find that there is a range in front of and behind that setting within which objects can also be filmed with an acceptable degree of sharpness. This is the depth of field for that setting. It varies according to the chosen aperture, the focal length of the lens and how critically you interpret the notion of "in focus".

If your camera has a mirror shutter, you will be able to see the exact image which the film will record at the taking aperture. A beamsplitter viewfinder, however, takes its light from the lens before the diaphragm (see p. 48) and so you cannot judge by eye how much of the subject will be in sharp focus. For absolute certainty, you will have to resort to depth of field tables (see p. 275). These will also help you maximize depth of field by focusing on the *hyperfocal distance*, so that infinity is the furthest point from the camera in sharp focus.

T stops

Because the f stop is a mathematical figure and takes no account of the fact that light is lost as it passes through the various glass elements of the lens, many cameras are also calibrated in actual *transmission stops* or *T stops*. In cameras with complex zooms and beamsplitter viewfinders the difference may be a full stop or more; f1.2 might actually mean that only f2 was reaching the film.

The effect of aperture on exposure

Wide aperture
In dark conditions, the lens aperture must be opened up wide – just as the pupil of the eye dilates to take in more light. But in normal conditions, too wide an aperture may result in an over-exposed shot.

f5.6

Medium aperture
When the aperture of the lens is accurately matched to the lighting conditions of the subject, exactly the right amount of light is allowed onto the film, and the shot will be correctly exposed.

f11

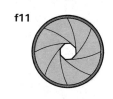

Small aperture
In bright conditions, the lens aperture must be "stopped down" – just as the pupil of the eye contracts to take in less light. But in normal conditions, too small an aperture may result in an under-exposed shot.

f22

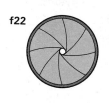

How to use depth of field

Shallow depth of field gives a selective focus effect in which only a part of the picture is sharply focused; a greater depth of field gives an effect known as "deep focus" in which subjects at widely varying distances from the camera are all in sharp focus (see p. 66). Deep focus is not always a good thing. There will often be times when you may want to isolate your subject; you may want to pick out a figure in a crowd, shoot a close-up of a flower against a distracting background, or film a backlit face against a screen of foliage. If this is the case, you can reduce the depth of field in any of the following ways:

● Use a longer focal length. In other words, zoom in close and move the camera further away.

● Use a wider aperture. Compensate for the exposure by altering the variable shutter (if your camera has one), by using a neutral density filter (see p. 94) or by using a slower filmstock.

● Indoors, use less light and open up the aperture.

How depth of field varies

The two primary factors affecting depth of field are the aperture and focal length of the lens.

At a wide *aperture* such as f1.4 the depth of field is very restricted; only a certain section of the picture is in focus. As the lens is stopped down and the aperture becomes smaller, the depth of field increases – bringing more and more of the picture into focus (see below).

The rule dictating how *focal length* affects the depth of field is simple: the longer the lens, the shallower the depth of field. In other words, a telephoto lens gives a very restricted depth of field, a wide-angle lens a much greater depth of field. The actual figure depends on the film format (see *Depth of Field Tables*, p. 275).

For more details on how to get the best out of depth of field, see *Choosing a Focal Length*, p. 66.

The effect of aperture on depth of field

Wide aperture
The wider the aperture, the shallower the depth of field. At a lens setting of f1.4, the small girl is the only part of the scene in sharp focus. The trees on either side of her are out of focus.

 f1.4

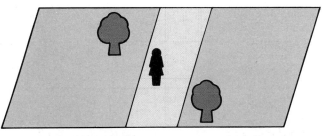

Medium aperture
In this shot, taken with an aperture setting of f8, depth of field has increased. The tree on the right of the girl has come into focus. This is because the depth of field is greater behind the point of focus than in front of it.

 f8

Small aperture
The smaller the aperture, the greater the the depth of field. With the diaphragm stopped down to f22, both the girl and the two trees are within the depth of field and are therefore in sharp focus.

 f22

The effect of focal length on depth of field

Telephoto position
The longer the focal length of the lens, the shallower the depth of field. In this shot, taken with the zoom lens in the telephoto position, only the subject and one of the columns are in sharp focus.

75 mm

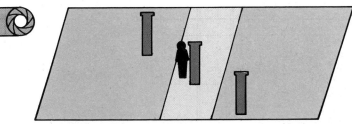

Wide-angle position
The shorter the focal length of the lens, the greater the depth of field. In this shot, taken with the zoom lens in the wide-angle position, the subject and all the columns are in sharp focus.

 10 mm

Viewfinder Systems

Whatever the virtues of the lens on your camera, a good viewfinder is vital. You should be able to see exactly what will appear on the film and also be able to tell whether it will be accurately in focus. There are two types of viewfinder systems: *direct* and *reflex*.

Direct viewfinders

The direct finder is a simple optical system which "looks at" the subject from a position parallel to the taking lens, but does not actually see *through* it. Unfortunately, it cannot be used to judge focus and will tend to produce problems of *parallax* when shooting close-ups (see right).

The system's chief advantages are that the image is very bright, because the viewfinder does not take away any light from the film. This makes it very useful on "existing light" or "XL" cameras, since as much light as possible is needed to expose the film.

Reflex viewfinders

Reflex viewing systems allow the subject to be viewed through the taking lens itself. They therefore show the exact image seen by the film, whether you are using a wide-angle or a telephoto lens. There are two types: *beam splitter* and *mirror shutter*.

The beam splitter

In beam splitter viewfinder systems a sizeable fraction of the light coming through the lens is diverted to the eyepiece by means of a half-silvered 45° mirror known as a *beam splitter block*. The remainder of the light passes on to the film. Since the light is taken from before the diaphragm in the lens, the image in the finder will not show the depth of field of the chosen aperture. However, the image remains bright, irrespective of the f stop, and focusing is easier because the lens is effectively at full aperture in the viewfinder. The beam splitter system is now standard on almost all super 8 cameras.

Parallax
On a direct viewfinder camera the image you see through the eyepiece will not be quite the same as that seen by the lens. This is due to their being some distance apart and the phenomenon is known as *parallax*. Normally the difference is so slight it can be ignored, but when filming close-ups it becomes critical. A subject framed perfectly in the viewfinder may turn out to have had her head cut off on the film.

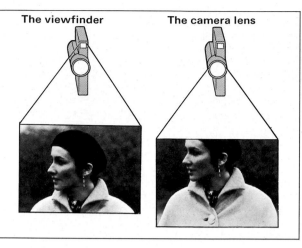

The viewfinder   The camera lens

The mirror shutter

In mirror shutter viewfinder systems a 45° mirror is incorporated into the shutter mechanism itself. The shutter is usually rotary (as in Arriflex cameras) in which case light is intermittently reflected sideways into the optical system of the viewfinder. Alternatively, the shutter can be of the "guillotine" type.

The advantages of mirror shutters are these: no incoming light is taken away from the film; interchangeable lenses can be used on the camera; and, because the light is reflected to the finder *after* the diaphragm, the image viewed has already been "stopped down". This allows you to see the effect of the aperture on the depth of field as you look through the viewfinder.

The only disadvantage is that, when actually shooting, the image in the viewfinder flickers with the movement of the mirror. This is not disturbing in practice, however. The mirror shutter system is now standard on all high-quality professional equipment.

How the beam splitter works
A half-silvered mirror within a prism block and set at an angle of 45° in the body of the lens diverts some of the light to the viewfinder eyepiece. The beam splitter is part of the lens itself and therefore lens interchangeability is ruled out on those cameras that have it.

Eyepiece

Film

Shutter

Image-forming lens

Beam splitter

Zoom lens

How the "guillotine" mirror shutter works
The camera shutter is actually a 45° mirror which opens and closes by moving up and down. It alternatively diverts *all* the light to the eyepiece when "closed", then *all* the light to the film for the period of the exposure.

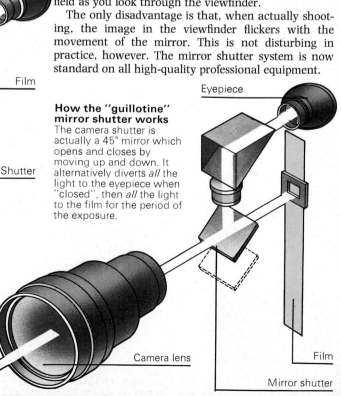

Eyepiece

Camera lens

Film

Mirror shutter

Metering Systems

All super 8, and some 16 mm, cameras are now equipped with built-in light meters which automatically adjust the aperture of the lens in response to the varying light. The principle behind them is simple. At the heart of the light meter is a small light-sensitive cell called a "photo resistor". It is usually the cadmium sulfide (CdS) variety. Its resistance to a tiny current sent through it by a battery varies according to the amount of light falling on it. If the light becomes brighter then the resistance drops, the current increases, and the aperture closes. If the amount of light falls the aperture opens.

Automatic metering undoubtedly works well in most situations. But there will be times when you need to be able to override the system. This is explained, together with the subject of separate hand-held meters and how to use them, on p. 90-91. There are two types of in-camera metering systems: *direct* and *reflex*.

Direct metering systems

In cameras with direct metering systems, the light-sensitive cell which measures the amount of light being reflected by the subject is situated *next* to the camera lens. The cell itself is usually of the CdS type, and this kind of system is often known as "electric eye" metering. The amount of light falling on the photo-cell is used to trigger a servo-motor which operates the aperture blades in the lens. Most direct metering systems are designed so that the angle-of-view of the sensor (generally about 40°) matches that of the lens. Unfortunately, however, such a meter cannot adapt to the varying angles-of-view produced by a zoom lens. Nor can it take account of any filters on the lens, and some exposure allowance must therefore be made, based on the appropriate factor for the filter being used (see p. 94). The chief advantage of this system is that the meter does not take any of the light from the film. As a result, it is most commonly used on XL cameras.

Viewfinder displays
Almost all cameras with automatic light metering systems have some form of display in the viewfinder. Depending on the camera, this may show either the f number selected or simply whether you are over- or under-exposing.

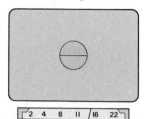

Moving f stop pointer.

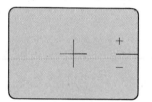

Moving scale of f numbers in top corner of viewfinder.

Moving pointer to show over- or under-exposure.

Reflex metering systems

In this system the light-sensitive cell samples the light which is actually passing through the taking lens. This is known as "through the lens" (TTL) or "behind the lens" (BTL) metering: the light sensor, which is usually a CdS cell, meters only the area viewed by the taking lens itself. As light passes through the lens, a beam splitter diverts some of it to the CdS cell – which may be designed to meter either the whole frame-area ("average" method) or merely the central portion ("center-weighted" method). Such meters are usually coupled by a servo system to the diaphragm so that they open and close the aperture according to changes in the brightness of the subject. The great advantage of TTL/BTL meters is that they automatically take account of both filters and changes in focal length: they see what the film sees. As a result, there is no need to make any correction for filter factors (see p. 94) or for the light-loss due to variation in the number of glass lens elements (see *T stops*, p. 46).

On the simpler cameras containing reflex metering systems, the diaphragm opens and closes automatically and a display in the viewfinder simply shows you what f stop has been selected. However, almost all good cameras with reflex metering now have a manual override which allows you to open up one stop or more to compensate for backlighting (see p. 91). This is frequently in the form of an "exposure lock". You can thereby exclude any parts of the scene which might fool the light meter – an expanse of white sky, for instance – and lock the meter at the correct setting for the shot. This can be done either by moving the camera up to the subject or, more easily, by zooming in to a representative mid-tone area on the subject, locking the exposure to that and then zooming back out again. Thus, the camera can be used in almost exactly the same way as a separate, hand-held "spot meter" (see *How to Get the Right Exposure*, p. 90-91).

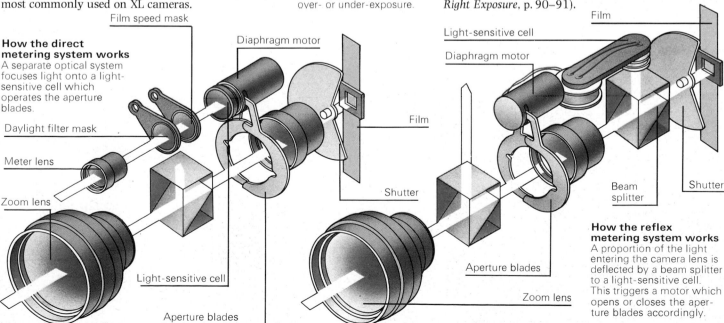

How the direct metering system works
A separate optical system focuses light onto a light-sensitive cell which operates the aperture blades.

Film speed mask
Diaphragm motor
Daylight filter mask
Meter lens
Zoom lens
Film
Shutter
Light-sensitive cell
Aperture blades

How the reflex metering system works
A proportion of the light entering the camera lens is deflected by a beam splitter to a light-sensitive cell. This triggers a motor which opens or closes the aperture blades accordingly.

Film
Light-sensitive cell
Diaphragm motor
Beam splitter
Shutter
Aperture blades
Zoom lens

The Principles of Color

Before you can understand anything about how film works (especially color film) you need to know something about the basic principles of light and color.

Light is the small sector of the electromagnetic spectrum which we can see with the eye; each different wavelength of light is perceived as a different color. Red is the shortest visible wavelength, and dark blue is the longest. Between these two extremes lie all the other colors. So-called "white light", such as that emitted by the sun, is a balanced mixture of all the colors.

The color circle

It is a convenient fiction to portray the colors of the visible spectrum in the form of a *color circle*. All the colors, or *hues*, in the circle merge gradually into one another, and they are all pure, or *saturated*, i.e. they contain no trace of either black or white.

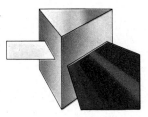

The visible spectrum
If white light is shone at an angle through the side of a glass prism, it will split up to form a rainbow-colored band called the "visible spectrum". The colors are seen as separate because each one has a different wavelength and is therefore "refracted" or bent differently.

Color circle

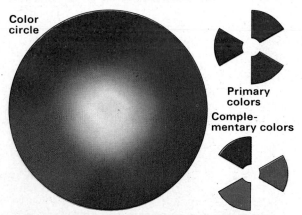

Primary colors

Complementary colors

Primary and complementary colors
The colors of the color circle fall into two categories: primary and complementary. For the purposes of film, as opposed to painting, the "primary" colors are blue, green and red; their "complementary" (or subtractive) colors, which are situated opposite them on the color circle, are yellow (which is white minus blue), magenta (which is white minus green) and cyan (which is white minus red).

Color contrast
When you are trying to create as much impact and contrast as you can, you should aim to work *across* the color circle. This is because the color which contrasts most strongly with any one primary color is its own complementary.

Color harmony
If you are trying to produce a harmonious effect, aim to keep all the colors within a narrow sector of the color circle. In other words, stick to closely related hues and avoid contrasting saturated colors.

Color addition/subtraction

All colors – whether in printing or on film – can be produced by a mixture of just three strategically placed hues. Forming complementaries by combining the three primary colors is known as the *additive principle*: if blue, green and red lights are shone onto a screen, complementary colors will appear where two primaries overlap; where all three primaries overlap, white light will form.

Forming primaries by combining the three complementary colors is known as the *subtractive principle*: if complementary-colored filters are held up to white light, primary colors will appear where two complementaries overlap; where all three complementaries overlap, there will be black – since no light of any color is able to pass.

Color addition

Any color in the spectrum can be created by combining blue, green and red lights.

Color subtraction

Any color in the spectrum can be created with yellow, magenta and cyan filters or "dyes".

Green and red lights together will produce yellow light.

Magenta blocks green; cyan blocks red. Blue is formed.

 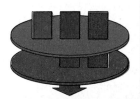

Blue and red lights together will produce magenta light.

Yellow blocks blue; cyan blocks red. Green is formed.

 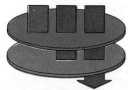

Blue and green lights together will produce cyan light.

Yellow blocks blue; magenta blocks green. Red is formed.

How Film Works

All film is sensitive to light. An image is recorded on the film because each part of the subject reflects a slightly different amount of light. In black and white film there is one layer of light-sensitive emulsion. It reacts to light of any color, but will only produce a black-and-white image. In color film there are three layers of emulsion, each of which is sensitive to a different color. These films are known as "integral tripacks". They all work on the principle that any light can be simulated by a combination of blue, green and red, and that these colors can be reproduced by a combination of yellow, magenta and cyan dyes or "filters". During processing, the metallic silver produced in each layer of emulsion is replaced by an appropriately colored dye. The dyes used are complementaries of the layers in question: the blue layer, for example, is yellow. In *reversal* film, the dyes produce a positive image; in *negative* film, a negative one.

The structure of film
Film is made up of a base, a backing and layers of emulsion. The "base" is simply a foundation for the emulsions, and is usually cellulose acetate or plastic polyester. The "backing" prevents light that has passed through the emulsions from bouncing back and forming a halo. The "emulsions" are thin layers of light-sensitive silver halides which convert to metallic silver when exposed to light. In color film, there are three layers – each sensitive to one of the primary colors – and also a yellow filter.

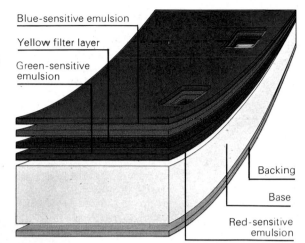

Blue-sensitive emulsion
Yellow filter layer
Green-sensitive emulsion
Backing
Base
Red-sensitive emulsion

Reversal film
The three emulsion layers are each affected differently by the various colors of the subject. The top layer records blue, the second green, and the third red. The areas *not* affected are then dyed in complementary colors to give a positive image.

Blue-sensitive layer
Blue is revealed during processing by dyeing all unaffected areas yellow – since yellow blocks blue.

Yellow filter layer
A yellow filter blocks any blue light not absorbed by the layer above and stops it reaching the layers below.

Green-sensitive layer
Green (and yellow – a mixture of green and red) are recorded by dyeing all unaffected areas magenta.

Red-sensitive layer
Red (and yellow – a mixture of red and green) are recorded by dyeing all unaffected areas cyan.

Positive image
When white light is shone through the developed film, a positive image of the subject can be projected onto a screen. It will appear in its original colors because, according to the subtractive principle, where complementary dyes overlap they will produce primary colors.

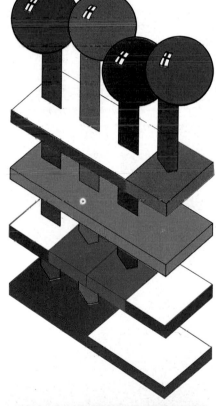

Negative film
The three emulsion layers are each affected differently by the various colors of the subject. The top layer records blue, the second green, and the third red. The areas which *are* affected are then dyed in complementary colors to give a negative image.

Blue-sensitive layer
Blue is revealed during processing by dyeing all affected areas yellow – blue's complementary.

Yellow filter layer
A yellow filter blocks any blue light not absorbed by the layer above and stops it reaching the layers below.

Green-sensitive layer
Green (and yellow – a mixture of green and red) are recorded by dyeing all affected areas magenta.

Red-sensitive layer
Red (and yellow – a mixture of red and green) are recorded by dyeing all affected areas cyan.

Negative image
After processing, negative film will show an image of the subject, not in its original colors, but in its "opposite" or complementary colors. A positive print can be made from the negative by shining white light through it and focusing it onto another strip of film – the print-stock.

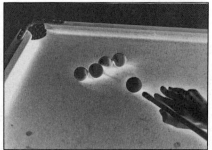

Choosing a Filmstock

Filmstocks vary considerably from type to type. They respond differently to light, they require different settings in the camera, and they produce very different results (see *Filmstock Specifications*, p. 272). When you come to choose your filmstock, it is useful to know what is meant by a number of technical terms.

Film speed

Different films have different degrees of sensitivity to light. This sensitivity is described as the film's *speed*. It is graduated in what are called "ASA" or "DIN" numbers. A "slow" film might have a speed of about 25 ASA, a "medium" film 100 ASA and a "fast" film 400 ASA or more. A 25 ASA film needs one stop more exposure than a film rated at 50 ASA and two stops more than a 100 ASA film in order to get the same result. However, all films allow a certain margin of error, or "latitude", in their exposure. The exposure latitude of any film is the range on either side of the rated speed which will give an acceptable image (see *Forced development*, p. 208).

Grain

We have seen that the light-sensitive emulsion layers in film are composed of thin coatings of silver halide particles. The smaller the particles, the finer and smoother the detail on the developed film. The degree to which individual particles are visible on projection is referred to as the *graininess* of the film. Fast film is more grainy than slow film: this is because fast film contains larger silver halide particles which are more sensitive to light than smaller ones. The grain of a film may vary from one part of the picture to another, but it is most visible on large neutral areas such as a gray sky.

Sharpness

The "sharpness" of film is a word used to describe a subjective impression of an image, and it is a combination of several factors which are easily confused: resolution, acutance and, to an extent, contrast.

A film's *resolving power* is its ability to record very fine detail. It is usually expressed in terms of the number of distinct vertical lines that can be recorded on one millimeter of film – over 100 in the case of slow film.

A film's *acutance* describes the sharpness of the boundary between the light and dark areas of an image. It determines the "bite" both of small details and of large areas of contrasting density.

Contrast

All subjects have areas of different brightness. A subject with a wide range of brightnesses – from dazzling highlights to deep shadows – is said to be of *high contrast*, and a subject with a narrow range of mid-tones is said to be of *low contrast*. Films vary in their ability to reproduce this range accurately. The degree to which any film has to compress the range of brightnesses is known as the "contrast gradient" or "gamma" of that film. If a film has a high "gamma" it will tend to exaggerate a subject of high contrast. If a film has a low "gamma" the image will be recorded in gray mid-tones and will tend to look "flat" (see also *High key and low key*, p. 97).

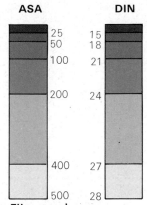

ASA	DIN
25	15
50	18
100	21
200	24
400	27
500	28

Film speed
The table shows the relation between the American (ASA) and the German (DIN) systems for rating film speed.

Grain
The top picture shows the increase in graininess when a frame of super 8 is blown up to 35 mm. Below left is an area of 25 ASA film, and below right 400 ASA.

Contrast
The top picture shows an area of film with a high contrast gradient. Beneath it is the same shot on low contrast film.

Negative or reversal film

Negative film produces a negative image. In black and white this means that the light areas of a subject are seen as black, and the dark areas are seen as white. In color it means that the original colors of the subject are recorded as their "opposite" primary or complementary colors. If the film is to be viewed, a print is made which has "normal" tonal balance.

Reversal or "positive" film, on the other hand, records the tonal values of the subject so that they correspond to the real thing. It can therefore be viewed directly, without making a print.

Both negative and reversal film are available in either color or black and white – except in 8 mm, which has no negative stocks. There are several advantages to using negative film: the process of printing allows you some room to correct the exposure or the color balance; it allows you to introduce "fades" and "dissolves" (see p. 186–7); and, if necessary, you can make a large number of prints from the original without loss of quality. Above all, negative film is *designed* to be printed. Reversal film, however, has the advantage of being cheaper, having a higher film speed and being easier to process. It is also said in some quarters to give greater sharpness.

Color or black and white film

It is only right that color film is now regarded as the normal filmstock, since our vision is in color. But black and white has great beauty and is often overlooked. It can formalize the patterns of light and shade and has a natural tendency to give atmosphere to a scene. Also, it is cheaper both to process and print, it is considerably faster (so it can save on lighting as well) and there are no worries about "color temperature" (see below).

Indoor or outdoor film

The color of light differs according to whether it is outdoors (sunlight) or indoors (artificial light), and is therefore said to have a different "color temperature" (see p. 92). All color film must be matched to the color temperature of the ambient light. There is a type of film called *daylight* film which is specially balanced for outdoor light. And there is *tungsten* (*Type A* or *Type B*) film for indoor light. By using a lens filter, it is possible to adapt one for the other.

There is also a third type of film (*Type G*) which is a compromise between outdoor and indoor color balance. It is for use in mixed light.

Fast or slow film

The film's speed is inversely related to its quality: the faster the film, the poorer the image. You should therefore choose as slow a film as will still give you a good exposure in the circumstances.

THE
ELEMENTS
OF
FILM

"The first quality of a director is to
see"   *Michelangelo Antonioni*

The Language of Film

Reference is often made to the "language" of film, because with film, as with language, the whole is greater than the sum of its parts. To take a melodramatic example, if you follow a shot of a woman crying with a shot of an empty baby carriage you have created a whole that is more complex and more potent than the two shots together. Film can leap from one snot to the next with the fluency of a dream so as to bypass our literal interpretation of images thereby striking directly at our imagination. For instance, when you watch an effective suspense film, you are often unaware as to what exactly causes unease or discomfort. In other words, watching a movie does not require any standard of literacy. However, the more movies you watch and the more carefully you look at them, the greater will be your understanding of the techniques invloved. You will begin to see *how* sequences are assembled.

Superimposed on our instinctive understanding of film language are a number of conventions that have evolved with the movies. These devices, usually known as the "grammar" of film (see p. 72), are concerned with such things as changes of direction, intercutting and transitions in time. We now accept these conventions so automatically that they pass unnoticed, and as a result they have often been mistaken for rules.

Because film "language" has so many variables, there is no doubt that the "rules" of film should only be discarded for good reasons and by someone who knows how to break them to telling effect. You have only to see one really incoherent (or "illiterate") movie to appreciate the value of film grammar. Imagine a page on which each word has a different size and color, could be moved across the page, zoomed in and out, have its own distinctive sound, and have a variable duration: these effects àre the fundamentals of filmmaking. And unless all these elements are first understood in isolation, they will never be combined successfully.

The place of editing

The best way to improve your films is to edit them. Some films can be "edited in the camera", but to shoot a film that really needs no editing requires a flawless filming technique and a mastery of cutting that only comes with years of experience. Unfortunately, and perhaps inevitably, this is how most people *begin* to make movies.

The results can be a little discouraging, for without editing you cannot juxtapose images, build a sequence, discard rubbish, tighten loose shots, intercut parallel actions, or indeed give any shape to the film beyond that of the original event. On the other hand, editing your footage can be a very exciting and creative activity. To hold film, manipulate it, arrange its images in time and judge the pace and flow of its movement, are enormously satisfying for the filmmaker.

There are, of course, films that may not need editing (such as a simple record taken for private consumption only). But even there, a knowledge of how a sequence is built will make all the difference to the shooting technique. Such knowledge can only be gained by editing film, and many of the shooting techniques that follow in this book pre-suppose that you *are* going to edit.

1 ⏱ 2 sec Gavino looks around at his friends

2 ⏱ 12 sec The friends walk away

Gavino's friends: "Remember: study vocabulary, learn the meaning of words"

The parade ground
As Gavino watches his friends walk off, there is an abrupt cut to a shot of the commanding officer addressing his men. Gavino is among then (shot 7).

Officer: "The flag ... All of you must know the meaning of the flag ...

5 ⏱ 10.5 sec The parade ground

You can forget your mother's name, your father's name, your brother's names ...

"Padre Padrone" (1977)
This sequence from the Taviani brothers' film, *Padre Padrone* ("My Father, My master") illustrates the freedom with which film can cross time and space. The hero, Gavino, is an illiterate Sardinian peasant who has enlisted into the army to ecape from the tyranny of his father. But on the parade ground in Turin, with the commanding officer's patriotic words hammering through his head, his new-found obsession with learning to read merges with his memories of his sadistic father – his master.

3 ⏱ 5.5 sec Gavino stares after him

4 ⏱ 15.5 sec The commanding officer

but not the significance of the flag, symbol of our mother country"

6 ⏱ 4 sec Raising the flag

7 ⏱ 8 sec Gavino

8a ⏱ 42.5 sec Raising the flag

8b Close-up of flag

8c Close-up of flag

The flag
From Gavino watching the flag being raised, there is a cut to a seemingly continuous shot of the flag itself. The camera zooms into a close-up of what at first appears to be the same flag. But this is a subtle transition to shot 8d. At the same time, Gavino's voice-over as he begins to recite words merges with the commanding officer's tirade on the Italian flag.

Gavino voice-over: "Banner ... bank ... band ..."

"Bandit ... bondage ... baritine ... Bantu ..."

"State ... stagnant ... staff ... stall ... stalagmite ... starred ... statue ...

Gavino as a boy
Leaving the *red* of the flag – a political statement in itself – the camera tilts down and pans around to the sheep and fields of Gavino's childhood. A boy appears in the frame and the camera cuts in to show him loading his barrow – for Gavino, it is a memory that is also a premonition of return to his Sardinian farm.

8d Sardinian landscape

9a ⏱ 9 sec Boy in fields

9b Boy in fields

"Station ... generation ...infant ... boy ... baby ... benumbed ... bloodsucker ... blistered ... blockhead ... savage ... wild ..."

The flag again
In shot 10a the camera again returns to the flag. Gavino's incantation of words (he is learning to read) has moved from "pastoral ... pasture ... pasteurization ..." to "languid ... horrid ... filthy ...", and finally the camera tilts down from the flag onto his father striding through the landscape.

10a ⏱ 17 sec Close-up of flag

10b Close-up of flag

11a ⏱ 17 sec Close-up of flag

"Mountainous ... bucolic ... idyllic ... Arcadian ... pastoral ... pasture ... pasteurization ...

"Deportation ... separation ... rejection ... masturbation ...

"Languid ... horrid ... filthy ... father ..."

Resolution
Finally, the logic becomes clear: for Gavino the flag symbolizes the paternalism of Italy itself – "father ... patriarch ... godfather ... master ..." This is both a political and a personal vision of his past, expressed through the color of the flag, the flashbacks of his father and the alliteration of the voice-over on the sound track. It also provides the title of the movie itself.

11b Gavino's father

"Patriarch ... godfather ... master ... Father Eternal ... patron ..."

11c Gavino's father

12 ⏱ 46 sec Gavino studying

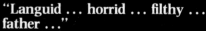

Steadying the Camera

If you want to make a movie which other people will enjoy watching, you should aim to keep the camera as steady as possible. The kind of shakiness produced by careless hand-held camerawork is unsettling to watch, and it should only be used to achieve special effects such as "earthquakes" and "explosions" or the view seen by a running fugitive or a staggering drunk (see *Subjective tracking*, p. 70). The most "natural" look comes from a steady camera: the film-frame then acts like a pane of clear glass through which we watch the action. If the movement of the camera becomes too erratic, this illusion is destroyed and we become excessively aware of the filming process itself.

The only certain way of guaranteeing that the camera is stable is to use a tripod. But there is a great deal you can do to improve your hand-holding technique.

Hand-holding the camera

There are many occasions – when you need to be able to move quickly or when space is restricted – where it clearly makes more sense to hand-hold the camera than to use a tripod. Modern cameras are extremely portable, and you should exploit this to the full.

When hand-holding the camera, move in close and use the widest angle you can justify. The picture will appear steadier and you will also have a greater depth of field. Remember that the longer the focal length the more your movements will be exaggerated by the lens. So, unless you have no choice, avoid sustained hand-held telephoto shots. If you want your subject to be larger, move nearer rather than zooming in.

The hand-held camera really comes into its own when following a moving subject (see p. 70). Aim to move in a smooth glide, keeping your steps short to minimize up-and-down motion. Practice keeping both eyes open so that you can see and avoid any obstacles in your path.

Camera supports

For sustained hand-held shots using one of the larger super 8 cameras, a *shoulder pod* is helpful. This enables you to brace the camera against your shoulder, rather like a rifle, so that it remains as steady as possible. Some shoulder pods incorporate a support around the waist.

The balance of the camera is as important as its weight, especially with 16 mm equipment. Aluminum body harnesses are available which support the camera and leave the camera operator's hands free.

How to hand-hold the camera
Almost all cameras are designed for right-handed people. Therefore, brace the camera by pressing it up against your eye with your right hand, keeping your right elbow pressed tightly against your side. Keep your feet slightly apart and stay literally on your toes. Use a wall, a tree, the corner of a building, a car roof, the back of a chair, or even another person to lean on whenever you can.

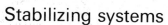

Stabilizing systems

A series of stabilizing systems have recently become available which enable a camera operator to perform a very smooth hand-held track or dolly shot. They are heavily damped so that they absorb all abrupt movement. The camera "floats" independently of the operator, enabling him or her to run up stairs or over rough ground with astonishing smoothness. They are very expensive but can be hired as required.

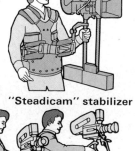

"Steadicam" stabilizer

Shoulder pods
These lightweight aluminum supports allow you to steady the camera by bracing it against your shoulder.

Tripods

There are many movie techniques and subjects for which a tripod is essential – for example, titling, time-lapse, remote-control, telephoto wildlife shots, architecture, landscapes, and macro photography. As a general rule, though, you should *always* use a tripod if you know that you will be shooting from a fixed position. Steadiness is the perfect example of invisible technique. You should therefore beware of intercutting between tripod work and shots which were obviously hand-held: the difference will be very noticeable.

Tripods come in various sizes and in various degrees of sturdiness. They have collapsible legs made of metal or wood which can be adjusted so that the tripod can be properly leveled on uneven ground. The legs may have rubber or spiked tips to give a grip on different surfaces.

The most important thing you will want from a tripod is steadiness, both in the legs and in the head. Therefore, go for the sturdiest model you can afford. The lighter and cheaper tripods are adequate for static shots but tend to move with the camera when you pan or tilt.

Setting up the tripod

Begin by setting the tripod up at the right height. Then attach the camera to it. Check the view and make certain that the camera is absolutely upright, especially when the shot contains strong vertical or horizontal lines. Some tripods have a built-in bubble level for this purpose. If yours does not, it is worth buying a small one and laying it on top of the camera to check the leveling. Remember that if you intend to pan or tilt, the camera must be level at the start *and* at the end of the movement.

On a slippery floor, the legs of the tripod are sometimes held in place by a *spider* or a *spreader*. However, standing the tripod on a blanket or taping around the legs can be just as effective as a way of keeping it steady.

The pan head

The camera is mounted onto the tripod by means of a *pan head*. This moves from side to side for panning, and up and down for tilting. Ball and socket heads, which move in every direction, though ideal for still photography, are unsuitable for movie work because the camera cannot be kept vertical when panning.

It is vital that the pan head should not only be very steady but that it should move as smoothly as possible. You should be able to pan the camera using only the slightest pressure; the movement should be perfectly even, without sticking or jumping; and it should stop when you do, without any backlash or overshooting.

The cheaper, lightweight tripods usually have *friction* heads which rely on the resistance between their moving parts to damp the movement. They are usually adequate for the smaller super 8 cameras, but they tend to "stick" at the beginning of a pan or tilt.

Although they are more expensive, *fluid* heads give the best results for normal work. They are hydraulically damped and give a perfectly smooth movement.

Geared heads are large, expensive and very accurate. They are used chiefly in professional movie work for supporting heavy 16 mm and 35 mm cameras.

Various types of tripod

Baby tripod (left)
This is smaller and lighter than the standard.

"High hat" (above)
This is used for difficult or floor-level shots.

Standard tripod (above)
This wooden-leg tripod is standard in professional movie work.

Basic tripod (above)
This simple aluminum tripod has twist-grip telescopic legs.

Monopod (above left)
This is a single extendable leg which supports a hand-held camera.

Cullmann tripod (above)
This tripod has quick-set clamps on the legs and will go very low.

Securing the tripod legs

Spider
This device stops the tripod legs from slipping.

Improvising with tape
Wrap tape or a length of string around the legs.

Using a blanket base
A rug or blanket prevents the legs from slipping.

Various types of pan head

Friction head (left)
A single handle allows the camera to be moved both horizontally for a pan and vertically for a tilt.

Fluid head (right)
This head produces very smooth pans and tilts. The movement is damped by a heavily viscous fluid.

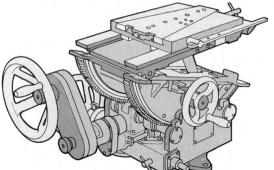

Geared head
This head is designed primarily for large studio cameras. They can be moved vertically and horizontally by rotating the separate handwheels, and produce very precise pans and tilts. Some models have a gearchange system which allows you to select different panning and tilting speeds.

The Basic Shots

It is customary when talking about film to divide shots into three main categories: *long shot*, *mid shot* and *close-up*. Although the division is a somewhat arbitrary one, the terms are usually used in connection with the human figure. In all cases, what is crucial is the amount of the subject in the frame. For example, a long shot usually includes a subject's feet; a mid shot usually extends below the waist; and a close-up does not include the hands. These three basic shots relate broadly to three different degrees of concentration: they narrow an audience's attention from the overall scene, through a group of people, to the single individual. The shots can be further divided into sub-categories such as "big close-up", "medium close-up" or "extreme long shot".

The three basic shots
Camera shots are conventionally divided into three categories: close-up, mid shot and long shot. They produce quite different effects, since each shot has its own specific characteristics.

The close-up isolates the head of one of the boys.

The mid shot reveals the immediate surroundings.

The long shot establishes an overall setting.

Cutting height
When framing your shot, remember that to include only half your subject's feet, their hands by their side, or their hands gesturing, is very irritating for an audience to watch. For this reason, a convention called "cutting height" has developed. You will find that if you cut the human figure at one of the points shown right you will get a more attractive composition. The cutting heights are usually regarded as being just below the armpits, below the chest, below the waist, below the crotch and below the knees.

Cutting heights

Close-up
The best cutting height for a close-up is just below the armpits (above). This will balance the composition.

Mid shot
The cutting height for a mid shot is below the waist. This makes it a "body" shot since the face does not dominate.

Long shot
A long shot should include your subject's entire body (above). It makes for bad composition to cut them off at the ankles (below).

The characteristics of the shots

The *long shot* is the most basic of all movie shots, and in most situations, if you have time for only one shot, this is the one it should be. It includes everything of importance in a given scene and can be used purely for conveying information – as an "establishing" or "master" shot. Alternatively, it can be used creatively, in direct and dramatic contrast to surrounding mid shots and close-ups. A long shot shows your subject's relation to nature, to their environment or to a group of other people.

The *mid shot* is the prime shot-size for establishing the interplay of character. It reveals enough detail of a character's face for us to be involved in what they are saying or thinking but not so much that we are *only* interested in that one person. Two or more people can be in shot at once, and all their reactions will be perfectly visible; you can then intercut close-ups as well.

A *close-up* concentrates exclusively on one person's face, or on any one detail of a scene. It can therefore give an insight into the interior life of the subject. The close-up is the most "compelling" shot, since it forces an audience's attention onto one single person.

Long shot (above)
The two girls cycling towards the camera are seen in long shot.

Mid shot (left)
This mid shot isolates the nun but shows her against a background of trees and a white fence.

Close-up (right)
The close-up of this girl shows her at close-range. It is basically a facial shot in which she dominates the frame.

Extreme close-up

Also known as a *big close-up*, this shot should not be used casually. It produces a "shock" effect by filling the screen with a single image, and is often used to focus an audience's attention onto a character's eyes or hands. Remember, however, that a face looks distorted if the camera is too close (see p. 67).

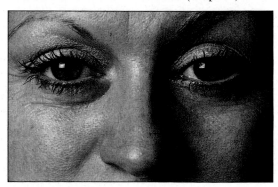

Extreme long shot

This is the shot to use if you want a panoramic view of a city or a landscape. In this way, it can act as a huge "master shot", establishing the location in which the action will take place. Very long shots can also be used to set a tiny human figure against a vast landscape, conveying a sense of dramatic isolation.

Extreme close-up (left)
In this shot, the subject's eyes and nose fill the frame. A blink of the eyelid at this range would appear to be a powerfully dramatic gesture.

Extreme long shot (right)
The lone figure in this shot gives a sense of scale to the ruined Armenian church, as well as emphasizing its precariousness.

Choosing the Right Shot

Movement in the frame

In still photography, composition is of primary importance because the image does not move. In movie photography, however, the movement itself is part of the composition, so when choosing a camera position you should make the most of whatever action you can expect to see in the frame. Bear in mind that with a moving subject the composition at the beginning of the shot may be less important than the middle or the end. When you select a spot from which to film, try to anticipate how things will develop during the course of the shot. There is no point in starting with a close-up if your subject is going to end up running towards you. Similarly, a long shot would be wrong in the facial details.

Remember that the focal length of the lens and the distance between the camera and the subject will affect the degree of movement in the frame (see p. 67).

Matching different shots

Because each type of shot has its own characteristics, you must constantly be aware of the effect you are creating when juxtaposing one shot with another. Cutting from a long shot to a mid shot will *concentrate* the audience's attention onto a smaller area of interest. But following a close-up with a mid shot often *reduces* the tension or intensity in a scene by opening out the shot and allowing other elements into the frame. Be careful when cutting shots from filmed positions and from different angles that your subjects are looking in the same direction (see opposite), that they are moving in the same direction (see p. 74) and that they are in the correct part of the frame (see p. 73).

When cutting from, say, a mid shot to a close-up of the same subject, you should try to match the lighting, the height and also the expression of the two shots.

You should also bear in mind that the difference in size and angle between two shots should always be large enough to be decisive but not so large as to jolt the eye.

Subtle facial expressions should really be close-ups, not long shots.

Long shot to mid shot
A "cut-in" from a long shot to a mid shot will focus the attention of the audience on your subject. From being merely a figure in front of a building, the man reading the magazine (right) suddenly fills the frame.

Mid shot to close-up
A "cut-in" from a mid shot to a close-up concentrates the attention still further. The background becomes scarcely visible and the girl's head and shoulders fill the frame.

Image size

Unlike the theater, where the distance between the audience and the actors remains fixed, a movie camera is able to move closer to and further away from the subject – either by zooming or by tracking in and out. This means that as a filmmaker you can control the viewpoint of the audience.

When choosing your shot, bear in mind that if you are very close to the subject, every action he or she makes will seem exaggerated. On the other hand, if you are a long way away, only large gestures will be visible.

As a general rule, remember that the smaller the gauge you are using, the more you will have to rely on close-ups. This is because the small screen of 8 mm formats is unsuited to sustained long shots; if they are to be successful, they must be powerfully composed and should not rely on the perception of minute detail.

Matching close-ups

If you are filming a couple talking to each other by intercutting separate close-ups of them, be certain that you match up the size of the shots. If they are different, the relative size of the faces will affect the way the audience "sees" the relationship.

Woman dominant
If the close-ups of the woman are consistently larger than the close-ups of the man, she will tend to appear the more dominant of the couple. If this is the effect you want, then the technique can be used to great advantage.

Man dominant
The reverse is true if the close-ups of the man are larger than those of the woman: he will appear as the more powerful character. Be careful when intercutting close-ups to match up the "eyelines" (see right and p. 76–7).

Eyeline

The *eyeline* of your subject is generally taken to be the direction in which he or she is looking – although it is a term whose meaning can vary according to the context in which it is used (see p. 102).

When filming a single subject, the closer the eyeline is to the camera lens, the more intense will be his or her gaze – and therefore the stronger the shot. For this reason, when cutting from a mid shot to a close-up, the increased intensity produced by the close-up should be matched by a narrowing of the angle between the camera and the subject's eyeline (see right).

Filming a person looking straight into the camera will allow the audience to "enter" the subject's mind. But if one subject in a dialogue is looking straight at the camera, however, then the camera becomes their interlocutor. In this case, the camera is as it were "inside" the head of the other person in the conversation.

When shooting a group of people by cutting from a master shot to close-ups and vice-versa, it is vital that your subjects are seen to be looking in the same direction in the close-ups as they are when we see them all together in the mid shot. The eyeline close-ups should be carefully matched to the overall geography of the scene.

In a dialogue, the eyes of each person are normally filmed slightly "off camera". One of the two usually looks left of the camera; the other right. This way, when the close-ups are intercut, the respective positions of the two people are maintained and the audience happily accepts that they are in fact talking to one another (see p. 76).

Narrowing the eyeline on a cut-in
When cutting from a mid shot to a close-up, narrow the angle of the subject's eyeline as shown.

Subject facing camera
A close-up of someone looking straight into the camera is one of the strongest shots available since the subject's gaze is directed straight at the audience. It is a shot often used with a voice-over soliloquy which represents what the subject is supposed to be thinking.

Incorrect

Correct

Matching close-ups to the master shot
Be careful that your subjects are looking in the same direction in close-ups as they are in the master shot – or they will appear to have moved and continuity will be lost.

Correct

Incorrect

Correct

Incorrect

Correct

Incorrect

Composing the Shot

The composition of a shot on movie film is different from still photography in two fundamental ways: first, it must be matched, in content and in style, to the shots around it; and second, it must frame a moving subject in a satisfying way *throughout its length*.

Good composition is not a science and therefore such "rules" as it has are most evident when they are broken. An unbalanced, cluttered shot or an ugly composition draws attention to itself; whereas it is hard to say exactly why a well-composed shot is good. Nevertheless, there are certain guidelines which are worth following: they concern where you position your subject, the lines of interest you create, and the relative balance of the elements in the frame.

The so-called "Rule of Thirds" says that you should try to avoid splitting the frame into two equal halves. The effect will be weak and static if you set the horizon midway between the top and bottom and then place your subject in the dead center of the screen. It is far better to divide the frame into thirds so that you create a tension between the various unbalanced parts. The strong diagonal lines of interest that this kind of composition creates will give the shot a feeling of depth and direction. This technique is particularly effective for set-ups containing two people (see p. 76–7).

Above all, remember that the golden rule of all composition is to *keep it simple*. A beautiful composition should never take precedence over clarity; the focus of attention should always be obvious. A cluttered shot, however well-composed, will always be confusing and will never be compelling on the screen.

Balance

A well-balanced shot is easy to recognize but almost impossible to define. You should try to get into the habit of weighing the subject with your eye, and asking yourself whether it would look better a little to the left, or higher in the frame, or more tightly framed.

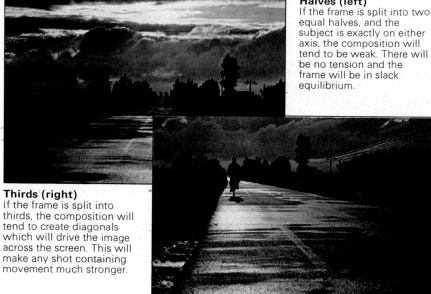

Halves (left)
If the frame is split into two equal halves, and the subject is exactly on either axis, the composition will tend to be weak. There will be no tension and the frame will be in slack equilibrium.

Thirds (right)
If the frame is split into thirds, the composition will tend to create diagonals which will drive the image across the screen. This will make any shot containing movement much stronger.

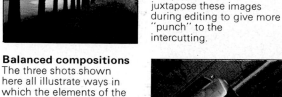

Opposing diagonals
Frame your shots so that you emphasize any diagonals in the composition. Then juxtapose these images during editing to give more "punch" to the intercutting.

Balanced compositions
The three shots shown here all illustrate ways in which the elements of the picture can be positioned in the frame to create a sense of visual balance.

Composing for color

Color can have as much effect on your composition as light or form. One small dot of red in an otherwise monochrome image can have an influence out of all proportion to its size; just as a well-balanced composition can look awful if the colors all conflict. Try to produce an overall color-balance throughout the film or sequence which matches the subject or mood of the movie.

The color spectrum

Coordinating the color
Although this shot features strong, saturated color – the blue gates in the foreground – the effect is not strident. The use of cool blues and greens conveys a sense of tranquility and harmony. This is emphasized by the symmetry of the composition, which leads the eye down the path to the door of the house.

Using strong colors
The strong, primary colors in this shot of two parrots convey a sense of liveliness and vitality. However, the vibrancy of the high contrast colors has been successfully controlled by the bold shapes and the simplicity of the composition. Balancing the color is as important as balancing the composition – although it is, of course, less easy to manipulate.

Framing

A powerful composition can be created by positioning the camera so that some foreground object "frames" the subject. The framing device may be anything from the branch of a tree, a doorway, or a window, to a person or group of people, and the effect may be used to focus attention on the isolated figure.

Framing
This shot of a small boy silhouetted in a doorway illustrates how framing can be used to create a simple but powerful composition. The two large, dark masses on either side balance each other and concentrate the attention onto the boy. Remember to take a light reading for the scene outside, not inside (see p. 91).

High angle shots

Changing the height from which the camera "sees" the subject is a useful way of introducing variety into a sequence. It is a technique that can also be used to create specific effects and moods. A *high angle shot* is one in which the camera is placed above the subject. From this angle, we look *down* on the subject, and he or she may therefore tend to seem dominated by the camera's point-of-view.

High viewpoint
A high camera angle emphasizes the abstract elements of composition in the shot below, and reduces the impact of the cowboy with the gun, right.

Low angle shots

By positioning the camera close to the ground and pointing it upwards, you can create a *low angle shot*. From this viewpoint, we look *up* at the subject, which therefore seems to assume greater size, strength and importance. It is a shot commonly used to emphasize height and dominance.

Low viewpoint
A low camera angle gives an unusual viewpoint on the small girl. It distorts the scale and seems to increase the stature of the cowboy, right.

The Zoom

A *zoom lens* is a lens with a variable focal length (see p. 43). It allows you complete control over the angle-of-view so that you can range from a telephoto to a wide-angle shot, or vice-versa, when and as you wish. The range of focal lengths covered by a zoom lens is commonly expressed as a ratio. For example, a 6 to 60 mm lens is said to have a zooming ratio of 10:1. This means that its telephoto setting is ten times longer than its wide angle. Remember, though, that knowing the ratio is not always as important as knowing what the telephoto or wide-angle settings actually are (see *Choosing a zoom lens*, p. 43).

Although zoom lenses are comparatively recent innovations in movie photography, they are rapidly becoming the norm. Their great advantage is that they give you a wide range of focal lengths without you having to carry around a lot of different prime lenses. But it also enables you to alter the angle-of-view during the shot – in other words, to produce zooms on film. Most zooms are now motorized and can be operated at the touch of a button. However, perhaps because of this, there is a tendency for beginners to zoom in and out too often. A zoom is a powerful instrument of expression and it should not be used randomly.

When to zoom

A zoom is essentially two dimensional; unlike a track, it does not alter perspective, only the angle-of-view (see p. 67). Therefore, you should only zoom when you cannot move the camera itself – with the reservation that a steady tripod-zoom is better than a wobbly, hand-held tracking shot. However, there are times when a zoom is the ideal tool; when picking out a figure in a landscape, for example, or shooting a scene across water – that is, when your subject is inaccessible. Choose the speed of the zoom carefully, and begin and end with "holding shots".

Wide-angle

Telephoto

Zooms in combination

In general, you should never zoom twice in succession – particularly not in reverse directions. Zooms should be separated by at least two static shots or pans unless, of course, you are aiming for an effect of frantic restlessness. It is possible, however, to combine a series of zooms in the same direction by quick dissolves or by cutting on the move. You must decide if the dissolves are to be made on the move or on holding shots at either end. Whichever you choose, follow the scheme through. Dissolves on the move are faster and more fluent. It is important that the speed of each zoom be consistent.

Variable focal length
A zoom lens allows you to choose the exact focal length you want.

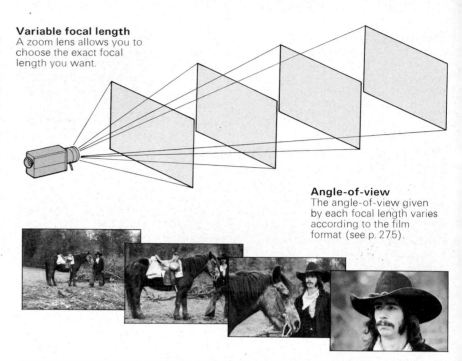

Angle-of-view
The angle-of-view given by each focal length varies according to the film format (see p. 275).

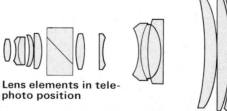

How the zoom lens works

A variable-focus zoom lens contains several elements divided into different groups within the lens barrel. The zooming is done by the central groups, which move backwards and forwards to alter the focal length. The front group of elements controls the focusing at different distances. And the group nearest the film actually forms the image onto the film plane. Almost all super 8 cameras have *auto* or *power zooms*, operated by a small electric motor, and sometimes having a variable speed.

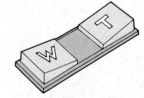

Power zoom
The zoom motor is controlled by buttons or a rocker-switch.

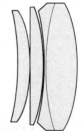

Lens elements in telephoto position

Telephoto
The zooming elements move back to give a narrow angle-of-view.

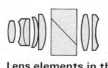

Lens elements in the wide-angle position

Wide-angle
The zooming elements move forward to give a wide angle-of-view.

Zooming in

A *zoom-in* is a narrowing of the vision and of the concentration. Unlike a simple cut from, say, a mid shot to a close-up, a zoom-in maintains an absolutely clear geography and forces the audience's attention onto the close-up. It has no parallel in our everyday experience and should be used sparingly. If you intend to use a zoom-in, *always focus up first* (see p. 44). If possible, use a tripod to avoid camera-shake and rehearse the shot.

The zoom-in
This focuses and concentrates the attention of the audience. Always begin and end with "holding shots".

Zooming out

A *zoom-out* is not a process of concentration, but of revelation. As you zoom out, a succession of new objects will continually enter the frame; it is vital, therefore, that the shot should become more interesting as it progresses. Try to preview the framing of the final wide angle before starting the shot, since it is more important than the initial close-up. There is usually no need to pre-focus for the end of the shot because depth of field increases.

The zoom-out
As the angle-of-view widens, more elements come into the shot and the surroundings or setting of the initial close-up are revealed.

Zooming and panning

One of the most satisfying ways of softening the relentlessness of a zoom is to combine it with a pan. Because they are happening at the same time, the sideways motion of the camera tends to disguise the change of focal length. It is a difficult camera movement to perform well so, where possible, try to rehearse the shot. Use a tripod, focus up first, and keep both the pan and the zoom slow.

The zoom and pan
It is essential to use a tripod for this sort of "combination" camera movement.

Initial holding shot
The movement begins with the lens set on wide-angle. The girl appears in long shot beside the lake. She is walking from left to right towards the camera.

Final holding shot
As the girl approaches, the camera pans around to the right and begins to zoom in. The shot ends with a "hold" on the girl's face in close-up.

Choosing a Focal Length

Whether your camera has a zoom lens or a selection of prime lenses, your choice of focal length will affect the depth of field, the perspective, the atmosphere and the sense of movement in the shot.

Depth of field and focal length

As we have seen (see p. 47), focal length is one of the factors that affects the *depth of field* – the range of distances from the camera within which your subject will be sharply focused. For any given aperture, the depth of field is smaller at long focal lengths than it is at short focal lengths. A telephoto lens will therefore tend to isolate a subject by throwing the background and foreground out of focus; it allows you to choose exactly what part of a scene you want in sharp focus.

Conversely, a wide-angle lens with a short focal length will give you an effect of "deep focus": everything in the shot is likely to be in sharp focus, even at quite wide apertures. Focal length is often used in movie photography to manipulate depth of field, because altering the aperture for the same effect will upset the exposure unless your camera has a variable shutter (see p. 42) or you use neutral density filters (see p. 94).

Deep focus (above)
A wide depth of field means that the gull and the background scenery are both in sharp focus.

Shallow focus (left)
A long focal length reduces depth of field and throws the background out of focus.

Isolating a figure (right)
A wide aperture reduces depth of field and blurs the background and the figures on either side.

"Pulling focus"

Because the lens can only be focused for one distance at a time, your subjects will tend to go out of focus if they suddenly move towards or away from the camera. At a wide-angle setting, where depth of field is greater, this is not often a problem; but for telephoto shots, where depth of field is very shallow, focusing is critical. When following a moving subject, you must be prepared to adjust the focus wherever necessary. The technique is known as *pulling* or *following focus*. It is not difficult as long as your camera has a reflex "TTL" viewfinder, although it is much easier if you know when and where your subject is going to move. It is always best to rehearse the shot before you start filming.

Selective focusing can be used creatively to shift the emphasis from one part of the scene to another. The method involves using a very shallow depth of field and changing the point of focus during the course of the shot. For example, a shot might begin with only a foreground subject in sharp focus. As the focus-pull begins, this subject will blur and another subject in the background, previously not visible, will come into sharp focus.

Focus pull
At the beginning of the shot, only the tree blossom is in focus. As the focus pull progresses the girl in the background slowly appears.

Perspective and focal length

Altering the focal length by zooming will vary the angle-of-view, but not the perspective. Zooming is flat and two-dimensional; although the subject is being magnified, the distance from the camera remains unchanged and so the subject's relation to the background is precisely the same throughout the zoom.

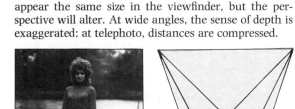

Zooming in (left)
Narrowing the angle-of-view by zooming in will increase the image size. But because the camera does not move in relation to the subject, perspective is unchanged.

Zooming in and tracking out (right)
It is possible to keep the same image size by moving the camera further away as you zoom in. But because the subject-to-camera distance changes, so does perspective.

Manipulating perspective

Only moving the camera changes perspective. This can be demonstrated quite simply: if you zoom in but move the camera away from your subject, he or she will appear the same size in the viewfinder, but the perspective will alter. At wide angles, the sense of depth is exaggerated; at telephoto, distances are compressed.

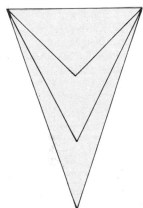

Atmosphere and focal length

Your choice of focal length will have a considerable effect on the "feel" of your shot. Wide-angle shots, which exaggerate depth, can be combined with short subject-to-camera distances to give "deep focus" effects and a certain ruthless clarity. The camera is unmistakably part of the scene, and the degree of impact and realism which this produces make wide angles common in documentary work. Close-up wide-angle shots of the human face, however, tend to be unflattering.

Long focal lengths, which compress distances, tend to produce more flattering shots – especially for portraits. If you use telephoto lenses and long subject-to-camera distances, the camera becomes a remote observer and you will produce detached, lyrical images.

Because the feel of a wide-angle shot is so different from that of a telephoto lens, the two can only be juxtaposed with difficulty. Try to decide on the atmosphere from the start and stick to it throughout.

Exaggerating distance
Wide-angle lenses are ideal for shooting in enclosed spaces since they have a large angle-of-view. However, they are unflattering for portraits, as they accentuate the nose and chin.

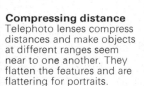

Compressing distance
Telephoto lenses compress distances and make objects at different ranges seem near to one another. They flatten the features and are flattering for portraits.

Movement and focal length

If your subject is walking towards the camera and you are using a long focal length, they will seem to be moving very slowly. To make movement seem faster, get closer to your subject and zoom out to a wide angle. They will then appear to grow rapidly in size and will move quickly through the frame.

How to emphasize movement

In each case, the car pictured below has traveled about the same distance. However, its movement seems faster in the wide-angle shots than the telephoto ones.

Start of a telephoto shot

End of a telephoto shot

Start of wide-angle shot

End of wide-angle shot

Panning and Tilting

A *pan* is a horizontal rotation of the camera about its vertical axis. Pans are used either to cover a wider scene than can be encompassed by the stationary lens, to follow a moving subject, or to relate one subject to another. Most pans are made on a tripod, since a steady hand-held pan requires excellent balance and control.

There is a great tendency for amateurs to use the pan far too often. The result, when combined with pointless zooming, tilting and tracking, is very unsettling to watch. You should never pan just for the sake of it. If you do decide to use a pan, try to get some action in the scene to "motivate" the camera's movement. Always ask yourself, "What am I panning to?", and plan the beginning, the middle and the end of the shot. Remember that any camera movement is easier to get into than out of, and that your pan should become more, not less interesting, as it advances.

It is ugly to come to a pan on the move, so give yourself a good, long static shot (or *holding shot*) at the start and end of every pan. The pan itself need not be continuous; it may well pause on its way. The pauses must be just long enough to be deliberate, but brief enough to retain the momentum – two seconds is a good average. Pans can be "intercut" with one another, but in general avoid a succession of different pans unless you have a moving subject to connect them. Finally, beware of changes in light-level (see *Metering for movement*, p. 94).

The pan
A pan is a shot in which the camera is moved around in a horizontal arc.

How to hand-hold a pan
Stand pointing towards the end of the pan. Tuck your arms into your sides, keep the camera upright, and avoid jolts.

Panning speed

When following a moving subject, the speed of the pan will depend on the speed of the subject. The blurred background does not matter because attention is focused on the subject. Decide before you start shooting whether you want the subject to leave the frame or stop within it, and if so where. In general, try to keep ahead of your subject during a pan.

Correct framing   **Incorrect framing**

When panning across a static scene, the speed must be very carefully judged to avoid a meaningless blur. Panning too fast is one of the commonest faults of the beginner. The wider the angle of the lens, the more rapidly you will be able to pan. A pan on the telephoto end of the lens must be very slow and very steady indeed.

A very rapid pan is known as a *whip pan*. It blurs the background completely and is sometimes used as a "jump cut" from one scene to another (see p. 83).

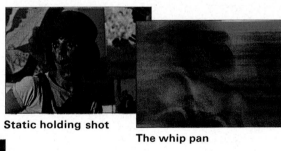

Static holding shot

The whip pan

1 The pan begins as the girl moves.

2 The pan follows her along the street.

3 The pan maintains a constant, steady speed.

4 The girl sees the man she is meeting.

5 The pan stops as they embrace

Panning with a tripod

Whenever possible, use a tripod for all pans. The tripod must be absolutely level and the camera vertical. A shot that looks vertical at the beginning of a pan may be hopelessly out-of-true at the end unless you have checked it first. A bubble-level on the pan head or camera is a great help. Set the friction on the pan head so that there is just enough resistance for the camera to turn steadily when pushed with two fingers at the end of the pan handle (see p. 57).

The problem with all tripod pans is where to put your feet. Because your eye is hard up against the camera, if you lose your balance at any point the camera will be jolted. Moreover, if the pan is a long one, you will have to move your feet – and it is very easy to kick the legs of the tripod accidentally as you swing around.

For a 90° pan, position yourself so that your basic orientation bisects the pan. You will then only have to move a maximum of 45°, and you should be able to do that without moving your feet or losing your balance. Set up the tripod with one leg on either side of you.

A 180° pan is difficult to perform smoothly, but a little practice will help. In order to reduce your leg movements to a minimum, aim to begin the pan in a rather uncomfortably stretched position; this will guarantee that as the shot proceeds things will become easier and you can end the shot comfortably.

How to perform a tripod pan

1 Stand facing the middle of the pan. Lean as far to the left as you can.

2 Slowly transfer your weight so that you are evenly balanced on both feet.

3 At the end, your weight should be on your right foot.

The tilt

A *tilt* is simply a pan in a vertical direction. It is most commonly used to film a tall building or a person without using a wide-angle lens.

As with the pan, remember that the tilt is a "developing" shot and that it should therefore lead up to something. For example, it is far more interesting to tilt up from a person's feet to their head than it is the other way around. Our anticipation of the face "energizes" the shot.

When tilting, try to use a tripod. Keep the camera perfectly vertical, put as much of your shoulder into the pan handle as you can, and aim to move your whole body, not just your arm or hand. This will produce a smoother movement.

The pan and tilt (below)
It is possible to combine a pan and a tilt in one single camera movement This is often useful for following a complex piece of action. In this sequence, the camera has panned along the top windows of the building and then tilted down to the fight in the street below.

The tilt (right)
A tilt can be used to establish an atmosphere of mystery or suspense. In the shot on the right, you might begin at the man's feet and then tilt up slowly to his face, revealing him lighting a cigarette.

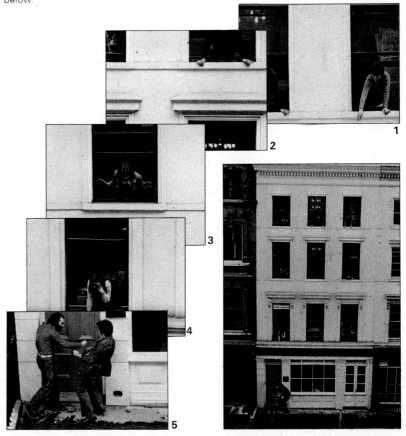

The Moving Camera

Moving the camera horizontally across the floor is known as *tracking*; moving it up or down in the air is known as a *crane shot*. It is *during* these movements that the movie camera really comes into its own. No other recording medium except video has this capacity to recreate three-dimensional objects on a flat screen. As the camera moves, perspective changes and a building, a person, or a sculpture takes on body and mass. This is film at its most dynamic and magical.

Tracking a stationary subject

A tracking shot is the best way of filming three-dimensional subjects which can be properly revealed only if the camera moves around them. Moreover, a track conveys a sense of exploration and a clear geography which cannot be achieved by a series of static shots from varying angles. Choose your speed carefully and rehearse the track before you start shooting.

In the case of people in a static dialogue, a tracking shot is normally dramatically motivated by the interplay of character. It is a visual metaphor for some aspect of the relationship and a clear manipulation of the point of view by the filmmaker: it should be used sparingly.

Tracking a moving subject

A tracking shot is an excellent way of keeping a moving subject in reasonable close-up. As the subject moves, so does the camera – and the distance between the two remains the same. The only other way of doing this is to use a telephoto lens and shoot from a long distance, but this will not have the force or impact of a tracked close-up. The subject can be anything from a person walking or running to someone in a moving car, or even a horse race. The speed can be slow and relaxed, or frenetic.

Tracking a moving subject is one of the most difficult of all shots. Hand-held tracking needs a good deal of coordination and practice (see p. 56) and so, if the situation allows, use some form of "dolly" to steady the camera. If you have a chance to plan the shot and rehearse it, do so. Decide whether you want to be in front, behind or beside your subject, and what distance you want to maintain. Outdoors, check for different light levels (see p. 94) and indoors set up your lights to give an even, consistent illumination (see p. 106).

The "subjective" track

A tracking shot in which the view seen by the camera represents the view seen by a character in the film is known as a *subjective track*. Imagine, for instance, a scene in which a man walks up to a door and opens it. As he walks through, the film cuts to a shot which represents what he sees. The camera is set up in the position in which we last see him; it then tracks as if it were the subject himself. If he stops, the track must stop. If he starts to run, the track must gather speed. If he looks to one side, so must the camera. We see the world as if through his eyes. In this situation, a steady camera is not essential. In fact, the slight wobble produced by a normal hand-held shot will convincingly suggest the subject's movement, especially if the man is supposed to be running, drunk, ill or deranged.

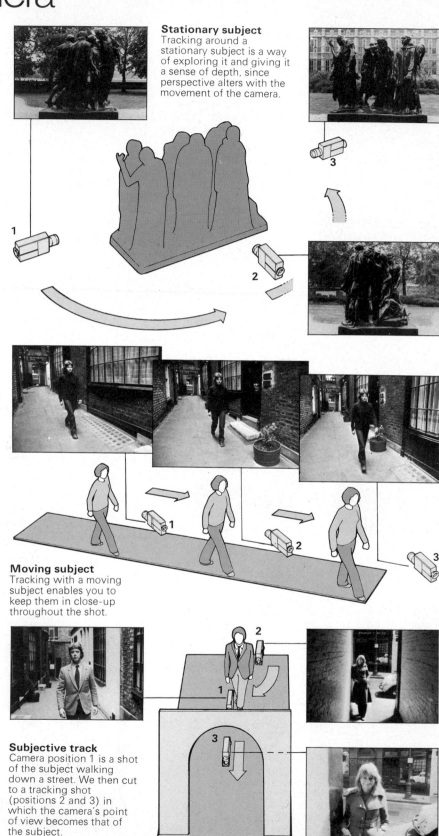

Stationary subject
Tracking around a stationary subject is a way of exploring it and giving it a sense of depth, since perspective alters with the movement of the camera.

Moving subject
Tracking with a moving subject enables you to keep them in close-up throughout the shot.

Subjective track
Camera position 1 is a shot of the subject walking down a street. We then cut to a tracking shot (positions 2 and 3) in which the camera's point of view becomes that of the subject.

How to track

A track may be made from a professional "dolly", a car or a wheelchair; or it may be simply hand-held. In each case, the big problem is keeping the camera steady. The powerful effect of a tracking shot will be spoiled if it is so wobbly that it draws attention to the filmmaking process rather than to the subject of the movie.

If you decide to hand-hold the shot, try to move as smoothly and evenly as you can. You may find it worth hiring one of the stabilizing systems specially designed for hand-held tracking shots (see p. 56).

Where possible, it is best to use some sort of "dolly". A professional dolly is simply a wheeled platform on which the camera is mounted. The camera-operator sits or stands on the dolly, and the entire unit is propelled on rubber wheels or tracks by a motor or by a second person. However, it is possible to improvise your own dolly using a wheelchair, a supermarket cart or even a baby carriage. But for tracking along a road, a car is by far the best. If the road surface is poor, try letting some air out of the tires to damp down the bouncing movement of the car. If you are shooting through the windscreen, make sure it is clean.

Start and end marks
Because focusing is often critical in close-ups, marks are sometimes made on the floor so that both the subject and the camera-operator can be in exactly the right spot at the start and end of the track. Either make your marks with chalk, or use pieces of gaffer tape.

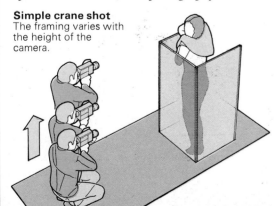

Wheelchair dolly
Use long wooden planks as improvised rails.

Home-made dolly
Mount the camera on a wheeled trolley.

Professional dolly
Both camera and operator sit on a special cart.

Tracking speed

The speed of the track is governed by the focal length of the lens, the subject-to-camera distance and the angle at which objects move past the camera. It can therefore only be judged by the camera-operator during a rehearsal. As a general rule, the wider the angle of the lens, the faster you need to track to achieve a given speed on the screen. And the closer the subject is to the camera, the slower you must track. If the camera is pointing straight ahead, the track will appear slower than if you pan around so that you are looking to the left or right of the direction in which you are traveling.

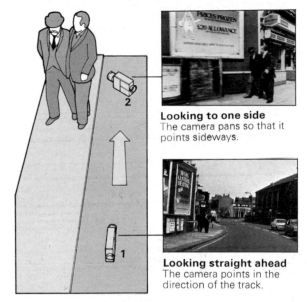

Looking to one side
The camera pans so that it points sideways.

Looking straight ahead
The camera points in the direction of the track.

Crane shots

A *crane shot* is a vertical track. The camera is either raised up into the air or lowered to the ground during the shot – thereby dramatically varying the height and the angle-of-view of the shot. Because this effect is outside our everyday experience, the crane shot can never be bland or neutral: it is probably the most spectacular shot in movie photography.

Simple crane shot
The framing varies with the height of the camera.

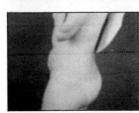

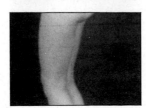

How to perform a crane shot

By hand-holding the camera and rising gradually from your knees to a standing position, you can perform a simple crane shot, but you must be very steady. It is possible to hire a large hydraulic platform designed for maintaining street lights, but they are expensive. Improvise by making use of escalators, elevators, fork-lift trucks or see-saws.

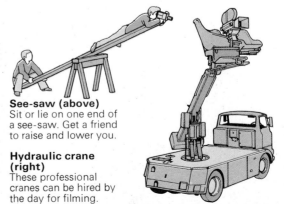

See-saw (above)
Sit or lie on one end of a see-saw. Get a friend to raise and lower you.

Hydraulic crane (right)
These professional cranes can be hired by the day for filming.

Creating a Sequence

All movies tell a story. No matter how impressionistic the treatment, the shots which you put together in any completed film will be in a fixed sequence; and that sequence is a statement which the viewer will interpret as a narrative. Unless you make it clear that what is being seen is a flashback or a dream, your audience will assume that the first shot occurred before the second shot, the second before the third, and so on. Indeed, our minds are so geared towards narrative and to recognizing cause and effect that film can easily generate misconceptions: if two quite unrelated images succeed one another, an audience will tend to create an imaginary link between them.

The story-telling aspect of film is as important for home movies or for documentary reportage as for drama. Say, for example, that you want to make a short film of your small daughter having a bath and going to bed. During the half hour which this takes, you shoot a 50 ft (15 m) cartridge of super 8 film. At 18 fps this will give you about three minutes and twenty seconds of screen time, which after editing might be reduced to about two minutes. Immediately, you come up against the following problems: you have to intercut various shots of the same person, using different camera angles and shot-sizes, without producing any ugly "jump cuts"; you have to maintain geography as the child moves from one room to the next; and you have to use "cutaways", "inserts" and close-ups in order to telescope the time-scale on the screen.

The art of the filmmaker is to take shots filmed at different times, from different angles and sometimes in different places, and to put them together to create a satisfying account of an event, or a place, or a mood. If the basic shots are thought of as the *vocabulary* of film, then the business of putting the shots together to create a logical, coherent sequence may be considered to be the *grammar* of film. It is what makes films work. The techniques outlined in the following pages provide the visual punctuation marks without which film would not make sense. They are not rules, but guidelines.

Abbreviations
There is a common convention for describing the basic shots in movie photography (see p. 58). The terms used are always abbreviated in the following way:

B.C.U. Big close-up

C.U. Close-up

M.C.U. Medium close-up

M.S. Mid shot

M.L.S. Medium long shot

L.S. Long shot

E.L.S. Extreme long shot

Shooting a simple narrative

Whatever the scene you are shooting, your job will be the same: you must film it so that the different shots can be assembled at the editing stage into one sequence of unbroken action. Some of the things you will have to consider will be: the *size* of the subjects in the frame; their *position* in the frame; the direction of their *eyeline* and their movement; and *continuity* of action. The example we have chosen to illustrate here is very simple. A girl is seen walking up a path, opening the door of a house and going in. The picture below shows the scene in plan and also some of the key camera positions which you might use. In the following pages, we discuss some of the ways in which you might film this scene and explain how to avoid the most commonly made errors.

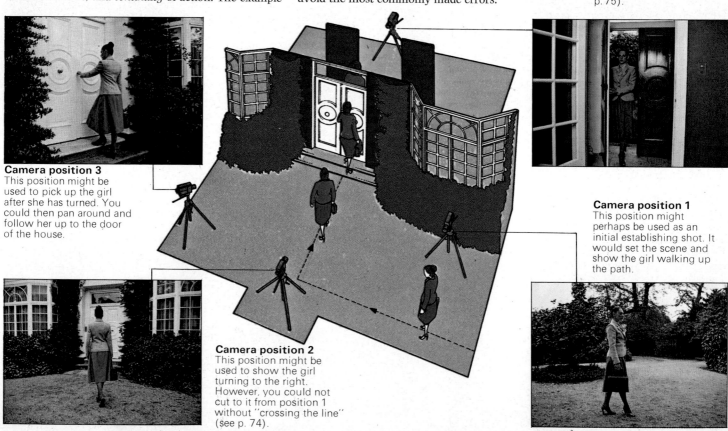

Camera position 3
This position might be used to pick up the girl after she has turned. You could then pan around and follow her up to the door of the house.

Camera position 2
This position might be used to show the girl turning to the right. However, you could not cut to it from position 1 without "crossing the line" (see p. 74).

Camera position 4
The camera is now inside the house. You might set it up on the same side of the "line" as position 3 or on the opposite side (see p. 75).

Camera position 1
This position might perhaps be used as an initial establishing shot. It would set the scene and show the girl walking up the path.

Image size

One way of opening the sequence would be to set up the camera in position 1 (see below) and begin with a long shot of the girl walking up to the house. This will establish the scene. You might then decide to pan around and follow her until cutting to another position when she turns. But it would probably help the sequence if, once the scene has been set, you cut in to a closer shot of the girl. This will guarantee that the audience's attention is firmly centered on her.

When making a cut of this kind, it is crucial that the difference in the size of each shot is right – or the effect will be either indecisive or shocking (see right). The usual technique is to use a mid shot in between the long shot and the close-up. You could shoot the whole scene from camera position 1, using the zoom lens to close in. But, in practice, it would be better to move the camera as well. Position 2 will vary the angle and give you a better mid shot; and for the close-up you could either pan around or track just in front of her to position 3.

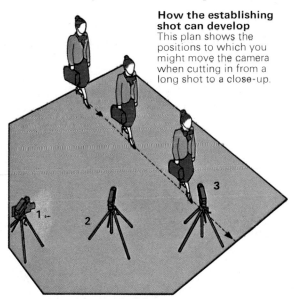

How the establishing shot can develop
This plan shows the positions to which you might move the camera when cutting in from a long shot to a close-up.

An "indecisive" cut
When cutting from a long shot to a mid shot, the difference in image size must be decisive. If the size of the girl does not change sufficiently, as shown here, you will get an unpleasant effect like that of a "jump cut" (see p. 83).

A "shock" cut
If, on the other hand, you cut directly from a long shot to a big close-up, you will produce a shock effect which may be inappropriate. For this reason, the usual compromise is to expose a mid shot.

L.S. (position 1)   M.S. (position 1)   B.C.U. (position 1)

L.S. (position 1)   M.S. (position 2)   B.C.U. (position 3)

Position in the frame

When cutting from one shot to another – say, from a long shot to a mid shot – the subject should occupy the same position in the frame. If your subject is on the left of the picture in the long shot then he or she should also appear on the left in the mid shot. This way the shots will juxtapose well and the audience will recognize instantly that the subject is the same person. If this rule is not obeyed and a subject formerly on the left of the screen suddenly appears in close-up on the right, there will be an awkward and distracting jolt.

Matching the position of the subject
In both the examples shown here, the position of the girl in the frame has changed from one shot to the next. Both the subject and the background appear to jump suddenly over to the right.

The Line

One of the greatest problems in filmmaking is that of maintaining a clear geography while changing the position of the camera in between shots. It is all too easy accidentally to juxtapose two shots in which the same person is seen to be facing or moving in opposite directions (a "reverse cut"). To prevent the confusion which this causes, there is a convention known as the "line": it is an imaginary line composed partly of the subject's eyeline, partly of the direction in which he or she is moving, and partly of the "line of interest" that stretches between two or more people. Both eyeline and direction will be confused if the camera positions for two consecutive shots are on opposite sides of the line.

Crossing the line

It would be an intolerable restriction if, having chosen to shoot from one side of the line, you were stuck on that side for the duration of the sequence. Three of the most common ways of "crossing the line" are shown below.

Get on the line
If the camera is placed exactly on the line itself, the "dead-ahead" shot can be used as a transition between two shots from opposite sides of the line.

Let the line cross the camera on a turn
If the subject changes direction, so does the line. If the camera is set up so that the change of direction is *seen* on the screen, then the new line will be clearly established.

Track across the line
In this method, the camera tracks across the line as the subject approaches and, in the course of the single shot, clearly shows her change of direction.

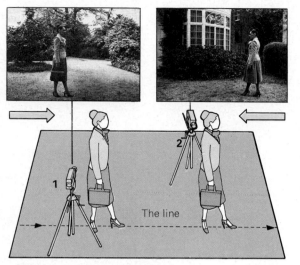

The line

Camera on the line
Cross the line with a shot in which the camera is on the line itself.

Cross the line in shot
Let the line clearly change direction in view of the camera.

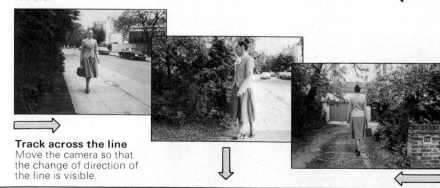

Track across the line
Move the camera so that the change of direction of the line is visible.

The "reverse cut"
In the example shown here, the "line" is the direction in which the girl is walking. The direction of any movement on film is what the eye sees first, and it should therefore be consistent. The stills show what happens if two camera positions are selected on either side of the line. Camera 1 shows the girl walking from left to right; camera 2 shows her walking from right to left. If the two shots are juxtaposed, then they will produce a "reverse cut" and the girl will appear to walk in the opposite direction.

Entering a doorway

As the girl in our scene walks up the path, she approaches a door. You are now faced with the problem of how to film her opening the door and entering the house. Unless you are going to settle for just one shot of her disappearing into the house, you will need a minimum of two camera positions – one outdoors and one indoors. The camera positions must be carefully thought out in relation to the "line" if continuity is to be maintained when you cut from the first shot to the second. In this case, the line may be taken to be the direction of the girl's movement – since this will always take precedence over the direction in which she is looking, and since there are no other people involved in

the scene. If the camera outside the house (position 1) pans to show her walking from right to left, then the camera inside the house must be set up on the same side of the line (position 2) or the girl will be seen walking from left to right and she will appear to have changed direction. The actual cut between the two shots might be made as she turns the handle and the door opens.

These words of advice must, however, be qualified: you will often see films in which the line is crossed as a subject enters a doorway, and you will often find that the action of opening the door is in itself sufficient identification to cover any confusion that is caused by the change of direction.

The line through a doorway
It is customary to use at least two camera positions to film a subject entering a doorway. By setting up the camera positions either side of the door on the *same* side of the line, the girl will appear to be walking from right to left throughout the sequence.

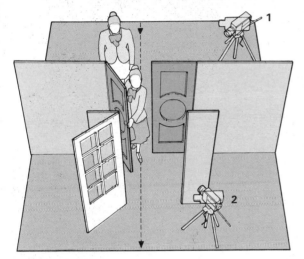

L.S. (camera 1)

L.S. (camera 1)

L.S. (camera 2)

Maintaining the line
Camera positions 1 and 2 are both on the same side of the line.

Disguising a reverse cut

You may find that the scene you intend to shoot inside the house demands that the girl is seen moving across the screen from left to right, not from right to left as in the case above. This means that you will have to "cross the line". You could use one of the techniques shown opposite to make the change of direction quite clear. But it might be simpler in this case to use a "buffer shot" to

disguise the reverse cut. Begin the sequence with a pan from camera position 1 of the girl walking up to the door. As she puts her hand out to open the door, cut to a close-up of the handle turning, shot from position 2 inside the house on the opposite side of the line. As the door opens, zoom out to show the girl entering the room; the change of direction will go unnoticed.

The buffer shot
An unavoidable reverse cut can sometimes be disguised using a "buffer shot". In this case, a close-up of the door handle diverts attention away from the fact that the camera has crossed to the other side of the line for the indoor shot.

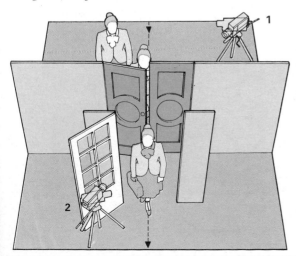

L.S. (camera 1)

B.C.U. (camera 2)

Crossing the line
Camera positions 1 and 2 are on opposite sides of the line.

L.S. (camera 2)

Shooting a Dialogue

A dialogue presents the problem of line-crossing in its simplest form, and will therefore serve to illustrate the challenges you will encounter in other comparable filming situations. You can shoot a dialogue either from one static position or with a moving, hand-held camera.

A tripod-mounted, static camera has many advantages, especially if the conversation is lengthy: for a start, it will not wobble as you begin to tire. However, your choice of camera position will inevitably force you either to favor one party, which makes for an interview rather than a dialogue, or (if you place the camera centrally, as in the illustration on the right) it will result in a pair of uncompelling profiles. Neither are really satisfactory, and the common practice in many dialogue scenes is to film the whole thing so that one person is seen face-on, and then to shoot a number of reverse cutaways of the other person so that both subjects can be seen from time to time. These cutaways may be staged after the main, sync shooting has been finished.

A better solution for any informal work is to hand-hold the camera and favor each speaker in turn as the dialogue progresses. In this way, you can respond flexibly to the flow of the conversation. Tracking is not recommended, but you could very well decide to use two cameras and cross-shoot from the same side of the line.

Single camera position
The master shot of a two-person dialogue may be shot side-on, but this will mean that the subjects are only seen in profile.

Camera positions
These are the shots you would get from various camera positions. They could all be intercut satisfactorily except numbers 1 and 9, which are on the wrong side of the line.

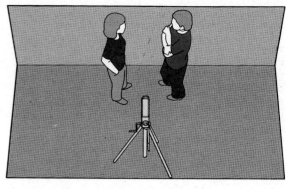

Establishing the "line"

For most purposes, the "line" in any two-person dialogue may be considered to run through the heads of the subjects. This is because the most important "line of interest" is the relationship between the two people. If one of the speakers should move, then the position of the line will change, but it will still be the straight line which connects them both. the only problem that might arise is if one subject actually looked so far from the other that his or her eyeline crossed a camera. The rules of the "line" should be respected.

Reverse angle
Camera position 1 is on the opposite side of the line.

Subjective shot
Position 2, on the man's eyeline, gives a subjective shot of the girl.

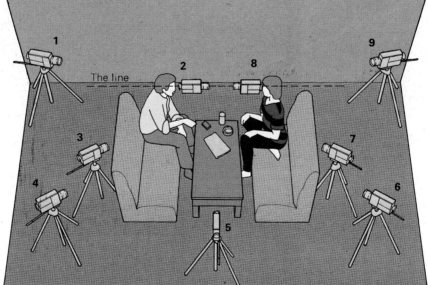

The line

Reverse angle
Camera position 9 is on the opposite side of the line.

Subjective shot
Position 8, on the girl's eyeline, gives a subjective shot of the man.

Close-up
Zoom in from position 3 to produce a single close-up of the girl.

Two-shot
A wide-angle shot from position 4 shows both of the subjects.

Master shot
From camera position 5, both subjects appear in profile.

Two-shot
A wide-angle shot from position 6 shows both of the subjects.

Close-up
Zoom in from position 7 to produce a single close-up of the man.

Eyeline continuity

When filming a dialogue, the position of the subjects in relation to one another *must* be clear to the audience, even when they are only seen singly in close-up. You can guarantee that the basic orientation is maintained by keeping the camera on one side of the "line" and avoiding reverse cuts (see opposite). But it is also very important that the subjects' eyelines are correct. When only one person in a dialogue is shown on the screen, the direction in which he or she is looking is the sole indication to the audience of the whereabouts of the other person. It is therefore vital that the eyelines be consistent (see p. 61).

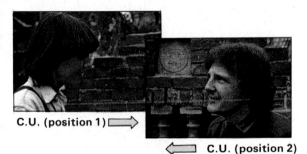

C.U. (position 1) ▭▷

◁ **C.U. (position 2)**

Composing for close-ups
The girl on the left in the master shot should be on the left of the frame in close-up, and should be looking from left to right. If the man looks right to left, the two will appear to be facing one another.

Telephone conversations

The conventional way of shooting a scene in which two people are talking to each other on the telephone is to film each person separately. You can then switch from one to the other, as the conversation requires, by editing the shots together later. In order to create the illusion that the two people are speaking to each other, one person should be on the left of the frame, looking right; the other should be on the right of the frame, looking left. Telephone conversations are sometimes filmed using the "split-screen" technique.

C.U. ▭▷   ◁ **C.U.**

Manipulating the image

Varying the camera angle can be used to influence the balance of the relationship between the two people in the shot. Tracking the camera in and narrowing the angle will enable you to shoot close-ups of the subjects. These can then be intercut at the editing stage. The comparative *size* of the close-ups will affect the audience's interpretation of the scene (see *Matching close-ups*, p. 60).

Varying the height of the camera and shooting over your subjects' shoulders enables you to establish a sense of "dominance". The subject who appears larger in both camera shots will seem the stronger.

Your choice of focal length will also affect the staging of the dialogue. Wide angles tend to exaggerate depth and telephoto lenses compress distance. Using a wide-angle will therefore seem to throw your subjects further apart whereas a telephoto shot will reduce the space between them and tend to bring them nearer together. Both of these can be used to great effect, but beware of intercutting shots that have a markedly different "feel".

Varying camera height
A low camera angle from one side and a high angle from the other guarantees that the subject on the right is always larger.

Telephoto lens (left)
A lens with a long focal length will tend to compress the distance between the two subjects.

Wide-angle lens (right)
The subjects in this shot are standing in exactly the same positions as in the shot on the left. However, the camera has moved nearer, and a wide-angle lens setting has increased the apparent distance between them.

Camera position 1

Camera position 2

Complex Line-Crossing Problems

Situations in which more than two people are being filmed can cause difficulties if the position of each person in relation to the others is to be clearly maintained while you cut from shot to shot on the screen. For this reason try to plan sequences of this kind before you begin shooting. In the case of a group of people, there will be several lines of interest, several eyelines and, if any of the subjects move, several lines of movement. How do you decide where the "line" which dictates the camera positioning runs? The answer is to make a choice of one of the many lines—it may be the dominant dramatic axis of the scene—and stick to it as far as possible.

In the example illustrated on these two pages, four people are sitting around a table eating a meal. The number of possible "lines" are shown right. The easiest solution is to select one of the outer lines, say the one between B and C, and remain outside it—that is, outside the whole circle. The two camera positions will allow you to cover all four subjects.

Multiple "lines"
Four people sitting around a table create a complex pattern of multiple "lines." Assuming that they all remain in the same position, each person has three lines of their own, depending on who they are talking to or who they are looking at. This means that the scene contains six possible "lines". When filming, you should choose one, and stay on the same side of it where possible.

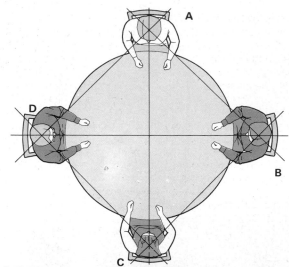

Camera position 1
From this camera angle it is possible to get three of the four people in shot—C, D and A—although you will not be able to get a close-up of C's face. The line passes between B and C.

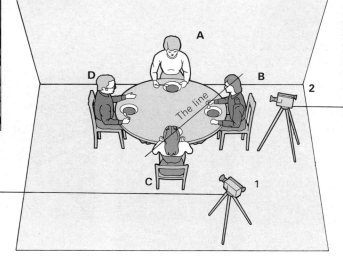

Camera position 2
The camera has now moved around the table, although it is still on the same side of the line between B and C. From the new position, you will get a shot that includes D, A and B.

How to cross the line
Although the two camera positions shown above will allow everyone sitting around the table to be in the shot, subjects B and C can only be seen in profile. However, occasions are bound to arise when you will need a close-up of B or C. These are likely to be while they are speaking or when they are reacting to what one of the others is saying. To get this close-up, you will have to cross the line. But how?

Let us say that C begins talking to A. You will be unable to get a good close-up of C's face from camera position 1 or 2—or indeed from anywhere on the right-hand side of the line running between B and C which you originally selected. The answer is therefore to cross the old line and select a new one. The obvious choice is the line of interest which has developed between C and A as a result of the conversation. Use this as your new line, and move the camera around to get your close-up of C speaking. But stay on the right of this line so that C is still seen looking left to right. If you cross over to the left of the new line, C will appear to look right to left.

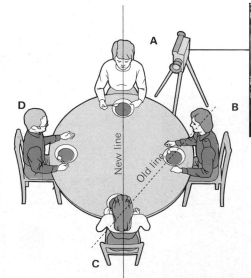

Close-up of C
By crossing the old B to C line and establishing a new one between A and C, you can move around the table and get a full close-up of C's face.

Establishing new lines

Having moved the camera to get your close-up of C, you can either return to your former position and reinstate the original line, or you can set up a new base of operations with both the master camera positions now established between A and B. Another alternative would be to move the camera to yet another position and establish a third line. You may find that this is essential.

Let us now say that B begins speaking to A. To get a close-up of B, you will have to move the camera further around the table, creating a new line between B and A. This time you must stay on the left of B's eyeline, so that B is still seen to be looking from right to left.

In complex situations such as this, work out well in advance what shots you are aiming for. Make sketches of the shots you are planning – with particular emphasis on the eyeline. If you apply the method of only establishing a new one when you have to cross the first, you should be able to foresee the results you will obtain.

Unplanned filming situations

Unfortunately, the kind of approach outlined above is only really feasible if you are able to make a detailed plan of the shooting beforehand. If you are filming at a real dinner party – where you cannot suddenly stop the conversation in order to change the camera angle – you are likely to find things more difficult.

Tracking around the table

While "two-shots" and "three-shots" tend to provide their own geography – since we recognize the relative positions of the people around the table – close-ups are very easy to confuse, and after three close-ups in a row an audience will no longer be clear about who is positioned where. In situations where you cannot plan the sequence shot for shot, the easiest way of establishing the geography is to hand-hold the camera and track around the table *before* cutting or zooming in to a close-up. That way, the change of position is actually visible.

Inserts and cutaways

When you are filming in unplanned situations, you should try as far as possible to "cover" yourself by getting plenty of reaction shots of your subjects as they listen and respond to one another. This will give you much more freedom when you come to the editing stage, and will enable you to get around difficult problems of continuity. Because the constant direction of eyeline is so important in maintaining a sense of geography (see p. 61), especially when intercutting close-ups from different camera positions, try to film a close-up shot of each person in the scene looking right, looking left and looking straight ahead. You can then insert these (see p. 80) as linking shots when you edit the film.

Similarly, try to film each of your subjects turning their heads across the line of the camera. These "mute" shots will be invaluable for maintaining continuity between shots filmed on opposite sides of the line.

Finally, if all else fails, it is always worth filming a few "cutaways" of the meal itself. These can be used to disguise the fact that the line may have been crossed.

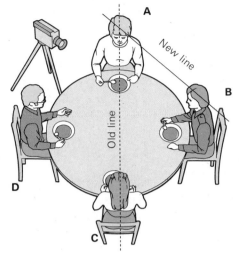

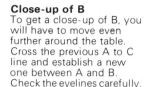

Close-up of B
To get a close-up of B, you will have to move even further around the table. Cross the previous A to C line and establish a new one between A and B. Check the eyelines carefully.

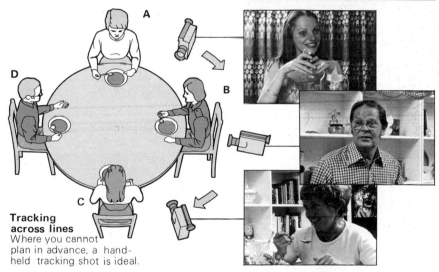

Tracking across lines
Where you cannot plan in advance, a hand-held tracking shot is ideal.

Subject looks left
Close-up of A looking off-screen to the left.

Subject looks at camera
Close-up of A as a head-on shot.

Subject looks right
Close-up of A looking off-screen to the right.

Wine
This shot of the wine will act as a cutaway.

Flowers
This shot is "neutral" in terms of the line.

Soup
Get some shots of the food being eaten.

Expanding the Image

The simplest way of recording an event on film is to set up the camera in one place and cover the whole scene from that one position. This is known as a *master shot*. It is the most theatrical of all cinematic techniques: the action takes place in front of a static camera, which acts as a passive observer. The pace of the sequence is determined by the actors or the events themselves.

However, the unique feature of movie photography is that it allows the filmmaker to manipulate the action, to create his or her own pace, and to expand the image of reality which we finally see on the screen. For this reason, the master-shot system is very rarely used on its own. What sometimes happens is that the scene is acted out several times, each time being filmed from a different camera position – one of which will be the master shot. The sequence is then built up at the editing stage by inserting close-ups and different angles into the master shot. This system allows you plenty of flexibility when editing and guarantees a certain inherent continuity, but it is wasteful of film. An alternative is to plot out the sequence, break the whole scene down into separate shots and shoot each one as a new set-up.

The master shot
A master shot is a record of the whole scene shot from one camera position in an extended "single take". However, it will look very static on the screen. To make the sequence visually more interesting, the master shot can be intercut with different angles, close-ups, inserts, cutaways or reaction shots.

Inserts

An *insert* is a shot of part of the scene covered by the master shot. It is usually filmed from a different camera angle and is intercut into the master shot to provide visual variety and to concentrate the audience's attention on a small portion of the scene. Inserts are therefore most often used to emphasize a significant detail. They can also be used as a bridge between two separate master shots. Be very careful when using inserts, especially if you are filming them at a different time; any continuity discrepancies will be instantly visible. Take great care that the camera does not accidentally cross the line, and that you match up eyelines if cutting in to close-ups.

Using inserts
In this sequence of a pistol duel, two inserts have been intercut with the master shot to provide close-ups of the protaganists.

An insert shot from camera position 2

An insert shot from camera position 3

Master shot

Master shot

Master shot

Master shot

Master shot

Cutaways

A *cutaway* is a shot of something not covered by the master shot. It is inserted into the main scene because it has some relevance to it, and to provide some kind of visual or dramatic enrichment of the central action. It might be simply a shot of something or somebody offscreen to which the main characters are referring. Or it may well be something at a distance – in either time or in space. Or it may be an image that is quite imaginary, inserted as a metaphorical comment on the action or on one of the characters. One of the most frequent, and unsatisfactory, uses of the cutaway is as a means of disguising an accidental reverse cut or a break in continuity (see p. 226).

Master shot

Cutaway

Master shot

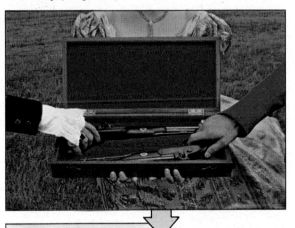

Using cutaways
By intercutting cutaways into the main action, it is possible to introduce an extra dimension to the scene. In the examples illustrated here, shots of the anxious girl, the pistols being taken from their box and a close-up of one of the guns have all been inserted into the master shot.

Reaction shots

As its name implies, a *reaction shot* is the silent response of one or many people to another person or event. Reaction shots are filmed in the light of the main shot – and therefore *after* it, unless you are using two cameras. Eyelines must be compatible, and in a dialogue you must judge carefully how you wish to balance the angle and the image-size of the respective faces, since this will affect their impact on the screen (see p. 60). In a confrontation, always position each face on the opposite side of the frame, or else your subjects will seem to be back-to-back.

Good reaction shots are surprisingly difficult to produce, since actors tend to overplay an isolated close-up. The best solution is to restage the whole scene from the new camera position. Alternatively, you can get your reaction shots from the listener or audience during some comparable subsequent moment in the action.

Master shot

Reaction shot

Master shot

Parallel Action

Cinematic devices such as inserts, cutaways and re-action shots (see p. 80–81) are all, in their own way, examples of "simultaneous" filming. In other words, the inserted shots are not so much consecutive with the master shots on either side of them as "parallel": they are another way of looking at the same scene. Film can create this simultaneity very easily. Indeed, the double vision is often extended to the point where two quite separate scenes are intercut. This technique is known as *parallel action*. Parallel action may be thought of as any related scene which is not occurring in the same place as the central action but which may be intercut with the master shot. In such a case, the two scenes are parallel in time – even if one of the two is a flashback to the past or a glimpse of the future. An intercut sequence of parallel action may therefore be a memory, a fantasy or a purely symbolic exploration of the main thread of narrative. There is no limit to the degree of intercutting, provided that direction and pace are maintained.

When to use parallel action

The technique of parallel action has been conventionally used to build up tension in a sequence since the beginning of movie photography. For instance, a blazing Western heroine stoked by Indians has for decades been intercut with shots of the cavalry racing across the plain. She looks left; they charge right. So familiar are we with the conventions of film language that we supply the implicit link between the two parallel shots.

Parallel action is not, however, confined to building up tension in thrillers and chase sequences. It applies to any film which attempts to do more than tell a two-dimensional tale. For instance, the reaction shots in a four-way conversation may tell a quite different story from the master shots. In this case the parallel action can be used to create another psychological or emotional dimension to the scene. The effectiveness of the technique depends on the skill and subtlety with which the parallel shots are intercut at the editing stage.

Intercutting for suspense
In this sequence, shots of the unsuspecting woman in the bedroom are intercut with shots of the murderer climbing the stairs. The feeling of increasing suspense is heightened by the dramatic lighting and by the contrast between extreme close-ups and wide-angle long shots.

2

6

1

3

4

5

7

Bridging time and space
In this example of parallel action, shots of a burglar breaking into a house are juxtaposed with shots of the policeman. The audience will supply the connection between the two scenes of action.

2

6

1

3

4

5

7

Manipulating Time and Space

Film allows you to distort time and space. You can compress a week of real time into a minute of screen time, or flash from one place to another, making "here" seem like "there". You can thus create a screen reality which need have no similarity to your actual settings – it will have its own time-scale and its own geography. Fades, dissolves, wipes, whip pans, cutaways and jump cuts are some of the conventional tools of film language which enable you to manipulate time and space.

Fade-out

Optical effects

A shot may be faded in or faded out (see p. 186). A *fade-out* to black is used to close a scene; a *fade-in* to open it. If a fade-out is followed by a fade-in, the audience will accept that time has passed or the location has changed.

A *dissolve* is a fade-out overlapped with a fade-in of equal duration (see p. 187). It is a transition shot, but is not as final as a fade-out. It is used to create a smooth visual flow between shots.

Dissolve

Editing techniques

Inserts, *cutaways* and *reaction shots* (see p. 80–81) are all used to compress action when you wish to disguise the fact that the time-span is being shortened. Perhaps the most familiar use of these is the cutaway of the crowd in a TV football game which enables the match to be condensed into, say, twenty-five minutes without any apparent discontinuity in the action. Cutaways may also be used to *expand* action. By overshooting a scene, you can, for example, stretch the last five seconds before a bomb goes off to thirty seconds on the screen.

A *jump cut* is a cut achieved by removing a length of footage from a single continuous shot and splicing the two remaining ends together again (see p. 226). On screen it may be glaringly abrupt or virtually invisible. Jump cuts are often used in documentaries to compress an interview without using cutaways. They are sometimes used with "locked-off camera" techniques (see p. 189) and with "freeze-frame" shots to produce a series of staccato images. Freeze-frames are usually produced in the film laboratory as an optical effect.

Master shot   **Cutaway**   **Master shot**

Varying the camera speed

Changing the speed of the camera enables you to distort time directly – rather than via one of the visual conventions used in movie photography. The effect can be very dramatic: *overcranking* the camera might produce a shot of a horse galloping in slow motion; *undercranking* the camera while filming from a moving car will produce an exhilarating fast-motion journey in which both time and space are compressed; and using *time-lapse* photography can show a crocus growing in as little as ten seconds.

However, more opportunities exist for varying the camera speed *very slightly*. Scenes such as a stunt, a fight or a crash are often slowed down slightly so that the audience has time to see what is happening. Likewise, chase-sequences are often speeded up slightly to make them more exciting. As a general rule, do not vary the speed by more than one third at the very most if you want it to go unnoticed.

Long shot   **Edited-out zoom-in**   **Jump cut to mid shot**

Wipes

Wipes are optical effects in which one image literally "wipes" another off the screen. They may be vertical, horizontal, round ("iris"), square, zig-zag or striped, and are usually produced in the laboratory, although you can perform simple wipes yourself (see p. 187).

Iris wipe
This iris wipe, which fades out on the last remaining coins in the hero's hand comes from Godard's film, *A Bout de Souffle* – a deliberate spoof of American gangster movies.

The Assembled Sequence

This sequence illustrates how the various elements of film outlined in the preceding pages – shot size, pace, camera movement, composition – create their effect by working not separately but in unison. Claude Chabrol's *Le Boucher* ("The Butcher", 1968), from which these frames are taken, is an example of discreet but highly refined technique. In this sequence, the schoolteacher – Chabrol's wife, Stephane Audran – is on a picnic with her pupils. We already know that there is a murderer at large. There is an atmosphere of apprehension, reinforced by the brooding music and relentless, slow tracking shots.

1 ⏱ **8 sec   The school picnic**

Establishing shot
In this long opening shot, we see that the children are literally on the cliff edge. This helps to emphasize the potential dangers of their position. The camera broods on the scene. There are distant children's voices on the sound track.

Pan and tilt
This lengthy (14 sec) top shot focuses our attention from the group onto the little girl in blue. We do not know yet why, and this again contributes to the tension of the scene. The children's voices are mixed with increasingly menacing music.

2a ⏱ **14 sec   The teacher**

2b   The schoolchildren

2c   The little girl in blue

Close-up of girl
From the long pan and tilt, Chabrol cuts to this shot which is a more intimate (and faster) close-up. It shows one of the shoolgirls preparing to eat a roll.

3 ⏱ **2 sec   The girl opens her roll**

4 ⏱ **2 sec   She is just about to begin eating**

Eye-level shot
The camera moves down and around and we are now right on the girl's eye level – although she is not yet in big close-up. The meaning of her question is still unclear and there is still no clue as to why the camera has selected her.

Girl: "Is it raining?"

Mid shot of teacher
This shot, in which we cross-cut to the teacher again is still quite lengthy (5 sec), thereby underlining the growing suspense. The use of mid shots here means that the big close-ups can be saved for later, more dramatic moments.

5 ⏱ **5 sec   The teacher**

Big close-up of blood
This is the moment when the tension is released. From now on the sequence accelerates and deals with large close-ups. The "rain" is blood, and it drips onto the little girl's roll.

Teacher: "Of course not. The sky is clear"

6 ⏱ **3 sec   Extreme close-up of blood dripping onto the roll**

Girl: "It's red"

Reaction shot
In a short close-up, the teacher looks around quickly to the little girl. It is the pace of the movement rather than the speed of the shot which accelerates the drama.

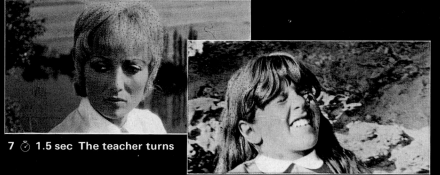

7 ⏱ 1.5 sec The teacher turns

Shock cut
Chabrol cuts back to the girl in another very fast, shocking shot. The blood which previously fell on the roll has now dripped onto the girl's face.

8 ⏱ 1 sec The blood hits the girl

9a ⏱ 6 sec Mid shot of boy

9b The camera tracks backwards to a big close-up of the teacher staring up

Track out
Using a track – which must surely have been hand-held – Chabrol links the children's world by retreating from a mid shot of the frightened boy to a big close-up of the teacher standing and looking upwards. We then cut to her eyeline

Boy: "It's blood"

Subjective shot
This is the teacher's view. The blood is revealed to be dripping from a hand hanging over a cliff-top and outstretched against the blue sky. This is the point at which the music reaches a climax.

10a ⏱ 6 sec Zoom-in

10b Zoom-in

10c Zoom-in

Zoom-in
This shot is a perfect example of a subjective zoom-in. The hand grows larger and larger in the frame, thus conveying the horrified narrowing of the teacher's attention on one object – the bleeding hand.

Continuity

The fundamental rule of *continuity* is that the action in one shot should match that of the next. To take the example illustrated on p. 72, if you cut from a long shot of a girl walking down a path to a mid shot filmed from a different angle, the girl must be seen to be walking down the same road, in the same direction, at the same speed, and wearing the same clothes. If she isn't, the audience will become confused, and continuity will have been lost. In feature films, where problems of continuity are likely to be very complex, a Polaroid camera is often used to take instant pictures of a shot so that it can be reconstructed later from a different camera angle.

If you cannot afford this luxury, remember that facial expressions and hand gestures (such as smoking) tend to be the most troublesome aspects of continuity. There is no foolproof way of guaranteeing a perfect shot-transition, but the most vital thing is to *watch the action very carefully at the moment you intend to cut, and to overlap the action* on the two shots. This will give you more flexibility while editing and will give greater fluency to the action. Finally, problems of continuity are much less noticeable if there is a substantial change of camera angle between the two consecutive shots. The change is dramatic enough to carry the discontinuity.

Polaroid camera

Continuity of movement
In the first three shots the girl is seen in mid shot walking down a road from left to right on the screen. But when we cut to the fourth shot, the camera has "crossed the line" (see p. 74) and the girl suddenly appears to be walking from right to left. This is known as a "reverse cut".

Red wine

White wine

Continuity of vision
These two examples illustrate the most common errors of continuity. In the transition between the two shots on the left, the glass of wine mysteriously changed from red to white. In the shots on the right, the girl's earring has inexplicably disappeared.

Earring

No earring

Continuity of sound and picture

When filming the separate shots which will go to make up a sequence, be careful to standardize the level of both sound and exposure. This is especially true if you are using reversal film; negative film does at least allow you some flexibility in the printing process (see p. 229).

If you have a manual VU meter for monitoring the sound level, try to keep to a fixed setting so that the level and the acoustic of the sound remains even throughout the sequence. You should also record a background "wildtrack" of the ambient sound. This is later used for dubbing to smooth out the edited sequence (see p. 245).

Continuity of vision is primarily concerned with a consistent quality of light. The problem here is usually the weather, since you cannot have the sun shining in every alternate shot. If you are lucky enough to get reliable weather, standardize the exposure for a given point of view. If possible, do all the shooting for one sequence in a single filming session: it may be weeks before the weather is the same. Remember, too, that the time of day will affect the color-balance of the light: it becomes very red at the end of the day (see p. 92–3).

Changing light
These shots of Bombay harbor were taken within a couple of hours of each other. The light has changed so much that it would be difficult to intercut them.

LIGHTING

"A film is never really good unless
the camera is an eye in the head of
a poet"   *Orson Welles*

Film and Lighting

Lighting is the key to all creative movie photography. Once you have got sufficient light onto the film to record an image, you can vary the lighting to achieve the mood or atmosphere you want. The shots on these two pages come from Ken Russell's film, *Mahler*. They illustrate how different forms of lighting can be used for various effects in movie photography.

Silhouette

Shooting against the light is one of the most exciting ways to film; and pure silhouette, with its total absence of modeling or relief, can be used to create strong, abstract images. In this scene, Ken Russell uses a shot of Mahler in silhouette to bridge a gap of time and space. The sequence begins with Mahler in a railway car, silhouetted against the passing scenery. Suddenly the film cuts to a shot of him in exactly the same pose, but this time silhouetted against a blue lake. We realize that we have flashed back to a memory in his past.

1a ⏱ 2 sec In the train

Shape and silhouette
A sudden cut between the train and the lake is linked by the shape of this distinctive silhouette.

1b ⏱ 3 sec In the train

2a ⏱ 2 sec Mahler beside the lake

2b ⏱ 3 sec He begins to speak

2c ⏱ 5 sec The camera zooms out

Light and reflection

A simple and effective way of enlivening any shot is to use whatever reflections you can. Light reflected off water, glass, metal or a wet street will emphasize any highlights in the composition and produce an attractive, high-contrast glitter. For the dramatic shot of Mahler shown right, Ken Russell devised an ingenious camera set-up which involved shooting through two windows and catching the reflections of the mountains in the first.

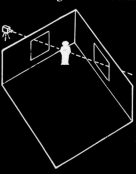

Reflections in glass
This shot comprises three elements. The camera is set up outside the lake-side hut in which Mahler stands. We see him through one window. It is this window in which the mountains across the lake are reflected. The patch of light behind Mahler's head is the view out of a second window on the other side of the hut.

Natural lighting

Try to take advantage of the variety offered by the changing light – for example, the soft, shadowless light on an overcast day, or the dramatic skies of a heavy thunderstorm. The scene shown here is set on the lake, outside the hut in which Mahler composed his music. The whole sequence is shot in late-afternoon sunlight. This creates warm, golden colors and strong contrasts between areas of light and dark.

Afternoon sunlight
The atmosphere of the idyllic setting is enhanced by the use of rich, golden sunlight.

1a ⏱ **5 sec The hut on the lake**

1b ⏱ **3 sec Mahler and his wife**

1c ⏱ **5 sec Mahler and his wife**

Artificial lighting

In indoor scenes, it may not be possible to film without using some form of artificial lighting. However, with careful planning and careful positioning of the lights, these shots can be very effective and need not look at all "unnatural". The sequence illustrated here is a perfect example. It begins with Mahler's wife standing in front of a window. The scene is lit by light from outside, and she is seen in silhouette. She then turns towards the camera and walks into the center of the room, where the children are in bed. This shot appears to be lit by a candle on the bedside table. In fact, the effect of candlelight is being simulated by a strong spotlight which is shining onto the wall behind the table.

1a ⏱ **6 sec Mahler's wife**

1b ⏱ **6 sec She turns towards the camera**

1c ⏱ **4 sec With the children**

Candlelight
The light cast by the candle is in fact a spotlight. It is switched off when Mahler's wife bends over and blows out the candle.

1d ⏱ **8 sec She bends over the child**

1e ⏱ **1 sec She blows out the candle**

Light Meters

In order that the film gets the correct exposure, the amount of light it receives must be carefully regulated. On a bright sunlit day far more light is available than on a gray cloudy day, and the adjustable diaphragm in the lens must be either opened up or "stopped down" accordingly. It is vital, therefore, that you know exactly how bright your subject is. A *light meter* is the device used to measure the intensity of light falling on, or being reflected by, an object. It is calibrated to give you a correct "average" exposure setting.

The light meter may be hand-held or it may be built-in to the camera. Built-in meters are always of the *reflected light* type (see p. 49), but hand meters come in the three varieties shown below. In each case the light is measured electrically by a photo-sensitive cell – made of either selenium, CdS (cadmium sulfide), silicon blue or GPD (gallium photo diode).

The very first thing to do before taking a measurement with any meter is to set the appropriate film speed on it.

Reflected light meters
A meter of this type measures the amount of light being reflected by your subject. It can be used to measure the whole of a scene or else, when close up, to compare different areas of brightness. When the meter is turned on, light falling on a photo-electric cell causes a needle to move across a scale of numbers, usually from 1 to 18. The indicated reading is then transferred to a dial, and the correct lens aperture can be read off against the frame-rate (fps) that you are using. If the meter only shows the time element in fractions of a second and does not have a "cine" fps scale, divide the time by two to give the frame-rate: thus 18 fps gives about 1/30th second.

Spot meter
A spot meter is effectively a reflected light meter combined with a telescope: it enables you to meter a very small area of a scene with great accuracy. Spot meters usually have a pistol grip, a viewfinder and a circle engraved in the eyepiece which represents the area being metered. The scale is read either by needle, by a rotating scale or digitally. Because these meters have such a narrow angle, you *must* select the right area to meter (see opposite).

A camera with a zoom lens can be used as an improvised spot meter by zooming right in to a small detail of your subject and taking a reading on the meter.

Incident meter
A meter of this type measures the amount of light falling onto your subject. It is held in front of whatever you are filming and is pointed towards the light source, in the direction of the camera. This means that it will not be misled by large areas of darkness or brightness in the shot and that it will infallibly render white as white and black as black – whereas a reflected light meter tends to reduce a snowstorm and a coalcellar to the same "perfectly exposed" average mid-gray. Incident meters are without question the most reliable way of metering and are standard for professional work. Many meters can now measure both incident and reflected light.

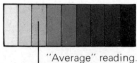

"Average" reading.

The tone scale
Every subject consists of a variety of tonal values. These may range from dark tones in the shadow areas to light tones in the highlight areas. The light meter is set to take a reading of the light reflected by an "average" 18 per cent gray subject. This means that the mid-tones will all be accurately recorded and the tones at either extreme will be acceptable.

Hand-held or built-in meters
Nearly all super 8 cameras now have built-in light meters. They measure the amount of light in the scene and automatically set the aperture in the camera to give the correct exposure. Provided that they allow you to override them manually, they are excellent. If they are of the reflex "TTL" type (see p. 49), they will also take account of any light lost during transmission through the array of lens elements, lens filters and beamsplitters. This is the big advantage which they have over ordinary reflected-light, hand-held meters. On all but the most expensive cameras, the marked f stop is not a true indication of the light which in fact reaches the film. When you use a hand-held meter you need to know the actual transmission stops, or *T stops*, of your particular lens/camera combination. It is worth working these out, by trial and error or by a series of controlled comparisons, since you will then be able to use both spot meters and incident meters.

Profisix light meter

Minolta meter

Spectra Combi meter

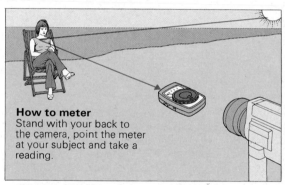

How to meter
Stand with your back to the camera, point the meter at your subject and take a reading.

How to meter
Stand beside the camera, frame the most important area of your subject in the meter viewfinder and take a reading.

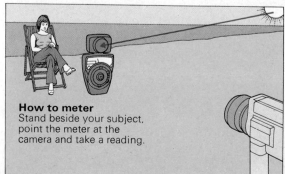

How to meter
Stand beside your subject, point the meter at the camera and take a reading.

How to Get the Right Exposure

Any one shot contains a wide range of brightnesses. A meter reading from one part of the scene may say f2.8; a reading from another part may say f22. This causes problems for any light meter. Most in-camera meters cope either by metering the whole frame-area and calculating an overall exposure (the "average" method) or by metering merely the central portion of the frame (the "center-weighted" method), assuming that this will represent the most important part of the picture.

If you are using a hand-held meter, either take readings of several different areas and work out an average setting yourself (see right), or measure an area which is as close as possible to the magic 18 per cent gray which will give the correct "average" exposure (grass, for instance). It is worth remembering that the pale skin tone of a white person gives a reading about one stop higher than 18 per cent gray; if you meter for that, then you should *open up* one stop more than the aperture indicated on the light meter.

Situations that fool the meter

The trouble with using a meter which takes an average reading is that it will be misled if there is a large bright area or a large dark area in its field-of-view. If you are framing your subject in a doorway or shooting from under an arch, for instance, the meter will tend to open up the aperture in order to render the dark areas as mid-gray. In fact, of course, they *should* be dark. You can avoid over-exposing by using an incident or a spot meter – or an in-camera meter that has either manual override or an "exposure lock". Set the camera up for the shot in the normal way, zoom in close to your subject and either set the lens aperture manually or "lock" the meter to the setting indicated. Then zoom back out and start filming.

Similar problems arise if you are shooting into the light. The meter will tend to expose for the bright sky behind your subject rather than for their face: the result will be an under-exposed face. Correct this by using your camera's "backlight control" to open up the aperture whenever the light is shining towards the camera or whenever the shot contains large areas of pure white (such as an object or snow, or even a few words on a sheet of white paper). If you have enough film to spare, "bracket" the exposure by shooting the scene at different aperture settings.

Exposure lock
An "exposure lock" button allows you to lock an automatic, in-camera meter onto one particular setting. On the Braun Nizo (see right), it is indicated by the word "fix". This camera also allows you full manual control of the aperture.

+1
aut.
fix.
man.

Backlight control
Most super 8 cameras have a "backlight control" button. It lets you open up the diaphragm by one stop or so when shooting into the light. On the Braun Nizo, it is indicated by the sign "+1".

+1
aut.
fix.
man.

A highlight reading will be under-exposed.

A shadow reading will be over-exposed.

An "average" reading over-exposes the central figure.

Stop down to give the correct exposure.

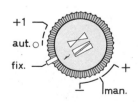
An "average" reading under-exposes your subject's face.

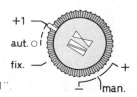
Open up to give the correct exposure.

Taking an average reading
In any scene the range of reflected light that you would find by metering different areas is astonishingly large. The small picture inset at the top left shows the result when a meter reading was taken from the bright area of sky (f16); the other small picture shows the result when the reading came from the dark shadow areas at the bottom of the scene (f2). The first is under-exposed and the second is over-exposed. The main picture was shot at f8 – an average of the two individual readings.

Contre-jour and silhouette

Shooting into the light is sometimes referred to as *contre-jour*. It produces a "backlit" subject. If you want to retain some detail in the shadow areas facing the camera but still want to catch the high contrast glitter of the highlights or the sun streaming over your subject's shoulder, take a reflected light reading but use the camera's back-light control. If you want to shoot in pure silhouette, meter the reflected light directly.

Contre-jour

Silhouette

Color Temperature

All light sources have a color cast. For example, lamplight is a very warm yellow whereas the light from a cloudy sky is very blue. A useful system of describing the color of light has been devised: it is called the *color temperature* scale and is expressed in degrees Kelvin (K). Every different light source has its own color temperature. Average noon daylight, for instance, is 5,500°K. This means that a theoretical "black body" would have to be heated to 5,500°K before the light it gave out was the same as noon daylight. Although red is thought of as a "warm" light and blue as a "cold" light, it is actually the higher temperature which gives the coldest (or bluest) light – hence the term "white hot".

Color temperature chart

Color temperature meter

This meter gives a measurement of the color temperature of incident light. It works by comparing the blue–red and green–red ratios in any light source. The reading is in degrees Kelvin and tables are supplied that indicate which filters should be used. The meter is used extensively in film and TV studios for matching shots and balancing color.

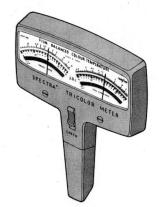

Mixed lighting

The picture on the right was taken just after sunset on daylight film. The light from the early night sky, which has a color temperature of about 7,000°K, gives the overall scene a bluish cast. The electric lights inside the house, however, have a much lower color temperature and record as a warm red–yellow light.

Color temperature and film

As a rule we do not normally notice the difference in the color of light, since our brain tends to compensate for our eye: if we "know" we are looking at a white sheet of paper, for instance, we will "see" a white sheet of paper, whether it is lit by the yellow light of a candle or by the blue light of daylight. Film is different. You can, of course, shoot in any light with black and white film, but color film will record the color cast of the light as it actually is. For this reason, there are two types of color film commonly available: outdoor or *daylight* film (which is balanced for 5,500°K) and indoor or *tungsten* film (Type A, which is balanced for 3,400°K, and Type B, which is balanced for 3,200°K). The difference between daylight and tungsten can be bridged using filters.

Outdoor lighting

The large picture was shot in daylight on daylight film. The small picture shows the same scene shot on tungsten film: it is unnaturally blue.

Color correction filters

These filters are placed on the camera lens to convert the color temperature of the light so that daylight film may be used in tungsten lighting and vice-versa.

If you are using daylight film to shoot indoor scenes, the result will be very red – since tungsten lighting has a low color temperature. To increase the blue and restore the color balance to normal, use a blue filter such as the Wratten 80A (see opposite).

If you are using tungsten film to shoot outdoor scenes, counteract the blue cast by using an orange filter such as the Wratten 85 or 85B. Almost all super 8 film is balanced for tungsten light. The orange "85" filter necessary to convert to daylight is built into the cameras where it can be operated either by a switch or a filter key.

Tungsten lighting

The large picture was shot in tungsten light on tungsten film. The small picture shows the same scene shot on daylight film: it is unnaturally yellow.

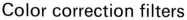

Color conversion filters

Whereas color conversion filters (see opposite) are strong and are designed to "convert" daylight film to tungsten or vice-versa, there are also *color correction* (or *color compensation*) filters which are weaker and can compensate for small differences between the film and the color temperature of the light source. They operate either towards the red or blue ends of the spectrum, and are therefore sometimes known as "warming" or "cooling" filters. The most common are the "Skylight" (1A) and the 81A filter. Also frequently used are *ultra-violet* filters which reduce blue haze and *polarizing* filters which darken blue skies (see p. 182).

Filters for controlling color temperature

There is a wide range of color filters designed for manipulating the color cast of light recorded on color film. They are most often used for color conversion and for reducing the excessive blueness of an overcast or hazy day. They are often classified according to the Kodak "Wratten" system.

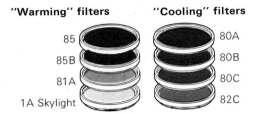

"Warming" filters — 85, 85B, 81A, 1A Skylight

"Cooling" filters — 80A, 80B, 80C, 82C

Ultra-violet   Polarizing

81A filter (left)

By using a warming filter such as the Wratten 81A, the unpleasant blue cast on this shot of Jerusalem has been reduced. As a result, the color appears more "normal".

Ultra-violet filter (right)

Ultra-violet light, which is unseen by the eye, records on film as a blue-haze — particularly at high altitudes. By using an ultra-violet filter or the Skylight (1A), this blue haze can be reduced.

Time of day

The color temperature of light varies enormously through the course of the day and will have a profound effect on the atmosphere, the color and the relief of your film. The changes in the color of the light can be turned to great advantage, and you should make a habit of using the prevailing light, not fighting it. However, if you do need to, you can use any of the color correction filters.

Changing color temperature

At sunrise, the color temperature of the light is likely to be about 2-3,000°K – a warm pink or yellow, according to the strength of the sun. The color temperature rises during the day, reaching a peak at noon and in the early afternoon. Towards evening it falls again, often producing a rich red color cast at sunset.

Sunrise   Mid morning   Noon   Mid afternoon   Sunset

Controlling Exposure

Neutral density filters

Apart from simple aperture adjustment, one of the best ways of controlling the amount of light which reaches the film is by using gray *neutral density filters*. They reduce the light by a number of stops so that the lens aperture may be opened up accordingly to give a shallow depth of field when you need it. They are available in a wide range of densities, and they in no way affect the overall color balance. They may also be used on occasions when there is too much light in the scene for the film that you have in your camera (when using 160 ASA film to shoot bright snow scenes, for example).

Graduated neutral density filters are effective only over their upper half, so that the sky can be darkened dramatically without affecting the exposure on the ground. Take care to position the filter so that the transition between the two halves does not show.

Filter factors

All filters absorb some of the light which passes through them and therefore reduce the amount which reaches the film. If your camera has a reflex "TTL" meter (see p. 49), it will take account of this and no adjustment need be made. But if you are using a separate meter you *must* know how much allowance to make for the correct exposure. This is indicated by the *filter factor*. It is expressed as a multiple (2X or 3X, for example) and is usually marked on the rim of the filter itself. Open up by one stop for a 2X filter, by 1½ stops for a 3X filter, by 2 stops for a 4X filter, and so on.

Neutral density filter
In this shot a neutral density filter has been used to reduce depth of field, throw the background out of focus and accentuate the Rolls Royce symbol.

Graduated neutral density filter
By reducing the exposure in the top half of the picture, the sky was darkened to create an overcast, stormy scene.

Metering for movement

If your camera has an automatic light-metering system, it will tend to alter the aperture *during* a shot whenever the subject changes or moves. For example, if you pan from a white house to a green field, the aperture will suddenly open up; or if a man removes his jacket to reveal a white shirt, the meter will stop down. The effect is unattractive and can be avoided with an "exposure lock" (see p. 91). Take a reading before the shot and then lock the aperture.

However, there are times when you will want to maintain the exposure difference between one end of the shot and the other, and some form of adjustment is essential. This is known as a "stop pull" and is done by hand so that the transition is as imperceptible as possible. It is best to plan the shot in advance, rehearse it through – checking the exposure at each point – and then film the scene as smoothly as you can. But, in general, avoid stop pulls if possible.

Light background
When the man moves in front of the light background, the camera will stop down to f16 to prevent over-exposing the white wall. This will be noticeable, since the man will suddenly become darker. To avoid this, "lock" the exposure at f5.6.

Dark background
During the first half of the sequence the man is filmed running against a dark background. The meter takes this into account and indicates an exposure of f5.6.

Shot at f5.6

Stopped down to f16

"Locked" at f5.6

Low Light Filming

Modern cameras, lenses and filmstocks permit filming in conditions that only a few years ago would have been considered impossible. In super 8, "existing light" or "XL" cameras, with their variable shutters and their "fast" f1.2 lenses, are now commonplace. In the larger gauges a lens as fast as f0.7 has been used.

Low light has no special intrinsic virtue. But low light capability means that you can fully exploit natural light without tampering with it. You can shoot a barbecue by the glow of the campfire, a street scene by the light of the shop windows, or a rock concert by the stage lighting.

However, if you are using the fastest lens–camera combination that you have and you still cannot get enough light for an acceptable exposure, there are three courses open to you before you are forced to bring in artificial lighting: use a very fast filmstock; "uprate" the film during processing; or "undercrank" the camera.

Using high-speed film
The fastest super 8 films on the market are nominally rated at 200 ASA (color) and 400 ASA (black and white). They all give acceptable quality, though they tend to be more grainy than slower films and they are less able to resolve fine detail. This is particularly noticeable in the smaller gauges, especially if you attempt to intercut Kodachrome 40 with Ektachrome 160, for example (see *Filmstock Specifications*, p. 272).

Uprating the film
To "uprate" a film simply means deciding to treat it as though it had a faster speed than its nominal rating and exposing it accordingly. For example, you might uprate Ektachrome 160 to 320 ASA (a gain in exposure of one stop). The film would then be given an extended development time in the laboratory to compensate for the lower degree of exposure received by the emulsion. This is known as "push processing" or "forced development" (see p. 208). It does, unfortunately, have some severe drawbacks: it increases the grain, reduces the definition and exaggerates the contrast.

Undercranking
To "undercrank" a camera simply means running it at a slower speed than normal so that each frame receives a longer exposure. You must choose a subject that is suited to the technique, since any movement will be speeded up (see *Fast Motion*, p. 188). You should always use a tripod when undercranking, and remember that any movement of the camera (such as panning or tracking) will look much faster on projection. You can work out the exposure by simple mathematics: if you film at 4 fps each frame will be exposed for 1/8th second – a gain of two stops over the usual 18 fps (1/30th second). You gain another stop if you shoot at 2 fps.

I once had to film the interior of St Sophia, in Istanbul, by undercranking to 8 fps and tracking very slowly across a rather bumpy floor. Despite the profound scepticism of the cameraman, but thanks to his prowess, the shots were quite acceptable. The lesson is clear: always try to use the available light, and if you have to augment it do so as sympathetically as you can.

Firelight
This shot was filmed entirely by the light given off from the bonfire. By using an XL camera with a fast lens and shutter, and by opening the aperture right up, it was possible to get a reasonable exposure. Remember that depth of field is very shallow at wide apertures, so focusing is critical.

Stage lighting
This shot of Mick Jagger was filmed using existing stage lighting. An XL camera with fast film was quite adequate to guarantee a good exposure. Stage lighting, which often comes from above or behind the performer, can produce strong, attractive back-lighting, but – unless it is an effect you desire – beware of the lights flaring into the camera lens.

Using a fast lens
When filming *Barry Lyndon*, Stanley Kubrick often used an unusually fast f0.7 lens. He was thus able to achieve marvellously naturalistic shots and can be said to have been responsible for the first feature film ever shot by candle power.

Undercranking
By running the camera at 8 fps, it was possible to achieve the first documentary shots ever filmed inside St Sophia, Istanbul. This avoided a lighting bill which would probably have been in the order of $40,000 per day.

Natural Lighting Conditions

The natural lighting conditions produced by the changing weather will dictate the mood of your sequence even more forcefully than the time of day. It is difficult to make a funeral look anything other than festive if the sun is shining brightly; and a wedding in heavy, gray drizzle is perhaps better not filmed at all.

If you are attempting to establish a particular atmosphere, film in weather that most closely resembles that mood, even if you have to wait a very long time.

Wet weather

It is always best to try and *use* the prevailing light and weather conditions that Fate provides. If it is raining, then film the puddles and umbrellas, the people running for cover, the water dripping from leaves, and so on. Your subsequent shot of a rainbow – if you are lucky – will then make sense chronologically as well as aesthetically. Always keep the camera dry: cover it with a plastic bag or stand under an umbrella. A plain glass or ultraviolet filter will keep raindrops off the lens itself, but remember that the drops are more visible at the wide angle than at the telephoto end of the lens.

After rain (above)
The light in this shot has a soft, pastel quality. It was taken in the early evening after a rainstorm.

Rainbow (far left)
This shot of a rainbow was taken during a summer storm.

Rainstorm (left)
The feeling of a sudden downpour is perfectly conveyed in this muted shot, taken through a rain-soaked window pane.

Filming a sunset

Sunsets are particularly dramatic when filmed using the "time-lapse" technique (see p. 189); they also make spectacular background scenery. Remember, however, that the light will be very red and will give an almost "raspberry" color cast to the overall scene. If this is the effect you want, however, you can exaggerate it by using red or orange colored filters.

Getting the right exposure will be your biggest problem when shooting sunsets, since, when the sun is still high in the sky, its presence tends to overwhelm the meter. One solution is to use your zoom lens to take a spot reading of the clouds near the sun, then lock the aperture and zoom out again for the shot. Alternatively, zoom to your wide-angle setting and, stretching your left hand as far forward as you can, try to mask the sun alone from the lens. This will give you an average reading of the cloud area. Finally, you may use a spot meter, and come to a compromise between the different cloud apertures.

Early sunset (above)
The sun is still above the horizon. If it is very bright, do not look at it directly through the viewfinder: the heat from the sun is reflected along with its light and it can cause permanent blindness.

Late sunset (below)
The sun has now sunk below the horizon. For the purposes of calculating the exposure, it may now be safely ignored: it will no longer be bright enough to mislead the meter.

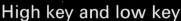

Cold weather

Seemingly poor weather is sometimes ideal for shooting certain kinds of scene. Snow, thick fog or a heavily overcast wintry afternoon all have a strong atmospheric "feel" of their own. But beware of under-exposing the film if you are shooting a sequence in snow (see p. 91).

Snow
The flock of crows landing in a field stand out starkly against the white snow and the dramatic winter sky. Remember, however, that if the temperature is very low you should keep the camera batteries in your pocket until you need them since they may run slow if too cold.

Fog
A thick, early-morning fog has drained all contrast and detail from this shot of a motor cyclist riding towards the camera. "Unfavorable" lighting conditions have thus been used to create a distinctly atmospheric and somehow mysterious shot. Fog effects can be faked using a special filter (see p. 182).

Hot weather

Filming clear blue skies, landscapes shimmering in the distant haze or the air rising off a hot road can all convey the claustrophobic feeling of stifling heat. But if you are filming in very high temperatures, keep the camera in the shade for as long as possible before shooting. Never leave it on the rear windowshelf of a car.

Heat
This shot was taken in the intense heat of the Kenyan desert. The mirage effect on the horizon has been produced by the hot air distorting the light. If you are filming in very hot conditions, you must keep the camera and film cool. Try using a cheap, insulated picnic-basket as a make-shift refrigerator.

High key and low key

Weather, time of day, backlight, silhouette, high or low contrast, hard or soft light, bright or muted colors, dramatic or restrained composition – all these factors interact to produce an image with a certain style of its own. And it is important that you match the style or "feel" of your shots when you put together a sequence. The phrases "high key" and "low key" are often used to describe both the intensity and the hardness of lighting.

High key

A *high key* shot is dramatically lit and composed, with strongly directional lighting and fierce relief. There is a wide tonal range between the highlights and shadows, and the colors tend to be deeply "saturated" and often of contrasting hues. A high key lighting set-up for interiors tends to produce an artificial, dramatic effect (see *Lighting for Dramatic Effect*, p. 104).

Low key

A *low key* shot tends to be flatly illuminated – usually from behind the camera and with a diffused light source such as a gray sky. Bright complementary colors should be avoided; pastels from within the same band of the color circle (see p. 50) will give a subtler, more low key effect. Low key lighting will make your subjects look more "natural" (see *Lighting for Realism*, p. 105)

Artificial Lighting

The function of any artificial lighting is to raise the level of illumination to the point where the film will be properly exposed. This level will, of course, vary with the film speed, and with the color, texture and angle of the subject, but the principal factors involved are the design and output of the light source that you are using and its distance from the subject you are filming.

Film lighting comes in every conceivable shape and size – from tiny "movie lights" which slot onto the camera to the "brutes" (225 amp arc lamps) of the motion-picture industry. The important thing to remember about artificial lighting is that *you* control it completely: the range of effects that can be obtained is limited only by your time, money and imagination.

The factors you should bear in mind when choosing a lighting system are primarily output and flexibility; can you vary both the intensity and the quality – the "softness" or "hardness" – of the light?

The inverse square rule

Light from a simple source (such as a candle) follows the inverse square rule: its power of illumination is inversely proportionate to the square of the distance from the subject. In other words, this means that if you double the distance between your subject and a lamp, it will receive four times less light than before. In practice, the loss is rather less, since all lights have some form of reflector which tends to reduce the light-loss due to distance.

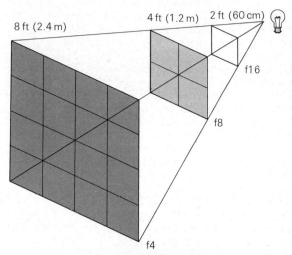

Hard light (left)

A "hard light" is one which is bright, sharply focused and has a narrow angle of illumination. It produces a high contrast subject with a strong, clear shadow.

Soft light (right)

A "soft light" is one in which the light is scattered to give a wide angle of illumination. It gives a gentle, diffused light and produces a soft, gray shadow.

High relief (left)

A strong ray of direct light, shone at your subject from a low angle, will bring out any textural detail and produce high contrast between highlights and shadows.

Low relief (right)

A diffused light source will produce a less dramatic shot, but the mid-tones will be richer, the shadows softer and more detail will be recorded.

Reflector design

A lamp without any kind of reflector will radiate light in every direction. By placing the lamp within a reflector, you can control the light and direct it where you want it. A *parabolic* reflector produces a hard light and is most commonly used with tungsten lamps. A *softlight* reflector has a shield in front of the bulb and so produces a diffused light. A *spotlight* enables you to vary the light beam. In each case, the light will be softer if the reflector surface is matted or dimpled rather than highly polished.

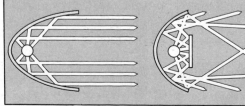
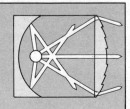

Parabolic reflector
This produces a concentrated beam of hard light.

Softlight reflector
This produces a broad beam of soft light.

Spotlight
This produces a variable beam of light.

Tungsten Lights

Tungsten lights are all basically similar to the standard domestic light bulb: they consist of a glass bulb filled with an inert gas and containing a metal tungsten filament. When an electrical current is passed through the filament, it heats up and gives off light. Tungsten bulbs are available in a wide range of power ratings – from tiny 100 watt modeling lamps to the big 10,000 watt lights used in the movie industry. However, a typical basic lighting kit containing three lamps and producing a total light output of 1,000 to 1,500 watts should not cost you more than about $100. Tungsten lights commonly come in two forms: standard tungsten-filament incandescent bulbs and special "photofloods".

Tungsten incandescent bulbs

Photographic bulbs with tungsten filaments have been widely used in the movie industry for years. They can be set in a wide variety of reflectors: a *floodlight* or "parabolic" reflector gives a fairly broad band of direct light (a "full flood"); a "diffusion" reflector generally has a shallower dish, with a less highly reflective surface, and a small cap to prevent direct light from the bulb hitting the subject; finally, there is the *spotlight* which is designed to give a hard light with a narrow angle of illumination (a "full spot"). Metal screens called "barndoors" can be fitted in front of the lamp; these can be opened and closed to select a particular lighting area. In addition, these lamps will accept filters, "scrims" and diffusers of various kinds (see p. 101). They are heavy when compared to the newer photofloods and quartz lights, but their versatility has made them the standard light for use in film studios or in any other set-up where portability is of little importance.

Photofloods

Photofloods are the cheapest form of artificial lighting. They look very like ordinary household bulbs and, since they have a standard screw-fitting, they can (in the USA, at any rate) be used in normal domestic light sockets. The bulbs are available in several versions, ranging from about 100 to 1,000 watts, and have a color temperature rating of either 3,200°K or 3,400°K. Many photofloods are what is called "over-run". This means that although they give out a substantial amount of light, they have a very short life. After as little as a few hours, the glass bulb begins to be blackened with deposits of tungsten, the light output starts to fall, and the color temperature drops – so that the bulbs begin to emit a red color cast. This effect can be very gradual and often goes unnoticed until the film is screened. It is important to be aware that the color temperature of tungsten lights also varies with the voltage of the power supply. You can keep a check on this by using a color temperature meter (see p. 92).

Photofloods are also available in a less over-run, "pearl" form. These do not give out quite as much light as fully over-run photofloods, but they last much longer – up to 100 hours – and for this reason are becoming increasingly popular. Some photofloods also have built-in reflectors; these are known as *reflector floods*. The light is reflected by a silver coating applied to the inside of the glass bulb, behind the filament.

Tungsten-filament incandescent bulbs

These bulbs, the traditional form of photographic lighting, vary greatly in shape, size and output. But they all contain a similar tungsten filament, which gives off light when an electric current is passed through it. Unfortunately, they all have a limited life.

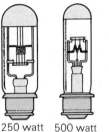
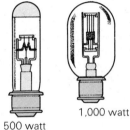
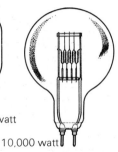

250 watt   500 watt

1,000 watt

10,000 watt

Floodlight (left)

A floodlight contains a single tungsten bulb set in a dish-shaped reflector. It casts an even light over a fairly wide area.

"Spot" position

"Flood" position

Spotlight (right)

These lights are designed to give a variable beam. They have a stepped-glass "fresnel" lens which allows the beam to be focused. The bulb and the reflector are both moved to and fro behind the lens to give a full flood or a full spot light.

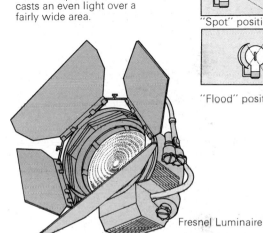

Fresnel Luminaire

Photoflood bulbs

These bulbs, too, vary in shape, size and output. They may have an opalized, pearl or satin-etched finish, and they may or may not have a built-in reflector. Although inexpensive, they may only last for a few hours. Their chief advantage is that they can often be used in standard domestic light fittings.

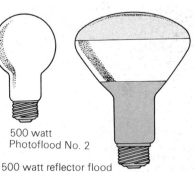

275 watt
Photoflood No. 1

500 watt
Photoflood No. 2

500 watt reflector flood

Lowell-Light (left)

Kits are available which often allow simple "barndoors" to be fitted to a photoflood. The bulb itself fits into a porcelain socket attached to a universal clamp.

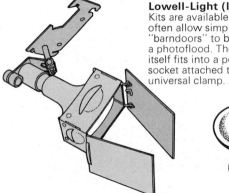

Barlight (above)

Fittings are available to hold more than one bulb. This one contains four 300 watt reflector floods.

Quartz Lights

Also known as *tungsten-halogen* or *quartz-iodine*, these lamps now dominate the moviemaking scene. They are smaller, lighter and more efficient than tungsten lights. They consist of a metal tungsten filament inside a small quartz glass tube filled with a halogen gas – usually iodine. The presence of the iodine guarantees that the bulb does not darken and that the light output and color temperature remain constant. Most quartz lamps last as long as 250 hours and have a color temperature rating of 3,200°K. Outputs vary from 150 to 350 watts for battery lights and from 200 to 10,000 watts for main power supply use. The quartz bulb itself should never be touched with a bare hand, even when unlit, as acid from the skin can cause premature failure of the bulb. Always handle the bulb with a small piece of tissue paper.

Quartz lighting kits

High output, long life and portability have made quartz lights very popular, especially for newsreel and documentary work and in other areas where mobility or one-person operation is important.

Movielights are designed to be attached to the top of a camera and are either designed to be plugged into the main electrical supply or to be powered by a battery. Sometimes they can be swiveled upwards so that the light is "bounced" off the ceiling. This is a big advantage because the light produced by a movielight tends to be hard, uneven and devoid of any relief.

Hand-held battery lights are often used professionally in night-shooting. They are usually known as *sunguns*, since they can also be used as a "filler" for facial shadows on dull days (see p. 108). When using a hand-held sungun, take care that it does not wobble while shooting because the motion will be visible on the screen.

Quartz bulbs set in open reflectors are probably the most common quartz lights. They are available in a wide range of wattages, usually from 200 to 2,000 but also as high as 10,000 watts. On many models the light may be focused by moving the quartz bulb to and fro. Nowadays, many of the better lamps are made with fiberglass housings to reduce transmission of the bulbs' heat.

Basic quartz lighting kits usually consist of three lights, each of which might be 1,000 watts. They are often equipped with "barndoors" and stands.

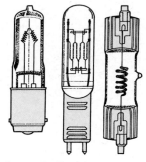

Quartz bulbs
The tungsten filament is set in a quartz glass bulb filled with halogen gases.

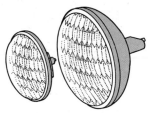

"PAR" quartz lights
These compact sealed-beam units have a built-in parabolic aluminized reflector (PAR) behind the bulb and a fluted or clear glass lens in front.

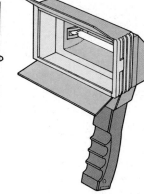

Movielights
Movielights are the most common form of artificial lighting for amateur movie-making. They can either be hand-held or mounted on top of the camera.

Sungun
Sunguns are small, lightweight quartz units. They usually range in output from, say, 150 to 350 watts and are powered by battery packs. Their chief advantage is their portability, and for this reason they are often used in newsreel work or in situations where heavy lighting equipment is not practical. However, the light they produce tends to be very hard if used directly.

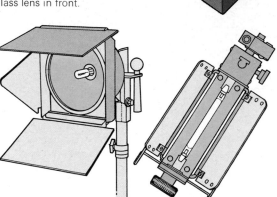

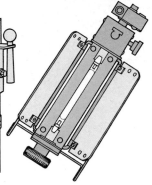

Color temperature of lighting

Both tungsten and quartz lamps are designed to produce light with a color temperature of 3,200°K or 3,400°K (see p. 92). They should, therefore, be used with film balanced for artificial lighting. However, if you are using quartz lights to *supplement* daylight and you are shooting on daylight film, you must raise the color temperature of the lights to 5,500°K by placing dichroic blue filters in front of the lamps. This will, of course, lower their output. Carbon arc lights may be either 3,200°K or 5,500°K. Metal halide lights are 5,500°K.

Remember that if the voltage supply to the light drops the color temperature falls.

Quartz reflector lamp
This lamp takes interchangeable bulbs of 500, 750 or 1,000 watts. The light-beam can be focused by moving the bulb backwards and forwards in the reflector. If the light is on a very tall stand, a system of chains enables you to do this by remote control. At full flood position the angle of the beam is 67°; at full spot it is 5°. A range of accessories such as barn-doors, filters, scrims and alternative reflector dishes are all available.

Quartz "Tota-Light"
This rectangular reflector lamp uses double-ended quartz bulbs ranging in output from 300 to 1,000 watts. It gives an exceptionally broad, even beam of light, ideal for "bouncing" off walls or ceilings. The angle of illumination can be adjusted by altering the position of the reflector doors. The lamp is rugged, very compact and extremely light (it weighs only 20 oz.). Reflector screens, "umbrellas" and filters are all available.

Quartz softlight
This lamp is designed to take two double-ended quartz bulbs, usually 750 watts each. The bulbs face inwards, towards the reflector surface. This means that no direct light hits your subject. All the light is "bounced" off the lamp's textured reflector surface. As a result, although the light is still bright, it is much "softer" than unreflected light. It is ideal for producing delicate lighting, especially if you are only using one light.

Lighting Accessories

The most important lighting accessory is the *stand*. It should be as strong as possible without being too heavy, and can be stabilized by draping a sandbag or water bag over the legs. Alternatively, use a *clamp* to attach the light to a door or a curtain rail, for example. The best kind is the "alligator clamp" or "gaffer grip".

Most of the other lighting accessories available are designed to control the quality, rather than the placing of the light (see below). Some of them – *barndoors*, spunglass *diffusers* and *filters* – are virtually essential. Many can be home-made: for instance, a large sheet of white polystyrene provides an excellent reflector for producing soft, diffused light. Large diffusers can also be improvised: simply hang up an ordinary white bed sheet and project light through it to soften it.

Alligator clamp
A spring-loaded clamp like this is ideal for securing fairly lightweight lamps such as medium-sized quartz lights.

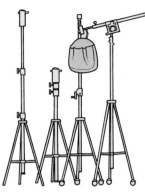

Lighting stands
The best stands are made of lightweight alloy and are telescopic. Ideally they should extend to about 6 or 7 ft (1.8 m to 2.1 m) and have wide, robust legs. They are also available in a "boom" form so that overhead lighting can be provided without the stand being visible in the shot.

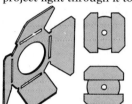

Barndoors
These are hinged metal flaps which fit onto the front of the lamp. By adjusting their position, you can limit the light area as you wish.

Snoot
Sometimes called a "nose", this is an open-ended cylindrical funnel which fits over the front of the lamp and gives a narrow, concentrated circle of light.

Diffuser
A sheet of material such as frosted plexiglass, spun glass or even tracing paper placed in front of a lamp will soften the light and allow you to control its "flavor".

Umbrella
These umbrellas open up to reveal a highly reflective surface on the inside. They soften the light and produce relatively shadowless Illumination.

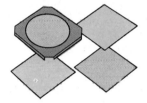

Filters
If you are shooting in mixed lighting (artificial and daylight), you can use dichroic glass or gelatin color-correction filters over the lamps (see p. 107).

French flag
This is an opaque black panel on a flexible strut which can be used to block light. You can make one yourself from black plywood or cardboard.

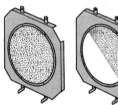

Scrim and half-scrim
Scrims are made of wire mesh. Placed in front of the lamp, they enable you to vary the output without moving the light and without "softening" it.

Cukaloris
Also known as a "cookie" this device projects shadows onto the background. The pattern can be either random or in the form of a window.

Reflector
A reflector allows you to soften and spread an otherwise hard light. You can also "bounce" light to fill in shadow areas that are too dark (see p. 105).

Window filters
As an alternative to putting filters on the lights for mixed lighting, you can put a filter on the window. Use a large roll of orange "85" gel (see p. 107).

Professional lights

For greater power than normal, a set of small "PAR" quartz lights can be used. Together they form what is called a *mini-brute* or *ninelight*. They require heavy cabling but give tremendous covering power.

Carbon arc lamps, also known as "brutes" are extremely large, heavy and powerful. They can produce either "tungsten" or "daylight" illumination in enormous quantities.

Metal halide lamps are enclosed mercury arc lamps. They are smaller and lighter than carbon arcs, and work on AC current. Like all these lights they are for professional use: their function is to turn night into noon, or a dull day into bright sunshine.

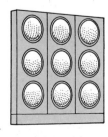

Mini-brute
This lamp is made up of nine 650 watt quartz sealed-beam units. They can be used separately.

Carbon arc lamp
The light is generated in this "brute" by a DC current passing between two carbon elements.

Metal halide lamp
The light is generated in this lamp by an AC current passing between two mercury elements.

Building a Lighting Set-up

Creative control of lighting is as important as proper control of the camera. You can vary the height, angle, intensity and diffusion of each of the lights in your set-up, and every change will affect the look and feel of your film. By positioning the lights where you want them you can produce a glossy, glittering image or a diffused, naturalistic effect; you can either allow yourself maximum flexibility for unpredictable locations (such as a party) or you can build a carefully structured and elaborately theatrical set-up for actors who can be guaranteed to be in the right spot at the right time. The techniques illustrated in the following pages can be adapted to any situation you wish. They can all be achieved using simple, inexpensive equipment.

Lighting for portraits

The human face is the most basic ingredient of any film, and an understanding of the ways in which it can be lit will help you to light other, more complex subjects. You are aiming to emphasize the best features of the face without producing excessive distortion. Although you are quite free to experiment with lights as you wish, most filmmakers agree that the best of way of lighting for portraits is to use a *key light*, a *filler* and a *back light*.

When positioning each of these lights, remember that there are two main factors involved: the quality of the light (that is, its "hardness" or "softness" – see p. 98) and the direction from which it strikes the subject.

Lighting direction
The direction of the predominant light source has a great effect on the shape and appearance of a face. Here, a strong spotlight has been used at different angles to show how the degree of modeling and the amount of detail change.

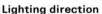

4 Sidelight

The effect ranges from complete silhouette when the light is directed at a white background behind the girl's head, through to a harshly lit face without any modeling when the light is shone straight at the girl from just above the camera. None of the lights, on their own, are very flattering.

1 Silhouette

2 Backlight

3 Backlight at 45°

5 Frontal light at 45°

6 Frontal light

Positioning the key light

The key light is the basis of all facial lighting. For this reason it is sometimes called the "main" or "source" light. Because it is the strongest light it is the one which gives modeling to the face and is almost always placed off to one side of the camera. It is very important to set up the keylight correctly in relation to your subject's "eyeline". The eyeline is an imaginary line projecting out from the face at an angle of 90°, at the level of the eyes. Unless your subject is actually facing the camera, the key light should in general be as close as possible to the eyeline, or else you will get unpleasant shadows from the nose. There is an arc of about 20° on either side of the eyeline within which you can move the key light to adjust the modeling without running into trouble, but beyond this point you are likely to have an unflattering image.

Horizontal angle
The key light is usually placed within an angle of 20° on either side of the subject's eyeline.

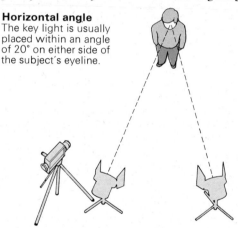

The height of the key light is also important. If it is too low, the effect is grotesque: the eyebrows, cheekbones and chin are all unnaturally exaggerated. This may be fine for filming a horror story, but not for a normal portrait. If the key light is too high, the eyes are invisible and heavy shadows distort the features. The best position for most subjects is found to be at an angle of about 40° above the subject's eyeline. This is hardly surprising since that is the position of most sunlight. It therefore produces a balance of highlights and shadow areas on the face to which we are accustomed and which we find "natural".

Vertical angle
Place the key light about 40° above the subject's eyeline.

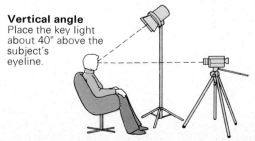

Key light only

The *key light* should be set up first and the others built around it. It provides the main bulk of the illumination, and therefore largely determines the exposure. When you have chosen the direction of the key light, you can then adjust the output and the degree of diffusion. If you decide to reduce the intensity of the light by moving it away from your subject, remember to increase its height so that the angle between it and the eyeline remains the same. The key light is normally a spotlight or variable-focus flood. It is not usual to diffuse it, but if it is the only light you have it should certainly be softened. No key light should ever be placed directly behind the camera. Having set up the key light, take a light reading.

Key light
This is the most important light in any set-up. It is often placed at an angle of 45° to the camera.

Adding a "filler" light

A *filler* light is added to the set-up to light some of the shadow areas thrown by the key light. It should be bright enough to relieve these shadows but not so bright as to fill them completely. The ratio between key light and filler light, called the *lighting ratio*, determines the degree of contrast and drama in the shot. In a classical set-up it would be about 2:1, the filler light adding perhaps one stop extra illumination. Always use a soft, diffused light for the filler. If your subject is looking straight at the camera, set it up on the opposite side of the key light. But if your subject's eyeline is off to the side, place the filler somewhere in the arc *between* the camera and the key light. Turn the key light back on and move the filler until the combined effect is just right.

Key light and filler
The filler is set closer to the camera and lower down than the key light. It reveals detail in the shadow areas.

Adding a back light

When the key light and filler light have been set, switch them off and add a *back light*. This light, which is usually a spot or variable-focus flood, is sometimes known as a "separation light". Its purpose is to rim-light your subject's hair and shoulders in order to "separate" the figure from the background and to give it greater mass and form. The back light should be just to one side of the line of sight, and on quite a high stand – at an elevation of about 50° from your subject's head. Use a "French flag" (see p. 101) to make certain that the light is not shining directly onto the camera lens, or you will get severe flare. Check too that the lighting stand is not so near that it is accidentally visible in the shot.

Key light, filler and back light
The back light shines from behind the subject and produces highlights around the shoulders and hair.

Lighting the background

The chances are that your subject will now be either set against a dark background that may distort the meter readings or against a light background that contains unwanted, confusing shadows. By setting up a *background light*, you can control this. A floodlight, focused onto the backdrop, is usually placed off to one side of the shot – the same side as the key light. This will soften the shadows cast by your subject and add a sense of depth to the scene. You can add a "cukaloris" (see p. 101) in front of the lamp if you want to break up the shadows still further. Alternatively, a light can be placed behind your subject or behind a stage prop so that it cannot be seen by the camera. But beware of this making the background too light and upsetting the overall balance.

The completed set-up
By adding a background light, the area behind the subject can be lit. In some situations this will produce a feeling of depth to the shot.

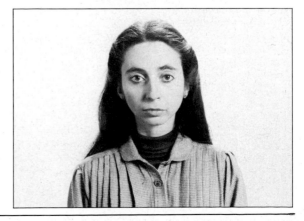

Lighting for Dramatic Effect

The classic lighting set-up of key light, filler and back light can be used to produce a glamorous, stylized effect. It is done by using a strong back light, to give an exaggerated halo around the hair and shoulders, and by establishing a high ratio between the key light and the filler. This kind of lighting is artificial and does not aim at naturalism, but at drama, glamor and glitter. At its best it can be beautifully polished and convincing. As a style of lighting, it was very popular in the Hollywood of the thirties, especially when combined with soft focus. This was partly because a brightly lit set was essential for the very slow filmstocks and camera lenses which were then all that was available to moviemakers, and partly a striving for romantic effect.

The "Hollywood" look
This shot of Marlene Dietrich as she appeared in Sternberg's *The Blue Angel* (1930) is a perfect illustration of the classical Hollywood lighting technique. The soft focus, the high key–high contrast lighting and the powerful back light all contribute to the impression of artificially exaggerated glamor.

How to build a high-key lighting set-up
Set a powerful key light off to one side of the camera to provide the bulk of the illumination. Use a spot or a variable-focus lamp with a narrow beam. Add a filler to light up the shadow areas. Keep the ratio between the key and filler light fairly high for dramatic effect. Finally, add a strong back light to emphasize the highlights in your subject's hair.

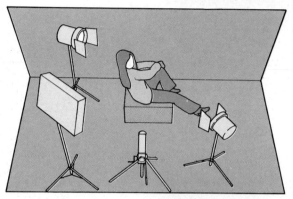

Lighting for melodrama

The best way to light for melodrama is to break all the rules. Instead of striving to achieve a "perfect" set-up in which all the lights are balanced and the result is an evenly lit subject with no heavy shadows, break up your shot into sharply contrasting areas of light and dark. This will create a strong sense of drama and tension. Use strong spotlights or adapt your open-reflector lamps by fitting "snoots" (see p. 101) so that you cast narrow beams of hard light across the scene. Above all, vary the *angle* of the lighting: a harsh light shone onto your subject's face from well below the eyeline will produce a very sinister effect, and is a technique used in countless horror movies.

Dramatic lighting
This frame enlargement is taken from *Citizen Kane* (1941). The two reporters, whose faces are never clearly seen, are rimlit by concentrated shafts of light across an almost totally dark projection-room. This is a case where the composition and the highly stylized lighting both generate a powerful sense of drama.

How to build a lighting set-up for melodrama
Use hard lights, preferably highly focused spots. Set the key light low down so that it shines up towards your subject's face at a sharp angle. If you wish, lighten the shadows slightly with a filler, set high up on the opposite side. Use a strong back light to emphasize one side of the face and throw stark, dramatic shadows onto the background.

Lighting for Realism

Outdoors, in natural lighting, we normally see things in soft sunlight or in the diffused light from a cloudy–bright sky. It is this light which we generally feel to be the most "realistic" and attractive. It casts few shadows and no pronounced, exaggerated highlights.

Because modern movie equipment no longer requires the brightly lit indoor sets it once did, it is now possible to shoot scenes using low key, realistic lighting. This kind of modern naturalistic filmmaking was pioneered by European directors and cameramen in the fifties and sixties; it has now spread to Hollywood, with all the gains in realism that you might expect. In view of the new XL cameras, it is also a "look" that any amateur can achieve with simple equipment.

Soft, misty light
Antonioni's film, *The Red Desert* (1964), from which this shot was taken, was among those European movies of the sixties which were breaking away from the traditions of artificial studio lighting. This shot of Marcello Mastroianni achieves its muted, atmospheric effect from the soft light, the misty gray sky and the muted colors and forms.

Using natural light
Both these shots are taken from *The Duellists* (1977). They both take advantage of natural lighting conditions. In the shot on the left, the couple are lit entirely by the light streaming through the bedroom window. No filler has been used, though the camera has some diffusion.

The shot on the right has the characteristically soft, shadowless light from a gray, autumn sky.

Lighting for naturalism

If you want your artificial lighting set-up to look as realistic as possible, you should aim to achieve the same soft overall light that you would get outdoors on an average day. The key to this is to use large, diffused light sources. Avoid hard lighting of any kind, keep the ratio between the key and filler light low and be careful not to overdo the backlighting. If you have a window in your shot it is a good idea to use the natural light coming through it to predominate as a back light for your subject. Unless you are using specially designed "soft-lights" (see p. 100), soften the illumination by either bouncing the light off a wall or ceiling, or by projecting the lamps through some form of diffusing material.

How to build a lighting set-up for realism
Diffuse any hard lights to produce a soft overall illumination. If you use a back light, keep it subdued.

Bounced and diffused light

All soft, relatively shadowless illumination comes from a diffused, broad light source. In other words, no direct light from the bulb must hit the subject. Lights which normally give a hard light can be easily adapted to produce soft light. The easiest method is to direct them away from your subject, towards a wall or ceiling, so that all the light is *bounced* or reflected. You can use a sheet of white polystyrene for the same purpose. Beware of colored surfaces since they will reflect colored light. Alternatively, you can *diffuse* a hard light by shining it through a sheet of tracing paper or spun glass. This will broaden the light and soften any shadows that it casts.

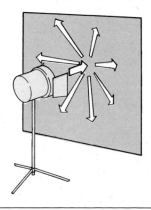

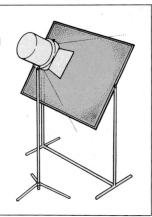

Bounced light (left)
Set up the lamp so that the light is softened and spread by being bounced off a reflective surface. Avoid colored walls since these will produce colored light.

Diffused light (right)
Place a sheet of semi-transparent material between your subject and the light source. The further it is from the lamp, the softer the light will be.

Lighting for Movement

If you are filming an indoor shot in which the subject, or the camera, or both, are moving, you will be faced with lighting problems. The perfectly balanced set-up for one position may be drastically unsuitable if your subject moves a few feet to the right or left. What is worse, because of the inverse square law (see p. 98), the level of illumination will change dramatically when your subject moves closer to a light or further away from it.

There are several things you can do to even out the light levels. By far the simplest is to abandon the whole enterprise of key lights and fillers, and shoot the scene with evenly diffused "bounced" lighting (see p. 105). The set-up is easy to build. There is no need to diffuse your lamps: reflecting them off the walls or ceiling will provide all the diffusion you need. However, when using bounced lighting, beware of colored ceilings or walls. Once you have set up your lights, check the overall evenness of the illumination by using an incident meter. Alternatively, get your subject to rehearse every possible move and check the exposure throughout the shot.

Lighting for a camera pan

When building a fairly elaborate lighting set-up for a moving subject, there are a couple of general rules that will help you to maintain a constant light level. First, keep the key lights as far as possible from the action. This may mean that you have to make them slightly more powerful, but it will reduce the importance of your subject's movements in relation to the lights and it will also help you to avoid the mistake of accidentally getting one of the lamps in the shot. Second, where you can do so without their becoming visible, fill the gaps between the main lights with soft fillers, so that the transition from the area covered by one key light to the area covered by the next is as smooth as possible.

In the example here, the girl moves across the room to answer the telephone. As she moves, the camera pans with her. The shot is best lit with two key lights – one to the left of the camera and one to the right – and a filler. The most accurate way to check that the lighting is even is to pace out the girl's path holding an incident meter at eye level. Any fluctuations in the lighting level will twitch the needle of the meter, and you can adjust the position of the lamps until the lighting is constant.

Lighting for a camera track

In the example here, the camera is tracking with the subject, consistently staying a short distance ahead of him as he walks down the room. If this shot were lit with only two sets of key light and filler – like the panning set-up above – the tendency would be for the light to be too bright as the subject passed the first key light and then too dark at the point between the two. For this reason, an extra small hard light could be added between the two keys to "lift" that dark area. A small soft filler on the camera could be added to keep the light level constant, but beware of it casting a moving shadow of your subject onto the background. Three softlights opposite the key lights will even out the light level further. Set them up high to avoid throwing shadows on your subject's face as you pass in front of them.

How to build an evenly diffused lighting set-up
This set-up allows you maximum flexibility. All the lamps are "bounced", and they are all placed so that if your subject suddenly decides to move he or she can do so without altering the exposure and without the lights appearing in the shot. Direct light 1 at a white wall to give a diffused key light for the principal position. Point lights 2 and 3 at the ceiling, away from the camera, to give an even flood of light in the far corners of the room.

How to build a lighting set-up for a pan (right)
Set up one key light for the girl's first position. Set up another for her position at the telephone. Use a soft filler for the area in between. Remember to keep the direction of the lighting constant since any change may be visible in the shot.

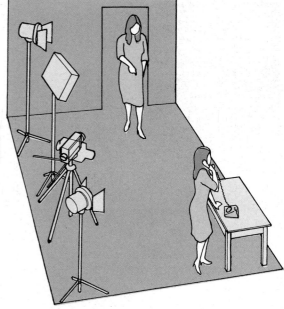

How to build a lighting set-up for a track (below)
Use three hard lights on one side of your subject, and three softlights on the other. Make certain that they are far enough away not to be visible in the shot.

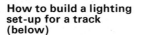

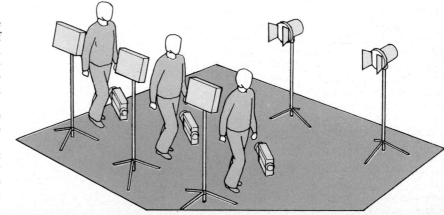

Mixed Lighting

If you are shooting an indoor scene which includes daylight coming through a window, you will be faced with two problems: exposure and color temperature.

In the example here, the subject is a girl sitting beside a brightly lit window. The important thing is to film her so as to see the view outside. However, there is a big difference between the level of light indoors and that outdoors. If the exposure is for the view outside, the girl will become a silhouette (see below left). If the exposure is for the girl's face, all the detail in the view will be lost (see below right). The answer is to use a diffused lamp inside the room to light the girl's face. This solves the exposure problem but, if you are shooting in color, creates another one of color balance. The daylight coming through the window will have a color temperature of, say, 6,000°K, whereas the artificial light is rated at 3,400°K. If you shoot on daylight film the foreground will be unpleasantly red. If you shoot on tungsten film the background will go blue. To avoid this, use filters to create a uniform tungsten or daylight color balance.

How to build a mixed lighting set-up
Set up a diffused light to illuminate the shadows on your subject's face. Either use a special softlight or diffuse the light through some form of translucent material (see p.105). This will give enough light on the girl's face to prevent her becoming a silhouette, but will still preserve the effect of natural daylight from the window (see below). Check through the camera itself to make sure that the softlight is not reflecting in the window and flaring into the lens.

Exposure for outdoors
If you take a meter reading for the background and shoot so that the view outside is correctly exposed, you will lose all detail in the girl's face. She will be silhouetted as a dark profile against the bright light outside.

Exposure for indoors
If you take a meter reading for the foreground and shoot so that the girl's face is correctly exposed, you will lose all detail in the view outside. It will be over-exposed and will look unnaturally "bleached out".

Using color correction filters

One method of creating a uniform color balance is to convert the color temperature of the indoor lighting to daylight. This can be done by putting a "blue" color conversion filter over your artificial light. You then key the "85" filter on the camera into position and shoot as for daylight. The result is fine, but you will find that you need a high level of illumination, since the filter on the lamp is cutting out a lot of the light and the in-camera filter is reducing the effective speed of the film.

A better solution is to cover the window with a sheet of orange "85" conversion film and shoot the whole scene at 3,400°K on tungsten film. This means that there will be no filters on either the light or the camera; the outside light will have been reduced by the window filter – making it easier to balance the light level.

Lamp filter (right)
These filters, known as "blues", convert artificial light to daylight. Made of dichroic glass or heat-resistant gelatin, they are fixed in front of the lamp as shown.

Window filter (left)
These orange "85" filters convert daylight to tungsten. They are available in rolls of flexible gelatin or in rigid plexiglass sheets. Tape them to the inside or outside of the window and beware of reflections or wrinkles in the gel.

Special Lighting Techniques

Supplementing daylight

Shooting daylight scenes outdoors rarely presents any problem as regards the light level. As long as there is enough light for the meter to register, you will get an acceptable picture – especially if you are using an XL or "existing light" camera. However, there may be times when you feel that you need some extra form of illumination to fill in dark shadows – if your subjects have their backs to the sun, for example, or if they are standing under the branch of a tree. In situations like this, the easiest thing to do is to use a *reflector* (see p. 101). These large sheets of reflective material are used to catch the sunlight and "bounce" it into the areas which are too dark. They can thus fill in shadow areas on your subject's face and help to balance out the light levels in a high contrast scene. Many varieties are available commercially, but you can easily make your own: a piece of white polystyrene covered on one side with tin foil will give you a choice of hard or soft light. If you are stuck, you can use a large sheet of white paper or even, for a close-up, a newspaper. Try to keep the reflector as steady as possible when shooting.

A battery-powered *sungun* (see p. 100) may also be useful for providing supplementary lighting outdoors. But it must be filtered for daylight and it has to be positioned very carefully. Beware of lighting the face so much that it is over-exposed, and take care not to cast any extra shadows. One valuable function of a sungun is as an "eye light", to highlight your subject's eyes.

"Faking" daylight shots

If you are filming an indoor scene which includes a window, you can avoid the problems of mixed lighting (see p. 107) by shooting at night and using artificial lights to "fake" a daylight effect. This is quite easy to achieve and, if done carefully, can be very convincing. Because all the lighting is artificial, there is no difficulty over balancing color temperatures.

Set up a lamp outside the window so that it shines into the room. For a "cloudy–bright" daylight effect, use either a large softlight or diffuse a floodlight by shining it through a pair of net curtains. For "sunlight", you need one single, very powerful light. When you set up additional lights indoors, keep them low key so that you maintain the impression of predominant daylight.

"Faking" night shots

Many night scenes shot in the movie industry are not actually filmed at night. They are mostly shot in daylight and under-exposed by two stops to give the impression of darkness. This technique is known as "day-for-night". If you are filming in color, you should also use a dark blue filter on the camera lens (see p. 183). Alternatively, simply remove the built-in "85" filter from the light path and shoot on tungsten film.

To make the effect convincing, select a scene with plenty of highlights and lots of clear outlines. Choose a bright, sunny day and shoot into the light; with luck, the resultant "rim-lighting" will look like moonlight. Avoid streetlights that are not switched on and cars driving without lights, as this will spoil the illusion.

Reflectors
These portable reflectors act as filler lights by allowing you to "bounce" sunlight into shadow areas. Check their position regularly in case the sun has moved across the sky.

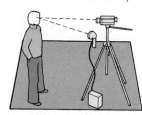

Eye light
You can produce a glitter in your subject's eyes by setting up a sungun next to the camera on their eyeline.

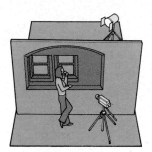

Artificial daylight
A diffused light, projected through a window, will appear as daylight.

Day-for-night
To create the effect of night-time by shooting in daylight, under-expose by two stops and use a dark blue filter. With negative film, the effect can be produced in the laboratory during printing.

Fluorescent lighting

Filming under fluorescent lighting can create rather complicated problems of color temperature. Fluorescent tubes do not operate quite like tungsten or quartz bulbs. Instead of giving out a constant light from one end of the spectrum, their spectrum is discontinuous. They cannot, therefore, be given a color temperature and have no real place on the Kelvin scale. In practice, fluorescent light often produces an unpleasant green or blue color cast. But even this can vary, since there are so many varieties of fluorescent tube on the market. Consequently, it is extremely difficult to match fluorescent lights to color film.

Manufacturers often recommend filters for use with color film, but these vary according to the type of film and the type of fluorescent tube. If you have the time, make tests with different filters. If you don't, it is generally best to shoot on tungsten film with the in-camera "85" filter in position. Kodak Type G film, balanced midway between tungsten and daylight, often produces good results. If you like, you can add some tungsten or quartz lights to "warm up" the effect.

Fluorescent lights emit a rapidly "pulsating" light. If the "beat" is not compatible with the camera, then you may get a sort of strobe effect.

SOUND

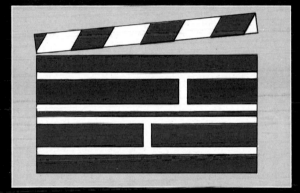

"I am sure that sound film is potentially the art of the future . . . it is a synthesis of each and every element – the oral, the visual, the philosophical; it is our opportunity to translate the world in all its lines and shadows into a new art form that has succeeded and will supersede all the older arts, for it is the supreme medium in which we can express today and tomorrow" *V.I. Pudovkin*

The Basics of Sound

Sound is the succession of pressure waves in the air caused by any vibrating object – a violin string, the human vocal chords or the diaphragm of a loudspeaker, for example. Air molecules move backwards and forwards until they meet the ear drum, which vibrates in response to these waves to produce the sensation of sound. Although the air molecules move to and fro, not up and down, sound is described as traveling in *waves*, which helps to describe the frequency of sound.

Frequency

A sound's *pitch* is determined by its frequency, or the number of times per second a complete wave passes a static reference point. The unit of frequency is the *Hertz* (*Hz*) (one cycle per second). The human ear can hear a range from about 16 Hz (a low rumble) to about 16,000 Hz (a bat-like squeak).

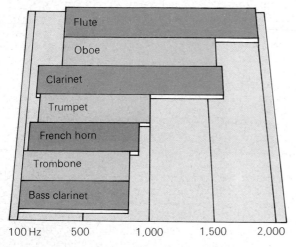

Volume

The human ear hears each doubling of sound intensity as a small single-step increase in a similar way as the camera sees each additional stop of exposure as a doubling of the amount of light reaching the film. This unit of sound intensity is measured in *decibels* (*dB*). As a guide, 120 dB is referred to as the threshold of pain.

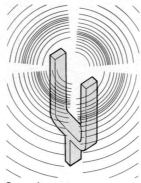

Sound waves
The tuning fork (above) produces a series of pressure waves that radiate in all directions.

Frequency
The selection of musical instruments indicated by the chart on the left all have a different range of frequencies. Those illustrated make up only a small part of the range of frequencies audible to someone with good hearing.

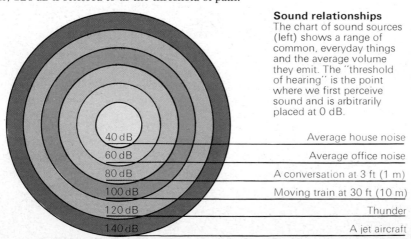

Sound relationships
The chart of sound sources (left) shows a range of common, everyday things and the average volume they emit. The "threshold of hearing" is the point where we first perceive sound and is arbitrarily placed at 0 dB.

40 dB	Average house noise
60 dB	Average office noise
80 dB	A conversation at 3 ft (1 m)
100 dB	Moving train at 30 ft (10 m)
120 dB	Thunder
140 dB	A jet aircraft

Frequency response

All sounds contain complex resonances that extend way up into the upper reaches of hearing, and it is these that give a piano note, for example, a quite different sound from the same note played on a violin. This is why the breadth of "frequency response" of any recording system is so important. "High-fidelity" is the sound equivalent of "high definition" in film.

The recording medium

The first step in translating sound waves into a sound track is the *microphone*, which converts the vibrations in the air into electricity. This can be done in a number of ways, and each microphone design produces its own pattern of frequency response, sensitivity and directional characteristics (see p. 122–3). The signal produced by the microphone can be recorded in one of two ways.

Magnetic sound
The microphone signal is amplified and passed on to a magnetic recording head. A length of tape or strip of film coated with oxide particles runs past the head, and is magnetized in response to the strength of the microphone signal. When the tape is replayed the original signals are reproduced.

Optical sound
This type of sound recording depends on the modulation of a beam of light. The brightness of the light varies according to the variations in intensity of the signal sent from the microphone. This fluctuating beam of light is recorded and, once developed, provides a photographic record of the variations of the electrical current.

Optical track prints cost less than magnetic, but the sound quality is inferior.

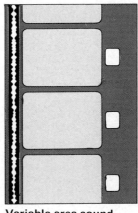

Variable area sound track (above)
This is a type of optical sound recording in which the track is divided into opaque and transparent areas. The trace on the film is the waveform of the recorded signal.

Variable density sound track (above)
This is another type of optical sound recording in which the sound is registered as a series of different densities extending across the width of the sound track.

Recording speed

The fidelity of any sound system is judged largely by its capacity to produce a full and balanced range of frequencies. In particular, the very highest notes require a large number of oxide particles to pass the recording head in a given second if they are to be properly rendered. The higher the tape speed, the better the frequency response. Reel-to-reel recorders are set to run at 15 ips (inches per second) for professional music recording; $7\frac{1}{2}$ ips for speech and normal music recording; $3\frac{3}{4}$ ips, which is barely adequate for speech, but not music; and $1\frac{7}{8}$ ips, usable only for dictation. Cassettes also run at $1\frac{7}{8}$ ips but can be fitted with Dolby noise-reduction circuitry, which gives remarkably good results even with demanding music. Modern cassette recorders can also use new kinds of oxide tapes (FeCr and CrO_2), which go a long way towards overcoming the disadvantages of the narrow tape width and slow speed.

The same criteria apply to magnetic film, whether *stripe* or *fullcoat*: on super 8 the head speed is 4 ips at 24 fps, and 3 ips at 18 fps – therefore 24 fps gives marginally better sound, but both these speeds are about *twice* as fast as a cassette and sound quality can be excellent. 16 mm gives just over 7 ips at 24 fps.

Any judgment of sound quality is subjective, and someone used to listening to good stereo is more likely to notice the difference. A good test is to shoot two lengths of film — one at 18 fps and the other at 24 fps. If you cannot hear the difference in sound quality, shoot at the slower speed. Remember, a 50 ft (15 m) roll of film shot at 18 fps will last three minutes and 20 seconds; at 24 fps it will only last two minutes and 30 seconds.

All these systems must run smoothly without speed variation, and playback must be at the identical speed of the original recording.

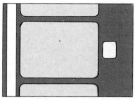

Super 8 sound film
A narrow band of magnetic particles (the sound stripe) is used on super 8 sound film to record the sound picked up by the microphone.

Magnetic fullcoat film
Another method of recording is to use magnetic fullcoat film. This material has exactly the same dimensions as the picture film and is perforated in the same way. It is used in a special recorder and produces a sound track that can be matched with the film later.

Sound on film

The sound available to the filmmaker is of three kinds: *actual sound* (either "synchronized" or "wildtrack"), *effect sound* and *added sound*.

Actual sound

If sound and vision are in the correct relation to each other, the film is said to be "in sync". The margin for error is very small – if the subject is a talking face in close-up, an experienced eye can spot a discrepancy of even one frame between sound and picture.

A "wildtrack" is a recording made at the original location but independent of the film-camera. This track might be played intact as a background to a sequence.

Effect sound

Sound effects recorded at the time of the action, such as the sound of breaking glass or footsteps, have a distressing habit of sounding thin and inadequate and even faked. On the other hand, genuinely faked sound effects can sound surprisingly real and are often better than the actual thing.

Added sound

Sound has been a part of films since they first began, but the modern filmmaker has the advantage that he or she, not the piano accompanist, can call the tune. Sound can be put on tape and played synchronously with the projector, or simply played in the background by a record player. Music, effects and commentary can also be transferred to the magnetic stripe found on single system sound film so that synchronization is effectively locked in place. The possibilities are endless, and in many ways the imagination is more free without the literal restrictions of "actual" sound.

Sound systems

Filming in super 8 gives you two alternative sound systems: single system and double system. With single system, sound is recorded directly onto a magnetic oxide stripe running down the length of the film, so combining the functions of the camera operator and sound recordist. Double system calls for a separate tape recorder. A pulse from the camera is recorded as a reference alongside the sound track so that sync can later be assured. Double system sound usually requires a sound recordist.

Single system at its best can be better than using a cassette, but it will never match the sound quality of a reel-to-reel running at $7\frac{1}{2}$ ips. The main variables are the quality of the camera's amplifier and film transport. With single system the camera must be running for any sound to be recorded, so it is best to use a separate tape to record a "wildtrack". This will provide continuity and fill any holes caused by editing. The early single system cameras were very basic, but now quite a few offer lap dissolves, fade-ins and fade-outs, as well as manual and automatic sound monitoring.

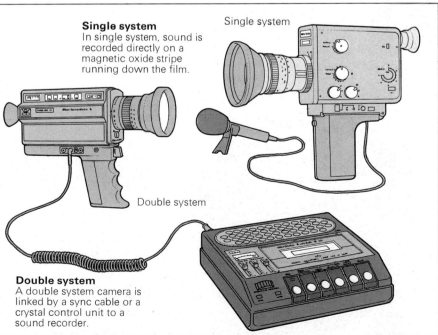

Single system
In single system, sound is recorded directly on a magnetic oxide stripe running down the film.

Single system

Double system

Double system
A double system camera is linked by a sync cable or a crystal control unit to a sound recorder.

Single System Sound

Super 8 sound cartridges were introduced by Kodak in 1973, and had a revolutionary effect on the home-movie industry – sound movies became almost as easy to shoot as silent super 8.

The basic principle of single system sound was not completely new: it had been available on 16 mm film stock long before 1973. Television had been aware of the ease and convenience of guaranteed lip-sync for years. For the advantages were obvious: with very tight deadlines, it was preferable to have a sound recording that did not have to be married to the pictures in the cutting-room: it was there, synchronized, as soon as the film was processed – this was especially useful if the film was not likely to be heavily edited.

Before the introduction of the Kodak super 8 single system sound cartridge, the only other company to make a serious attempt to enter this field was the Williamson Camera Company of California, USA. Their idea involved modifying the Minolta D 10 camera to take a 200 ft magazine. Then they added a sprocket drive and sound head equipment to the standard camera body and sold the revamped model for $5,000, almost exclusively to the news media. Fortunately, single system cameras available today are only a fraction of this price and are easily accessible on even a modest budget.

Single system is by far the easiest method of shooting sound film. With the microphone mounted either on the camera body itself or held in one free hand, the process of shooting synchronous sound can easily be carried out by one person. The only serious drawback with this system of sound shooting comes at the editing stage, and the problems associated with this aspect are discussed more fully on p. 234–7.

Shooting single system
The all-in-one operation of single system filming and sound recording is based on an 18-frame separation of film gate and sound head. Both the sound and its corresponding picture are recorded at precisely the same time, but on different parts of the film. The sound is recorded on the stripe 18 frames before the corresponding piece of film is simultaneously exposed to the light.

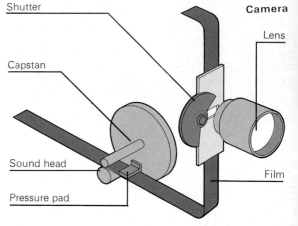

Projecting single system
In order that sound and pictures appear to be in sync when they are projected, the 18-frame separation has to be maintained (see right). The projector is designed so that when the sound stripe is passing over the sound head the corresponding picture is being projected.

Sound and pictures
As the film is exposed, sound is recorded 18 frames ahead.

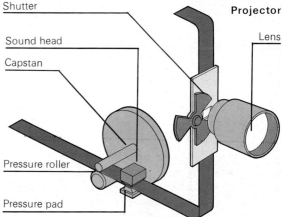

The film

Single system sound film requires a stripe of magnetic oxide to be laid down one side of the film. Although this stripe is not very thick (it stands off the film surface only 1/4,000th inch), it needs to be offset by a *balance stripe* on the other side of the film. Without this, the film would not sit completely flat on the reel (see diagrams below right). This balance stripe serves another role. Because it is composed of the same material as the recording stripe, some advanced projectors will allow you to record on it, so giving you the chance to place additional music, commentary or sound effects in permanent sync. This second sound track is usually added after the film has been edited, and an increasing number of projectors will allow you to play the two sound tracks in "duo-play" or in stereo (see p. 250). This is unavailable in 16 mm.

The cartridge

Super 8 cartridges come in either 50 ft or 200 ft lengths. Cameras designed to take the 200 ft cartridges will also accept the 50 ft cartridge, but not vice versa. Sound cartridges will not fit into a silent camera.

Film formats
The size of the film referred to in the name is an indication of the width of the film from edge to edge – 16 mm means the film is 16 mm wide; 8 mm means it is 8 mm wide. Note also that the perforations are differently placed in 16 mm and 8 mm film.

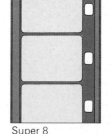

Super 8   16 mm film

Balance stripe
The sound stripe running down the length of super 8 film, although very thin, needs to be balanced by a stripe on the other side of the film. Its function is simply to make certain the film sits evenly on the reel, but it can be used to record on with a projector after the film has been edited.

The camera

While each frame has to be held stationary in the gate while being exposed, the sound track needs to be running smoothly over the sound head. For this reason, the gate and sound head need to be physically separated. On single system sound cameras the sound head is a set number of frames ahead of the picture (28 frames for 16 mm and 18 frames for super 8). In other words, the sound track next to any given frame really belongs to the frame about one second behind (see opposite). The film in between forms itself into a loop to enable the juddering of the film across the gate to be ironed out into a smooth, continuous flow before reaching the sound head. For projection, the sound-to-image differential needs to be maintained, and as long as there are the right number of frames between the projector gate and the projector sound head, the projection is bound to be in perfect lip-sync (see opposite).

All this clearly depends on how precisely the camera has maintained the gap between sound and vision. In 16 mm this is achieved by an exact arrangement of sprocket wheels, which engage the film to produce the right loop. In super 8, separate motors are used for the film transport and sound head, linked by means of a servo-motor mechanism. In effect, the sound track runs at its pre-determined speed and the shutter speed is adjusted to match it. This is done through a sensor that detects any change in the size of the slack film (the loop) between sound and vision, and adjusts the film transport to correct it. This system is based on the sound-speed motor because any minute variation in pitch, especially in music, is clearly audible, whereas the equivalent minute change in exposure is not so noticeable.

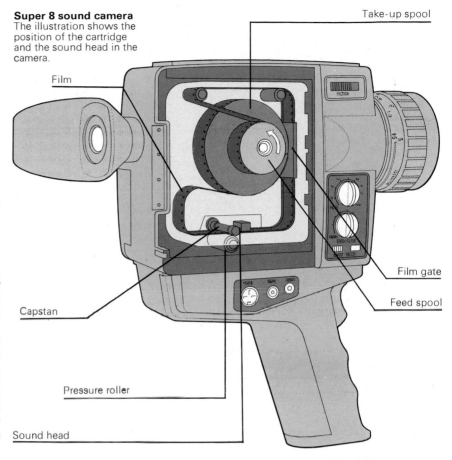

Super 8 sound camera
The illustration shows the position of the cartridge and the sound head in the camera.

Take-up spool

Film

Film gate

Feed spool

Capstan

Pressure roller

Sound head

Soundproofing

When the microphone is camera-mounted there is a danger that it will pick up unwanted noise from the camera motor. A *barney*, or silencer, made from foam rubber with apertures cut out can be fitted over the camera body. A barney should not be confused with a *blimp*, which is a much heavier, rigid, case.

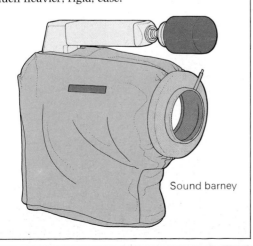

Sound barney

Super 8
The film on a super 8 sound cartridge (left) is on a triacetate base. Loading takes only a few seconds and the cartridge is not reusable.

Single 8
The single 8 film format (right) is the same as super 8. The basic difference is in the film base (polyester) and the shape of the cartridge.

Sound fades
The fade-in control on the camera (above right) allows you to begin a shot in darkness and, by slowly turning the control, to bring the image up to normal exposure (see p. 186). On some cameras the sound automatically fades in also. A fade-out is the reverse process, in which the picture fades to darkness and the sound to silence.

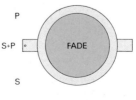

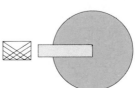

P

S+P

S

FADE

Sound dissolves
The dissolve function on the camera (below left) allows you to superimpose one series of pictures on top of another. It is accomplished by fading out one series of images, backwinding the film and then fading in another set on top (see p. 187). Several sound cameras will overlap the sound as well as dissolving the picture.

Monitoring the Sound

In any sound recording the incoming signal must be matched to the capacity of the tape (or stripe) receiving it. Too little signal, and the sound becomes degraded by the "hissy" noise inherent in the magnetic oxide material; too much signal, and the stripe becomes overloaded, resulting in an "out-of-focus" sound, especially noticeable on high notes. Sound input is monitored automatically on many super 8 cameras, but on others it is monitored manually with the aid of a calibrated *VU meter* (see above right). The needle of the meter should remain solidly in the middle of the white area, and just nudge the red section when the loudest noise is recorded. When the needle enters the red section of the scale the recording is overloaded. Many cameras allow you to monitor the sound level by means of an indicator in the viewfinder.

Automatic gain control

Automatic sound monitoring, known as *automatic gain control (AGC)*, approximates an average sound level, and this system works best in conditions of steady ambient sound. However, problems arise whenever there is a sudden lull, as the amplifier in the camera pulls up the sound level to maintain an average level, and surges of background noise appear in every pause. Despite this disadvantage, AGC can give better, more consistent sound recordings than manual sound monitoring in one-person operation, and it also leaves you with more time to think about the shooting.

Recording sound

For the average home-movie-maker only a limited knowledge of microphone construction is necessary. The most important thing to bear in mind about most types of microphones purchased with the averagely priced super 8 camera is their lack of sensitivity. To test the sensitivity of your particular microphone, shoot a test film with the microphone at varying distances from the sound source and note where its performance is best.

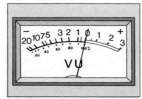

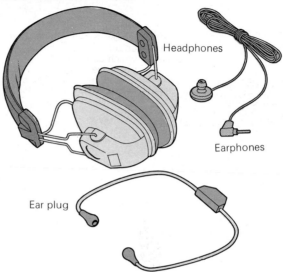

Headphones

Earphones

Ear plug

Sound meters
Both the VU meter (left) and the frequency peak indicator (right) are manual systems for measuring the amount of signal entering the recording medium.

Sound monitoring
Monitoring the sound coming into the recording system through headphones, earphones or an ear plug has many advantages. It tells you immediately if the microphone is properly connected and properly positioned. Another important aspect of monitoring is that you only hear the sound picked up by the microphone. Without these aids you might hear a car start up and immediately try to filter the noise out, although the microphone may not have responded to it. Above all, monitoring helps you to balance the various recorded sounds.

Unless you are shooting an interview or documentary you will not want the microphone to be visible in the shot, and yet it must be close enough to the sound source to give a good recording level. To overcome this problem without purchasing a better quality microphone (see p. 122–23), a boom or long pole can be used to suspend the microphone over the sound source. To avoid having to buy a boom, use a lighting stand.

Microphone positions
The illustrations below are only a few of the many ways you can position the microphone when shooting single system.

On the camera
Mounting a directional microphone on the camera (left) is the most convenient method of one-person filming and sound recording. With the microphone in this position, camera noise could be a problem. If so, use a barney to dampen the noise of the camera motor.

On a small stand
A small microphone stand (left) is a great help. If you do not want the microphone to appear in shot, adjust the central column until the height is right. The disadvantage with this system is that the microphone cannot follow a moving sound source.

On a boom
A light-weight boom or pole (left) allows you to get the microphone above the sound source.

Hand-held
If you are filming an interview or recording a documentary (right) you may not mind if the microphone is in the shot.

On a table stand
Like the small floor stand, the table stand (left) is low enough not to be in shot unless a wide-angle lens is in use.

Out of sight
Props can be used to hide the microphone, but make sure they do not muffle the sound.

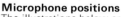

Tips on Shooting Single System

The most difficult aspect of using single system sound film is the 18-frame discrepancy between sound and picture which will permit the film to travel smoothly over the sound recording head in the camera. On stripe film the sound remains ahead of the images right through the editing and projection processes. In the case of super 8 this 18-frame separation means a discrepancy of $\frac{3}{4}$ second at 24 fps or one second at 18 fps. This presents no problems on projection, because the projector's sound head is also set 18 frames ahead of the projection gate (see p. 112). But special techniques are required to overcome this separation when editing.

Demagnetizer
A sound head demagnetizer is used to remove the magnetic build up on the sound heads, which can lead to excessive "hiss" on recordings. It can also be used to demagnetize the sound head of your camera.

Removing unwanted noise

After many hours of recording, the heads of cameras and sound projectors can become permanently magnetized, resulting in an annoying background "hiss" on record and playback. A *sound head demagnetizer* is useful for demagnetizing the sound heads and gives a much cleaner record and playback. The demagnetizer can also be used to remove any extraneous noise and unwanted "pops" that inevitably seem to show up on recordings. However, the demagnetizer does not descriminate between wanted and unwanted noise and a safer method of removing this type of interference is to cover the relevant section of the stripe with a little piece of splicing tape. The tape covers the oxide stripe itself and this method is much more flexible, as the tape can be peeled off and re-positioned until it covers exactly the right section of the stripe.

Adding wildtrack

A non-synchronous sound recording, or wildtrack, made at the same time and place as the filmed action can be transferred to the magnetic stripe; this fills in any dead spots on the sound track caused by editing and helps make the transition from scene to scene smooth and logical. Some projectors have the facility of superimposing sound on top of the original: a "trick" effect. If so, then music, commentary or sound effects can be used in the same way as a wildtrack.

1 One second silence at beginning

2 She starts to play

3 Music continues

4 Music continues

5, 6 One second silence at end

Editing in the camera

With the fixed relationship of sound to images firmly in mind, it is possible to make allowances while filming that will make the task of editing in the cutting room (see p. 234–37) much easier.

First, aim for a longer take than you might normally do if shooting silent film. Try to allow at least one full second of silence at the front of each shot, so that when you cut for the action you will not be removing the beginning of the sound. Also, allow the film to run on for one full second after the end of each word or note of music you can use of each scene. In this way, you will not have to choose between losing the last few words or notes or having one second of the next scene in vision.

Shooting single system
When starting a new shot, instruct your subject to leave one second's pause after filming has begun before starting to play or speak (represented by the picture above left). At the end of the shot, keep filming for one second after the final note or word (represented by the picture on the right). The shots can then be physically separated when editing, since sound and pictures will not overlap from scene to scene.

Double System Sound

Double system sound is any synchronous recording system in which the sound track is recorded outside the camera. The magnetic recording medium and the film are entirely separate at the time of filming. Recording the sound separately from the film is the major advantage double system has over single system, because the sound track is not in a fixed position in relation to the image. This means that during editing the sound track can be shortened, altered or moved: the trick is to be sure that, after shooting, the sound and vision can be put in sync for viewing and editing. Perhaps the major disadvantage of double system is the need for an extra person to operate the sound recording system. Compact cassette recorders can be carried by the camera operator, giving him or her the dual role of filming and sound monitoring

as in single system; but to fully exploit the flexibility of double system it does make more sense to have a separate sound recordist.

There are three main methods of achieving synchronous sound when using a separate tape recorder. Two of them, *Pilotone sync* and *digital sync*, involve connecting the camera and tape machine with a *sync cable*. This is used to transmit an electronic pulse to the tape recorder's sync head, and the pulse acts as a reference to the camera's speed. The third system, known as *crystal sync*, does not use a sync cable and allows the tape recorder and camera to move independently. A cable is fragile, and unless you are operating the recorder yourself it is preferable if the sound recordist is not connected to the camera.

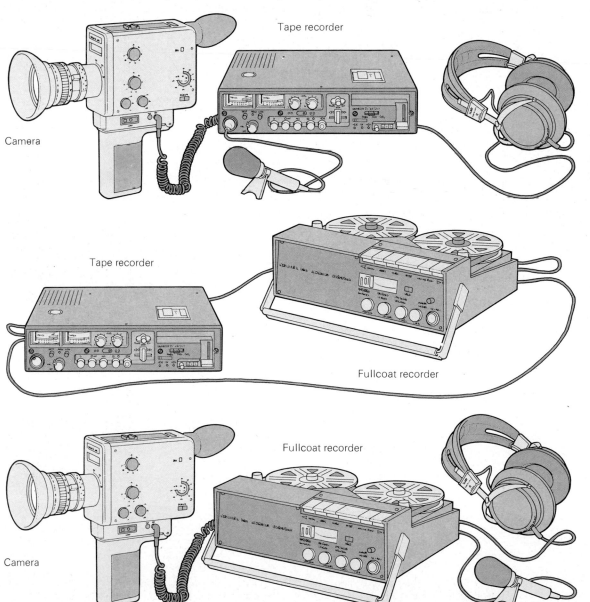

Camera

Tape recorder

Tape recorder

Fullcoat recorder

Fullcoat recorder

Camera

Recording on tape
If you are using Pilotone or digital sync to record double system, the camera and the tape recorder (or cassette) have to be connected by a sync cable. A crystal sync controlled camera and recorder, on the other hand, do not need this physical connection. Headphones should always be used to monitor the sound being picked up by the microphone to check whether it is correctly positioned and connected.

From tape to fullcoat
The reference pulse transmitted via the sync cable is recorded on the tape alongside the sound track. This reference pulse is used later by a fullcoat recorder to resolve (transfer) the sound track onto magnetic fullcoat film in frame-for-frame sync with the pictures. This step is necessary because it is the fullcoat and not the original recording that is used in editing.

Recording on fullcoat
The step above can be bypassed by recording directly onto magnetic fullcoat, if you have the use of a portable fullcoat recorder. The recorder needs to be linked via a sync cable to the camera if you are using Pilotone or digital sync. But fullcoat recorders can also be crystal controlled to produce a length of magnetic film in frame-for-frame sync with the film produced by the camera.

Pilotone sync

Pilotone is the system used almost universally on 35 mm and 16 mm equipment. For super 8 users it is available on some Nizo and Beaulieu cameras. The camera motor generates a 60 Hz (cycles per second) "pilot-tone" (the sync pulse), which is sent down the sync cable to the tape recorder. If the camera is filming at 24 fps, then $2\frac{1}{2}$ *cycles equals one frame*. The 60 Hz frequency was chosen because it corresponds to alternating current (AC), so cameras fitted with AC motors could be run off the main power supply in those countries where the main power supply is 60 Hz.

With the Pilotone sync system the motor of the camera and the motor of the tape recorder or cassette are completely independent and running at different speeds. For editing and viewing purposes the tape must be transferred onto sprocketed magnetic film or sprocketed tape, and during this process (known as "tape-transfer" or "resolving") the pilot-tone pulse acts as a reference signal so that the magnetic film recorder can vary its speed in response to it.

For this transfer the tape is played back into the magnetic film recorder, which looks somewhat like an ordinary reel-to-reel tape recorder. The film recorder constantly monitors the passage of the pilot-tone sync pulse, which has been recorded in parallel to the sound track, and transfers the sound onto fullcoat film. The magnetic film recorder works on the principle that every $2\frac{1}{2}$ cycles of sound equals one frame of film in producing frame-for-frame sync.

Digital sync

Digital sync is widely used on super 8 cameras for double system sound recording. At least 40 different camera models are fitted with the necessary attachments to make them suitable for sync sound recording without any modification. The system utilizes a *PC (Prontor Contact)* switch to produce *one pulse*, which is recorded along with the sound track, every time *one frame* of film is exposed. If the speed of the camera varies, so does the number of pulses produced. The PC switch was originally designed to permit electronic flash to be used in conjunction with time-lapse photography (see p. 189), and it opens and closes once for every frame that passes through the camera gate. If instead of connecting the flash to the PC socket you plug in a tape recorder, the *one-frame (1/F)* switch will produce a single on/off pulse for every frame of film. The tape recorder must be modified to include a *tone generator* because there must be an electrical impulse sent up the line to the camera for the 1/F switch to interrupt. Some Nizo camera models contain their own tone generators, and can be used with any unmodified tape recorder. The tone generator can also be added to other camera/recorder combinations in the form of a 1000 Hz unit, which is patched into the sync cable between the camera and recorder. The camera's 1/F switch interrupts the tone once per frame. The pulse or tone recorded on the tape acts as a reference, which is used by the magnetic film recorder to produce a synchronized magnetic fullcoat sound track for editing in sync with the picture.

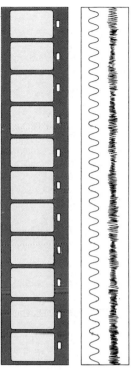

Pilotone sync
In this system, every $2\frac{1}{2}$ cycles equal one frame.

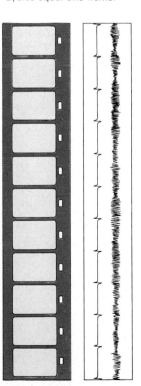

Digital sync
In this system, every pulse equals one frame.

Crystal sync

Crystal sync overcomes the major disadvantage of double system sound recording; it does away with the sync cable itself that somehow always manages to get in the way no matter how much care is taken.

The system is based on two crystals – which can be thought of as two extremely accurate clocks. One regulates the speed of the camera motor and the other lays down an equally accurate pulse on the tape coinciding with the sound track. The two crystals have no electrical or physical connection at all, but they are accurate to within at least one frame in ten minutes. The system has several advantages over other double system sound recording methods: the recordist can hide out of sight of the camera, but close to the source of the sound, even while the camera operator films from a distance using a telephoto lens; or you can film in a jostling crowd without any fear of the sync cable being torn out of its socket; or more than one camera can be run in sync with no interconnection at all. Shooting with more than one camera helps overcome the problem of the $2\frac{1}{2}$ minute film cartridge. As one camera comes to the end of its footage, a second camera can start filming. Two cameras are also used to cover a shot from different angles.

If recording with a portable magnetic fullcoat recorder, the crystal regulates the speed of the recorder in exact relationship to the speed of the camera, producing a length of magnetic film in frame-for-frame sync. If using an ordinary recorder, the crystal lays down a reference pulse from which the tape can be resolved.

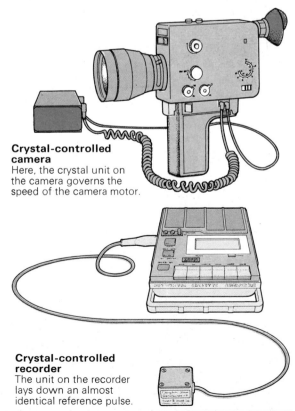

Crystal-controlled camera
Here, the crystal unit on the camera governs the speed of the camera motor.

Crystal-controlled recorder
The unit on the recorder lays down an almost identical reference pulse.

Double System Sound

Establishing sync

Having recorded the sound track on either a cassette or reel-to-reel recorder and then transferred it onto full-coat magnetic film or sprocketed tape, you will have in your hands the basic materials for synchronous sound and images. The magnetic fullcoat recorder will lock onto the sync pulse to produce magnetic film of identical length to the film shot, and in frame-for-frame sync: but, unless a *common start mark* for sound and vision has been established for each shot, you could be in trouble. In the editing room the common start mark (a simultaneous sound and visible action) is used to establish the precise starting point of both elements.

The clapper board

The usual method of establishing a common start point is to use a *clapper board*. This is simply a piece of board with a hinged section. The camera points at the board (positioned in front of the intended action) and when the camera is running and the recorder is registering the sync pulse properly, someone calls out the shot number and "claps" the two sections of the board together. This simple device identifies the shot in both sound and vision and, because you can not only hear but also see exactly when the clapper falls, you have a completely accurate sync reference point for each shot. This sync point can be established at the front or end of each shot.

Clapper board
When shooting double system, each shot should begin with the closing of the clapper board. This provides a common start mark for synching up sound and picture.

The electronic alternative

As an alternative to the hinged piece of wood, the camera can be fitted with an electronic device that performs the same task of establishing a common start mark. When the camera is started, a press switch makes a connection that records a "bleep" on the sound track and simultaneously shines a light on the film and fogs a few frames. In the editing room, the first frame of fogging and the first frame of the "bleep" are matched to establish sync for that shot. This method has one big advantage – it does away with the clapper operator.

A third alternative is to put the microphone into shot and tap it sharply to establish the start mark.

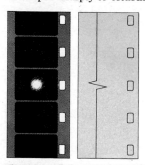

Electronic alternative
A device can be used that simultaneously fogs the film and registers a "bleep" on the sound track. This performs the same function as the clapper board in providing a common start mark for matching up sound and picture in editing.

Establishing sync with the clapper board

1 All relevant information, such as scene and shot number, should be written on the clapper board and the sound recorder should be switched on.

2 When confirmation from the sound recordist is received that the sync pulse is being registered and the sound is being recorded, start the camera motor and wait a second or two for it to come up to its correct running speed.

3 When both camera and recorder are operating at their correct speed, place the clapper board in shot where all relevant information can be recorded by the camera.

4 Have the clapper operator verbally identify the shot and then bring the two sections of the board together to make a clearly audible sound. Then quickly remove the board from the camera's view and refocus the camera before starting the action.

Magnetic film recorder

If you are lucky enough to own a magnetic film recorder, such as the Super8 Sound recorder, you will have at your disposal perhaps the most versatile and useful piece of equipment available to the super 8 filmmaker – in fact the very heart of double system sound recording. It can be used for original recording of a sync soundtrack, resolving sound recorded on an ordinary sound recorder, and at the dubbing stage (see p. 248). The magnetic fullcoat recorder also can be used to build up a multiple sound track.

This portable machine can be linked, via a sync cable, to many unmodified cameras with a digital sync pulse output (see p. 117), and the recorder will produce up to 380 feet of magnetic film in perfect sync with the camera film. The Super8 Sound recorder can also be used with cameras operating the Pilotone 60 Hz signal used on some super 8 Beaulieu and Nizo cameras. If you are using cameras fitted with crystal sync (see p. 117), the recorder will match its speed to the rate of the film passing through the camera, using its internal crystal control, without the need for a connecting sync cable. If you prefer to do the location recording on a cassette or reel-to-reel recorder, the magnetic film recorder can also be used to resolve the recording (transfer it onto magnetic film) using the pulses transmitted via the sync cable or crystal control as a reference.

Combining sound and images

After editing both the sound film and the camera film, you are still left with two separate strips. For the purposes of projection it is usually more convenient to combine the two rather than run two machines locked together. The first step in this process involves adding a magnetic oxide stripe to the camera film so it can then accept the sound track (most film laboratories provide this service or you can do it yourself, see p. 233). Next, the film is threaded onto a magnetic sound projector. The projector needs to be fitted with a single-frame switch, similar to the one found on the camera. Then the magnetic sound recorder must be cabled up to the projector. When both machines are running, the single-frame switch on the projector interrupts a current once per frame and controls the speed of the recorder so that the sound from the recorder is transferred onto the film's magnetic stripe in frame-for-frame sync. It is also a good idea to include an equalizer between the two machines to make final corrections to tonal balance.

It is easy enough to start both machines at the same moment by plugging both, via an adaptor, into a common lead. The difficulty is that each machine will reach its proper running speed at a different moment. This can be somewhat improved by measuring the exact amount of footage that passes through each machine before they are running at full speed and then splicing that amount of leader onto the front of each shot. The best method is, however, a "common start" device, which is accurate to a frame. This will automatically start a recorder as the first frame passes through the projector gate, whether used for dubbing or for sync projection of the finished film.

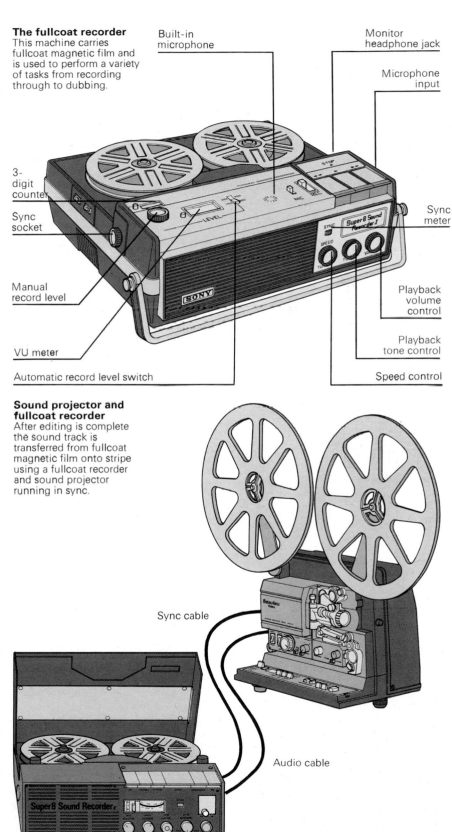

The fullcoat recorder This machine carries fullcoat magnetic film and is used to perform a variety of tasks from recording through to dubbing.

Built-in microphone

Monitor headphone jack

Microphone input

3-digit counter

Sync socket

Manual record level

VU meter

Automatic record level switch

Sync meter

Playback volume control

Playback tone control

Speed control

Sound projector and fullcoat recorder After editing is complete the sound track is transferred from fullcoat magnetic film onto stripe using a fullcoat recorder and sound projector running in sync.

Sync cable

Audio cable

Sound Recorders

It is tempting to apply the same criteria to sound recording for film as you would for sound reproduction on home hi-fi – but unless recording music, this is not appropriate. For practical purposes, only a portable sound recorder that can be comfortably carried in one hand will normally be used. A recorder suitable for film sound can be a simple cassette or a professional reel-to-reel recorder, depending on budget. Unless you are aiming at the very highest quality, satisfactory sound results can be achieved with a recorder costing less than an averagely priced super 8 camera.

How sound recorders work

Magnetic sound recorders work on the principle of the interaction between electrical currents and magnetic fields. The microphone converts sound (from a human voice, disk or any other sound source) into an electrical current, the strength of which fluctuates depending on the intensity of the original sound. After amplification the signal passes over a *recording head*, which produces a magnetic field that also varies in accordance with the strength of the sound input. As the tape passes the recording head (an electromagnet), the magnet changes the orientation of the oxides coated on the tape. To play the recorded sound, the tape must pass over the *playback head*, which is another electromagnet. On some machines the recording and playback heads are combined. When the rearranged oxide particles on the tape enter the magnetic field of the playback head a current is induced, which is again amplified and sent to the speakers or headphones.

Which system?

The choice of recorder usually lies between reel-to-reel (sometimes called "open reel") and cassette. Fullcoat magnetic recorders, although able to record high-quality sync sound on location are expensive and you could purchase two or three cassette recorders for a comparable outlay of money.

Reel-to-reel recorders

Whether recording a wildtrack or fully synchronized sound, a reel-to-reel recorder offers optimum flexibility. A wide choice of tape speeds, which have a direct bearing on sound quality, is standard – on many machines ranging from 15 ips to $1\frac{7}{8}$ ips. In double system, the original sound recording has to be transferred to magnetic fullcoat film and then, if you wish, transferred again, after editing, onto the magnetic stripe on the picture film. At each stage, some loss of sound fidelity is to be expected – so it is important that the original recording is as good as you can make it. The $\frac{1}{4}$ in. (6 mm) tape and higher tape speed on reel-to-reel recorders actually allows more room for the recorded signal than on a cassette.

Unfortunately, many reel-to-reel recorders are too heavy for comfortable use on location and are really designed for home recording. Also, many of these machines need to be connected to the main power supply. But good-quality, battery-operated reel-to-reel machines are available.

The principle of sound recording

How sound is recorded
Vibrations are picked up by the microphone and amplified by the recorder before being sent to the recording head. On playback, the signal is again amplified before being sent to the speaker.

Recording and playback
The recording head produces a magnetic field, which rearranges the oxide particles on the tape as it passes. The playback head produces an electrical current, which varies in response to these rearranged oxide particles.

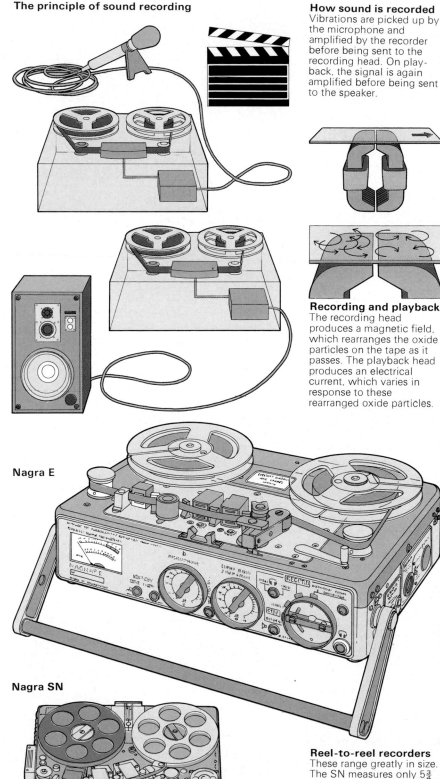

Nagra E

Nagra SN

Reel-to-reel recorders
These range greatly in size. The SN measures only 5¾ × 4 × 1 in. (147 × 100 × 25 mm) and has a recording time of 30 minutes.

Cassette recorders

The major advantage cassette recorders have over reel-to-reel recorders is portability. Their light, compact construction is a great asset in the field, and if necessary a cassette recorder can easily be carried by the camera operator, removing the need for a sound recordist. With better quality cassette machines this lightness is not at the expense of robustness. When filming, the action is frequently tightly scripted and time spent rethreading a reel-to-reel recorder could mean that an unrepeatable shot is lost. With a cassette recorder, loading a fresh tape takes only a few seconds and there is less chance that any action will not be covered by the sound track.

Since the introduction of Dolby noise-reduction circuitry, the main drawbacks of cassette recorders – their slow tape speed (only $1\frac{7}{8}$ ips) and high "noise" level – have largely been overcome. Despite the tiny size of the recording area on cassette tapes, modern tape designs are steadily reducing the lead in quality that the $\frac{1}{4}$ in. reel-to-reel tapes have enjoyed in the past. If using small, "uncritical" speakers, the difference in sound quality between the two systems is difficult to detect.

From the filmmaker's point of view, the drawback with using cassettes comes in editing the tape. If recording a wildtrack, editing is essential and the narrow tape width means that cutting and splicing can only be done with extreme care. You might find yourself transferring the whole sound track to wider tape simply to edit – and running the risk of losing sound quality in the process and increasing overall costs.

Which system for added sound?

If you do not intend to shoot sound on location, but simply wish to add sound effects, music and perhaps commentary to a film, then it is preferable to use a reel-to-reel recorder. The $\frac{1}{4}$ in. tape of the reel-to-reel is more flexible than the cassette tape, and it can be edited. A stereo recorder, with two tracks running in each direction, gives you the option of using combinations of different types of "added sound". If your recorder has a *sound-on-sound superimposition* facility (able to record one sound on top of another without erasing the original), then music and commentary, for example, can be locked together in a fixed relationship. When recording this type of sound track it is vital that the recorder has an accurate *digital counter*. Unless you know how much of a particular sound you have recorded, combining it with the images might be hit-and-miss.

A tape machine to fill all these requirements would not have to be a portable unit with built-in loudspeakers as it will never have to leave the house.

Building sound on tape

	Commentary
	Music and commentary
	Commentary
	Music and commentary
	Effects replace commentary
	Music and commentary
	Effects

Super8 Sound recorder

This machine is one of a range of six cassette recorders produced by Super8 Sound. Five of them use the 1/F digital pulse system and the other accepts the 60 Hz Pilotone sync pulse. The digital pulse facility means that this type of recorder is compatible with over forty different super 8 cameras without any modification, making it the ideal type of machine for recording sync sound on location. The 60 Hz model can be used with any 16 mm or 35 mm double system sound camera.

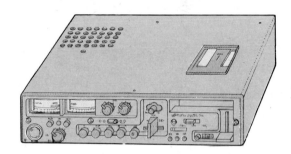

Uher CR 240

This cassette recorder offers Dolby noise-reduction, plus 2-track stereo recording in addition to a third pulse-reference track. Quality is very high.

How cassettes work

The cassette consists of a thin plastic container housing the magnetic tape, which runs between two hubs. When the tape finishes it cannot come loose because it is attached to the hubs by a length of leader tape. This is because the cassette is designed as a sealed unit and the tape is not thick enough to allow it to be handled, as would be necessary for rethreading. A series of rollers and guides hold the tape in contact with the driving rollers, and recording and playback heads of the cassette machine.

Cassette tapes

It is vital that the "bias" of the tape matches the characteristics of your machine. CrO_2 tapes for example, require special switching on the recorder for correct replay and correct recording.

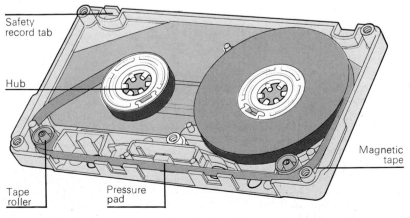

Safety record tab

Hub

Tape roller

Pressure pad

Magnetic tape

Microphones

The function of the microphone is to convert the physical motion of the air molecules (see p. 110) into an electrical impulse, and the construction of the microphone has a direct bearing on this – and hence on the quality of the sound produced at the other end of the system. There are five basic microphone designs: crystal carbon, ribbon, moving coil and condenser – all of which work on slightly different principles. In the cheaper, less efficient range, the crystal and carbon types give relatively poor results. Ribbon, moving coil and condenser microphones can all be excellent, as can the cheaper variant of the condenser type, the electret.

From the point of view of the ordinary user, the most important thing to know about the microphone is its *directional characteristics*. Not all microphones respond equally to sounds from all sides, and the most convenient way to classify them is in terms of their *directional response*. There are three principal types: omnidirectional, cardioid and shotgun.

Omnidirectional

This type of microphone theoretically covers an arc of 360° with equal response, and therefore receives a broad, unselective sound. It is ideal for recording unfocused atmospheric sound – at a party, for example – but it is a poor instrument for rejecting unwanted sound, such as camera noise. It is unfortunate that this type of microphone is so often supplied by manufacturers of single system cameras. Also, these units are all too frequently of poor quality and, if this is the case with your microphone, you would do well to buy a more directional one for your filming. This would probably be of the cardioid type.

Cardioid

Cardioid microphones are so-called because of the heart-shape of their response patterns. They are much more sensitive to a sound source dead ahead than behind or to one side. This characteristic is particularly useful if the microphone is to be mounted on top of the camera, since the camera noise will be behind the microphone, and the sound balance will automatically match the subject in the shot rather than some sound source the camera cannot see. It is equally suitable for recording an "atmosphere" track, but it needs more careful placement than the omnidirectional microphone – perhaps up high on a boom, "overlooking" the sound source.

Shotgun

Shotgun microphones are even more directional versions of the cardioid, with an area of sensitivity of about 40°, and are sometimes known as "supercardioids". Their limited area of sensitivity means that all sounds coming from the sides are registered only faintly. This type of microphone is particularly useful when you cannot move in close to the sound source – because the sound recordist might be seen by a camera fitted with a wide-angle lens, for example. Shotgun microphones tend to be on the expensive side and their sound quality is not always as good as the omnidirectional or cardioid types when used close to the sound source.

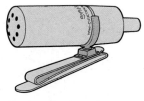

Personal microphone

Radio microphone

Omnidirectional microphone
The omnidirectional (or nondirectional) microphone is the ideal tool for recording a general, non-specific sound, the type that is needed for an "atmosphere" sound track. It is not often used attached to a boom because of the general need for a more specific pick-up response pattern.

Cardioid microphone
This type of microphone is probably the most commonly used of all. Although the exact response pattern varies from type to type, its ability to reject unwanted noise from the sides and back makes it a good, all-purpose microphone, and especially useful when it is camera-mounted as camera noise will not be registered.

Shotgun microphone
This type of microphone is also known as a super-cardioid or ultradirectional microphone because of its very narrow sound acceptance angle compared to other types. It is believed by some that only sound in a narrow strip in front of the microphone is picked up, but this is not so as it has an acceptance angle of approximately 40°.

Personal microphone

These tiny and unobtrusive personal microphones can be either clipped to clothing or hung around the neck. The microphone cable is channeled down a sleeve or trouser leg out of sight of the camera. You must take care that clothing does not rub against the microphone as it will be recorded as a "rustling" sound or could possibly muffle the sound altogether. These microphones are particularly useful in noisy surroundings as they can be positioned very close to the mouth.

Radio microphone

Radio microphones are now offered as accessories on many amateur cameras, and they are extensively used in professional filming. They consist of a microphone, a short-range transmitter and a receiver on the camera or recorder, and they operate on the FM (frequency modulation) waveband. They allow a moving subject greater freedom since there is no lead to get in the way.

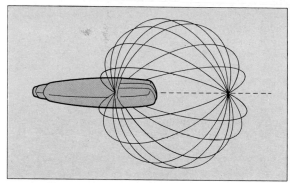

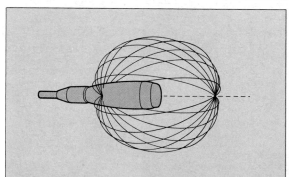

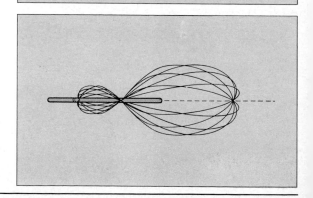

Positioning the microphone

In all films that strive after realism there is a convention that the microphone is never seen. On the other hand, in a documentary the reporter often brandishes a hand-held microphone to advertise the actual process of filming. Deciding where to place the microphone depends on the type you are using and on the acoustics of the surroundings. In the following discussion of how to use and position the microphone for the best results, it is assumed that you will not want it to be visible.

Making use of acoustics

Even in the open air, sound travels to the microphone from the subject by a devious route. In a "live" acoustic, such as a bathroom or gymnasium, the hard surfaces reflect the sound to and fro many times before it dies, and the high frequencies in particular may become muddled as they reverberate round the room. In a "dead" acoustic, such as a room thickly carpeted and with curtains or tapestries, the sound dies quickly, with little reverberance or echo. A dead acoustic always helps the clarity of music or speech, but clarity is not everything, and for music you may decide you want an attractive touch of echo. Either way, your choice of acoustic has a great effect on microphone placement. In general, if you want to reduce the effects of excessive reverberation, move the microphone nearer the sound source – it will then be louder in relation to the reflected sounds. You can also deaden the acoustic by drawing the curtains or throwing down a carpet. Conversely, moving the microphone further away from the sound source will "open up" the sound, giving it more spaciousness at the expense of detail. The proximity of the microphone to the walls will also have an effect on your recording. To get the most out of your chosen acoustic, experiment with different positions.

A "live" acoustic
An empty room and hard sufaces reflect the sound.

A "dead" acoustic
Furnishings tend to absorb sound.

Microphone impedance

Impedance is the total resistance offered by the electrical system, and is measured in ohms (Ω). Microphones are usually grouped as high, medium or low impedance, and they should be connected to a socket of equivalent impedance on the recorder or single system camera. Your dealer will advise you if you are in any doubt if you take along the specification sheet. As a rule, microphones of high impedance are of low quality and those of low impedance are high quality.

One person talking
When recording a single sound source, a cardioid or omnidirectional microphone should be positioned in front of the camera to minimize the camera noise.

A conversation
If using two microphones proves impossible, then a single cardioid or shotgun microphone can be used instead.

A crowd
When recording the generalized noise generated by a crowd, the broad response patterns of the omnidirectional and cardioid microphones can equally be used.

Recording one person talking

If you do not have a personal microphone, you will probably be using either a cardioid or omnidirectional microphone. The cardioid should be between two and four feet from the sound source (depending on the ambient noise), and the omnidirectional type slightly closer. Both types must be *in front of the camera*, just out of frame, in order to minimize camera noise being picked up by the microphone. Even when using an omnidirectional microphone, which is really unsuited to the job, it must be placed on the axis of the subject's "eyeline" (see p. 102) to record the best sound, though it may be above or below head height. Always check that the microphone is well clear of the camera's field-of-view or it will be visible in the shot. If it proves difficult to position the microphone close enough to the sound source to obtain a good recording level with the cardioid or omnidirectional types, consider using a shotgun microphone placed further from the subject.

Recording a conversation

A conversation between two or more people can be recorded in a number of ways. Ideally, it requires two microphones. If you only have one, you could place an omnidirectional microphone between them, but it would probably be in shot. If a cardioid or shotgun microphone is used it must either be mounted on the camera or else skilfully operated by a sound recordist to follow the course of the conversation. At the same time the recordist has to keep a sharp eye on the movement of the camera to avoid getting into shot and to make sure that he or she is covering a sound appropriate to the image. The recordist can also balance the different voice levels. This, however, is quite a complicated technique, and for most simple filming the on-camera position should produce fairly acceptable results.

Recording a crowd

Since an overall effect is called for here, a well-edited "wildtrack" (see p. 115) may well give a more effective sound track than a sync recording. Either an omnidirectional or cardioid microphone may be used to equal effect, especially when combined with a recorder hung over the shoulder. For specific "spot-effects" of someone speaking, the wildtrack can be overlaid with sync effects shot on a single system camera.

Recording music

Filming music is a very broad topic and the problems of microphone placement can only be talked about in general terms here. There is one golden rule – *always monitor the sound before shooting and adjust the microphone position accordingly*. Decide whether you want a live acoustic or a dead one; one microphone or several; one master track or one track for each instrument. Most important is to thoroughly familiarize yourself with the music beforehand; have the players rehearse the loudest notes so the recordist knows when to expect them. Finally, be aware that music is the most testing of all subjects for your microphone so use the best one possible.

Music on Film

The sound track for any filming of music must be uninterrupted. This means that you *must* make at least one continuous recording of the piece of music, whether filming single system or double system. Always remember that when filming music you are inexorably bound by the sound track: in other words, you must have some visual material to cover every inch of the sound or you will be left with a gaping hole.

Filming

To simplify the editing of a musical performance, the standard practice is to shoot one "master take", followed (in a repeat performance) by numerous shorter cutaways that can be overlaid in vision over the master sound track. These additional takes are best *filmed to playback* (see below), but they can be used for brief periods when shot "wild" if the players are consistent in their timing. Another trick that helps in editing is to shoot a lot of takes that do not betray their precise musical location – the conductor's head (without his hands being in shot); the pianist filmed from across the piano; the score; a row of organ pipes; or the glint of light on a violin case. All these will help to fill in any visual gaps and guarantee that the music track is fully covered. Remember that you cannot cut from one camera position to another in the middle of a musical phrase unless you are also running a separate cassette or tape recording of the whole musical piece, which can be overlaid in the editing. If you intend to splice together two master tracks (of different performances), make certain that the shot-size at the end of one roll matches the shot-size at the beginning of the next.

Know the music beforehand

Music, whether classical or popular, is very demanding to record, and it is advisable to prepare thoroughly. If possible, obtain a recording of the music to be performed and listen to it with the sheet music in front of you. Even if you cannot read music you will soon learn to follow the ups and downs, and you can mark where the sound is going to peak (and overload the recording medium). Knowing the music thoroughly also allows you the chance to mark any particular solo passages or areas in the music where particular instruments are to be accentuated. The most tricky part of following a score for non-musicians is the repeat marks, which indicate that the previous section is to be played again. If recording loosely structured rock music, talk to one of the performers beforehand to get some idea of what you can expect in terms of musical peaks.

The location

Music is best recorded in a room with a relatively "dead acoustic" – generally a well-furnished room with only a few hard surfaces. Set up the recorder in a quiet corner as you will want to monitor the sound through headphones without being overpowered by the direct sound. Professional studios provide a glass-fronted booth to deaden the direct sound and allow you to see what is going on. After inspecting the location a decision has to be made on equipment and microphone placement.

Covering the sound track
When filming music, shots that do not indicate their musical position, as the example above of a conductor as seen from the orchestra's viewpoint, can be intercut to make sure the sound track is covered.

Pianist
Another example of the type of shot needed to cover the sound track could be of the pianist, filmed so his hands cannot be seen.

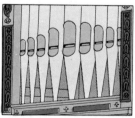

Using the surroundings
Do not feel limited to shots only of musicians as "fillers". If the music is being performed in an attractive room or auditorium, the surroundings themselves can be used as an accompaniment to the sound track. For example, the sound of an organ could be linked to a shot of organ pipes (above) and, as the music swells, so the camera could pan up the pipes to settle on some architectural feature above the organ, or even the ceiling if it incorporates some interesting design or pattern.

Equipment

A single system camera is not really ideal for music recording. The frequency response of stripe film, even at 24 fps, is inferior to $\frac{1}{4}$ in. tape at $7\frac{1}{2}$ ips. In most cases sound recorded on a separate recorder will be transferred to striped film or fullcoat, but the rule holds true – *the better the original recording, the better the final sound track will be*. If you must use a super 8 stripe camera, choose one that accepts a 200-foot magazine and lock the recording level manually. If not, the AGC will tend to flatten the peaks and "pull up" the quiet passages. Make certain whichever camera you decide to use is well soundproofed so not to intrude onto the sound track. The running time of the tape should be worked out accurately so that there is no chance of its ending in the middle of a shot. Super 8 users who own a stereo projector should consider a two-track stereo recording; in which case a stereo recorder able to record two tracks plus a sync pulse will be needed.

Two double system cameras, both equipped with crystal sync, are ideal for filming live music. When one camera is about to run out of film, the other camera can start, overlapping the first a little. Both will produce images in perfect sync with a common sound track.

The microphones you choose should be of the best quality your budget allows. The directional characteristics you select will largely be determined by the number and disposition of the performers. Finally, make certain you have enough cable for the distance between the microphones and the recorder, and remember to allow enough sync lead to reach the camera if you are not using crystal sync control units.

Filming to playback

When filming music with only one camera, it is often necessary to intercut separate takes. If a cutting point cannot be found in the music, the vision from Take One might have to be laid over the sound from Take Two, for example. The snag is that performers never play or sing in exactly the same way twice in succession. The result will be an out-of-sync shot as the pictures and sound slowly drift apart. To remedy this, you need to use two recorders. One plays back the sound from the master take while the performer mimes to it. The other recorder is used to record a "guide track", which is used as a reference when it comes to editing. Without the guide track it may be difficult to know which piece of mime belongs to which piece of master take. It is vital that the playback should be at a constant speed, and the best system is for the recorder to be locked into crystal sync. For the playback to be convincing it is essential that the performers put everything they have into the act. A singer's throat must be seen to strain, and a pianist must move his or her fingers in time to the music; the director must make sure the mime is in sync.

Positioning the microphone

Whether using one microphone or several, it is an enormous advantage to be able to listen to a rehearsal and, by trying different positions for the microphones, arrive at the ideal placement. If only one microphone is in use it should be sited so it does not unduly favor one instrument or group of instruments. For even coverage, it should be placed high up and face diagonally across the room to minimize any resonance that might build up between two parallel walls. Using a single microphone is, in some ways, the purest way to record – no artificial coloration or rebalancing being introduced by the recordist. More commonly, several microphones are used. They are placed and monitored individually during a rehearsal of the music and their relative balance adjusted using a *mixer*. It is common practice to use one "master microphone", the sound from which is enriched with close-up detail of individual players provided from more directional microphones on stands among the players and out of sight of the camera.

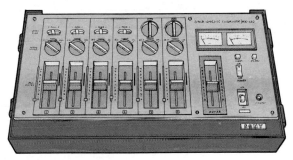

Sound mixer (above)
The Sony MX-650 mixer features six different micro-phone inputs, each with a separate volume control, so the sound from six different instruments, or groups of instruments, can be finely balanced. The MX-650 can also be battery operated for location use.

Recording a group (below)
If you use only one microphone, it should be positioned diagonally across the room to reduce the build up of resonance between parallel walls.

Recording separate instruments

Piano

Choose a microphone position that does not ex-cessively favor one end of the keyboard at the expense of the other. The best all-round position is approxi-mately one-third of the way round an arc from back to side, pointing down so that the microphone can "see" all the strings. The further away the micro-phone is placed the higher it should be.

Singer

A singer may be separately "miked" to allow the sound recordist to finely balance instrumentation and voice. Unless you are recording rock music, the microphone should not be so close that the sound becomes "breathy" – about 2 feet (·6 m) should be regarded as the minimum. If the voice level is low, screen the microphone from the instruments so that it does not pick up unwanted sound.

Woodwind

The sound from woodwind instruments is largely emitted through the first few holes and is fairly omnidirectional. Few problems are likely to crop up except in the case of the flute. Here it may be best to place the microphone above and behind the player. This should minimize the breathiness that sometimes can be picked up on a frontal microphone and ruin the recording.

Strings

All string instruments radiate their sound from the sounding board and not the strings, and the high frequencies go upwards rather than out. A high microphone position will tend to emphasize the highest frequencies, so an eye-level position is gen-erally best. The larger string instruments are quite omnidirectional in their sound radiation and mic-rophone placement is less critical.

Brass and percussion

Both these types of instruments are likely to produce a sudden, loud sound, and it is important to know exactly when they may be expected to crash onto the sound track. Choosing a microphone position is difficult here, but a spot forward of the brass and not too high is probably best. This is much the same way the audience hears the sound.

Electric music

With heavily amplified music the noise emitted by the players is utterly swamped. Ignore the players and place the microphone in front of the sound source – the speakers. The best position should be along the axis of the speakers' high frequency response. Two rear microphones are needed for the drums and a frontal microphone for the bass drum. A singer will need to be separately miked so that the voice can be properly balanced.

Manipulating the Sound

Sound filters

All microphones add their own coloration to a sound, and this continues at all points in the chain of recording and reproduction. To rectify this distortion, "sound filters" are used in a process known as equalization. These filters are termed either "active" or "passive".

Active filters

These filters can actually be used to boost one portion of the frequency range as well as to lower it. Most of us know these filters as the bass and treble controls on domestic hi-fi amplifiers. Active filters are also used to lift the mid-range, which has the effect of adding "presence" to the sound. At their most complex, active filters can provide a separate control for each octave and these permit very fine control of the recorded sound.

Passive filters

These filters merely reduce the signal at one end or the other of the scale of frequencies. Their most familiar forms are as the "rumble" filter (or bass-cut) and the "scratch" filter (which removes high frequencies) found on hi-fi amplifiers. Passive filters are principally used to correct mechanical faults in disk reproduction.

Equalizers

In a professional recording studio, each input channel would have its own filter, or equalizer, so that each instrument could be correctly balanced. The non-professional user would be more likely to have only one equalizer circuit to work with, and this would be placed between the mixer and the recorder. However, it might be better to delay the process of equalizing the sound until the dubbing stage. Sound, once removed, can never be properly replaced, and except in the case of a serious distortion (rumbling traffic noise, for example) you should try to leave the sound as it is first recorded.

Echo and reverberation

Echo (also known as reverb) can be added to any sound track. It is used to brighten a dead acoustic, to glamorize a wobbly top note, and to conceal clumsy sound edits. This effect can be generated in three ways. An *echo chamber* is a small, soundproof room with hard walls and floor containing a speaker and microphone. The sound is fed in through the speaker and is altered by the acoustic qualities of the room, so that by the time it reaches the microphone it will have acquired a new resonance. Alternatively, a *reverberation plate* can be used. This is a large steel sheet fitted with two "transducers" (devices for transferring energy from one form to another), one of which vibrates the sheet while the other picks up the reverberant sound. The third method involves creating an echo by using the feedback from any tape recorder that possesses three heads and a sound-on-sound control (see p. 121). The idea is that the recorded sound is returned from the playback head to the recording head, where it is added back to the master track. This method is not recommended for use where a natural sound is required, but it can produce a useful science fiction or horror movie electronic warble.

Noise-reduction adapter
The most effective method of improving sound quality is to use the Dolby noise-reduction unit each time the sound track is re-recorded, as most "hiss" and other high-frequency noise is picked up at these points. Decoding the signal takes place when the film is projected.

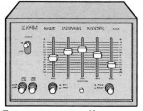

Frequency equalizer
A frequency equalizer is very useful when dubbing the sound onto the final master track. Slider controls on the equalizer (above) are used to boost or cut a specific range of frequencies. The equalizer can be thought of as a tone control that splits the frequencies in the audible range into very fine divisions, each of which is controlled by its own slider.

Compressors

Compressors are extensively used to boost the apparent loudness of amplified rock music while preventing any overloading of the recording medium. They are rarely used for classical music.

Noise-reduction systems

Any tape recording contains a degree of "hiss", which cannot be heard if a strong signal is present on top. If, however, the signal is weak, as in a quiet passage of music, or if the equipment is poor, tape noise can build up to an unacceptable level. All noise-reduction systems aim to improve the signal-to-noise ratio and thereby reduce tape "hiss". The most commonly used is the Dolby system, which is known as Dolby B in its amateur form. The principle is that, on recording, the higher frequencies are boosted, to a greater or lesser extent, depending on the volume at the time. On playback, the reverse process occurs and the boosted frequencies are returned to normal. Since the tape "hiss" has not been boosted it is lost in the decoding process. Dolby systems are invaluable for cassette decks, where tape noise is particularly evident, but Dolby tapes require Dolby equipment for proper reproduction.

Stereo recording

Stereo recording depends on the information from two separate microphones being fed to two separate speakers through two entirely separate chains of amplification and reproduction. The effect produced of spaciousness comes from the fact that our ears are given all the information they need to establish the direction of the sound. It is absolutely vital for all stereo recordings to be played back into speakers that are correctly *in phase*. As the cone of a speaker moves in and out, the air is alternately pressurized and depressurized. If the positive and negative terminals on the projector (or amplifier) outputs are not connected to their appropriate counterparts on the speakers, the left and right speakers will be moving the air in exactly opposite directions at any given time. When this happens the speakers are said to be *out of phase*, and the effect is to destroy the stereo image, as well as resulting in a severe loss of bass response and possible damage to the amplifier.

Duo-track and multi-track

A two-track recorder need not necessarily be used to record a stereo track. It can also be used to record two tracks that will later be mixed down into one composite mono track. For example, one track might carry a piano and the other a vocalist. It is known as a *duo-track*.

Professional recording studios have extended this system of recording with the use of eight-track and sixteen-track recorders using $\frac{1}{2}$ in. (13 mm) tape. These professional *multi-track* recorders record each channel separately and without mixing them. These tracks can then be subsequently mixed, juggled and manipulated in a wide variety of ways without affecting the original recording in a procedure called *post-balancing*. The main use for these machines is in the recording of rock music, where many of the effects are electronic.

MAKING A MOVIE

"The real work was thinking, just thinking" *Charles Chaplin*

The Basic Equipment

Whatever your budget, the camera you choose must be compatible with your projector and other equipment. It is pointless buying an expensive camera if your projector is not of an equivalent standard. By considering the system as a whole, individual pieces of equipment can be updated without rendering the rest obsolete. The most crucial decisions about buying cameras are usually to do with the sound rather than the visual side: decide whether you intend to use sound and how you want to record and therefore edit it (see p. 232). The equipment we discuss here deals with both single and double systems. Accessories like tripods, cable releases and light meters are essential for successful filming, while additional lenses and filters are useful for enhancing it.

Single system super 8

A single system super 8 camera is ideal for both the filmmaker who wants to progress from a silent super 8 camera and the beginner who wants a sound camera. This is because with single system the camera itself records both the sound and the picture. There is no need to carry around extra sound recording equipment because the microphone attached to the camera picks up the sound and records it on "striped" film (see p. 111). In addition to sound recorded at the time, sound effects and commentaries can be added to the sound track later. Sound cameras are similar in price to silent cameras, and can also be used for silent filming. However, they are heavier and bulkier than silent cameras.

1 Microphone
2 Cardiod microphone
3 Close-up lenses
4 Lens cloth
5 Blower brush
6 Shoulder brace
7 Film cartridges
8 Lens filters
9 Movielight
10 Battery box
11 Battery recharger
12 NiCad batteries
13 Light meter
14 Cable release
15 Standard tripod
16 Nizo 4080 camera
17 Sound barney
18 Equipment bag

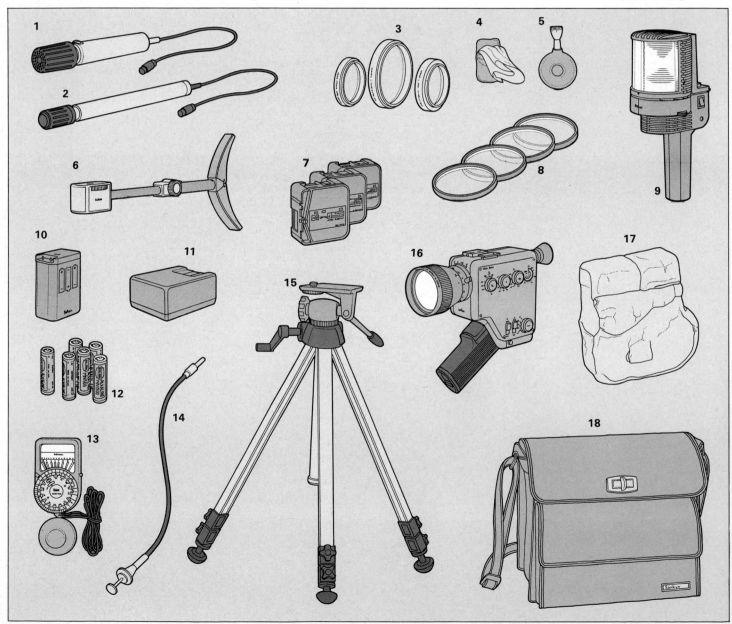

Double system 16 mm

The double system 16 mm set-up shown below is suitable for the more experienced filmmaker. The separate shooting and recording equipment require a more professional and planned attitude to filming.

In double system the camera does not record the sound; instead it is recorded by a separate tape recorder, and an electronic reference pulse from the camera is placed onto the tape parallel to the recorded sound. The pulse may be thought of as a form of "electronic perforation", and the tape is subsequently transferred to fullcoat magnetic film for editing. The great advantage of this is that the sound and picture can be edited separately. This allows for greater freedom – for example, a sound can be edited to overlap a previously unrelated image. Another advantage is that the recorder can be used to make extensive "wildtrack" recordings (see p. 115) which can be overlaid at the dubbing stage to provide a fully professional sound track without any embarrassing gaps.

Double system 16 mm is standard procedure for most high quality TV work. The cameras and accessories, though bulkier and more expensive than amateur super 8 equipment, are much cheaper and more portable than 35 mm. There is a wide range of 16 mm filmstocks, in both negative and reversal forms, and because of the larger frame area, the quality of the image is significantly higher than that of super 8.

1 Clapper board
2 Lens filters
3 Blower brush
4 Lens cloth
5 Changing bag
6, 7, 8 Additional lenses
9 Film magazine
10 Bolex H16 EL camera
11 Sound barney
12 Shotgun microphone
13 Headphones
14 Nagra sound recorder
15 Crystal sync pulse
16 Spider tripod
17 Cable release
18 Spot meter
19 Shoulder brace
20 Equipment box

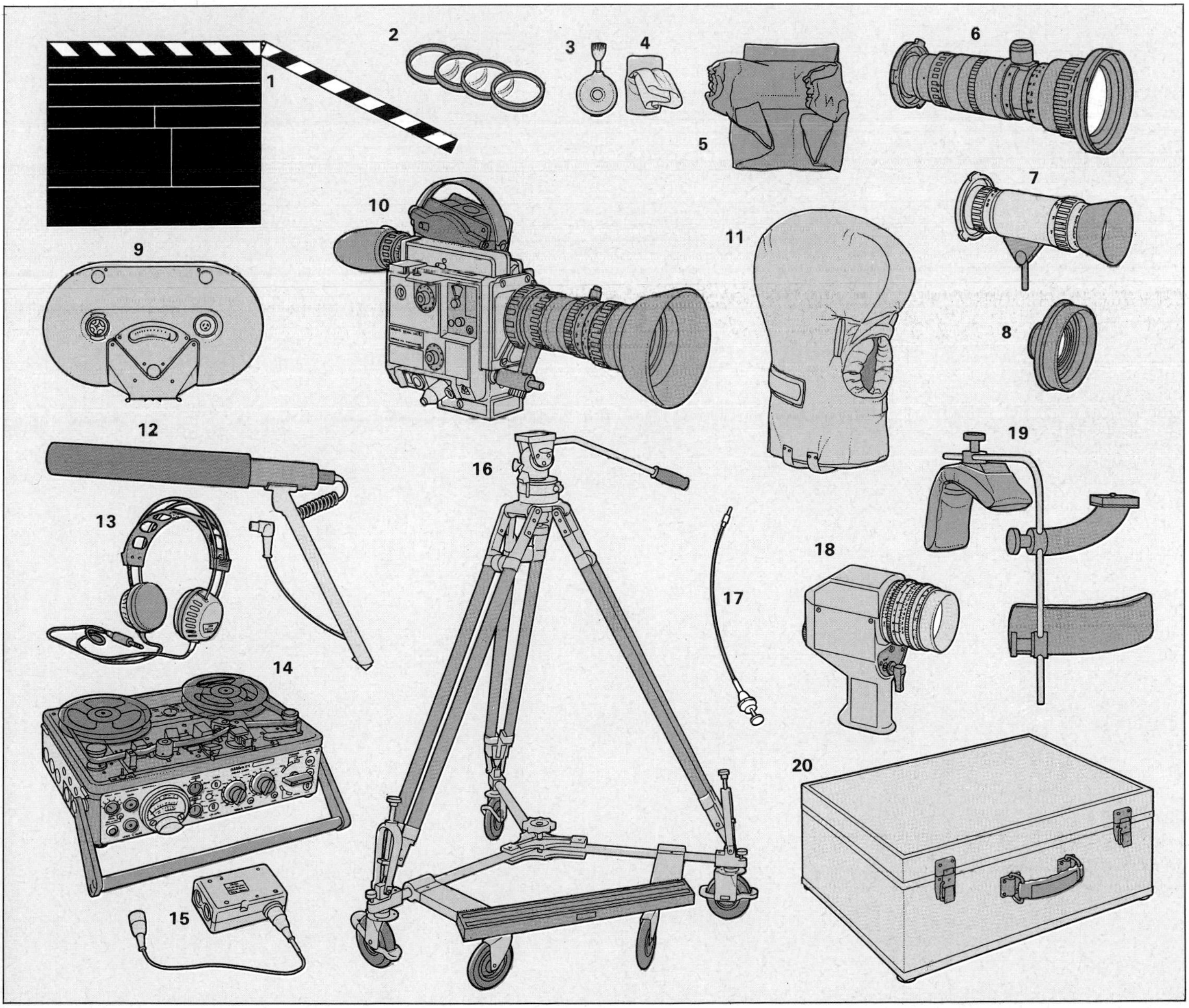

It has to be faced that "home movies" have acquired a rather unfortunate reputation over the years, largely because it is so easy to confuse what is interesting to oneself with what is interesting to others. A wobbly sustained shot of a baby crawling across the lawn may move your family to tears, but the effect on your sleepy after-dinner guests, who remember neither baby nor lawn, will be more on the lines of a yawn. There is nothing wrong with shooting a simple family record, but making movies out of the same material for *others* to watch is a far more demanding task. You will get far more pleasure from your movies if you try to give each subject form, pace, atmosphere and narrative continuity. Aim to make every reel "tell a story", even if the story is an evocation of part of your family life. Your job is to create a pattern that is both attractive and truthful to its subject and this is done partly through judicious editing (both in-camera and at the editing bench) but more especially through pre-planning.

A child grows up

There are three main ways of approaching the filming of children. The first is to shoot at every opportunity. This is by far the easiest method, but the results are poor since each shot is separated from the ones on either side, with no continuity: it should therefore be avoided.

The second method is to choose one particular time or event and to film it in detail, the idea being to freeze time rather than to show its passage. This gives you a chance to watch and film the child in detail and allows you to build a sequence which makes sense and has atmosphere, while still retaining a strong narrative thread. Say you decide to shoot a picnic: there are certain structural elements which must be shown for the movie to have a narrative sense – the packing of the food, driving away, eating, playing and coming home. Keep an eye open, also, for any cutaways so that the time scale can be compressed without strain.

The third method is to make the passage of time itself the subject. In effect this is a "compilation movie" and will almost certainly involve more intensive editing than the single-subject approach. For example, you might decide to shoot the various stages of a child learning to read. The shooting might be spaced out over the course of a year and you might want to punctuate the final movie with some indication of the date: instead of a calendar, try intercutting the child's reading with the growth of the garden and the passing of the seasons. Show the transition from stories being read to the child, to when the child begins to read from memory.

The challenge of making any movie about children is to capture them acting unselfconsciously in front of the camera. There are several ways of making this task easier. Use a telephoto lens setting where possible so you can keep the camera at a distance. And, to get them used to the presence of the camera, try shooting for a while without any film. But the most important thing is to *give the children something to do*. This will not only make for a more interesting film, but, with luck, their absorption in their own activity will outweigh their interest in you and your movie camera.

Filming children

One of the main problems that face you when filming children is to make them behave in an unself-conscious way in front of the camera. If they are very young they can easily be distracted by someone else. But if they are older, film them when they are playing together, perhaps on the long end of the zoom, or else while they are absorbed in some kind of game. Holiday trips to the country or the beach also provide a marvellous opportunity for memorable filming.

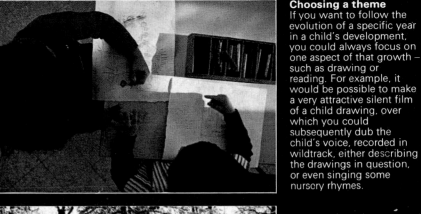

Choosing a theme

If you want to follow the evolution of a specific year in a child's development, you could always focus on one aspect of that growth – such as drawing or reading. For example, it would be possible to make a very attractive silent film of a child drawing, over which you could subsequently dub the child's voice, recorded in wildtrack, either describing the drawings in question, or even singing some nursery rhymes.

Making a film of the children's party

Parties are marvellous locations for filming, because the children will certainly not be distracted by the camera so long as there is cake on the table or games to play. Try to avoid using movielights on the camera, however, unless you have absolutely no choice. They are glaring and will drown the light of the candles on the cake. Use an XL camera and fast film instead. Sync sound is strongly recommended – either single system or double system according to your equipment.

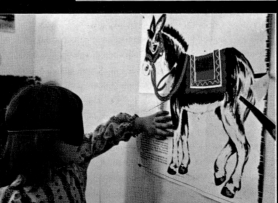

Filming a Wedding

Like all social ceremonies, a wedding contains certain key moments which have to be covered: the arrival of the bride and groom, the marriage ceremony, the walk up the aisle and the departure. There will also be unexpected incidents such as the fidgeting uncle or the cloudburst and these should be allowed for in the overall plan of action. Make certain that you have the minister's permission to shoot. Then go to the church before the day, if possible at the same time as the wedding will be. Take a light meter and your camera with you. Draw up a plan of the church and mark down your proposed camera positions. Your aim throughout should be to lead the eye from the cars to the altar and back again in one smooth sweep. Never work out camera positions first and the flow of shots afterwards, or the action will appear disjointed. If it helps, write a script so that the progression of the action is clear in your mind before you get to the church on the day.

Camera positions

Find out the exact order of the service, with rough timings if possible, and think where you can put the camera for the key moments. For your main position, you must be near enough to get close-ups of the bride and groom but far enough away to get a wide-angle, with the other end of the zoom, of the whole ceremony. The greater the zooming range of the camera the greater your choice of position. Try to make the background as attractive as possible because you will not be able to move around during the service. In the quieter moments you will have to be in a good position to shoot cutaways. These are vital shots, since the main editing problem in a sequence like a wedding will be to compress the time-scale without destroying the atmosphere. If you are planning to record sound as well, you will probably need both single system sound and a separate recording of the whole service (see p. 111). At this point you will have to decide on the microphone positions. To record both the participants and the music, and to do justice to both, you may need two microphones.

Lighting, exposure and film

Inside the church, shoot on fast film as for daylight, with the "85" filter in position. It is impossibly expensive to light even an average church, and the color temperature of unfiltered tungsten lamps is too yellow to mix with the predominant daylight inside. The size of the windows and the color of the walls will determine what exposure you use and also the type of film. Take an average reading, preferably with an incident meter. Keep in mind that on the day itself it may be four stops less bright. If so, you may not have enough light to shoot at all, even with fast film and an XL camera. Always overestimate the amount of film you will need. Do a rough calculation based on how long the finished movie will be and how much you need for editing. In super 8 a 50 ft (15 m) cartridge runs for about 3 mins 20 secs at 18 fps, and in 16 mm a 100 ft spool gives you about 2 mins 47 secs at 24 fps. Longer runs are available, for some cameras, in both gauges. Always carry a supply of fresh batteries, and clean the camera before filming.

The arrival
The arrival of the bride is one of the key moments that you must catch. Starting the camera as soon as the car can be seen will give you a long, sweeping shot of the arrival. Make certain the camera position is absolutely right as the car comes to a halt. The Rolls Royce mascot gives a useful built-in cutaway to the bride getting out of the car.

Entering the church
The camera, hand-held now, tracks around the columns as the bride enters the church with her father. Try not to leave tripods or other pieces of equipment in the shot as this detracts from the final image.

The ceremony

It is often impossible to position yourself in front of the bride and groom. In such cases you might go for a high top-shot, from where you can also get close-ups. The back stairs give an unobtrusive way of moving around during the service.

Filming inside

When filming inside the church, try to use as fast a film as you can. If you have an XL camera – with a fast lens and a shutter with a larger than normal cutaway (see p. 42) – then you should be able to get a satisfactory exposure. Try to take a test light reading before the ceremony itself.

Close-ups

When all is said and done your film will stand or fall on capturing people's faces. Go for strong, frame-filling close-ups. It will help if you ask both sides of the families in advance who they would like to see in the film. People are easily offended if you leave them out.

The departure

The cutaways (above) of the bouquet and of the church clock will be invaluable when you come to edit your sequence together. In practice, there might be several minutes in the action which you have to bridge with a cutaway. The departure of the car provides a tidy end to the sequence at the church.

Capturing Character

People's characters are made visible through their behaviour, their appearance, what they say and how they say it, and even at times by inaction. It is the very expressiveness of human character which makes it such a rewarding subject for the movie camera. The camera is there to record, not create. Choose an activity or a scene which is both typical of the subject and sufficiently absorbing for them to be able to forget the camera. The activity you show should not be violent – it is possible to show character with a passive, delicate study, as well as a more active pursuit. Keep instructions to a minimum and do not ask for actions to be repeated – it will be unnatural. Stand well away from the scene and, using the long end of the zoom, shoot good, solid close-ups. Get into a position where the subject's eyeline is close to the camera, but not looking directly at it. Use plenty of film to make sure that you get the full range of expression that you need. In fact, the longer you film, the more relaxed people will become, especially children. A good tip is to shoot for some time without any film in the camera so that the subject gets used to your presence and to the filming. By the time it comes to the real shooting they will have forgotten you are there. It is often best to use diffused or bounced lighting – it looks more natural and gives you more flexibility of movement. On closer shots, only use a tripod if it is needed to steady the camera or if you are certain that the subject is not going to move; avoid tracking shots as they are very cumbersome.

Woman knitting
It is often the case that an elderly person's face reveals the most character. Try to catch your subject while they are absorbed in a typical or favorite activity. This should hold their attention so that they behave naturally in front of the camera. Light them in a sympathetic way – for example, harsh, artificial lighting would be completely wrong for a delicate study of someone sitting by a fire. In such a case you might want to film them, bathed in firelight, with cutaways to the cat asleep on the mat, the slow burning fire and the glint of the needle.

The motorcyclist

In the case of a study of a keen motorcyclist, try to shoot him polishing and maintaining the bike, revving it up and roaring away into the open country. Get him to give you a ride so that you can take some subjective shots, looking over his shoulder. These can be inter-cut with telephoto panning shots or else, to maximize the effect of speed, with low level, static wide-angle shots.

The sound track

There are three sources for the sound track which you can develop for character: *sync dialogue*, *wildtrack recording* or *commentary* which can be added at the end of editing. Music can also be added at this stage.

Sync dialogue is the most revealing source, but all too often the best snatches of conversation fall neatly between rolls of film. Any good dialogue you do record tends to be scattered and it is therefore common to strengthen the sound track by adding some wildtrack sound. The procedure is simple and also cheap. Take a lengthy recording of the conversation on cassette or $\frac{1}{4}$in. (6mm) tape, edit the recording and use this compressed version for editing or dubbing purposes. It can either be edited in parallel with the movie after being transferred to fullcoat magnetic film (see p. 240) or dubbed directly from tape onto the stripe after editing (see p. 247). You cannot use one person's voice while their non-synchronized mouth is visible, but you can easily lay the sound over a reaction shot of the person to whom he or she is talking. You can also use the whole sound track "wild" as a backdrop of voices. At a party, for example, you could combine sync shooting with a long, continuous wildtrack on a separate recorder. The number of people present in the shot will effectively disguise the variable sync, while the wildtrack will be full of dialogue.

Wildtrack voice-over is a rather different procedure, with different aims. In this case the recording is made directly with the person or persons that are the subject of the movie. It may be an interview from which you subsequently remove your own remarks and questions. For example, you might decide to use the edited tape as a continuous sound background to someone's reminiscences where they are only heard, not seen. An alternative would be a commentary after editing but this is surely the least satisfactory form of sound track.

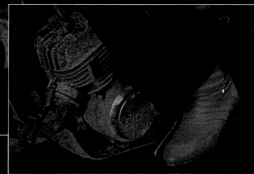

The Film Essay

This category of filmmaking may sound a little imposing at first, but it is in fact one of the most creative areas of film, and one that is quite accessible to the relative beginner. The film essay should not be confused with a documentary type report, which deals with a given subject or topic in a very literal, factual manner: instead, the subject is, if you like, *the film itself.* It should be made clear from the beginning that a great deal of this type of filmmaking is "created" at the editing stage. The juxtaposition of one sound with another image is fundamental to this kind of many-layered film and, as a result, is responsible for much of the challenge.

The abstract film

This is a film about an idea – an abstraction. The concept might be grandiose, common-place or perhaps even erotic, according to taste. But the concentration on one idea gives you enormous scope to work within a narrowly defined area: you will have to plan it all the way through, and you will almost certainly have to write an outline, if not a proper script. The sources to be drawn upon are innumerable – live action, poetry, music, nature, animation – almost anything that suits your purpose. What you should aim for is some organizing structure that will simplify all this rich but unwieldy material and hold it together and that will give discipline and directness to the film. For example, you might take the subject of "Time". Though time rules, and eventually ends, our lives, it has the misfortune, from the filmmaker's point of view, of being invisible. Your material then is time once removed: the effects of time, the memories of the very old and the indifference of the very young, the seasons, the clocks and the mechanics of time-keeping, the movement of the sun across the sky and the movement of the tides, the prodigious body of poetry and prose on the subject of Time and, of course, music. You could use the progress of one calendar year as your framework: from spring (childhood) through to winter (old age). To illustrate the transitions you could use Shakespeare's sonnets, for example, which are largely about time, as a recurrent theme. Once you have decided on some form of framework, the job of sifting the material becomes much easier.

The types of ideas and examples mentioned here are only intended as a guide. All the crafts of man can be marvellous subjects for your camera and you will soon learn to steer a path between over-literalness on the one hand and wilful irrelevance on the other.

Equipment

A film essay of the type we are describing here is often a very personal statement – representing the individual view of the filmmaker – and, as a result, it does not always lend itself to the film-crew approach. Though 16 mm will give undeniably excellent results for large-scale projection, and will also yield good-quality prints for multiple copies, for most private purposes super 8 is perfectly adequate. The savings in weight and complexity, and the possibility of discrete, one-person operation of camera and recorder, are strong arguments in favor of the smaller format.

The single-subject film

There are many subjects in the arts and crafts that can be used as the basis for a single-subject film. If, for example, there is a piece of music that excites you, it can be "illustrated" with the images it suggests. The music score can become the script to which you can refer during shooting and editing (see p. 242). Paintings also form the basis of many short films but they require all the camera movements to be smooth and precise.

A craft process lends itself admirably to a single-subject film. It is always fascinating to watch a person at work, especially when you are able to watch a single object being made from beginning to end. However, the process must be followed very carefully from stage to stage, with a careful eye for detail.

Glass-blowing
Glass-blowing proved to be ideal for the single-subject film as it deals almost exclusively with one person and their craft. Also, as most of the action is concentrated in quite a small area, it can easily be covered by one camera.

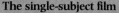

The molten glass
This glass-blowing sequence is typical of the kind of craft process that you might decide to shoot. It offers a wide variety of visual material – the glow of the furnace and the molten glass, the glitter of the finished article – and it also gives you an opportunity to study the character of the glass-blower himself if you wish. In this case you would almost certainly decide to follow one single object – a goblet – from the furnace to the display case.

Forming the glass
One of the difficulties in filming a sequence such as this is that the process is very fast and it cannot be halted in the middle. You will have to move swiftly and keep shooting.

Forming the stem
The likelihood is, however, that you will miss out on some of the action. If possible, choose a subject that you can repeat. Film it twice and intercut the two takes in editing. This will also help with the inevitable continuity problems that are involved in any detailed subject. In the shots illustrated here, for example, of the glass stem being formed, images from two different takes have been intercut to form one continuous sequence. This technique will only work if careful attention is paid to camera position and subject lighting. Continuity can also be helped by wide variations of camera angle, and by inserting cutaways.

Attaching the base
Concentrating on a detail can often be more effective than a full-figure shot. Go for all the cutaways you can, so that the time-scale can be compressed without discontinuity or jump cuts.

Also, get all the sound you can, even if you record it "wildtrack". Be certain to shoot an interview with the craftsman talking about his work – it can be used as a voice-over at the dubbing stage, perhaps with a musical track too.

Zooming in
The final sequence of this film essay deals with the finished articles – the glass objects. The reflected light on the glass decanter was the final shot of a slow zoom-in.

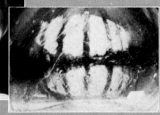

Zooming out
A cut to a zoom-out was used to finish the essay. Beginning where the last sequence ended – on a close-up of the decanter – and zooming out to show the setting helps place the objects in their proper perspective.

Making a Documentary

Probably the most common form of the documentary film is the social documentary. This umbrella term takes in a wide range of possible causes, from opposition to a new road scheme to a charitable organization wishing to raise funds. Many individuals and organizations find the short polemical film the ideal medium for putting across a social or political viewpoint. When a television network, for instance, makes a documentary, it will go to great lengths to present an apparently rounded view of any question. Whether the resulting film can ever be genuinely "balanced" is arguable: after all, films are made by people who have opinions and a moral sense. If the documentary you are planning is committed to a particular cause, the only reason you need any balance at all is to make your own committed position more credible. You will also find that your film carries more conviction if the message emerges from the body of the film rather than from your superimposed commentary. In other words, *do not say it if you can show it.* This can be done in two principal ways: through the words and actions of the people in the film; and through the power of the visual imagery.

Your equipment needs for a documentary are very similar to those for a film essay (see p. 136) – because of its low-light capability, super 8 may well be the best choice. This allows you to dispense with lighting equipment and is a great help in making people feel at ease.

Adding a commentary

Wherever possible when shooting a documentary you should try to find others to say what you are trying to convey – although there will probably remain quite a few ends to be tied, points to be made and conclusions to be drawn. You will, in fact, need a commentary. Try to keep it as brief as possible and do not fill every frame of film with sound – rather, let the images tell their own story. The best person to record the commentary may well be someone who is utterly indifferent to the issues at stake (for details on writing and recording a commentary, see p. 244).

Recording an interview

Interviews can be conducted in two ways: as a two-way conversation where you would expect to retain the questions as well as the answers after editing, or where you intend to remove all trace of the questions during editing, leaving the final version "clean" of the interviewer's presence. In the later case, your questions will have to be carefully phrased so that they do not allow a "yes" or "no" answer. In general, a bullying technique should not be adopted. It may well antagonize any non-committed viewer and it will not draw the best response from the interviewee. Also, do not interrupt during the answers, especially if you are not in shot. A friendly nod or encouraging smile is best, and a period of expectant silence often triggers a better response than a hastily put question. It is worth remembering not to overlap your next question over the end of the previous answer – you may want to separate them in editing. Especially if using single system, leave a full second's silence (see p. 115). Finally, do not be so mesmerized by your next question that you fail to listen to your subject. They are thinking about what they are saying, even if you are not.

A film about waterways

The shots on this page illustrate one of the ways in which you might go about putting together a documentary film to convey a personal point-of-view. In this case, the subject is canals and waterways – the barges and the people who live and work on them, the landscapes, the industrial architecture, and the controversial environmental issues involved. Remember to go for the shots and the juxtapositions that will make your points for you, and do not underestimate the power of the unaided image. Above all, try to avoid relying too heavily on the commentary to get your message across.

Opening shot
Your film might well begin with this kind of image. As an establishing shot, the snow-covered canal boat could be used to lead gradually in to increasingly controversial topics.

The locks (above)
An interesting sequence may be created simply by following a single boat through the lock system. In this case, long shots are intercut with a close-up of the prow of the boat.

Industrial landscape (right)
Shots filmed from the boat can illustrate the contrasting environment that the canals encompass – here, the industrial panoramas of warehouses and gas storage tanks.

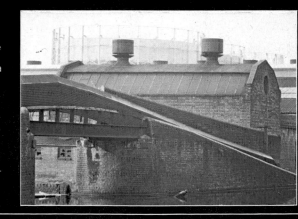

Cutaways (left)
The architecture alongside waterways can provide rich visual material. Abstract compositions made up from the lock gates, machinery and the waterfront buildings can all be used as cutaways to enrich the overall feel of the film.

People (right)
These shots portray some of the people working on the canal boats, as well as those in factories on the canalside. If you have recorded wild-track interviews of people talking about the life on the canals, the sound could be used as a voice-over with shots such as these.

Details (below right)
Exploit the bright, strong colors of the traditionally painted barges as far as you can. Powerfully composed, color-saturated shots like these should be allowed to tell their own story

Closing shots (below)
You might decide to end your film on a strident, controversial note. Alternatively, you could go for a quiet, peaceful atmosphere such as that suggested by these shots, filmed in the warm yellow light of early evening.

A Simple Scripted Film

Once you make the jump into fictional film, your whole approach to moviemaking will change. You no longer look for shots, you create them. And you are no longer on your own. Even if you write the script, direct, edit and project the film yourself, the business of setting it up and shooting it will inevitably involve others. If you are prepared to listen to what they have to contribute, this collaboration can be enormously rewarding.

First, you need an idea. And your choice will depend very much on your reasons for wanting to make a movie in the first place. One person will opt for a thriller, another for a comedy. But all good ideas for a simple fictional film must fulfil fundamental criteria. The number of actors should not be greater than you can muster, nor should the parts be impossibly demanding in an amateur film. The locations should not be inaccessible or expensive. And any stunts, special effects, opticals or graphics should be within your means – both technically and financially. Above all, the characters and the plot should be as *interesting* as you can possibly make them.

Character
For an actor to sustain the illusion of a "real person" on the screen, he or she must have something to go on. It is the job as scriptwriter or director to provide physical mannerisms, an outline of character and, most important of all, a clear and visible motivation for the action the subject is supposed to perform. You must make certain that the human reasons for each stage of the plot are perfectly clear. If one man is trying to kill another, we want to know why. If the motive is not jealously, greed or mistaken identity, then what is it?

The plot
The conventional wisdom is that the plot should have a distinct beginning, middle and end. But a good plot can just as easily have a slow-fuse opening, two or three successive "middles" and a double-twist ending. The only requirement is that the audience's attention should be held – by guile, mystification, comedy or sheer brute force – from beginning to end. Above all, remember that, if the story is strong, keep it simple.

The treatment
After deciding on the outline of your plot, you should write out a treatment of the whole film. This should contain quite a lot of detail but only a general indication of dialogue. You are not yet concerned with specific shots or camera positions, so concentrate on getting the story itself into shape. This is the point at which you should assess the balance and structure of the film, and build in all the undercurrents, red herrings, false clues and subtleties of character you need. Ask yourself at every stage of the treatment exactly what is providing the "dynamic" at any given point – is it suspense, curiosity, laughter or the clash of two wills? Make certain that you know what effect you want, so that you can put all your effort into its achievement.

Scripting the film
A script is essential when dealing with a fictional narrative, even if it is later altered to accommodate the circumstances of shooting. Suppose you have written a simple story in which a boy is kidnapped, driven off and held for ransom. From this idea you can write a treatment, the final sequence of which might run as follows: the boy, bound and gagged, is squirming on the back seat of a car as it races toward a railroad crossing. A train is due and the kidnapper is desperately trying to beat the train as the boy's father, in another car, is catching up. The gates at the crossing close, the father's car screams up, the boy frees himself and the man runs off to avoid capture.

The following film script is one possible treatment. There is no dialogue, only effects, and music if needed.

A simple scripted film

#	Shot	Description
1	L.S.	Car, low angle, right-to-left. Car passes rapidly through frame. *Sound:* throughout, squealing tires, roaring engines, as appropriate.
2	M.C.U.	Man from passenger's front seat. Man looks around to rear. As he looks, pan to boy on rear seat. His head is on offside.
3	C.U.	Boy's face, gagged, frightened.
4	M.S.	Over man's shoulder. Road ahead.
5	C.U.	Man's eyes. They look down to clock.
6	C.U.	Clock on eyeline. Second-hand moves around. Clock says 10:58.
7	L.S.	Train travels left-to-right.
8	B.C.U.	Man's eyes. Up to mirror.
9	C.U.	Mirror. Other car visible.
10	M.S.	Tracking with other car, M.S. of father in pursuit right-to-left.
11	C.U.	Boy's face, more determined. Pan down to hands as they slowly work loose.
12	C.U.	Gear-change by man. White knuckles.
13	B.C.U.	Man's face, eyes to clock.
14	B.C.U.	Clock 10:59.30.
15	C.U.	Father, anxious.
16	M.S.	Train rushing through frame left-to-right.
17	L.S.	Cars both pass very fast, close together, right-to-left. *Sound:* distant train whistle.
18	B.C.U.	Boys hands finally loose.
19	V.B.C.U.	Massive close-up second-hand 11:00.
20	L.S.	From across *far* side of railway crossing. Gates close just as car arrives. As train wipes the shot *very close* to camera, cut to.... *Sound:* loud train whistle.
21	L.S.	Car stops. Father's just behind. (Camera has now crossed line.)
22	B.C.U.	Man's face. Jumps out. Runs away.
23	M.S.	Boy jumps out. Pan with him to father.

The storyboard

To help you to gauge the cumulative effect of the story as you have conceived it, and to help to communicate this to any others involved in the production of the film, it is often useful to make rough sketches of the successive images. This process of visualization is known as a *storyboard.* In this particular example, shots 1 to 25, representing the final sequence of the film, could be laid out as illustrated below. It will be seen that to enhance the suspense, the long shots are intercut rapidly with increasingly large close-ups of the action. Mid shots, wherever possible, have been avoided. The pace of the shots will build up through the sequence.

1 L.S. Car

2 M.C.U. Man looks to boy

3 C.U. Boy's face

4 M.S. Over shoulder

5 C.U. Man's eyes

6 C.U. Clock

7 L.S. Train

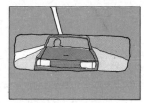
8 B.C.U. Man's eyes

9 C.U. Mirror

10 M.S. Tracking shot

11a, b C.U. Pans from boy's face down to hands

12 C.U. Gear change

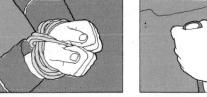
13 B.C.U. Man's face

14 B.C.U. Clock

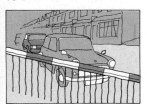
15 C.U. Father's face

16 M.S. Train

17 L.S. Both cars

18 B.C.U. Boy's hands

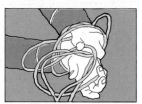
19 V.B.C.U. Second hand

20a, b L.S. Gates close, train passes

21 L.S. Car stops

22 B.C.U. Man's face

23 M.S. Boy and father

The shooting script

When you come to shoot the film, it is not always possible to film each sequence as it will finally appear on the screen. For example, you might have a scene near the beginning of the film that requires you renting a car. The same car could also be needed briefly near the middle of the film and again near the end. As your film may be a part-time, week-end production, shooting might be spread over many months.

From a planning point of view, it makes more sense to film all the scenes involving the car on the same day, rather than hiring the same car on three separate occasions. This principle, of course, applies to making the most economical use of all your resources, including the actors. The order for filming the shots is known as a *shooting script.*

A Simple Scripted Film

1 L.S. Kidnapper's car

2a M.C.U. Kidnapper

2b M.C.U. He turns his head

2c M.C.U. He looks around

2d Pan to C.U. of boy

The chase sequence

The sequence opens with a shot of the kidnapper's car rushing through the frame. We then cut to a shot of the kidnapper from the passenger's seat inside the car. As he turns his head, the camera pans around to reveal the boy bound and gagged on the back seat. Throughout, there are "wild-track" squealing tires and roaring engines on the sound track.

3 C.U. Boy's face

4 M.S. Over kidnapper's shoulder. Road ahead.

5 C.U. Kidnapper looks at his watch

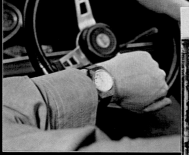

6 C.U. His watch 10:58

7 L.S. Train traveling left to right

8 C.U. Kidnapper's car. He looks up to mirror

Building suspense

The kidnapper knows that he must beat the train to the railroad crossing and that it will arrive at exactly 11:00. He looks at his watch, and we cut to a "parallel action" shot of the train. Meanwhile, a subjective close-up of the kidnapper's car mirror reveals the father's car in close pursuit. Tension increases with the slow pan down to the boy struggling to free his hands.

9 C.U. Father's car in mirror

10 M.S. Tracking shot of father's car in pursuit

11a C.U. Boy's face

11b Pan down to hands

The chase accelerates
In this series of shots, close-ups of the kidnapper (shot 13), the father (shot 15) and the boy's hands (shot 18) are intercut with rapid long shots of the train and of the two cars. The train is seen nearing the railroad crossing, the father's car is gaining on the kidnapper, and the watch shows 11:59.30.

12   C.U. Kidnapper changes gear

13   B.C.U. Kidnapper

14   B.C.U. Watch 10:59.30

15   C.U. Father driving in pursuit

16   M.S. Train, now closer than in shot 7

17   L.S. Both cars pass through frame

18   B.C.U. Boy's hands

19   B.C.U. Watch 11:00

20a   L.S. Gates close as cars arrive

20b   L.S. Train passes in front of camera, right to left

The escape
From an enormous close-up of the watch showing the time at 11:00, we cut to a shot from the other side of the railroad crossing. The gates close just as the cars pull up. The train hurtles past and wipes the shot close to the camera. The boy, his hands now free of the rope, jumps out and runs to his father. The kidnapper runs away.

21 L.S. Kidnapper's car stops, father's behind

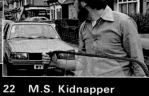

22   M.S. Kidnapper runs away

23a   L.S. Boy gets out

23b   L.S. He runs towards father

23c   L.S. They embrace

143

Shooting an Unscripted Film

Instead of opting for a sustained account of, say, a holiday from beginning to end, you may well prefer to select just one episode and film it rather more intensively. This has the great advantage that your narrative line is automatically provided by the event itself, leaving you plenty of time to explore the character and atmosphere of the day. However, you cannot just arrive at the location and shoot at random. You will need to consider the requirements of smooth action, continuity and so on, exactly as though you were shooting a drama. At the same time, try to build into your shooting a time-structure which firmly reflects that of the day itself – this involves a number of otherwise abstract shots to establish the scene and to relate each sequence to its successor. In the example shown, you would be aiming to capture the sunlit atmosphere, the excitement of the fishing and some of the characters involved.

1 Long shot of stream, establishing locale

Establishing the setting
A long shot of the stream with no-one visible, followed by a macro close-up could be used as a gentle, low-key introduction.

2 Atmospheric close-up of dragonfly

3 Wide-angle establishing three-shot

4 Mid shot of one of the group

5 Two-shot cut to boys

6 Mid shot of boy fishing

7 Cutaway to close-up

Dramatizing the catch
Shots 3 to 10 progress from extreme long shot, through single shots of the fishers, into tighter close-ups ending in the capture of the fish.

8 Medium close-up of the young boy

9 Close-up of the boy

10 The fish is caught

Varying pace

By using a large number of reaction shots and cutaways, you can easily compress the events of a whole afternoon into a few minutes. But be careful to vary the cutting pace so that you do not destroy the peaceful character of the day. Also, since the catching of the minnows will be a repeated action, you can intercut two different versions of the same event. Thus, a dramatic top shot of one fish can be intercut with another.

11 Top shot, dropping the fish into the bag

12 Cut to close-up of fish and bag

Line-crossing and angle

It is not quite so vital to respect line-crossing problems in this type of filming, but if you are carefully following the process of one particular catch try to stay on one side of the line throughout. Alternatively, you could easily use a cutaway or a dramatic change of angle to give yourself latitude in editing. When you do go for close-ups, make sure they really fill the frame. Vary the size, angle and composition of your shots to give variety and visual excitement. While close-ups can easily be staged, both rapid action and facial close-ups should almost always be shot spontaneously for a natural effect.

13 Tighter close-up

14 Big close-up, completes capture of fish

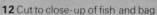

15 Cutaway to river acts as buffer shot

16 Another top shot, last view of family

Sound track

The question of sound track may well arise in a sequence such as this. The sound of the stream, the birds, the chatter of the fishers, will all add greatly to the atmosphere you are trying to recreate. Even if you are shooting with a non-sync silent camera it will be worthwhile to record a lengthy wildtrack on tape or cassette. This can be used later as a running background over which you can superimpose music or commentary.

17 Atmospheric shot of rock and river

Summary

The structure of this small example is completed as the fishers walk home, leaving one rejected minnow on a stone and ending with a fish on a plate. The passage is further helped by the shots of the bag being filled and the water rippling downstream. It is often these anonymous shots which lend a single-subject movie its principal charm and character.

18 Close-up of dinner

A Fictional Adaptation

To produce a script for your first fictional film you may find it easier to adapt an existing work of fiction rather than originating your own. A novel will almost certainly be too long for your needs, but a short story can easily be condensed into a manageable length. It should not be necessary to change the story too much and you should never change the dialogue if it can be avoided.

If you find a story that you think might suit you, but you intend to enter the film for a competition, or some other form of public showing, then you must consider the question of copyright. If the work is more than fifty years old then there is no problem, but if it is more recent you must get permission from both the author and the publisher. In addition, there is a copyright attached to any new translation, even if the original work is more than fifty years old. If your film is only for local or film-club showing there should be no difficulty in getting permission, and the charge for use should not be too high. Publishers are generally only interested in claiming their due if it looks as if your film may make money.

What to look for in the story
When considering a story for adaptation always consider its suitability for film. For example, it may be easy to imagine concepts such as a twinge of remorse or a shortage of money while reading about them, but it is not so easy to translate them onto film. Inner thoughts and conflicts *can* be shown on film but they must be clearly translated in terms of sound and vision. An amateur filmmaker is therefore better off finding a story with a strong plot, only a few characters, plausible dialogue, and not too much "psychological" action.

Once you have chosen the story, decide what the treatment of it will be. The *treatment* is a synopsis of how the writer "sees" the film. From this, the *storyboard* is drawn up, and with it the *film script*. When the locations have been chosen the *shooting schedule* can be drawn up. Choose the locations with as much care as the story itself because they greatly affect the look of the film. They should have adequate light and be free of onlookers, cars, planes and all unwanted noise.

Locations
It is a good idea to take polaroid pictures of locations as reference material, both for the script and the storyboard.

The original story

Henry James' story *The Middle Years* can be used to show how interior life is expressed and visualized on film. It is an account of an ailing but inspired writer, recuperating in Bournemouth, a seaside resort in England. Here he receives a copy of the last book he will ever write. The opening scene is as follows:

"The April day was soft and bright, and poor Dencombe, happy in the conceit of reasserted strength, stood in the garden of the hotel, comparing, with the deliberation in which there was still something of languor, the attractions of easy strolls. He liked the feeling of the south so far as you could have it in the north, he liked the shady cliffs and clustered pines, he liked even the colourless sea. "Bournemouth as a health resort" had sounded like a mere advertisement, but he was thankful now for the commonest conveniences. The sociable country postman, passing through the garden, had just given him a small parcel which he took out with him, leaving the hotel to the right and creeping to a bench he had already haunted, a safe recess in a cliff. It looked to the south, to the tinted walls of the Island, and was protected behind by the sloping shoulder of the down. He was tired enough when he reached it, and for a moment was disappointed; he was better, of course, but better, after all, than what? He should never again, as at one or two great moments of the past, be better than himself . . ."

Dencombe stares at the sea, observes a group of figures and opens his parcel.

Plan out the shooting locations with the story in mind. Make a note of the times of day when the light is right, and check with any property or land owners that permission will be granted to film at the times you have in mind. If you intend to film with a tripod in a street you may need to check beforehand.

The treatment

The scriptwriter's task is to rearrange the chronology of the story so that flashbacks, memories and the preoccupations of the characters are comprehensible to the film audience. It is sometimes necessary to add small actions to link scenes, but avoid adding extra dialogue.

It is Bournemouth in the late 1890s. An early spring day. We see the sandy cliffs over the sea, across which a postman is riding, whistling as he goes. He tethers his horse to the gatepost of the hotel, and walks across the garden with his bag of post. As he does so, a gentleman walks out of the hotel, leaning on a cane, and walks unsteadily towards the pines. The postman calls him and tells him that there is a parcel for him. Dencombe takes it, and walks down towards the right of the hotel, to a bench overlooking the sea. He is in his late fifties, but gaunt and clearly in bad health. The effort of reaching the bench has almost exhausted him. He looks closely and with a trace of humor at a group of three people on the beach below – a young man, a young girl, and an older woman – then picks up the packet. We read the address (Bournemouth) and the name. He opens it, and we see the brand new book title, *The Middle Years*, by Dencombe himself. This will act as the main title for the film. He leafs through the book, then sighs to himself "Ah, for another go, ah for a better chance." (the original dialogue).

This is a more compressed treatment of the opening scene than you would actually have, but it gives some idea of the technique involved, The chronology has been straightened out, and the postman is now first. The name, profession, and location of the writer are now both seen and heard, and his frailty is visible.

The storyboard

The next stage in the production of this adaptation is to convert the treatment into a full script. This is also the stage to look for a location and to produce what is known as a "storyboard". This is a large grid of drawings representing consecutive frames, each of which stands for one shot. In the case of a complex shot, such as a track or a pan, more than one frame can be used. The sketches can be very rough as their only purpose is to help you visualize a shot and to see it in relation to the shots on either side (see below).

1a,b Pan from sea to hotel   **2** M.S. over shoulder

3 M.C.U. of Dencombe   **4** C.U. of Dencombe   **5** M.L.S.

6 M.S. Dencombe   **7,8** Dissolve to L.S., becoming M.S.

9 a,b Over-shoulder subjective L.S. Zooms to M.L.S.   **10** B.C.U. of Dencombe

11a,b Shot over shoulder. Zoom to C.U. of book   **12** Pan from hands to B.C.U.

The film script

Scene 1. Exterior. Day. Early morning, early spring. 1893. Location: Hotel Splendide, near Bournemouth, England.

Shot	Action and dialogue	Description
1a,b	Camera pans from the sea onto the land to show the postman on horseback riding along the cliffs. As he comes to the hotel he dismounts and walks in with his satchel.	L.S. pan right to left
2	In over-the-shoulder shot we see the hotel door towards which the postman is walking. Dencombe emerges from the door. He wears a top hat and frock-coat. He looks around and walks right.	M.S.
3	Reverse two-shot with Dencombe in foreground. He walks towards camera, not seeing Postman. Postman calls "Mr. Dencombe, Sir!" Dencombe turns.	
4	Dencombe sees the postman, looks pleased, and exits left.	B.C.U. Dencombe
5	A distant conversation ensues which is heard only as a civilized mutter. The postman hands over a parcel and exits right. Dencombe exits left, parcel under his arm.	M.L.S. two-shot towards gate
6	Dencombe looks around reflectively to decide on the direction for his walk: exits right.	M.S. towards hotel.
7	Dencombe walks towards the sea. Dissolve to:	L.S. towards sea
8	Dencombe now approaches bench, panting heavily, and flops into the seat. The package is on his knee.	L.S. becoming M.S.
9 a,b	Reverse over-the-shoulder shot reveals sea, beach, and three figures. Camera zooms into M.S. of the group – one old woman, one young companion, and a man behind, reading a red book.	L.S. zooms into M.S. three-shot.
10	Dencombe's tired face twitches with a knowing smile, and he looks down at book.	B.C.U. Dencombe
11a,b	Over-shoulder high shot to show book, which Dencombe begins to unwrap. Camera zooms in to show address (Bournemouth) and then, as the book is revealed, the title (*The Middle Years*) and the author (Henry Dencombe).	M.C.U. zooms to B.C.U. of book.
12	He picks up the book, and as he opens it, the camera pans up to his face. He whispers sadly: "Ah for another go, ah for a better chance!"	C.U. book from *in front of* D., panning up to B.C.U. his face.

Directing the Film

The director's job in a fictional film is to compile the shooting script, choose locations, rehearse and direct the actors, select the shots, and to tell everyone else (lights, sound, camera) what to do and when. In short, he or she is busy. However much collaboration has gone into the preparation of the film, only one person should be responsible for the creative decisions during shooting. Even in a small film where the actors are your friends and where helpers are few and far between, you will find the job of directing much easier if your eye is not glued to the eyepiece of the camera. However, many one-person, single system movies are made, when the only directions the filmmaker has to give concern the actors (see right). In any larger unit, involving double system sound, it is well worth following the standard professional procedure for shooting which includes making a shooting schedule, slating the shots and checking continuity.

The shooting schedule

No film is shot in the same order as either the film script or the final, edited film. This is inevitable because of the difficulty of coordinating actors, weather, camera and lighting with the actual order of the script. It is common sense to shoot the film in whatever order is dictated by location, props and weather. For example, while the camera is in position for the first shot it may be possible to shoot the last scene of the movie as well. Similarly, an actor who has finished one scene may well be able to shoot another, if his or her clothes, the lighting and the weather are right.

It is because of this that the *shooting schedule* is drawn up. This is one of the most important parts in the preparation for filming. The schedule simply breaks down the original film script into convenient work sessions for the camera. It groups together all the scenes to be shot in one location, all the actors for each scene, the estimated times for each scene, the camera equipment, the props and the costumes required. It should also note the dates for the scenes, the times the crew and actors should arrive, parking and possibly accomodation arrangements. Travel and time details may be unnecessary if the cast is your family, but they are essential if you are coordinating a number of people. If one person is late, the whole day's shooting may have to be abandoned. As soon as you have decided on the shooting order, type it out and give a copy to everyone concerned for their comments and suggestions. You are sure to have missed something, and you should be grateful for advice before you actually start shooting.

The final stage of preparation is a *shooting script* which is a kind of breakdown of each day's work. In the shooting script drawn up for the Henry James adaptation (see p. 147), it would obviously be easier to shoot shot 10 and then shot 12, rather than moving the camera around to the back of the actor in between. The shooting order for the whole sequence would probably be: 1, 2, 4, 3, 5, 6, 7, 8, 10, 12, 9, 11. If this sequence was used you would need an extra dummy book, *The Middle Years*, for shot 12, since the parcel is still closed in shot 9. The costumes would have to be organized as well as permission for the location.

From film script to shooting script
The film script breaks the action down into scenes and shots. The type of shot is noted, with a brief description of the action. The shooting script organizes these shots into a logical shooting order. It is basically a list for the director, camera operator, actors and crew.

Film script
1a Pan starts from the sea
1b Pan continues to hotel
2 Two-shot over shoulder
3 M.C.U. of Dencombe, turns
4 C.U. of Dencombe
5 M.L.S. of Dencombe
6 Dissolve to L.S.
7 Dissolve to L.S.
8 Dissolve to M.S. of Dencombe
9a Subjective L.S.
9b Zoom into M.L.S.
10 B.C.U. as Dencombe smiles
11a Over shoulder zoom
11b End zoom on book
12 Pan to B.C.U. of Dencombe's face

Shooting script
1a, b Linked by pan
2, 4 Same direction of shooting
5, 6, 3 Same direction of shooting
7, 8 Same location
10, 12 Both C.U. and same location
9a, b, 11a, b Zoom, linked by same location

Dealing with actors

If you are an amateur filmmaker you will probably be working with actors you have known for some time. You will probably have less choice than you would have liked, but if you do have a number of applicants for a part, ask them to audition for you. Give each actor a script and get them to read a section of the text. Then, even if you have enjoyed their reading, ask them to modify it slightly. In this way you can assess their flexibility, their willingness to take direction and their feelings about you as a director. These factors are often as important as their raw acting ability. Another important factor is their appearance. If a person looks right on film you can often disguise their lack of ability, but no amount of acting brilliance can save a miscast face. A great deal of movie acting is in fact a form of typecasting: finding the right person for the right part.

Talk to each person about the part they will play, encourage them to think themselves into the character's state of mind, and then organize a script reading for the whole cast. Afterwards, discuss the characters, the dialogue and the plot. There will almost certainly be things to change in the script as the actors get used to their parts. There may also be some changes in the cast needed, and it is at this stage that these decisions should be made rather than later in production.

Start rehearsals as soon as you have finalized the cast and the script. Try to rehearse at the proposed location, but if this is impossible measure it up and duplicate the equivalent acting space at home or in a hall. Either arrange the furniture to match the layout of the location or stick masking tape to the floor to mark the position of the walls. Whatever you do, you must rehearse the dialogue to establish the identities of the characters before you get to the location for shooting. To guarantee that the camera is accurately focused for the "take" give an actor a mark by sticking a small piece of masking tape on the rehearsal floor. During filming he will have to stop exactly on that mark, without looking down (see p. 71).

Directing actors is not as autocratic as it sounds. You should always ask actors for their own interpretation before offering your own. It may be helpful for the actor to give his interpretation *only* through movement – for example, by lighting a cigarette or stroking a cat. Use description and analogy to explain how you want them to perform and only demonstrate your own version as a last resort. Make your suggestions as precise and practical as you can and always encourage the actors. Acting can be very depressing when it is not going well, and constant criticism makes matters even worse. You must learn to recognize the point beyond which a performance will not improve (you may also discover that the first of fourteen expensive takes was the best after all). Although learning lines is not as difficult for the movies as it is on stage you should insist that the actors know the whole of the scene in which they are involved. Without this you will lose both the flow and the pace of the action. This is particularly true if you are using the technique of one master shot plus intercut close-ups (see p. 80).

Preparing to shoot

Your shooting schedule will have told you which actors and what equipment you need at specific locations. Set up the camera and if necessary, the lights. Check that the camera, the recorder and the links between them both are running efficiently. Rehearse any camera movements thoroughly, especially the more complicated shots like tracks and pans. Finally, check the clapper board (see right). The clapper board serves two purposes: it guarantees sync and it identifies the shot in both sound and vision.

Rehearse the actors both with and without the camera and check that the sound recordist, the camera operator and the lights are ready. Shout both "Standby" and "Quiet please everybody", then start the sound and camera. In Hollywood, this somewhat dramatic moment would be heralded by "Lights!" "Sound!" "Camera!" and "Action!", but in any smaller-scale film unit it is more likely to consist of some mutually acceptable phrase such as "turn-over." When both sound and camera are running to speed and when (if you are using a sync cable, the sound recordist has confirmed a sync-pulse) the shot can be slated by the clapper board operator. He or she holds the clapper board in front of the lens so that it can be read. This will usually mean refocusing the lens and may, very occasionally, mean using a special light. The shot, scene and take numbers are then announced within range of the microphone, and the clapper is snapped shut. The whole procedure takes about eight seconds, and is called *slating the shot*. The shot may also be marked at the end. This is sometimes a preferable arrangement if your subject is very nervous, or if there is any danger of unsettling them. Hold the clapper board upside down and as the board is shut say "End board".

When the clapper is clear of the shot and the camera is ready for shooting, shout "Action" for the shot to begin. During the shot watch the action closely, but keep an eye on the camera. Stand as close as possible to the camera lens, with your eyeline matching that of the camera. By watching the zoom you can see if the zooming speed is right, and by watching a pan you can see if there was a perfectly smooth movement. In either case, you may need to use some tact if you want to re-take a shot for technical reasons without offending the cameraman.

If the shooting is mute (*mit-out sound* or *MOS* in the USA), you can give running instructions and cues to the actors from behind the camera during the take, and you can also talk to the camera operator. This is one reason why many Italian films are shot entirely mute, with the sound added later at a post-synchronization session. When filming sync sound you still cue an actor to begin a speech or a move by standing in line with them, but make certain that you are not visible in 'the shot, dropping your hand at the appropriate moment. You can also work out a series of codes with the camera operator before the shot: for example, one light tap for a close-up, two taps for a mid-shot and three for a long shot. This is particularly useful for interviews.

The clapper board
The beginning of every "take" should have an identifying shot of a clapper board. Write the movie's name, the roll number and take number on it with chalk. The board provides a common start mark which guarantees sync between sound and picture.

The scene breakdown
This tabulates the action for each scene in the movie and contains all notes of costume, characters, props and continuity.

Continuity in shooting

In large productions people are assigned to look after the script and the continuity of the movie (they were originally referred to as script-girls and continuity-girls). They keep track of the action in relation to the script and make sure that consecutive shots, which may be filmed days or weeks apart, will intercut flawlessly (see p. 86). If you are filming out of sequence, or even if you plan to intercut two consecutive, complex actions, you must take similar precautions and this can only be done at the time of shooting. Every time you pass an anticipated cutting shot in the course of a shot, note the relative positions of the cast, their expressions, what they are holding and the clothes they are wearing. A Polaroid camera is handy for taking quick reference shots.

For example, in the storyboard on p. 147 there are two areas in particular where continuity could be a problem. These are between shots 2 and 3, and between shots 11 and 12. In the first case, the postman's position in relation to the gate must be the same in both shots. In the second, Dencombe's hand and the wrapping paper must be the same in relation to the book. Other areas which might cause problems are the weather and pace. Be sure that the sun is not shining in one shot and hidden in the next. Watch out for this in shots 9a and b. Also, when cutting from a long shot to a close-up of a person walking, try to match the pace of the footsteps in the two shots. This would occur between shots 3 and 4.

A *shot list* will also help you keep track of the shooting (see p. 214). This gives details of the film-roll number, the duration and description of each shot, the comments made at the time relating to each take and any notes on continuity. These notes might be on the weather, time of day, clothes, action, make-up and eyeline. This is obviously a full-time job, so if someone offers to do it for you, accept. Even if you are doing the filming by yourself, write down a short description of each shot, noting the best take and the content of each roll or cartridge as they are changed. Both cans and cartridges can be labelled with white tape and marked with a fiber-tip pen.

The scene breakdown

Title: The Middle Years

Location: Bournemouth, England. The Hotel Splendide

Time of day: Early morning

Estimated shooting time: 2 hours

Scene sequence number: 5

Characters: Dencombe, postman

Dress: Early twentieth century

Synopsis of the action: M.L.S. (two-shot) of two men talking

Props: Walking cane, postman's bag, parcel

Additional considerations: Crossing the line. Dencombe should enter from the right of the frame since he left the previous frame from the left.

Atmosphere and Character

Instead of intercutting from long shot to close-up or mid shot, it is often possible to use one single extended tracking shot to vary the distance between the camera and the subject throughout a take. If the actors, too, are moving, then you are dealing with a very subtle and complex camera movement. The results can be dazzling.

One of the greatest modern masters of this technique is Bernardo Bertolucci. But he is well aware that the technical problems are such that they can threaten to constrain the actors. He said recently that he likes to give his actors freedom to improvise – within certain limits, obviously. But supposing the actor suddenly decided to walk out of shot? That, said Bertolucci, was a matter for intelligent compromise. In extended shots such as these, the camera can itself become an active participant in the drama. And the very need to reconcile the demands of the camera's movement with the freedom of the actors can produce a tension that lends the shot its power or distinction.

An example of how this works in practice can be seen below. This is a selection of frames from the final *third* of a very long tracking shot (the whole shot lasts a full 3 minutes and 4 seconds). The film is *The Spider's Stratagem* (1970). Athos, the young man, has returned to his home town to discover the truth about his father's assassination. He is both confused and seduced by his father's former mistress, who sits at the center of a complex web of lies and deceit.

1a ⊘ 1 min 30 sec. He enters shot from left

1b She removes his jacket

1c He turns and faces her

1d They walk off

Creative camera movement
In the course of this shot, Bertolucci uses the camera movements to enhance the dramatic tension of the scene. The woman removes Athos's jacket, we are in close-up, and she repeats "You can't go away any-more!". At this point she leads him through the door-way. The camera follows them.

Tracking through the corridor
During part of the track through the corridor, the couple actually move out of the frame altogether – this is perhaps what Bertolucci meant by an "intelligent compromise" between spontaneity and formal camera movements. It is as though we, in the shape of the camera, are actually rush-ing after them from room to room. The sudden long shot (1h) provides visual variety and anticipates the long, in-tense close-ups to come.

1e They vanish through door

1f Camera remains on window

1g Camera follows

1h Camera reveals her sitting

1i She walks around him

1j She circles him again

Focusing for a camera tracking shot
One of the major problems encountered when tracking is that the focus varies con-stantly at different points in the track. Normal practice is to rehearse the shot very slowly (a "stagger-through" checking the focus at each point, and marking the focus points on the lens barrel. The camera assistant (or "focus-puller") then operates the focus during the shot.

1k Still circling him

1l She passes in front of camera

1m She moves behind him

The spider
In these shots, as the woman attempts to persuade Athos to live with her, she circles around him as though she were literally ensnaring him in her web. The camera has now moved into close-up again to match the renewed intensity of this moment in the scene

1n He walks away, she remains in frame

1o She talks off-screen

1p She follows him

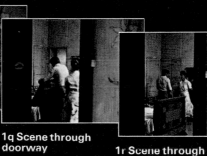

1q Scene through doorway

1r Scene through doorway

1s She turns

1t She walks through doorway, in front of camera

1u Camera tracks with her

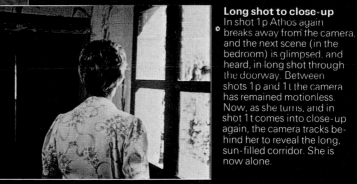

1v She looks out of window

Long shot to close-up
In shot 1p Athos again breaks away from the camera, and the next scene (in the bedroom) is glimpsed, and heard, in long shot through the doorway. Between shots 1p and 1t the camera has remained motionless. Now, as she turns, and in shot 1t comes into close-up again, the camera tracks behind her to reveal the long, sun-filled corridor. She is now alone.

Summary
Even in this brief section of the single shot, we have seen three distinct sections of close-ups interposed between long shots and mid shots. Also, the lighting balanced for daylight because of the windows in shot 1w, has remained even; the focus has been accurately maintained; and the movements of both camera and zoom have been perfectly coordinated with the action. This is an outstanding example of unobtrusive technique.

1w She passes through doorway

1x She walks out into sun-filled corridor

1y Camera follows

Creating Suspense

The melodramatic sequence on these two pages comes from Carol Reed's *The Third Man* (1949). Three separate groups of people have mounted an ambush for the elusive Harry Lime. Reed establishes the scene by intercutting shots of the waiting soldiers and the deserted Vienna streets, and then builds up a carefully controlled atmosphere of suspense. The pacing of the sequence, achieved largely by skilful editing, is masterly. A regular cutting pattern of tighter and tighter close-ups, broken once by a long, continuous shot, is finally brought to a climax, and the tension released, as the shadow is revealed to be not Lime, but a balloon-seller.

1 ⏱ 3 sec Martins looks left

2 ⏱ 8.5 sec The street

3 ⏱ 2.5 sec Martins looks right

4 ⏱ 3.5 sec The street

Martins in the café
The sequence begins with Martins (Joseph Cotton) waiting in the Café Marc Aurel. In the background is heard the slow zither music that haunts the film. The shot is tilted. The camera establishes first Martins' view out of the window to his left (shot 2), then to his right (shot 4).

5 ⏱ 3.5 sec Waiting German soldier

6 ⏱ 1.5 sec The empty street

7 ⏱ 1.5 sec German officer

8 ⏱ 2 sec The empty street

9 ⏱ 2 sec Waiting German soldier

10 ⏱ 2 sec Alleyway

The waiting ambush
Progressively larger static shots of the soldiers waiting for Harry Lime are intercut with point-of-view shots of the empty streets to build an atmosphere of distorted tension.

11 ⏱ 2 sec Waiting German soldier

12 ⏱ 2 sec Empty alleyway

13 ⏱ 2 sec Close-up of German officer

14 ⏱ 2 sec Empty street again

15 ⏱ 2 sec Martins still waiting in the cafe

The café (left)
The camera cuts back to another shot through the café window, taken from the same position as shot 1. Martins waits, morosely pondering his coffee.

The shadow appears (right)
The camera shows the soldier, as in shot 5, but from further away. He moves suddenly as if he has noticed something. We cut to his view across the street. A huge shadow appears against the side of a building.

16 ⏱ 2 sec The soldier moves

17 ⏱ 2 sec Shadow appears

18a ⏱ **15.5 sec German soldier**

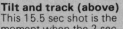

18b Camera tilts slowly down

18c Tilt continues

18d Camera tilts and tracks in

18e Track in to reveal British officer **18f Two British officers wait**

Tilt and track (above)
This 15.5 sec shot is the moment when the 2 sec cutting rhythm is broken. A long track reveals the two British officers waiting in the shadows.

Suspense increases
The tension now centers on the growing shadow. Seen from the same camera angle as shot 17, it now advances and spreads menacingly across the wall. The German soldier turns as he spots it, so does Martins from his table in the café. The same music is still playing in the background.

19 ⏱ **2 sec The shadow in the street grows**

20 ⏱ **1.5 sec Soldier looks around**

21 ⏱ **2 sec Martins looks around**

The climax (right)
We cut back to the same camera position as shot 19, the view across the empty square. The suspense reaches a peak as the figure on the wall grows even larger.

22a ⏱ **9 sec The shadow advances**

22b The balloon- seller appears

The dénouement (left)
The built-up tension breaks as the shadow rounds a corner, disappears and is revealed to be an innocent balloon-seller. At the moment he appears, the music changes character and tempo, becoming almost a waltz.

23 ⏱ **3.5 sec British officers**

24 ⏱ **1.5 sec German soldier**

25 ⏱ **2 sec Martins turns away**

The pace relaxes (left)
The British officers look quizzically at each other, and retire again into the shadows. The German soldier, too, moves back. Martins turns his head away from the window, the music slows down, and the pace of the whole sequence relaxes, in preparation for another climax to come.

Filming Comedy

Early comedy films were almost exclusively composed of visual gags, but with the coming of sound, the comedy films of the thirties veered largely towards verbal humor – one tends to remember what W. C. Fields or the Marx Brothers *said* rather than what they did. In films such as the famous Ealing comedies that emerged during the fifties, there is more of a balance between the visual and the verbal. You cannot apply general rules to comedy, but in this extract from *The Lady Killers* (1955) certain devices are obvious: the build up of the gag through reversal of our expectations; rapid intercutting; good sound effects; strong images and, above all, clarity and timing.

1 ⏱ **6 sec Professor Marcus and Louis on railway bridge**

2 ⏱ **2 sec C. U. Professor prising away ladder**

3 ⏱ **2.5 sec Cut to L.S.**

Louis: "What are you doing?"
Marcus: "I won't keep you, Louis"

4 ⏱ **1.5 sec C. U. Professor's hand again**

5 ⏱ **2 sec Cut back to L.S.**

6 ⏱ **1 sec Train approaching**

7 ⏱ **2.5 sec As shot 4**

8 ⏱ **1 sec Cut to L.S.**

Setting the mood

In this sequence, Louis (Herbert Lom) is hanging onto a ladder above a railroad line. Professor Marcus (played by Alec Guiness) is trying to kill him, as he has killed both his other hopelessly incompetent accomplices – by dropping him from the bridge into the empty wagon of a passing train. In a series of rapid and precise close-ups we see the ladder, the approaching train and the struggle for the gun. The train whistle just precedes the sonorous "clang" as the ladder gives way.

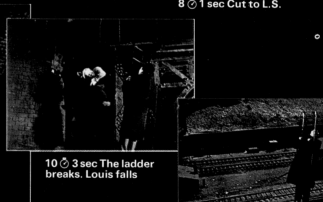

9 ⏱ **1 sec C. U. Louis grabs the gun**

10 ⏱ **3 sec The ladder breaks. Louis falls**

11 ⏱ **3 sec Reverse angle of Louis falling**

12 ⏱ **1 sec Gleeful Professor**

13 ⏱ **4.5 sec Ladder begins to return**

14 ⏱ **1 sec Professor ready to kick**

Rapid intercutting

Shots 10 to 14 show the first of several classic "reversals" – just as we are convinced that Louis is doomed (11), with the train approaching and Professor Marcus triumphant (12), Louis starts to roll back again (13). However, the professor again manages to kick him off (14). Between shots 2 and 17, only one shot is longer than 3 seconds, and most are much less.

Louis' sticky end

There are more comic surprises in store. Louis is doomed (15) but he still has the gun. Professor Marcus has forgotten this. Louis fires (16) and the professor's shock is registered (17). Louis vanishes into the mist, followed by a huge "bong" as he lands in the train. Professor Marcus, who seems unhurt, stands victorious under a signal (19) gazing down to where Louis has fallen (20). He is counting his chickens before they are hatched.

16 ⏱ 1 sec Louis fires as he falls away

15 ⏱ 2.5 sec Professor Marcus kicks Louis away

17a ⏱ 1 sec Reaction shot

17b ⏱ **Professor's shock at being fired at**

18 ⏱ 4 sec Louis falls

19 ⏱ 4 sec Professor stands

20 ⏱ 5 sec Rail trucks

21 ⏱ 4 sec As shot 19

Just deserts

These last shots complete the series of rapid comic reversals and, indeed, the film. As the music rolls on, the train suddenly starts, and just at the end of shot 23 the music abruptly cuts. The signal falls (24) and hits Professor Marcus on the head (26). He joins poor Louis in the wagon and the train steams away.

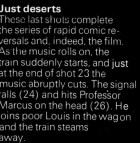

22 ⏱ 8 sec Train moves

23 ⏱ 3.5 sec Professor

24 ⏱ 1.5 sec Signal falls

25 ⏱ 0.5 sec Signal hits Professor Marcus

26 ⏱ 1 sec He falls

27 ⏱ 2 sec Body falls into truck

28 ⏱ 5 sec Train pulls away

155

Staging Fights

All stunts are potentially dangerous; if misjudged they may be lethal. Always plan the stunts out fully and rehearse them until all your actors understand what is required of them and can perform their parts perfectly. Never take chances or overstep your knowledge.

Staging a fist fight

A fist fight is the stunt most easily performed by the amateur filmmaker. First, plot each punch, slap or flying bottle, right down to the collapse of the actors. It is unnecessary to have one sustained master shot filmed from one camera angle. Instead, shoot each phase of the fight from a wide range of heights and angles. This allows for the rapid intercutting necessary to produce successful, action-packed fights (a certain amount of undercranking increases the speed of the action, but this effect should not be overdone). To really convey the physical sense of the action, use a hand-held camera and get in close to the actors. Shoot the fight without sound so that you can give directions during the fight. All grunts, crunches and shouts can be added after editing. In a fist fight make sure that the actors just miss each other, and that the chin receiving the punch reels away at the right time. The subsequent sound effect will complete the illusion, especially if there is a change of shot at the moment of impact.

Parts of the set can be constructed so that they break safely on impact, your actors can then break chairs, overturn tables, and smash through windows during the fight. Construct "prop" windows with balsa wood struts, loosely slotted together and held in place with putty, never nails. The glass can either be specially made "soft glass" or previously ripped plastic. As long as you shoot at an angle, or only shoot the window as the actor goes through it, the fact that the glass is already broken will not show up in the finished film.

Staging a sword fight

The rules for planning and filming sword fights are the same as those for fist fights. However, there is even more reason to plan and execute the fights carefully because of the points on the swords or daggers. "Property" knives with retractable blades should be used. These have parallel sides, short, blunt points and are spring-loaded so that the blade retracts into the handle. If the blade is constructed with a tube down the middle then the handle can be filled with blood. This will squirt out when the blade retracts. It is more difficult to film a stabbing with a sword or rapier because their blades cannot retract. Film the fight from a suitable angle, cutting to the loser just after he receives the final thrust. He will appear to be run-through if two half swords are fitted either side of his body.

It is also possible to fake arrows or knives flying though the air and thudding into their targets, using a whip pan. First, fix a duplicate knife or arrow into the target. Set up the camera so that you film the real weapon being thrown, well to one side of the actual target. Whip pan rapidly from the real weapon being thrown and stop when the duplicate weapon and target are in frame. No one will notice that they differ.

Staging a fist fight

1 In preparation for the punch the assailant grabs the victim, pulls back his arm and clenches his fist.

2 As he moves forward the victim tries to pull away from him. He moves back and prepares to recoil.

3 The assailant, careful to miss the victim's jaw, punches past his chin. The victim recoils as if hit.

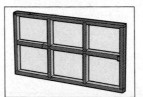

Props
Props, designed to break easily, are sometimes necessary in fight scenes to protect the actors. Their value can be seen in the shot from *Shane* (below left).

Sword fights
The two shots (below) are from Ridley Scott's *The Duellists*. Apart from the skilful sword work, one of the most important factors in the scene's success is the sound track. This accentuates the noise of the clashing swords and when combined with very atmospheric lighting makes a frighteningly realistic fight.

Arrow trick
This trick relies on camera work to produce its effect. It is simple to produce and can be done with complete safety for the actor, who is positioned with an arrow in place. The camera whip-pans from the arrow being fired and stops when it reaches the second arrow in the target.

Producing Explosions

Regulations concerning the acquisition and use of explosives vary from place to place so you *must* make the relevant inquiries before you begin. The type of explosives an amateur filmmaker will use are the "deflagrating" variety, like gunpowder. When these are ignited they go off with a loud bang. The powder should either be packed into a cardboard tube and sealed to make a "thunderflash," or contained in an open "flash pot" which directs the blast upwards. Gunpowder is fired by a *pyrofuse*, which is a small inflammable charge. The pyrofuse can be triggered electrically with either batteries or magnetos. The amount of explosive needed must be determined before you perform the stunt. This means testing a small amount and gradually increasing it until you have the effect that you want. Always test a blast inside if it is designed for use indoors, and *never* connect up the firing batteries before wiring up the charge, even if you are sure that they are switched off. Finally, never store any powder near the scene of your test explosion. And if you have any doubts at all about using explosives, seek professional advice.

To produce the effect of bullet-hits small plastic-covered charges are placed under the ground or just under the surface of scenery. A string of them, detonated in sequence, produces a machine-gun effect. They should only be placed on an actor's body when absolutely necessary. In these cases special shielding must be worn by the actor to protect him or her from flying debris. Put the bullet-hit between the actor's clothes and a plastic blood bag, and place both of these on top of the actor's protective shield.

Blank bullets can also be used, but they are dangerous. They should never be fired at a closer range than 10 feet (3 m) because small particles of copper and wadding can fly out and hit someone. Even out of this range it is best to aim off to one side of the victim.

Faking explosions

If you do not want to risk using explosives you can quite easily fake them. For example, say you want to show a bottle being hit by a bullet. Take a small mouse trap and tape a strong nail onto the trap bar so that it extends about $1\frac{1}{2}$ in. (3.8 cm) beyond the wooden base. Tie a wire to the trap's release catch and set the assembly carefully behind the bottle. On cue, pull the wire; the nail will swing up and smash the base of the bottle. This is even more effective if the bottle is full of liquid. The explosive "bang" will have to be put on the sound track at the dubbing stage (see p. 244).

An equally easy trick is one frequently used in Western fights – the water butt riddled with bullet holes. Drill two holes in your barrel – one in the front (the cork hole) and one about 1 ft (30.5 cm) higher at the back (the pull hole). Cut a piece of cork to fit the bottom hole snugly, trimming it so that it will be flush with the barrel surface. Screw a picture hook into it and thread this with wire, then pass the wire to another hook positioned opposite the cork hole. This wire should then be passed up and out of the pull hole (you may need another hook to help to guide it upwards). Fill the barrel with water, about half way between the two holes.

Simulating bullet-hits
In these shots from Michael Winner's film, *The Lawman*, a protective plate was placed on the actor's stomach, covered by a blood bag, and the small explosive charge detonated.

Producing explosions
The extremely effective explosions (below) were both performed with stunt men. Unless you have expert advice, it is safer not to attempt any major explosions of this sort.

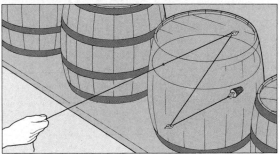

Simulating explosions
It is quite easy to simulate bullet hits, without risking the use of explosives. A nail, on a carefully positioned mouse trap, can be used to fake bottles being shattered (left). Similarly, a barrel can appear to be riddled with bullets by pulling the wire on cue. If the barrel is full of water it will spurt through the hole when the cork comes out (left).

Filming Stunts

The sequence on these pages comes from William Friedkin's film, *The French Connection I* (1971). It is only 13.5 seconds long, yet it has become one of the most justly celebrated car-chase sequences of the recent past. It contains sixteen shots and many of them seem, in the context of the movie, to last a lifetime. Gene Hackman plays the Narcotics Division officer, Popeye, who is chasing a man whom he believes can lead him to the center of a drug-smuggling ring. Popeye snakes through the iron posts of the subway as the suspect edges his way forward through the hijacked train, above, with a gun.

It is essential that each second be carefully scripted and rehearsed. You cannot just put a camera in a car and crash it. The subjective shot from inside the car must match the speed and direction of the exteriors, and the progressively tight close-ups of the cop's face must match, in expression and intensity, the action shots themselves. The complexities of even a very brief sequence like this are such that they are often handed over to a second unit director. He or she will have to clear the police permissions, organize the stunt drivers in their various cars, coordinate the different assistant directors with walkie-talkies, and shoot endless different takes of the same sequence of action.

What lessons are there for the amateur in all of this? First, plan all stunts with great care, preferably with a detailed storyboard (see p. 147). You can get away with outrageous deceits on film if the effect is carefully planned. Next, allow time for lengthy rehearsal before shooting. Finally, use rapid action-cutting and editing tricks to cover those actions which would otherwise be impossible to stage.

Intercutting inserts
This sequence opens with Popeye's subjective point-of-view, shot through the windscreen. It is intercut with a shot of his foot on the gas pedal, then the brake. Needless to say, these would have been shot in the studio. However, shot 3, with the overhead reflections visible in the windscreen, would probably have been shot on location with the camera on the car hood.

1 🕑 0.5 sec **Popeye's view**

2 🕑 1 sec **Foot on gas pedal**

3 🕑 1.5 sec **Popeye through screen**

4a 🕑 6 sec **He sees the car**

4b **He avoids the car**

5 🕑 2 sec **Popeye through windscreen**

The car swerves
After Popeye's dead-ahead shot, we again cut to his point-of-view. An orange VW swerves to avoid him and Popeye himself then swerves to avoid another car. These stunts would of course be performed by highly-trained drivers. The camera might well be undercranked to increase the effective speed through the frame.

The soundtrack
Throughout this sequence the soundtrack consists of incessant squealing of tires and honking of car horns. In fact, a great deal can, and should, be done with sound to strengthen a stunt-sequence. A perfectly innocuous crash can sound like the end of the world if it has the right sound accompaniment. Good synchronization is vitally important.

6 🕑 1 sec **He sees the mother**

7 🕑 0.5 sec **Close-up of Popeye**

The mother and child
The horrific sight of a mother wheeling her pram across Popeye's path (a fast, subjective tracking shot) is cross-cut to a 180° reverse shot (number 6) in much larger close-up than shot 3. Needless to say, there is no baby in the pram, and the two shots have no physical relation to each other. Indeed, it is doubtful if Gene Hackman ever saw the woman standing-in for the mother.

8 ⏱ **0.5 sec The mother screams**

"Crash zoom"
The camera zooms, not tracks, rapidly in onto the mother's face until it fills the frame. For these nine frames – less than half a second – the zoom is as effective as a rapid track, and far less dangerous. This kind of rapid zoom is generally known as a "crash zoom".

9 ⏱ **0.5 sec Popeye swerves violently**

Hits the garbage
Popeye swerves violently to avoid the mother and pram, and in shot 11 we see that he is veering towards a pile of garbage. This subjective shot crosscuts to a head-on view of the car careering towards the camera. In these circumstances it is often best to use a remote-control camera.

10 ⏱ **0.5 Popeye's view**

11a ⏱ **1 sec Car hits garbage**

11b Close-up of car

12 ⏱ **0.15 sec Car rushes past**

13a ⏱ **1 sec Car rushes past**

13b The street

The pace increases
Shot 12 is only 3 frames long. At this point in the stunt it is perfectly possible to include a blurred shot such as this which actually cannot be read in its own right. It is there to add to the sense of violent chaos.

Conveying speed
Finally, in shots 13 and 14 the car rushes past the camera very close to the lens and Friedkin cuts back to Popeye. Popeye looks back over his shoulder, then grimly settles down at the wheel.

14a ⏱ **3 sec He looks around**

Summary
These 13.5 seconds of film contain only four basic elements, but with these simple, meticulously timed and planned ingredients, the stunt is created. In all this, only one dangerous event actually occurs, in shots 11–13, and then it may be presumed that the camera, which the car so narrowly misses, was unmanned.

Filming Sport

Sports movies can provide some of the most exciting footage, but they are difficult to produce well. One of the greatest problems is maintaining continuity in the action. Although cuts can be made away from the action, the restrictions of shooting from one position – which is how most amateurs have to shoot – are considerable. However, there are certain techniques which can be recommended for shooting specific sports.

Filming team sports

To get the best coverage of the game there are certain pieces of equipment you should have. Although you will get a good impression of the game without them, the coverage will neither be as interesting nor as varied. The camera must have a reasonably long zooming range (for example, 8:1), to reduce the disadvantages of shooting from one position. Because you will frequently be working at the telephoto end of the zoom (especially in football coverage) you will also need a tripod and a good pan-head. If possible, use an extended magazine run (200 ft for super 8 and 400 ft or 1,200 ft for 16 mm) to avoid running out of film at a critical point in the match. A single system sound camera also simplifies the sound-track recording, because no slating or additional recorders are needed. For indoor sports you may need an XL camera if the lighting is poor.

Get permission well in advance to shoot the game and arrive with plenty of time to set up. Take adequate filmstock, spare batteries and a gadget bag with the usual accessories (see p. 128). Next, decide where you want to film the match from. To give each team equal coverage set up near the center of the pitch, about one third of the way back into the stands. Make sure that the view is unobstructed and that you do not block the view of someone behind you (if you are directly in front of a pillar the tripod can be as high as you like without affecting anyone else). It may be necessary to buy more than one ticket to be sure of a clear view. For a more dynamic angle, but more biased coverage, set up just next to the goal of your team's opponents – this will give you very powerful shots of your team's triumphs and virtually nothing of their failures.

For indoor sports, also check the type of lighting in advance. If fluorescent lights are in use, either shoot on Type G film or on fast tungsten film with the daylight "85" filter in position, (see p. 92). Automatic metering systems tend to become confused as the camera pans across light and dark areas especially when you are shooting from a high angle onto a shiny floor or icerink, so take an overall exposure reading and lock the aperture at this if the camera has a manual override.

If you can use two cameras set one up in the center and the other by the goal. Both cameras *must* be on the same side of the goal since in a team game the camera positions are governed by the "line of action" (see p. 74), which passes down the middle of the pitch, running through the middle of the goals. To maintain continuity from right-to-left you can shoot from anywhere on one side of that line. Coordinate the two cameras so that they are both filming at the same points in the game. The two angles can then be intercut during editing.

Soccer
All of the action, no matter how many cameras you use, must be strung together without any jump cuts; try shooting long takes so that extensive editing is unnecessary. Use the zoom to vary shot size, but do not "trombone" in and out too much. Make sure you take plenty of cutaway shots – for example of the crowd or the trainer's bench.

American football
You could also begin each shot by panning into the main action from the crowd or from another part of the field. This provides a built-in cutaway at the front of each shot and no editing may be needed to effect the transition. It can however become monotonous if used too frequently.

Filming tennis

In tennis there are only two positions from which you can cover all the action, and those are actually on the "line," at either end of the court (the center position cannot be used in tennis because the speed of the action creates a series of whip-pans). The fact that you are shooting from one position is less restrictive in tennis because the players change ends every two games. The height and distance from which you shoot are essentially pre-determined. The height is determined by the fact that there must be a sufficient gap between the top of the net and the service box for the bounce of the ball to be seen. The distance of the camera from the court is determined by the extent of zoom. Aim to cover the whole court on the wide-angle end of the zoom, without moving the camera. Any further away from this position and the telephoto will be restricted; any nearer and you will have to pan backwards and forwards to follow the action. Remember to take plenty of cutaways – they are just as important in tennis as in any other sport. The score board between games and sets is a very useful bridging device, as are shots of the players towelling down or changing ends. As an alternative approach, try shooting a "sports portrait" of one player and make no attempt to follow the course of the game. In this case you will want to get in close and go for the most exciting shots without regard to continuity.

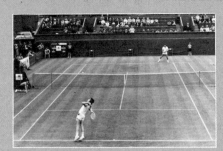

Position
From the central camera position you will not only be able to cover the whole court on a wide-angle, but also, by using the zoom, you will be able to get an acceptable shot of the player at the other end of the court. You can also get a closer shot of the player at the other end.

The service
During a service, leave the zoom quite wide, or you will lose the ball. For a more dynamic view of one player, get down to ground level and shoot from the side.

Cutaways
Cutaways are vital in tennis – as in the making of any film. The scoreboard and the crowd are always useful as punctuations. You can also pan off the crowd onto the game, or vice-versa, to provide a buffer shot.

Filming a Motor Race

If you only have one camera it is difficult to shoot a full version of a motor race since each car will probably be out of sight for most of the time. It is therefore easier to aim for an evocative compilation-film which captures the spirit of the race and perhaps focuses on one or two of the drivers. This means that you will have to move around during the race, so plan your positions beforehand, bearing in mind the "line of action", (see p. 74). This is particularly important in a race because the cars must be traveling in the same direction when you cut from one shot to another. Find at least one position where the cars are actually coming towards you. This is not only visually exciting but allows you to "cross the line" since the change of direction will be visible in the shot, (see far right). Vary the shooting as much as possible, both in content and in the type of shot. Film the

pits, the start, one high speed section, one series of hairpin or S-bends where the cars are slow enough to be visible in some detail, the finish and the lap of honor, but make certain that you shoot plenty of cutaways, of the crowd or the marshals, as these will be invaluable at the editing stage. Mix wide-angle and telephoto shots, and try experimenting with focus – for example fill the screen with the image you want, pulling focus with the action. Go for all the speed, color, noise and action that you can find. Remember that what matters is not absolute "real" speed, but the speed of the image across the screen. A close-up, medium or wide-angle shot when a car is coming towards you gives a much greater impression of speed than a telephoto shot of the same car (see *Movement and focal length*, p. 67). You may have to cheat at the editing stage by using fast action-cuts.

The zoom (below)
To convey the tension of the start of the race the camera zoomed in rapidly on the face of the driver. For this sort of crash-zoom both pre-focusing and a tripod are essential.

The start (above)
To vary the style of shooting as much as possible, set up in at least one position where the cars are coming directly towards you. The position chosen (above) made it possible to follow the cars as they turned the corner.

Cutaways
The wide-angle shot (left) and the crowd scene (right) were used as cutaways in the final movie. They were inserted in such a way that continuity of the film was preserved.

Cutaways

It is essential to take plenty of cutaway shots in any high-speed action sequence. They not only vary the pace of the action, but also help to string the movie together at the editing stage.

Crossing the line

If you start shooting from position A on a sharp S-bend the car will be traveling from left-to-right across the screen. If you pan around to position 3, any change in direction will be clearly visible. But if you have to cross the line, cut when the car is at position 2 and move to camera B. Start with a head-on shot and then pan – the change of direction will be clear, although the car will now be traveling right-to-left.

The pits (left)

In this shot the pace of the action is varied by juxtaposing images of the car back, front and side. The energy and speed conveyed as the mechanics move around the car in the pits is an integral part of the race and balances the speed of the cars.

The presentation (below)

The presentation of the winner's cup, laurels and the bottle of champagne are a classic way of ending a movie on "The race".

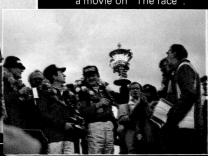

Special Effects

On occasion you will want to control the weather situation yourself – for example, it may be glorious sunshine outside but you want to convey a wet, windy scene. For large-scale *wind* effects use a large, multi-bladed fan, pointed towards the action; for close-up shots just point a cool hair-drier at the subject. Fake *rain* by directing water from a hose into the air, either over the action, or between it and the camera. To simulate rain on windows either hose above the window or fix a perforated water-pipe along the top edge. To produce *lightning*, first paint a lightning flash on black cardboard. Then under-expose a cloudy-bright sky by two or three stops, backwind the film to the middle of the scene and expose the painting for a couple of frames. The most commonly used subsitutes for *snow* are shredded paper, polystyrene balls or salt. The first two can either be dropped from a trough above the action or, like the salt, they can be sprinkled on the ground. For *smoke* you can either hire a professional smoke gun, smother a bonfire upwind of the scene or sprinkle oil on top of glowing charcoal. For a low-hanging *mist* drop dry-ice into a bucket of water placed just off camera, it defrosts rapidly and can be fanned across the scene, or left to float into the shot. Simulate *fire* by hanging red and yellow strips of gelatin in front of your key lights, and shaking them during the shot.

Wind
Position a hair-drier, just off camera, to blow cold air onto the subject's face and head.

Snow
Drop the paper or polystyrene balls from a trough above the set.

Rain
Point a hose directly into the air over the actors. They must look drenched and the ground wet.

Mist
Wear thick gloves and drop a handful of dry-ice into a bucket of water. Fan the mist over your scene.

Raindrops
Spray water from a hose just above the top of the window so that it trickles down the glass.

Fire
Cut some strips of yellow and red gelatin and dangle them in front of your key lights.

Lightning
Superimpose a painted lightning flash on a previously filmed black sky.

Smoke
Place a burning charcoal briquette in a metal container and sprinkle oil on top to produce smoke.

Costumes and Sets

In any film where you cannot use existing locations or props, new ones will have to be specially designed. If possible, make one person responsible for the overall appearance so that you have a continuity of design. Much of the success of movies like *Bonnie and Clyde* or *Barry Lyndon* was due to their unified period look and feel – the settings and costumes were impeccably authentic. The designer should decide which props and clothes are needed for each scene and arrange to have them borrowed or made. Props which cannot be found easily can be made from plaster of Paris, polystyrene or latex. If you are making the costumes be sure that their colors are not too garish and that they are not obviously new. Film is mercilessly revealing in close-up and if you have any doubts about your ability to produce a good version of period costume, you might be well advised to rent the clothes from a theatrical rental agency. These are readily available and are not usually expensive.

Historical costume
In this lavishly appointed set from *Nicholas and Alexandra* the colors of red and blue predominate and they have been used to set off the glittering jewels, table setting and drapes.

Artificial lighting
In this scene from *Butch Cassidy and the Sundance Kid* lighting has been used to create the mood of the set. The warm light on the characters' faces, angled from below, echoes the warmth of a Bolivian evening.

Make-up

Make-up for a film demands a far greater degree of realism than stage make-up. In inexperienced hands excessive make-up can ruin a film, so try to avoid using it if you can. However, make-up is necessary if you want to show an actor ageing, or if you want to alter his appearance. For the best results, consult an expert if you plan to use make-up extensively. The basic techniques for ageing and "deforming" an actor are shown below.

Ageing

1 Clean and tone the model's face. Saturate a sponge with cream make-up and smooth thinly over the face and neck. Blot all over with a tissue.

2 Apply brown shadow either side of the nose, around the eyes, mouth and on the neck muscles. Ask the model to frown and fill in the lines.

3 Take a lighter shade than the foundation and highlight above the shadows. Put white lining color onto the eyelashes, and also onto the pursed lips of the model.

Monster

1 Clean and tone the model's face. Apply a gray or white foundation to the face, neck and ears. Blot with a tissue. Shadow the nose, mouth and forehead.

2 Take a thin brush and apply pink highlights to the previously shaded areas. This throws the shadows into even greater relief, especially if metallic make-up is used.

3 Paint the lips green and spray the hair black with a safe dye. Use black eyeliner to draw in an outline along the hairline to exaggerate the pointedness.

The Holiday Film

Before you leave, make sure that your camera is working properly and check that all the necessary equipment has been packed (see p. 128). Be sure to take plenty of filmstock but check before you buy as some countries have restrictions on the number of rolls that can be imported. Look after the filmstock both before and after exposure (see p. 259). If you are going to be shooting in dusty or sandy conditions pack the correct protective and cleaning equipment. Remember that film emulsion is softer at higher temperatures and therefore scratches more easily. The film is also more prone to shed particles of emulsion as it passes through the gate, so pay particular attention to cleaning this area when changing the film. If your camera has rechargeable NiCad batteries and you are going abroad, make sure that the voltage and plugs of the country you are visiting suit your equipment. If they do not, you will need a transformer and adapter, respectively. If you are traveling by air your baggage will be X-rayed. The machines supposedly operate at low enough levels to allow several examinations without damaging filmstock, but it is safer to carry equipment and filmstock as hand baggage and have it inspected manually.

There are two basic sorts of movie you can make of a holiday: the *beginning-to-end account* and the *single-subject movie*. The first attempts to cover every phase of the holiday while the other concentrates on a specific event or situation.

The beginning-to-end account

The beginning-to-end movie needs to be planned beforehand, and is therefore more time-consuming. Because the movie is meant to show the passage of time, you should take plenty of traveling and transition shots. To convey geographical locations, make the most of shots of road signs, maps, travel brochures and luggage labels. Within this framework of shots aim to show three or four episodes from the holiday that you want to record (it is unwise to show more than this in a short movie because the action will appear too disjointed).

Beginning-to-end account
In the kind of movie which attempts to convey the whole course of a holiday from beginning to end, you will need a lot of linking shots such as these: cars traveling right-to-left and left-to-right; planes taking off and landing; aerial shots; packing and unpacking; road signs passing the car; and so on. These will combine to give a sense of direction to and from the location and thereby give structure to the film.

The single-subject movie

The single-subject movie, because it concentrates on one day or episode, allows you to develop a scene in depth. For example, you might decide to shoot "a day on the beach", retaining the original sequence of events: packing the car, driving, swimming, sunset, return. Alternatively, you could make the whole movie an atmospheric evocation of sea, sand and sun, or even a simple narrative sequence. In this kind of film, it is vital to choose a subject that is lively, self-contained, and that will give plenty of opportunity for character to be revealed. For instance, you might shoot two children playing ball by the water. Shoot both of them together in a two-shot and use this as the master shot. Get close-ups of them both throwing and catching the ball, from the same side of the line (see p. 74). Get cutaways of someone watching further up the beach. To end the movie see if you can find an elegant way of titling it. In this case try shooting the children writing "A day on the beach" for the opening and having this washed away by the sea for the closing title.

Single-subject movie
A typical single-subject movie might be a day on the ski slopes. You should take the obvious precautions such as winterizing the camera and taking plenty of fresh batteries and film. Get all the single shots you can as well as ones which convey the atmosphere. These elements could either be intercut or constructed into the progressive account of one single day. In all these cases you should be careful of underexposing when filming snow scenes.

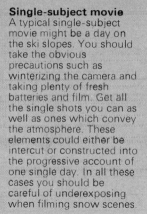

Conveying mood
In this kind of film, you are aiming to create an overall impression of a day skiing. You can therefore combine wide-angle shots of the landscape or the mountain village with crowd scenes and candid shots of the people on the ski slopes. Go for strong shots and sequences that will convey the general atmosphere of the day.

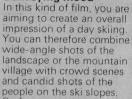

The Travel Film

In the strictest sense, a "travel film" is a documentary in that the subject is the place that you are traveling to and not "you traveling". It is less personal than a holiday film and should be planned much more thoroughly. Decide on the area or town that you want to film and do some research before you leave. Find out about its history, famous citizens, well-known buildings and work out how these elements can best be put together in a film. Do you want a straighforward "travelog", showing the physical structure and layout of the town, its buildings and the people living there, or do you want something more specific? For example, you may choose a region famous for its food or wine. In this case you might concentrate less on the historical aspect and more on the landscape, the restaurants, the chiefs, their clientèle. The final movie may well differ from your original plans, but that is part of the excitment of making a documentary. Do not forget the equipment when you make your plans. Take plenty of filmstock with you, because you may not be able to buy the correct type where you are going, and if you are going to be moving around a lot think of taking a shoulder brace instead of a tripod for quick and relatively steady shooting.

Moghul palace (above)
The aim of these shots was to concentrate on the way sunlight filters through stonework onto the marble reliefs of the interior. Careful metering was needed to avoid over-exposure.

Architectural composition
Try framing a building in an arch which is itself part of the scene. If you use a wide-angle lens keep the camera level to avoid converging verticals.

Customs and character

The experience of travel is in no way restricted to the Baedeker guide: the people, life and landscape of any place, from Damascus to Detroit, are more vivid a subject for the filmmaker than any monument could ever be. But you must be sensitive and responsive to their own culture – in the East many Muslims, especially women, may object on religious grounds to being photographed. Neither bully your subjects nor bribe them. Try to become friends, and ask their cooperation; alternatively, use the very far end of the zoom and if necessary be prepared for a quick getaway. Finally, the more you know about the local life, the better your footage will be.

Filming Buildings

A movie camera is ideal for filming buildings because their three-dimensional form is really only revealed by a camera which moves across, around, up, down and eventually through them. The time of day affects the appearance of a building, especially where there is strong relief on the facade, so choose the time with care. Begin by relating the building to its surroundings, perhaps using a tracking shot, and then start to explore the building. If it has a spire, or if it is very tall, use a tilt to emphasize the height. Film with a tripod and make sure that the camera is level before shooting because the perfect verticals you are filming will reveal any inaccuracies. Use plenty of static shots in between the pans, tilts, zooms and tracks or the film will become fussy. When you shoot details in close-up make sure that it is clear where those objects stand in relation to the rest of the building. Zooms are the easiest way to do this, but they can become tedious. You may prefer to cut straight into one, or a series of, close-ups.

Establishing shots
To establish St Paul's Cathedral in its London setting, you might decide to use a long shot across the Thames, followed by a closer shot which gives an atmospheric impression of Fleet Street.

Track and tilt
This long tracking shot was only possible because of the road running around St Pauls. The camera was pointed out of the window of a smoothly moving car, which gives a dynamic, sculptural view of the building.

Track
You can cut between tracks while they are on the move as long as the movement is in the same direction as it is here.

Cutaways
Having covered the large mass of the exterior, the camera now begins to explore the details. Their location has been established in the earlier wide and medium shots.

Filming interiors

The challenge of filming interiors is that of showing what you want to show without losing a grasp of the building's layout. It is a great advantage if you can follow someone so that the building is seen through their eyes. It will then be credible to use tracking shots to follow them from room to room, and to use tilts or zooms as their eyes move from one object to another. Always aim to make the whole movement through the building as orderly and smooth as possible. Decide before you enter the building where you want the film to finish – for example, when filming in a church you might decide to track down the aisle, slowly tilting up to hold on the roof. Then after a short sequence of details tilt down again to the chancel, ending with a zoom to the rose window.

Tilt
Having tracked into the church and down the aisle in previous shots, a slow tilt up to the roof was used. The camera, with a wide-angle lens, was of course mounted on a tripod.

Cutaways
Having established the overall plan and flavor of the building you can begin to explore its detail: the organ could be used as a cue for a sequence of close-ups cut to music.

Zoom
A musical climax could be constructed so that it ends with a zoom into the dome.

Final shots
Having reached the dome, the camera can now be reversed to give the view from above. The final shot is another reverse angle.

Filming Landscapes

It is often the most theatrical landscapes which attract the filmmaker. But even the rolling chasms, waterfalls and geysers of the American West will become tedious if you have just pointed your camera and photographed a series of repetitive long shots. Plan your shooting as though you were shooting a drama: give it a structure. You might establish your position in the landscape with a pan, then use the zoom to pick out details within the scene (you could also try a slow pan on the telephoto end of the zoom which will exaggerate the distance traveled into the landscape). Build up the film by taking close-up shots, juxtaposing large with small, dark with light.

Even if your landscape does not appear to have an immediate impact, it is always possible to find varied and interesting shots. As a general rule, the weakest position for the horizon is in the center of the frame – so use the "thirds" rule discussed on p. 62. A flat landscape often derives its scale and drama from the sky, so compose your shots with the horizon low in the frame and use a wide-angle lens. Shoot in the early morning or evening, when the slanting light will bring out the full relief of the land. Make use of any changes in the weather and make the most of all cloud formations, possibly using a polarizing filter to darken the sky.

Landscape (left)
The slanting evening light across this Turkish landscape both emphasizes the relief and saturates the color. At noon, this field would be quite unremarkable.

Snow scene (right)
Here, too, the snaking lines of the landscape hold the composition together. But beware of the exposure problems when shooting snow scenes.

Middle Eastern Castle
A zoom can be used to relate detail to the overall large scale landscape – in this case a castle isolated from its setting.

Thirds rule
This is one practical example of the so-called "thirds rule" (see p. 62). The horizon is always at its weakest when it bisects the screen. Here it is placed both high (left) and low (right) to emphasize earth and sky.

Evening scene
Make sure that the continuity of time of day is maintained between shots of a given landscape. Here, all three shots share the same golden evening light.

Grand Canyon (left)
One of the best ways of articulating a landscape film is to make it an account of a journey – for instance a mule trip to the bottom of the Grand Canyon.

Clouds and horses (right)
The natural brilliance of the complementaries yellow and blue give an almost unearthly quality to this Arizona landscape

Farm machinery
Tracking through landscape is only effective if a strong foreground is used to establish motion and scale – as in the case of this farm machinery

Cutaways
The wide-angle shot, left, and the close-up shot, right, were used in juxtaposition.

Wildlife

A wildlife film, whether shot in your back-yard, local park, zoo or wildlife sanctuary, will demand a lot of patience and ingenuity, but the rewards will be enormous. Aim to capture key scenes in the animal's life. For example, a film on a bird might show flying, feeding, territorial fighting, courtship, nesting and the feeding of its young. You may decide to concentrate on one of these aspects, or use them all to show the animal's life over a period of time. Whatever your subject, you must be absolutely familiar with the animal's life style. Do this by both reading about and observing the animal's habits. Get to know where it feeds and at what times, where it nests, and how sensitive it is to human presence. Even if you have chosen a spot where there are no apparent disturbances, you may find that you have to use a hide or some form of lure to get the film you want.

Wildlife equipment

The most important piece of equipment will be a powerful telephoto lens. On super 8 cameras use the longest zoom lens you can (a 60 mm zoom lens on a super 8 is equivalent to a 250 mm lens on a 35 mm still camera). In some cases, a 35 mm still camera telephoto lens can be also be used if your movie camera accepts interchangeable lenses and if you have the correct adaptor. In 16 mm, use a zoom lens of at least 120 mm. Because telephotos show up any camera shake, a solid tripod, preferably one with a good pan head, is essential. Another way of minimizing camera shake, and also of making the image sharper, is to film in slow motion (see p. 188). The camera must run as silently as possible to avoid disturbing the animals. You may need a "self-blimped" camera or a "sound barney". Try to use the longest reels of film you can, as animals have a way of waiting until the film has run out before they do what you want them to. To actually trigger the camera you may find that a remote control device is useful. This can be set off manually using an FM radio attachment or a long cable release (the best cable is an extension vacuum cable which works by air pressure), or it can be set off automatically using a trip-wire or photo-electric cell. Focusing is critical at long focal lengths so pre-focus and adjust the camera to give the greatest depth of field possible. This will allow for any unforseen movements on the part of the animal.

A telephoto lens
A long telephoto lens is not only useful for filling the frame: it can save your life. Even the most picturesque wild animals can be dangerous when they are accompanied by their young. Always keep the engine of your car running and reverse up to the herd.

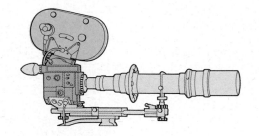

Close-up shots
Here, the long telephoto lens has the added attraction of separating the sharply-detailed whiskers of the lioness from the dark background. For moments like this you will need patience and a lot of film.

Filming herds
For a really sustained sequence such as a lion-hunt, or the study of a herd of impala, you will have to embark on a serious study of the animals' life style and habits. In these cases, you should get all the help you can from the game wardens and be prepared for many long waits.

Setting up for filming

To avoid scaring the animals it may prove necessary to film from a hide. Many wildlife sanctuaries have permanent hides (built for viewing bird's nests, for instance). Alternatively, one of the best and most readily available hides is a car. For some reason, animals will accept the presence of a car, even though there are people visible inside, where they would never accept people on foot. Make sure all the windows are clean, especially the front and rear ones which cannot be rolled down. You should also consider buying a clamp attachment for the car. This can be fastened to the side door or dashboard and provides the solid support essential for telephoto settings. Animals frequently have to be lured to the filming area and the most common way of doing this is with food or water. Place the food regularly in the chosen spot until a visiting pattern is established. Three-dimensional models (like duck decoys) or tape recordings can also be used to reassure the animal.

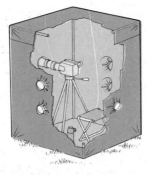

Hides
Hides are easy to build but should be put up as quickly as possible to avoid disturbing the animals.

Using the hide
Hides are indispensable when filming birds, particularly if you want a close view of the nest. Take care not to disturb any nesting bird or it may desert its young. This particularly applies to rare species such as eagles and ospreys.

Building a hide

In inaccessible areas you may have to build yourself a hide. The most common form consists of four upright stakes hammered into the ground, with horizontal cross-pieces at the top. This box is then covered with green or brown canvas tarpaulin so that it blends with the background. One of the sides should have a hole or zipper in it for the camera lens to peep through. The front leg of the tripod may also have to poke through the canvas to get the lens close enough to the hole. Build your hide as quickly and quietly as possible, at least twenty-four hours before you plan to use it. Since your stay inside may be a long one, equip the hide with a folding canvas chair (preferably one with a back), binoculars, notebook, pens, reference books, food and drink. When it comes to filming, one trick is to take an "assistant" with you. When the assistant leaves, the animals think the hide is empty and start to behave as they would normally.

Filming in zoos
You can often get quite remarkable film sequences in an ordinary zoo. Feeding times provide a reliable action sequence with the advantage that you can predict its occurence to the minute. To avoid the bars getting into the shot, shoot with the camera parallel to the cage and use a long lens to defocus them.

Underwater Filming

Underwater scenes are ideal for movie photography. The fluid movements of plant and animal life match themselves perfectly to the smooth tracking shots which you can produce with your own buoyancy.

One of the best introductions to underwater filming is through snorkeling. The only pieces of equipment you need for this are a camera housing, a snorkel, mask and flippers. To shoot you float on your stomach with the camera pointing downwards. Try to find an area which will provide a fair amount of relief and variety. If you find snorkeling enjoyable and want to try actual scuba-diving, you must first become properly qualified (underwater, you must be a diver first and a filmmaker second). This is most easily done by joining a sub-aqua club: they provide the instruction and also the equipment.

Turtle
The camera housing used for this shot permitted the camera's zoom lens to be used in the normal way.

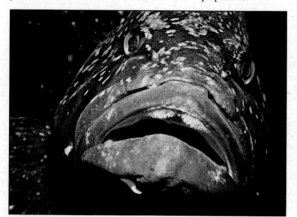

Grouper fish (top left)
For close-ups like this it is best to use a wide-angle lens and get as close to the subject as possible.

Sweetlips (top right)
The colors of these fish were retained by using fast film and bright lighting.

Queen Angelfish (center left)
The brilliant colors of this fish, which are scarcely visible below a certain depth, were revealed by the strong lighting.

Diver (center right)
Because this was shot below 100 ft. (30.2 m) blue was the predominant color. Fast film was used and no artificial lighting.

Diver (bottom left)
Artificial lights are kept away from the camera to minimize fogging.

French Angel fish (bottom right)
The close-up of this fish was taken without artifical lighting. The shot was taken towards noon.

Underwater equipment

For filming underwater your camera must have a watertight housing. Housings range from the clear plastic bag variety to plastic or aluminum cases molded to the camera's shape. They all provide a means of operating the shutter release, and some are even capable of zooming. The housing is fitted with weighted arms so that the whole assembly floats level in the water (this is called "neutral buoyancy"). One of the problems with underwater housings is the condensation which occurs in cold water. It will help to put a small bag of moisture-absorbing silica gel inside the housing. Another common problem, especially with plastic housings, is the reflection in the housing of the camera itself. Either use a lens hood, or put black masking tape on the inside of the housing to prevent this.

The best light for underwater filming is the natural light that you get between ten o'clock and two o'clock, when the sun is almost directly overhead. However, the intensity of the light drops off rapidly the deeper you go, and below about 20 ft (6.40 m) some form of artificial light may well be necessary. Battery lights are the most suitable. Always light your subject from the side to prevent any reflections bouncing back and causing a "foggy" effect (like you get if you use full beam when driving in fog). The lights can either be mounted on a wide bar, at an angle to the camera, or they can be held well to one side by an assistant. Artificial lights reveal all the reds and yellows which disappear below about 30 ft (9.15 m). After 100 ft (30.2 m) greens disappear, leaving blue the dominant color.

Choosing the filmstock

The most commonly used filmstocks are Kodachrome 40 (K40) and Ektachrome 160 (E160). K40 tends to give redder, warmer tones which is useful in depths where red has been absorbed. It is also good for close-ups under artificial lighting. However, if you are planning to dive into very poorly lit shallow areas, or below about 20 ft (6.40 m), it is a good idea to use E160. Its relatively fast speed gives perfectly good exposures at depths of up to 150 ft (27.45 m) with no auxiliary lighting. It should also be used for filming at night, with artificial lighting. Keep the camera on its automatic metering system – even if this means getting an occasional under-exposure of a bright object in the foreground.

Filming underwater

When you first get into the water check your housing carefully for any leaks. Next, test that it is neutrally buoyant and that it hangs motionless in the water if you let it go. Guide the camera in front of you in a steady glide to produce the underwater equivalent of a tracking shot. Stick to a wide-angle setting, use plenty of close-ups and mid-shots, and move towards your subject slowly and steadily. You will get the best color results by keeping as little water between the camera and the subject as possible. Keep an eye on your film counter – since 50 ft (15.55 m) film does not last long. When you get out of the water to reload or store the camera, make certain that you wipe the housing carefully before opening it. Rinse it thoroughly in fresh water before putting it away.

Focusing underwater

Objects underwater always appear nearer than they really are because they are magnified by about a quarter. This is due to the "refraction", or bending, of the light rays as they pass through the water. The focal length of the camera lens is increased so that a wide-angle gives a normal image, a standard lens gives a telephoto one and the telephoto lens becomes unusable. For this reason always use the widest lens you can (or a wide-angle, aspherical attachment, see p. 185). It is easier to focus using the focusing screen in the viewfinder rather than the focusing scale, because of the refraction problem. However, if you must use the scale, set it at roughly two thirds of the actual distance. For example, if the object is 30 ft (9.15 m) away, set the scale for 20 ft (6.40 m).

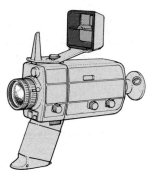

Eumig Nautica
This watertight camera can be used without a housing.

Canon Underwater
This super 8 camera is fitted in a traditional plastic housing.

Lionfish (top right)
This highly poisonous Lionfish was shot in East Africa. On this occasion you might well prefer a longer lens.

Divers (below left)
These divers, on their way to investigate a wreck in the Bahamas, were shot from below with the sun directly above them. This gave the silhouette effect.

Feather star (bottom right)
A high-speed black and white film was used. The light was coming from behind the subject, giving high relief.

Close-up Photography

Macrophotography

Macrophotography is a method of filming extreme close-ups to produce a magnified image of the subject. Many super 8 cameras have a "macro" setting on their zoom lenses which allows subjects to be filmed at very short distances with high magnification. The exact technique varies from camera to camera, but usually when the zoom lever is placed in a certain position the "macro" setting is engaged. This moves the rear group of lenses inside the camera further away from the film plane. The further away they are moved, the greater the magnification. With the lens on "macro" you cannot zoom; the zoom lever is used for focusing.

If your camera does not have a macro lens you can use *close-up* or *diopter lenses*. The advantage of these is that you can still use the zoom. They screw into the filter threads of the lens and come in varying degrees of magnification (from $+1$ to $+5$). Two or more can be used together, with a cumulative magnifying effect. Place the strongest lens nearest the camera, with the convex surface of additional lenses towards the subject. If your camera has an interchangeable lens you can use a *bellows unit* or *extension tube* to produce the same effect. Unscrew the lens and fit the bellows or tube between it and the camera body. At large magnifications the depth of field is very shallow, so you must use the smallest aperture possible and focus very carefully.

Bellows

Diopters

Macro setting

Lily (top left)
A close-up diopter lens was used for this shot.

Butterfly (top right)
Two diopter lenses were used for this shot.

Bee feeding (bottom left)
To reduce the swaying movement of this flower the camera was overcranked slightly.

Dewdrop (bottom right)
This leaf, protected by a windbreak, was shot with the camera on macro.

Microscopy

Some super 8, and almost all 16 mm, cameras can be made to fit onto the eyepiece of a microscope using a specially designed adapter. Alternatively, if the camera has a removable lens, the camera body can be fitted directly to the microscope adapter. In this way it uses the microscope's own optical system. For support, use a copying stand or a tripod with the camera pointing downwards between the legs.

Microscopy
These thyroid sections were stained with fluorescent dye. A copying stand was used to keep the camera completely rigid. The lens, with diopters attached, joined onto the microscope with an adapter. The set-up was lit equally from either side.

How to set up for a macro shot

At large magnifications the movement of a swaying flower or an insect scurrying up a branch will appear unrealistically fast. To correct this either steady the subject or overcrank the film (see p. 188). Steady a flower branch by securing it to a garden cane, positioned out of the shot, or build a clear plastic windbreak around the subject (the shallow depth of field will keep the plastic out of focus). Alternatively, overcrank the camera by about 8 fps. Bear in mind that the depth of field will be reduced because of the larger aperture required by this technique. Set up your camera on a tripod with a cable release to minimize vibration. A minipod or "high hat" is most suitable for extreme close-up work.

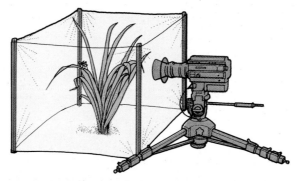

Macro set-up
The camera was securely attached to a tripod, and angled down towards the bush. A length of clear plastic was set up around the bush to act as a windbreak.

Bush cricket (left)
Two close-up, or diopter, lenses were used together to shoot this insect. Because these lenses were used, the camera was still able to zoom in on the cricket's head. A small aperture is best used with diopter lenses, since this gives maximum depth of field.

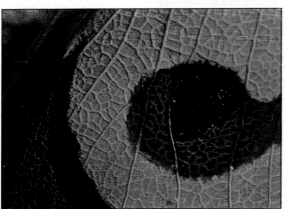

Moth wing (left)
This moth was shot using a +5 diopter lens. This gave a large magnification of the markings and veins on the wing.

Chameleon (right)
The camera, with its macro lens setting, was set up in position on a tripod. A cable release was used to avoid disturbing the animal.

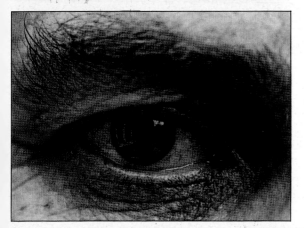

Eye (left)
A camera, with an extendable bellows tube, was used to shoot this eye. It was shot outside and no additional lighting was needed.

Dragonfly (right)
This dragonfly was shot with the camera on its macro setting. No additional lighting was necessary.

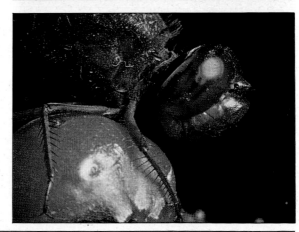

Aerial Filming

Aerial shots are ideal whenever you want to show the layout of a town, landscape, or large building. They are also effective for tracking moving objects – for example, a herd of stampeding animals or cars moving around a race track.

The biggest problem for the amateur filmmaker is the expense of chartering an aircraft. The one you choose will depend on your budget. The helicopter is the movie-industry's vehicle for filming because of its versatility of movement. Fixed-wing airplanes, although more accessible to the amateur, present two problems: they fly too fast and cannot hover. However, they can bank 360° so a subject can be held in the center of a shot while it is filmed on all sides. Only film on clear, unturbulent days and try to shoot in the early morning. Shoot into the light to give the image good relief, and to guarantee that the shadow of the aircraft is not visible.

Film with the aircraft door open, so you can look down with an unrestricted view, and secure both yourself and the camera to the plane's body. One difficulty with aerial photography is the vibration caused by the aircraft. The best way to minimize this is to use a vibration isolation mount, which insulates the camera from the operator and the aircraft. The alternative is to hand-hold the camera. When you hand-hold the camera, avoid telephoto lens settings, which dramatically increase camera shake. Instead, get the aircraft close enough to the subject and use a wide-angle lens.

For a slow, floating shot, overcrank the camera and use a wide-angle lens. If you want a dramatic shot get close to the subject and use the speed of the subject. This is especially effective when the foreground falls away to reveal a vista beyond (as when shooting over the lip of a canyon, or over the top of trees).

Vibration isolation mount
This mount isolates the camera from both vibration and the vagaries of aircraft motion. The zoom and focus may be servo-controlled.

Hatfield house
For this kind of zoom-out it is essential to overcrank and to mount the camera securely. You will have to zoom in and wait until the helicopter has entered a patch of steady air before zooming out using the servo-control. The effect of such a zoom can be quite dramatic, though less so than moving the aircraft itself to change perspective.

Wase rock (top left)
Aerial photography gives an incomparable sense of scale, but beware of intercutting a series of shots facing the same way out of the aircraft. They become monotonous.

Mount Kenya (top right)
Some landscapes are either invisible or inaccessible from the ground. It is essential to brief the pilot and to rehearse before shooting.

Palmanova (bottom left)
The impact of the plan of this town is only really revealed from the air, making it an ideal subject for aerial photography.

Castle (bottom right)
Flying rules vary, and you will almost certainly need permission to approach buildings closely.

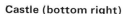

SPECIAL
TECHNIQUES

"The only technique worth having is
the technique you invent yourself"
Jean Cocteau

Special Filter Effects

Many spectacular effects are possible with the aid of gelatin or glass lens filters. In general, gelatin filters are slotted into a holder held in front of the lens with an adapter ring. Glass filters generally screw onto the lens but, like gelatin filters, they can be made to fit a variety of lenses with the use of different sized adapter rings. Filters absorb some of the light passing through them and therefore reduce the amount which reaches the film. To compensate for this, the exposure will have to be increased. The degree of increase required is known as the *filter factor* (see p. 94).

Lens

Lens

Adapter ring

Filter

Holder

Filter

Retaining ring

Attaching the filter
The glass filter, far left, is screwed onto the front of the lens. The gelatin filter, near left, is dropped into a holder which is attached to the lens with an adapter.

Polarizing filters
These filters eliminate reflection from non-metallic surfaces such as glass, plastic or water by allowing light to pass through only at a certain angle. They also reduce haze and darken blue skies. Fit the filter and rotate it to the correct position before taking any meter readings. When panning, you will get a variety of effects.

Diffusion filters
These filters give a glamorous effect while maintaining a sharp image. They bleed light from the highlights into the shadow areas and they reduce overall contrast. They are most effective on a glittering, high-contrast backlit subject.
    As an alternative, spread petroleum jelly onto an ultra-violet filter until it gives the required effect. Never put jelly on the lens.

Fog filters
These filters give the illusion of fog without destroying definition. The effect is similar to, but more pronounced than, diffusion filters. They are available in different densities and the effect can be controlled by lighting and exposure.

Graduated filters
These filters can be used to produce a dramatic sky without affecting the tone and exposure of the rest of the scene. They have a tinted half which diffuses into clear glass and although the boundary of the two halves is usually placed on the horizon, the filter can be twisted so that it is either vertical or diagonal. The tinted half is usually neutral density gray.

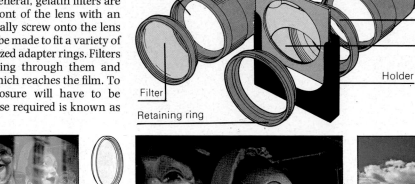

Color filters

On color film, these filters can be used to alter the natural color balance of the scene. Deep color filters give very interesting results when used on high-contrast or backlit sources. The overall color will be that of the filter, plus an amount of black in certain darker areas. However, pale filters give a subtle overall tint to the scene and thus "warm up" or "cool down" the colors in the frame.

On black and white film, a yellow filter is often used to darken a blue sky and a green filter to brighten foliage. To lighten a specific color, use a filter of the same color; to darken a color use a filter of the complementary color.

"Day for night"

A blue filter used in bright sunshine with the camera under-exposed two stops produces the effect of night time. Shoot directly into the sun to "rim-light" the subject to give the high-contrast effect of moonlight.

Color spot filters

Color spot filters produce a softly graduated color around the outside of the picture and a clear circle in the center. The best results are gained by using these filters with a wide aperture. The narrow depth of field throws the hard edge of the filter out of focus and gives a softly diffused effect.

Dual color filters

These filters, as the name implies, produce a two-colored image. Once fitted to the lens, the filter can be rotated so that the division of colors lies horizontally, vertically or diagonally, according to the effect desired. Generally, the wider the aperture and the longer the focal length, the more graduated the effect of the two colors will be.

Special Lenses and Attachments

There are various special lens attachments available, all of which can be used to manipulate the image on the film. The *prism* lens has a multi-faceted surface and produces two types of pattern – radial and linear (that is surrounding, or parallel to, the central image). The *starburst lens*, as its name implies, produces a starred effect as it picks up highlights of reflected light. A diffraction lens is similar, but the highlights are colored like spectrums.

Split-field diopters allow for focusing on two separate planes at once, thereby overcoming depth-of-field problems. *Ultra wide-angles* and *extreme telephoto* lenses can both produce dramatic effects. Ultra wide-angle lenses and attachments are particularly useful when shooting in restricted spaces, since they greatly increase the angle-of-view of modern zoom lenses.

Adjusting the lens
Rotate the attached lens until you achieve the desired effect.

Attaching and adjusting the special lens
Prism, starburst, attachments and split-field diopter lenses either screw directly onto the front of the lens or screw onto a suitable adapter. They can be used alone or, when there are threads on the front as well as the back, can be used in conjunction with other lens or filter attachments. If you are using a camera with a reflex viewfinder, the effect you see will be the effect that you get on the film. In the case of starburst and diffraction grating lenses the attachment should be rotated as you look through until the desired positioning of the highlights is reached. Extreme wide-angle and telephoto lenses usually interchange with the regular lens of the camera. However, where the camera's lens is not interchangeable, a converter attachment can be used to adapt the existing lens.

Radial prism lens

A radial prism lens produces duplicate images in a circular pattern. The lens may have between three and six faces, each of which produces a separate image. If a colored filter is  used with the prism the image will appear tinted. If you want a static image, fit the prism lens into position on the camera and leave it in this position. If you want to produce movement during filming, rotate the lens in its mount as you shoot. There is no need to adjust the exposure when using the lens.

Radial prism lens
The faceted surface of this lens produces three images in a radial pattern. The central image is static, but the surrounding images can be made to move by rotating the lens.

Parallel prism lens

Parallel or "repeater" prism lenses produce up to five adjacent duplicate images. One half of the lens is faceted and the other half is plain. The lens can be rotated so that the faceted 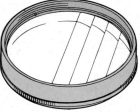 half lies at any angle, thus giving a horizontal, vertical or diagonal effect. To produce a sharp picture use a short focal length and a small aperture; use a wide aperture for more diffused images. Colored filters can be placed in front of the prism lens to produce tinted images. There is no need to adjust the exposure when using this lens.

Parallel prism lens
The faceted surface of this lens produces three parallel images. The colors, right, are very subtle, but the composition has been given weight by using the multi-image effect.

Split-field diopter lens

A split-field diopter allows you to focus on two subjects at once – one very near the camera and one a long way away. The lens consists of two halves – the curved half of the lens is  an ordinary close-up lens, and the other half is made of plain glass. Set the camera up so that the edge of the half lens coincides with an equivalent line in the scene. This way the lens can be used either horizontally or vertically, and the borderline between near and distant focus will be disguised.

Split-field diopter lens
One half of this lens acts as a close-up lens, the other half is plain glass. To keep the houses and tulips in focus the half lens was attached diagonally, covering the tulips.

Starburst lens

A starburst lens produces star shapes of reflected light. The plain glass surface of the lens is engraved with radiating or cross-hatched lines. The number of star points produced by  the lens depends on the number of radiating lines. The lens is particularly effective when it is used to shoot over water and into the sun, or with candlelight. The position of the highlights changes as the attachment is rotated in its mount and their width increases when the aperture is reduced. It is most effective when used on subjects with small, intense highlights against dark backgrounds and the effect varies considerably according to the aperture.

Starburst lens
A five-pointed starburst lens was used on this subject to highlight the reflections from the water. The effect was heightened by shooting directly into the sun, silhouetting the figure of the man.

Starburst lens
A simple cross-screen lens was used on this night scene to pick up the highlights from the headlamps and street lights.

Ultra wide and extreme telephoto lenses

An ultra wide-angle lens has a very short focal length and therefore wide angles-of-view, resulting in more of the overall scene fitting into the frame. They can be used on any camera that accepts interchangeable lenses. In 16 mm there are 5.7 mm and 5.9 mm lenses (from Angénieux and Kinoptic) which have a horizontal angle-of-view of 90°; and in super 8 there is a 1.9 mm or "fisheye" lens from Karl Heitz with an angular coverage of 197°. On cameras which do not have interchangeable lenses, attachments are available which bring the effective focal length of a standard zoom down to about 4 mm.

An extreme telephoto lens has a very long focal length and therefore a narrow angle-of-view, resulting in a high magnification of the image. Although extreme telephotos are specifically manufactured for movie cameras, it is also possible to use long-focus lenses designed for 35 mm still cameras if your 16 mm or super 8 camera has an interchangeable lens and is fitted with the correct adapter. These give gigantic magnification when used on super 8 cameras. For cameras without interchangeable lenses, telephoto lens converters are available. These screw onto the front of the existing lens and increase the effective focal length.

Wide-angle attachment
An ultra-wide lens attachment such as the one shown above was used to film these camels. Perspective is distorted and the front camel appears much nearer than the distant ones.

Telephoto converter
An extreme telephoto attachment was used for this shot.

In-Camera Effects

Fades

A *fade* is an in-camera trick whereby the image either disappears to leave a black screen or slowly appears out of nothing. Fades are an ideal way of showing the passage of time and the transition from one scene to another and can be made automatically or manually.

In many cameras the variable shutter can be automatically moved by a "fade-control" button and this is sometimes linked, on single system sound cameras, to a corresponding fade on the sound control. In these cases, the fade is especially useful as a way of bridging discontinuous filming on stripe sound. If the camera does not have this automatic facility, but has a variable shutter, then the amount of light allowed to reach the film can be altered by opening or closing the shutter using a lever or drive mechanism (see p. 44). Depth of field is not affected in the case of a shutter fade, since neither the lens aperture nor the focal length are altered during the course of the shot.

Fades

A fade-out is often used to signify the end of a scene. The shot starts with a normal exposure. The light is then gradually reduced until the image disappears.
A fade-in is often used to convey the change from one scene to another. The image gradually appears as the exposure increases.

Aperture fades

If you can close the camera diaphragm manually you can produce aperture fades. To film a fade-out the aperture is gradually closed down to prevent the light from reaching the film; to film a fade-in it is opened up. The effectiveness of a fade depends on the number of stops moved through. For this reason always make the aperture go through at least four stops, starting with the aperture as wide as possible. If the working stop is f8 and the camera only goes down to f22 then the fade to black will be too fast because you are only fading through three stops. Keep the lighting low and use a slow film. A neutral density filter can also be attached to ensure that the camera operates at a wider aperture. This is especially important if you are filming in bright sunlight where, without a filter, a wide aperture at the beginning of a fade-out or the end of a fade-in would result in over-exposure. Remember that altering the aperture during a fade will also affect the depth of field.

Aperture fade

Shutter fade

Fade-out

Fade-in

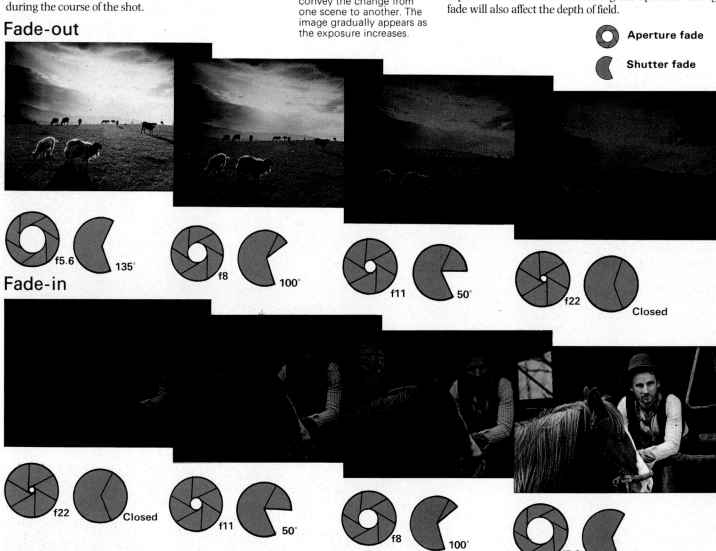

f5.6   135°

f8   100°

f11   50°

f22   Closed

f22   Closed

f11   50°

f8   100°

f5.6   135°

Dissolves

A *dissolve* is a double exposure in which one image melts into another and it is produced by filming a fade-in in the same position on the film as a fade-out. To produce a dissolve on any film there has to be some way of backwinding the film before the second exposure. On some cameras this can be done automatically, but bear in mind that no super 8 cartridges can be rewound more than a hundred frames.

Super 8 backwinder

To produce a dissolve manually, make the fade-out and allow the camera to run for an extra three seconds at the end of the shot. Note the number of frames shot on a frame counter (in some cameras this is a built-in feature) and then rewind the film the length of the fade plus the three seconds, using a backwinder (see left). The fade-in of the new scene can then be filmed "on top" for the correct amount of time.

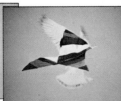

Wipes

A *wipe*, whether horizontal or vertical, is used to obscure one image and reveal another. End the first scene by gradually passing a black card in front of the lens and then start the next shot with it in position. The new scene replaces the old as the card is slowly removed. For variation, the subject of the film can also act as the wipe by passing close enough to the lens to obscure all other objects. The new scene should open with a black screen and then reveal the new setting for the action.

Like all in-camera effects there is an element of risk in producing a wipe. You must be careful that you slide the card across the camera lens at a consistent rate – both when you wipe the first image out, and when you reveal the second. Wipes (and dissolves) for 16 mm can be produced in the laboratory; and, as many labs are now offering this facility for super 8, it is worth bearing in mind as an alternative to the in-camera effect. Optical laboratory wipes come in many different forms, the most common being vertical, horizontal and circular (see p. 83).

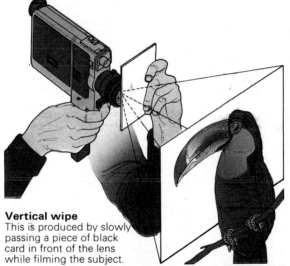

Vertical wipe
This is produced by slowly passing a piece of black card in front of the lens while filming the subject.

Revealing the image
The first image is obscured by passing the wipe from left to right. The new image is a right-to-left wipe.

Superimposition

Superimposition is a double-exposure effect where one image appears on top of another. It can be used for titling by superimposing white lettering over a dark background or it can be used for a wide variety of trick effects. A ghostly figure can wander down a hall and through the wall; fireworks can explode in a church or even underwater; images can be linked in a surreal blur.

In order to make these superimpositions at the shooting stage the film will have to be rewound, so this cannot be done in super 8 cameras without the use of a backwinder. Shoot the initial scene and take note of the frame counter so that you know exactly where you are on the image you have just shot. Rewind the film shot by this amount and then shoot the second scene directly on top. When filming each shot designed for superimposition, remember that the exposure of that stretch of film will be cumulative. If both backgrounds are to be visible in the final mixed shot the exposure of each should be reduced by at least one stop to avoid over-exposure.

Superimposition
The road, left, was shot first. The film was back-wound and the sunset filmed on top.

Slow and Fast Motion

Slow motion

Slow motion is produced by filming with the camera at a faster running speed then the eventual projection speed. This is called *overcranking* and the amount you over-crank depends on the subject and the effect you are aiming at. A fifty per cent increase in frame-rate (from 18 to 27 fps) will produce good effects when used to slow down very fast action like a car crash. But for more exaggerated slow motion you should film at 54 fps or more. This produces such classic effects as a horse floating through fields of swaying grass. Remember that slow-motion filming uses up film very fast indeed.

Slow motion
To produce this slow motion effect of the girl running, the camera was overcranked and the film was then projected at normal speed.

Adjusting the exposure for slow motion

Any change in the frame-rate affects exposure. For example, filming at 36 fps exposes the film to half as much light as filming at 18 fps, so the aperture has to be opened up to compensate for the shorter exposure time. On super 8 cameras this is done automatically, but on other gauges it has to be done manually. Work out the approximate exposure by doubling the chosen frame-rate and treating it as a reciprocal of one second – 50 fps gives 1/100th second; 80 fps gives 1/160th second. (Remember to give shutters on XL cameras $\frac{1}{3}$ stop less exposure time.)

Fast motion

Fast motion is produced by filming with the camera at a slower running speed than the eventual projection speed. It is called *undercranking*. In fact, the reason why the old silent movies appear so jerky is that we project them too fast. Slight undercranking effectively speeds up action sequences like chases and fights, but undercranking by more than ten per cent results in unrealistically fast movement (the most glaring example of this is the 100 mph horses in the Westerns). Undercranking can also be used to film areas that would otherwise be too dark (see *Low Light Filming*, p. 95).

Fast motion
For comic effect, the camera was undercranked to compress the action from a few minutes to five seconds. As a result, the girl appears to blow up the beach ball absurdly fast.

Steadying the camera for fast motion

The slower the camera's running speed the more important it is to use a tripod to avoid camera shake. Below about 12 fps this is essential since any movement of the camera during filming will appear in the final shot as a judder or blur. To avoid this, it is advisable to operate the camera with a remote control mechanism. Use a shutter mechanism operated by a cable release, or a self-timer. Some cameras incorporate complex timing controls which can be triggered by FM radio links (these are especially useful when filming shy wildlife, since the camera can be triggered from a distance).

Reverse action

In some cameras a reverse action effect such as a man diving backwards onto a diving board can be produced automatically. If your camera does not have this facility shoot with the camera held upside down. Cut this part of the processed film and turn it end to end and back to front, so the perforations still run down the same side. Because the film is reversed the emulsion for that shot will be on the wrong side, which may result in a slight loss of focus on projection.

Time Lapse Photography

Time lapse enables you to see events which normally happen so slowly that they cannot be seen by the naked eye, the classic example being a flower bud opening. In this technique one frame is exposed at regular intervals using a single-frame release mechanism (this feature is common to most cameras). The single frame can be exposed manually, with a cable release and stop watch (a very time-consuming task), or automatically with an *intervalometer*. This is a form of clock which operates the single-frame release at a pre-determined interval and can be attached to almost any camera if not built-in. Work out the intervals of shooting by estimating the length of the event to be filmed, and deciding how long you want it to last when projected at the chosen frame-rate. Say the event is going to take seven hours and you want the whole shot to last for 30 seconds on the screen. At 24 fps, a 30 second shot will contain 720 frames. If this is to be spaced over seven hours (25,200 seconds) then each frame will have to be 35 seconds apart. You would therefore set the intervalometer to "trigger" the camera every 35 seconds. At a projection speed of 18 fps you would need to shoot one frame every 47 seconds. It might be advisable to run a test the day before to see how long the actual event will last and work out your mathematics accordingly.

Set-up for time lapse

Time lapse
A room being gradually lit by the rising sun as the candle burnt down was an ideal subject for this time lapse sequence. The camera was set up on a tripod and attached to an intervalometer. This was set to shoot at ten minute intervals. No extra lighting was needed for this shot.

Setting up for time lapse
Set the camera up on an absolutely firm tripod. Do not touch it during filming as even the slightest movement will be visible as a jolt in the final shot. Since the camera will be switched on for the entire filming period, check the batteries periodically between frame exposures. If they do fail, replace them as gently as possible between shots (if the camera is mounted on its handle this may prove impossible without actually moving the camera).

Lighting for time lapse
Time lapse filmed with continuous sunlight presents no lighting problems, and exposure can be left to the automatic metering system of the camera. In some cases extra lighting will be needed. Electronic flash is the most efficient means of lighting time-lapse sequences as it can be synchronized with the flash socket on quite a few cameras but their aperture must be set manually. Find the "guide number" for the film-speed that you are using (from the flash gun manual) and divide it by the number of feet between the flash and the subject. This number will give you the correct aperture. Always use fresh batteries. As electronic flash is balanced for daylight, the "85" filter should be in place in the camera when you are shooting on tungsten film.

The locked-off camera

This simple comic effect can be produced without having to edit the film and involves stopping or "locking off" the camera. It can be used to make twenty people walk into the same telephone kiosk or a man walk behind a tree in evening dress and reappear in rags. Set the camera on a tripod and use a cable release mechanism so you can avoid any camera shake. After the first part of the action, stop the camera, prepare the second part of the scene, and go on to film the rest of the sequence.

Models and Miniatures

By filming with models and miniatures, it is possible to show elaborate or unusual sets without having to go on location or spend vast amounts of money.

Static models

Static models can be used in conjunction with a fully-sized set by placing them between the camera and the rest of the scene. They can either be suspended above the camera (as in an extra part of a vaulted ceiling) or supported with wooden poles, set wide enough apart not to appear in the frame (as in an extra part of a wall). The advantage this has over a glass shot, which is used in a similar way (see p. 194), is that a convincing model can be constructed more easily (though more laboriously) than a realistic painting on glass. Also, the model is automatically lit in the same way as the rest of the scene. The camera can pan, tilt and zoom, so long as it is mounted with the center of the tripod directly under the focal plane. Tracking is not possible however, and a very good depth of field is essential to hold both the model and the scene in focus.

Models can also be filmed on their own so that they form the whole set and it is in this way that most amateur moviemakers will use them. Almost anything can be done with model sets – space stations can be explored or whole towns destroyed – with no danger and little expense. What is more, the camera can move in any way that you want, so you can track, tilt, zoom and pan, depending on the effect desired.

How to build a model set

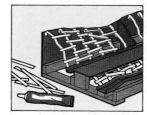  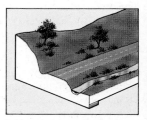

1 Build a framework of wooden sticks and then cover it with chickenwire to give the rough contours.

2 Drape burlap over this. Stiffen with plaster of Paris so that you have a firm foundation.

3 Use dyed green sawdust for grass, cellophane or glass for water, and card, tin or plastic for buildings.

Space station
This miniature set was lit from one side and shot from a low angle to appear more realistic.

Moonbase
In this model set, left, the hills were made from polystyrene, the buildings from pieces of tin can and cardboard, and the moondust from wood shavings and flour. It was made by the BBC special effects department and was shot against a black background.

Space station
The depth of the model's framework can be seen in this picture which also illustrates its scale in relation to the man. It was shot against a black background to represent the night sky, with beads for stars.

Moving models

The moment a model begins to move, some compensation has to be made for its lightness or lack of mass. This lack of mass affects both the speed and the way in which the model moves – for example, real cars do not bounce backwards off walls, nor do real ships bob up and down in choppy water. The solution lies in the structure of the model and in the speed of the filming. First, build the model as large as possible. The larger the model, the more realistically it will move and the more convincing it will look because of the amount of detail possible. The second thing to do is to slow down the action by "overcranking" (i.e., by increasing the frame-rate, see p. 188). The rate of increase is governed by the scale of the model, and it can be worked out using the graph on the right. For example, for a ship built to the scale of 1/16 (1 in. to 16 ft or 2.5 cm to 3.7 meters) the frame-rate must be increased by four. If your normal shooting speed is 18 fps this means you must shoot at 72 fps; if it is 24 fps you must shoot at 96 fps. It can be seen that a high-speed camera is essential for good action-filming of moving models. However, beware of too much overcranking as the slow motion can itself appear unrealistic.

The other difficulty in filming moving models, apart from the speed of movement, is the lack of depth of field in the shots. Try to shoot in sunlight so you can use a small aperture, even at a high frame-rate. If you have to shoot indoors, use variable quartz lights (see p. 100).

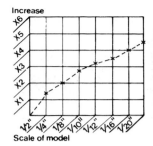

Scale of model

Camera speed adjustments
The increase in the frame-rate is the square root of the scale of the model. The filming speed for a 16-scale model needs to be increased by four.

Space ship (right and below)
The picture, top right, shows the suspended model with the camera on the left and a video view-finder below it. The picture, bottom right, shows the image as it appears on film.

Alien ship (left)
This model, from the film *War of the Worlds*, was shot with strong lighting from underneath.

Landing ship (bottom left)
These model spaceships were suspended above the miniature set-up and lit evenly from each side to avoid confusing shadows.

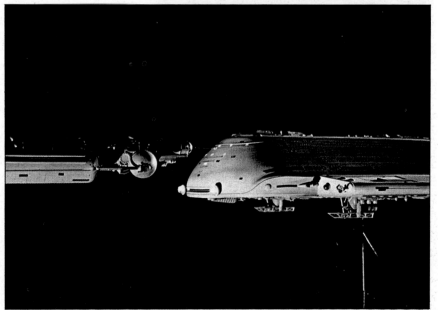

Matte Effects

A *matte* is a kind of mask which is placed in front of the camera lens to screen off part of the action. It enables you to produce simple but dramatic in-camera effects. Mattes are made of black card or metal and come in a variety of shapes. The most common are the keyhole and binocular shapes. You can, however, make your own mattes with black card or sprayed tinfoil which allow you to design your own shapes.

Mattes are usually held in position in front of the camera in a *matte box* or *compendium*. This is usually a bellows-like device which screws onto the filter threads of the lens and has slots at the back or the front for the mattes or lens filters.

To produce a sharp matte image use the smallest aperture you can. This will give you greater depth of field and will guarantee that the edges of the matte are sharp.

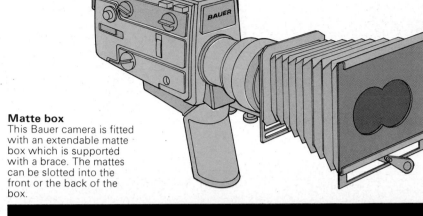

Matte box
This Bauer camera is fitted with an extendable matte box which is supported with a brace. The mattes can be slotted into the front or the back of the box.

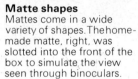

Matte shapes
Mattes come in a wide variety of shapes. The home-made matte, right, was slotted into the front of the box to simulate the view seen through binoculars.

Traveling mattes
This is a laboratory process for superimposing one scene on another. First the background scene is filmed as normal. Then the scene to be superimposed is filmed against a blue screen. In the laboratory all parts of the second scene which are colored blue are replaced with the first background. It is a complex and expensive process and is unsuitable for smaller gauges, although it is used widely in the movie industry.

Composite matte shot
Background and foreground are combined.

Background
The proposed background, in this case Buckingham Palace, is filmed as normal.

The image
The image to be superimposed is filmed against a blue screen.

Split-screen shots

In this effect the two halves of the frame are exposed separately and when screened they form a split picture. The technique is frequently used to show an actor with his or her double, or two people talking on the phone. The position of the mask in relation to the lens affects the definition of the dividing line. If the mask is placed 2 in. to 3 in. (5 cm to 7.5 cm) in front of the lens the join will be very soft; if it is placed further away it will be sharper.

Set the camera and attached matte box on a steady tripod to avoid any camera shake. Put in a mask which covers half of the frame and film the actor in the half of the set still visible. Note the number of frames exposed and then backwind to the beginning of the shot. Place the mask over the other half of the frame and film the second part of the action for the same number of frames.

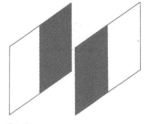

Split-screen
This is an ideal technique for linking two images on the screen. One of the best uses is for telephone conversations. Always make sure that you have your actors "facing" each other.

Multi-screen shots

This technique is an extension of split-screen filming: by progressively masking off different portions of the frame and backwinding each time you can build up a multi-picture that contains any number of different images. This enables you to show many aspects of the action in one image. The amount of space taken up by the individual images depends on the shape of the matte and the way you choose to put them together in the final film. Keep track of the framing of the images by slotting a clear glass reference slide into the matte box. Look through the viewfinder and mark the matte positions.

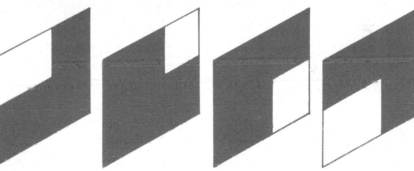

Multi-screen
This is a more elaborate version of the split-screen effect, and can be used to "tell-a-story" in one image. This is done by carefully masking off areas of the lens, as above, backwinding and then filming another area. In this case, two long shots of the city (top left and bottom left) are used to establish the location and set the scene. These are juxtaposed against two details: a close-up of a small girl sneaking a look over a wall (top right); and a shot of two women talking, completely unaware of the camera, outside a doorway (bottom right)

Glass and Mirror Shots

Mirror shots

This technique is used for superimposing ghosts, titles, 35 mm slides or 3-D models and is ideal for super 8 users because no rewinding of the film is necessary. The main set should be in front of the camera and the subject to be superimposed should be to one side. Take a partially silvered (or two-way) mirror and set it at an angle of 45° to the camera. This mirror allows fifty per cent of the light striking it to pass through, but reflects the remaining fifty per cent. For this reason the camera films both the scene beyond the mirror and the reflected side scene. Place the subject at the side against a black background and light it in the same way as the main scene. Both images will appear transparent so try to position the "ghost" image over the darker parts of the scene.

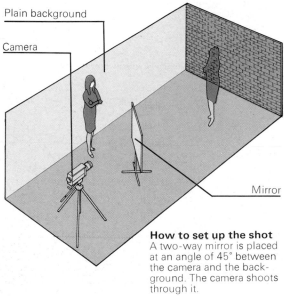

How to set up the shot
A two-way mirror is placed at an angle of 45° between the camera and the background. The camera shoots through it.

Plain background
Camera
Mirror

Mirror shots
This scene was produced using a blank brick wall with the subject set against a plain background.

Glass shots

An inexpensive though difficult way of transforming or adding to the background or foreground of a scene without having to build extra scenery is to use a glass shot. Additional parts of the set are painted onto glass which is then placed between the main scene and the camera. While you paint the scene keep looking through the viewfinder to make sure that color, line and perspective blend completely with the scene. Cut-out photographs, provided they are big enough, are an alternative to this. Whichever method is used make sure that the camera is rigidly mounted on a tripod, that it is kept in a darkened area so that the camera is not reflected in the glass, and that the depth of field is adequate to keep both the glass and scene in focus.

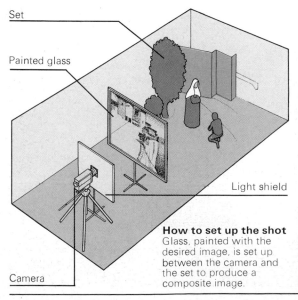

How to set up the shot
Glass, painted with the desired image, is set up between the camera and the set to produce a composite image.

Set
Painted glass
Light shield
Camera

Glass shot
In this scene from *Black Narcissus* all the scenery was first painted on glass as shown

Scenic Projection

Front projection

In this form of projection a highly-reflective glass-beaded screen is used. Set the projector up at 90° to the camera then place a partially silvered (two-way) mirror at an angle of 45° to the camera. The projector beam will reflect off the mirror and onto the screen and the camera will film the composite image through the mirror. By covering parts of the set with the same material as the screen the actors can appear to walk behind parts of the projected background. Say you have a picture with two elements – a house and a hill. This can be projected so that the house appears against an exact cut-out of its shape, while the hill is framed directly onto the reflex screen at the back of the set. An actor can walk out from behind the reflective-covered "house".

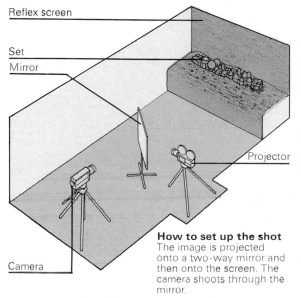

Reflex screen

Set

Mirror

Projector

Camera

How to set up the shot
The image is projected onto a two-way mirror and then onto the screen. The camera shoots through the mirror.

Front projection
This model was filmed with a front projected sky.

Rear projection

In this form of projection the projector is placed behind a high-diffusion screen which is itself placed behind the actors. Amateurs will find it easier to film static back images, using a 35 mm slide projector. The quality of the projected image must be high and the lighting must compare accurately, both in direction and intensity, with the background. If you choose to use a moving background *interlock* (or synchronize, frame by frame) the projector and camera to avoid strobing. Rear projection is commonly used professionally, and is most frequently used to show the view from car and train windows constructed in the studio. It provides foreign locations without traveling and allows hazardous scenes to be shot without endangering the actors.

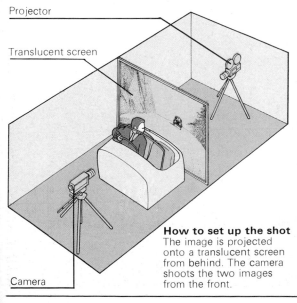

Projector

Translucent screen

Camera

How to set up the shot
The image is projected onto a translucent screen from behind. The camera shoots the two images from the front.

Rear projection
In this shot from *Dr No*, the car chasing James Bond was produced using rear projection.

Basic Animation

Animation replaces live action with the simulated movement of models, drawings or other inanimate objects. It is done using a camera (preferably reflex) capable of single-frame exposure. The scene being animated is filmed, frame by frame, and the position of the object required to "move" is altered slightly between frames. On projection these single-frame shots are seen as continuous movement through the phenomenon of "persistence of vision" in which the eye retains an image for a brief instant so that consecutive images appear to be fused into a continuous sequence. To understand animation you will have to develop a whole new way of considering action. Try watching a movie film frame by frame to see how the movements flow together and how the pace of the action varies throughout its length, then try animation yourself.

Basic equipment
For successful animation it is essential to provide a solid base for the camera so that there is no movement during filming. Any movement of the camera in between single-frame shots will be visible as a "wobble" on the screen. The cheapest way to make certain that the camera remains absolutely still is to set it up on a tripod and use a cable release. You can also use a still camera copying stand. This consists of a flat base board with an adjustable vertical frame to mount the camera on. Specially designed animation stands are expensive, so consider making your own (see p. 198).

Basic animation of shapes
The simplest way of producing animation is to arrange three-dimensional objects on a flat surface and then to move them slightly between frames. When the film is screened they will appear to move about on their own. Always keep the shapes simple and avoid complicated movements. Remember that the more you change the object's position between frames, the more jerky the action will appear. The objects that you can use are limitless: beads, sequins, buttons and pebbles; kitchen items like beans or pasta; even metal objects like paper clips or iron filings. The latter can be used in an imaginative way by placing a magnet underneath the horizontal, flat surface on which they are lying. Movement is produced by changing the magnet's position.

Copying stand
A camera copying stand is ideal for animation. Lights are usually attached to the central bar, at an angle of 45° to the base board.

Tripod
The camera is attached to a tripod and angled downwards to the animation board placed directly beneath.

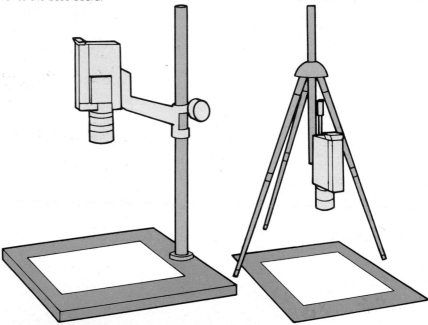

Simple animation
This is one of the easiest ways to produce animation. In the example shown here, various different nuts have been arranged in the shape of a face. The mouth was very gradually moved until it was pulled down into a frown. A couple of frames were shot each time the nuts were moved into the different positions.

Simple animation
A selection of cooking ingredients were used to make up this animated scene. The cloud of flour was gradually moved across the sky. The stages of movement were each shot for a couple of frames. This technique is known as "doubling up".

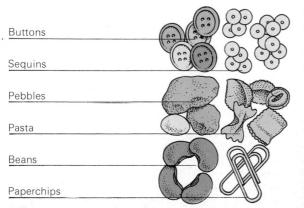

Buttons

Sequins

Pebbles

Pasta

Beans

Paperchips

Paper cut animation

This form of animation is the most similar to cel animation. Paper or cardboard cut-out figures are used and movement is simulated, not by drawings, but by hinging the figures' "joints" with thread. If you cannot draw use cut-out photographs mounted on card; move and film the same way as for basic animation.

Cut out the figure and then hinge the movable parts by taping a length of thread to their undersides, as shown on the right. Secure the main body of the cut-out to the background with non-sticky fixative so that it does not move during filming and place on a horizontal surface. Set the camera up so that it is above the animation and light the scene equally from both sides. For a silhouette effect use simple cut-outs made from thin cardboard but place them on a light-box.

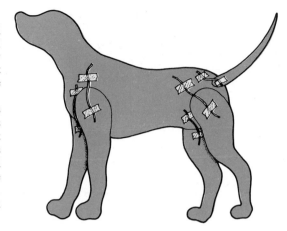

Paper animation
The jointed dog was shot using a tripod pointing downwards. A lightbox could have been used for a silhouette effect.

Three-dimensional animation

This form of animation uses solid figures with limbs capable of movement. Hand-made clay or pipe cleaner figures can be used or, as an alternative, store-bought toys or puppets. These three-dimensional figures are plotted and moved in the same way as in basic animation – that is, by moving them slightly from frame to frame. The difference is that they are filmed free-standing and therefore it is essential that their limbs are stiffened so that they can be left in position and photographed without any movement.

Place the figures on a flat surface and use a blank piece of cardboard or photograph as a background. Set up the camera and tripod and light in the same way as for models and miniatures (see p. 190).

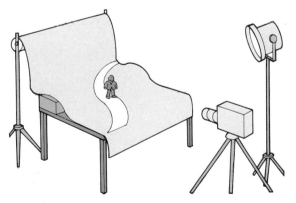

Three-dimensional animation
This clay model was set up against a plain gray background. A white path was pasted on and the figure was placed on the path. The set-up was lit from one side only so that a solid shadow was cast to one side. The figure was moved into "walking" positions, each of which was shot for a couple of frames. This guaranteed a smooth walking pace.

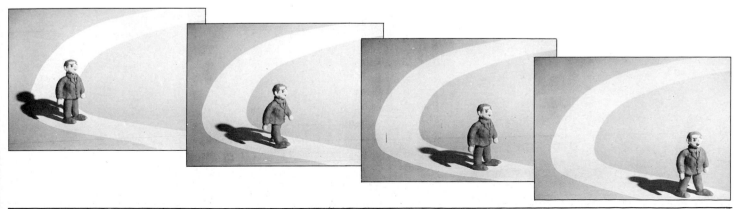

Cel Animation

In this form of animation the images are drawn onto a series of transparent sheets made of cellulose acetate, called *cels*. By using cels instead of individual paper drawings you can avoid having to draw in the background and foreground every time there is a change in position. Where only a small part of the action needs to move between frames you can simply draw this new action onto a separate cel and leave the rest of the scene undisturbed. Do not use more than four cels at a time or the background will not be properly exposed.

The drawings are initially outlined on animation or layout paper, held in place on a *registration pegbar* (this is a two or three pronged device which corresponds to the holes punched along one side of both the paper and the cels). This guarantees accuracy when positioning one drawing in relation to another. Each cel is then placed on top of the registration pegbar and the drawing traced off with a chinagraph or audiovisual pencil. Always wear cotton gloves when handling the cels to avoid any grease marks. When all the cels have been traced in this way they are painted on the reverse side with acrylic paint and placed in the correct order on top of the background, which is also held on the pegbar. The background is usually drawn on cartridge paper and painted with water colors. Crinkled tissue paper can be put between the background and artboard so that any unevenness is smoothed out. The whole assembly is held in place by a piece of clear, good quality glass called a *platen*. The weight of the glass guarantees that no shadows are caused by bumps in the cels.

Animation stand
This Oxberry animation stand has all the features necessary for advanced animation work, and is complete with angled lighting.

Angled light

Registration peg bar

Adjustable column

Camera

Camera bracket

Glass platen

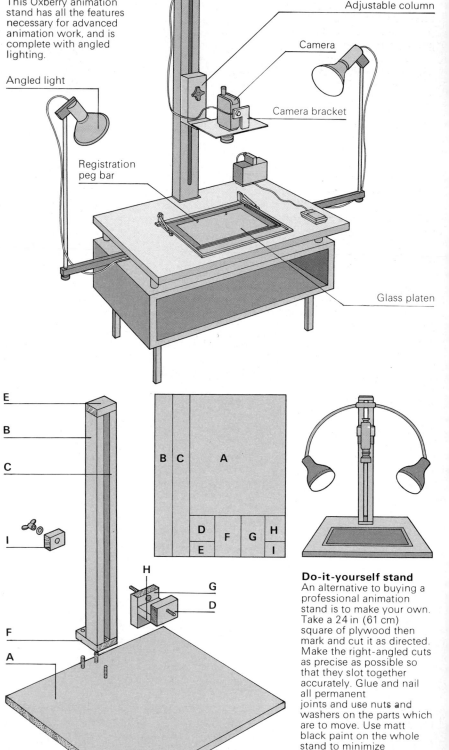

Cel make-up
Here, different areas of the action have been put on different cels so that they can be changed individually. Keep the number of cels constant even if it means using a blank cel.

Do-it-yourself stand
An alternative to buying a professional animation stand is to make your own. Take a 24 in (61 cm) square of plywood then mark and cut it as directed. Make the right-angled cuts as precise as possible so that they slot together accurately. Glue and nail all permanent joints and use nuts and washers on the parts which are to move. Use matt black paint on the whole stand to minimize reflection.

Animated Movement

To make an animated movement look convincing you must know three things before you begin: how long the action lasts in reality, what the major positions within the action are, and how you want the intermediate positions to be spaced out.

Work out how long the action takes by timing yourself as you imitate the movement. Say it lasts half a second. At 18 fps this gives you 9 frames into which the action is to be divided. For simplicity, think of any action as split into sections known as *key positions*. Once these positions have been decided on, the intermediate frames of the section, or *in-betweens*, are drawn in. Each portion of action – from one key position to the next – is known as a *phase*. When the phase from one key position to the next is the same, it is known as a *cycle* (for example, a walker's feet, which return to the same position at regular intervals). Always look for duplicated cycles in the action because they reduce the amount of drawing and therefore save the animator both time and money. Another economy is to shoot two frames per drawing instead of one. This is known as *doubling up*.

Draw the first key position on translucent animation or layout paper, held in position by the registration pegbar (you might find it easier to do this on a lightbox). Then place a fresh sheet on top and draw in the next key position, in correct registration to the first. Continue until all the key positions have been drawn. Then fill in the in-betweens according to the number of frames decided on. When the action is fully roughed out, transfer it to the cels and then paint them (see p. 202).

Key positions
In this animation of a boy jumping numbers 1, 3, 6 and 7 are key positions. The movement looks realistic because the boy's knees are bent in preparation for the jump. As he lands, at 6, his knees bend again. He straightens up at 7 still moving forward slightly.

In-betweens
Numbers 2, 4 and 5 are the in-between or filling shots which guarantee that the movement is smooth.

Cycles
This cycle of drawings can be used repeatedly to show the cat running.

Acceleration

In reality no object moves at a constant pace. There is always an element of speeding up or slowing down. This is conveyed in animation not only by altering the in-between drawings as the action progresses but also by shooting them for a varying number of frames. The slower the action, the less the drawing will change from one frame to the next and the more frames of it there will be. For example, a ball thrown in the air rises at a fast speed then decelerates towards the top of its arc. If the flight takes half a second to complete, at 18 fps you will have 9 frames to distribute across the arc of the ball. Frames 1 and 9 are key positions.

Acceleration
Nine frames have been used to draw the cannonball, but you could use more to emphasize the sense of deceleration – as the ball slows down you could double up the frames. Notice how the ball is elongated to give the impression of speed and how it is flattened when it hits the man's head.

Animation Techniques

Movement and speed

Apart from the number of frames given to each drawing, there are other ways to convey the sense of movement. One of these is to distort the drawing to create the effect of speed. The most common technique for showing this is to elongate the drawing away from the direction of movement. The speed of the character can be exaggerated even more by drawing lines alongside it with flurries of dust or sprays of water behind. Show deceleration by compressing the object. For example, bunch a cartoon car up to half its normal size and hunch the back wheels over the ones at the front. This technique is often known as "squeeze and stretch".

Conveying Speed

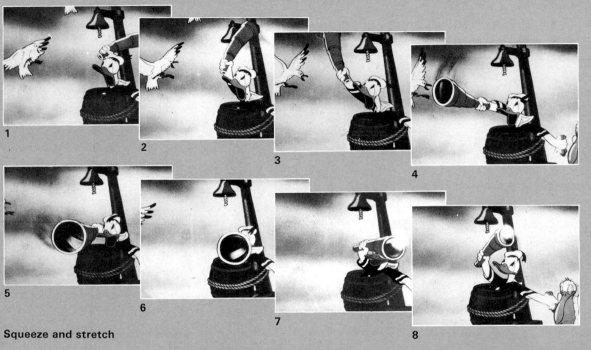

1 2 3 4 5 6 7 8

Speed

This sequence is taken from the early Walt Disney film, *The Whalers* (1938). It demonstrates admirably the way in which speed can be conveyed in the drawing. The telescope has been bent backwards to give an impression of the speed and force with which it is being wielded by Donald Duck. As it accelerates, speed lines have been added behind it. The frames illustrated are all consecutive.

Squeeze and stretch

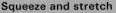
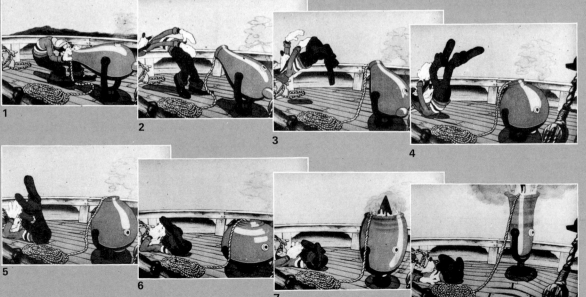

1 2 3 4 5 6 7 8

Squeeze and stretch

This sequence also comes from *The Whalers*. In the second frame Goofy falls backwards and his elongated arms exaggerate this movement. The cannon becomes gradually shorter and fatter as the pressure builds up inside. When it comes to the explosion it is absurdly elongated to convey the power and speed of the ejected anchor.

Transformation

Once you have become familiar with the techniques of animation you should be able to experiment with your drawings. Remember that there is no need to stick to realism: the effects that you produce can be as bizarre as you want them to be. Through your drawings you can visibly transform one image into another on the film.

The effect is easily produced by gradually changing the drawing every few frames. On projection at normal speed the image seems to appear from nowhere. It is very important to use a registration pegbar so that each shot is correctly positioned in relation to the previous ones (see p. 197 for details).

Metamorphosis

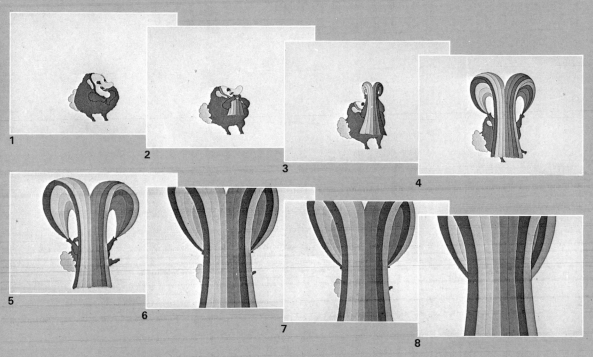

Metamorphosis
The most bizarre effects can be produced with animation techniques, as this sequence from the Beatles film *Yellow Submarine* (1968), illustrates. In this single shot, the cartoon character is transformed into a shower of multicolored ribbons. This is animation at its most abstract, free and inventive.

Editing in animation

In conventional moviemaking the film is edited once it has been processed (see p. 210). This gives the filmmaker much greater freedom because images can be cut and juxtaposed regardless of the order in which they were shot. However, this form of editing is not practical for animation. Because animation is so time consuming and involves so much work, it is essential that all the moves are plotted out in advance and then drawn as the film progresses. This means that there is very rarely any spare footage; editing is built into the planning of the film. Nevertheless, when cutting from one shot to another try to follow the guidlines described on p. 54–86.

Cutting-in
These two shots come from Bob Godfrey's film, *Great* (1976). The first cel shows the scene in long shot, the second in close-up.

Action cut
The cutting point from the big close-up to the long shot has been made at a moment of strong visual action. The frames come from a scene in *Heavy Traffic* (1973).

Filming Animation

Place a clean, grease-free cel on top of the completed drawing. Both layers should be held by the registration pegbar. Carefully trace around the outline of the drawing with a grease pencil, audiovisual pencil or rapidograph. Turn the cel over and paint in the outlines with acrylic paint. It is important to have enough of each color to last the entire film because it is impossible to mix a second identical "blend". The painting should be flat and opaque, so take a well-saturated paint brush and work from the center outwards in a series of pushing strokes. Spray the finished drawing with fixative. Handle all cels with great care, picking them up by their edges, well away from the area containing the drawing. An alternative is to wear cotton gloves.

Before you start to film the cels you must draw up a *dope sheet*. This is the animator's shooting script and it is a visual breakdown of the action. It lists the frame numbers and, against them, the background to use, the order of the cels, zooms, pans and sound effects.

Shooting the film

The actual filming should be straightforward if all of your preparatory work has been done properly. Run through your dope sheet and check that you have all the necessary cels in the correct order for shooting. It is a good idea to stack them by your animation stand in the correct order. Make sure that the artwork base is steady, and that the cels are clean. Wear cotton gloves so that no finger marks are transferred to the cel and be careful not to bend them or the paint might crack. Set the cels up on the animation stand with an 18 per cent gray card on top of them. Take an exposure reading using the camera's built-in meter then fix the exposure in that position using the "exposure lock". The exposure can be left in this way as long as the lights are not dimmed or moved during filming. Zero your frame counter if you have one and tick each frame off on your dope sheet after you have filmed it. Always use a single-frame release to avoid vibration and organize your filming so that you do not have to reload in the middle of a scene.

Zooming

In animation, zooms are done manually so the camera should have a manual zoom lever. Tape white paper around the lens and mark the position of the lever or ring at the start of the zoom. Look down the viewfinder, zoom manually to the end position, and mark it on the tape. The distance between the two marks is the extent of your zoom. For a constant zoom divide this amount into equal portions, then shoot one, two or three frames at a time, moving the lever from one mark to the next.

Panning

To make the image look as if the camera is panning from left to right, the artwork is moved from right to left. Make certain that the background is wide enough to move from right to left without the edges coming into the picture. Mark out a slate along one edge, with an arrow in the center of the shooting bench (see right). Move the background away from the arrow, along the scale – the larger the calibrations the faster the panning movement.

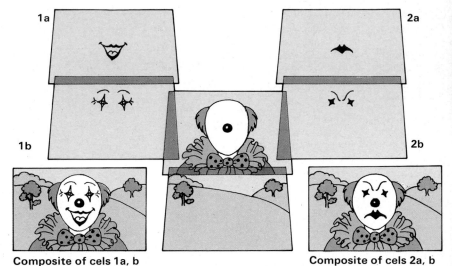

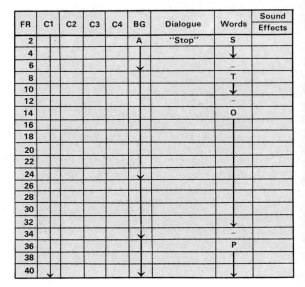

Composite of cels 1a, b

Composite of cels 2a, b

The cel
The expressions have been changed on the cels above with the minimum of work by using the same background and basic face.

The dope sheet
This is an essential part of the planning of animation because it lists the order in which the cels are placed on the background and the order in which they are shot. Sound effects and camera movements are also plotted.

Key
- FR Frame
- C Cel
- BG Background

Panning
This effect can be produced in animation by gradually moving the background in between shots while the cels are held in position by the pegbar. The background is moved betwen tacks.

FR	C1	C2	C3	C4	BG	Dialogue	Words	Sound Effects
2					A	"Stop"	S	
4							↓	
6					↓		–	
8							T	
10							↓	
12							–	
14							O	
16								
18								
20								
22								
24					↓			
26								
28								
30								
32							↓	
34					↓		–	
36							P	
38								
40	↓				↓		↓	

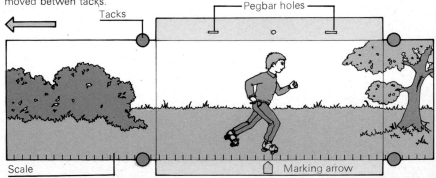

Tacks — Pegbar holes

Scale — Marking arrow

Animated Sound

Sound

Music, speech or special sound effects can easily be added to an animated film. To make animated drawings match a sound track, it is best to pre-record the sound on $\frac{1}{4}$ in. (6 mm) tape before the artwork is done. This should ideally be done on a machine equipped with "synchronized pulse" (see p. 245), which guarantees that the sound recorder runs at the same rate as the projector. Before you start to draw the animation you will have to "break down" the sound. If it is a music track note the changes in tempo; if it is speech note how long each talking part lasts and what syllables it is made up of. One way of doing this is to run the tape through the tape recorder and to time the speech or sound effects.

Alternatively, if the recorded sound is transferred to fullcoat magnetic film (see p. 116), it can be analyzed frame by frame on a synchronizer. The exact sound cues can be written on the shiny side of the "mag. film" with a spirit felt-tip pen or a grease pencil, and they can be referred to frame by frame when you come to make up the dope sheet. You can also use a frame counter and note the frame number of each cue as it passes the sound head on the synchronizer.

Animating voices

First listen to and "break down" the sound track using one of the methods described above. It is unnecessary to animate every vowel and consonant; often, the simpler the mouth actions, the better the results. However, at the moments where the lips meet in pronouncing a *b*, an *m* or a *p*, for example, the drawing should be in perfect synchronization with the sound, because these are the movements which people will notice most.

Pencil in the "key positions" for the movements of the mouth that you have decided are the most important and then add the "in-betweens" (see p. 199). You can make the drawing more realistic if you change the facial expressions according to what is being said. For example, make the eyes larger if the character is scared.

Mouth shapes
For every vowel or consonant there are specific mouth shapes. These can be reduced to nine basic forms – as shown below. However, you will find that it is unnecessary to draw every single letter of a word. You can also save yourself some work by only making the mouth and not the whole jaw move (draw the mouth on one cel and the head on another).

Drawing onto the film

It is possible to produce animation without a camera by drawing directly onto the surface of unexposed film. This technique is unsuitable for super 8, but a film made on 16 or 35 mm can be reduced by optical printing for conventional 8 mm showing. Scratch the image onto the emulsion with a sharp instrument like an awl or stylus or, if you are using clear film, draw onto it with a fiber-tip pen or "blooping" ink. Hold the film steady on a registration pegbar.

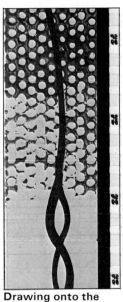
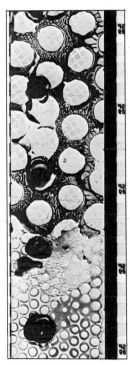

Drawing onto the film
The shapes, right and above, were drawn directly onto the film using blooping ink.

AI E O U WQ

MBP CDGKNR STHYZ L FV

Titles and Titling

All films benefit from well-made titles, whether the title is being used to introduce or end the action, or clarify parts of it half way through. Front titles which are well-composed, short and to the point, will give your whole film a more professional look. The design of the title should suit the subject of the movie – for example, use strong colors and forceful shapes with an action-packed story. Keep the titles simple and unpretentious: *Yosemite* is a more suitable title than *Wonderland of the Sierras*. Make them novel enough to catch the audience's attention, but resist labored puns and quirky in-jokes. Show the titles long enough to be read in comfort, but not so long that the audience gets bored.

If you want to keep commentary to a minimum during the film, or if there is no sound, titles and sub-titles are an ideal way of identifying a person, date or place. Captions like *Meanwhile*, or *1800* can be shown between action shots, or alternatively they can be superimposed, see p. 206.

The End is an unambiguous way of bringing your movie to a close and is a possible way to finish if you are not planning any credits. However, for any film which goes beyond the simple family record, or for one that you want to enter for public showings, it is important that credit be given to the production team. If the movie is a one-person show the credit is sometimes given at the beginning (*A film by . . .*), but normally all credits go at the end. In the interests of democracy, keep the credits the same size and duration, dividing the title cards into the areas of work done – the cast, the writer, the sound recordist and the director.

Lettering

The simplest way to make up titles is to use lettering kits which are produced in a wide variety of styles, shapes and sizes and can be bought from art or photographic stores. Stencil and three-dimensional letters can be re-used; transfer letters can only be used once. In stencil kits the letters are traced with a special pen, using a template. The height and slant of the lettering is often adjustable. Three-dimensional letters are usually made from white plastic and are either stuck to the background with Velcro, magnetized, or clipped into slots. The main alternative to these re-usable systems is dry-transfer sheet lettering. This can be transferred to any flat surface using a burnisher.

Layouts

Whatever method of lettering you choose, an accurate layout of the finished title must be worked out before you start. Always leave sufficient margin around the title. To do this, measure the height of the background which is visible when the camera is in position for shooting. Make your margin at least an eighth of this measurement all around. Align your letters – either with a T-square or with a steel ruler. Space the letters according to what looks good, rather than by measurement (see right), but place them no further apart than the width of the capital N of the type used. If they are spaced out any more than this they will be difficult to read.

Front titles
The obvious background for a movie on New York is the skyline of the city itself and a 35 mm transparency of this was projected on the titling unit described on p. 206. Titles should always be simple, and a bold white typeface was chosen for the lettering in this movie.

New York, New York

Mid-film titles
These titles are sometimes necessary to identify people, places, or dates mid-film. The typeface is the same throughout the movie to maintain consistency.

New York

1970

End titles
If you start with a front title you should really finish with *The End*. If the production team is of any size they should be credited at the end of the movie, along with the director.

The End

Directed by Pietro Henrietta

Stencil letters
Stencil kits come in a variety of typefaces and can be re-used.

Margins
Always draw up an accurate layout before you place the lettering on the background and position the lettering sensibly within the margin.

Spacing
Fairly tight spacing tends to look better than very wide spacing. Always go by the look of the title, not the actual measurements between the individual letters.

Three-dimensional letters
Always use a ruler to align these letters on the title-board.

Transfer letters
These letters can be transferred to most surfaces, but are not reusable.

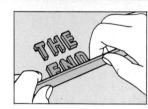
Week-End

Correct

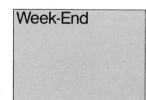
Week-End

Incorrect

Interpol

Correct

Interpol

Incorrect

Backgrounds

The simplest and best background to use for titling is black card. It provides a good contrast for white lettering, drawing attention to the letters and not to itself. Other colors can be used for the background as long as they contrast with the lettering (colored or otherwise). The darker, richer tones, especially red or brown, are most successful; pastel shades should be avoided as they can appear "muggy" on film. If you are using a colored background with transfer lettering, you can give the title more depth by adding a "shadow". Make up the title with white lettering on an acetate cel, then make up a duplicate cel with black lettering. Lay the white cel on top of the black, slightly out of register to create a shadow effect.

The background need not be plain; it can be textured or patterned. Design it in such a way that it suits the title and make sure that it does not detract from what the title is trying to say. If you are using a photograph as a background make sure that the letters are against a suitable part of the picture. For example, do not place white letters against the pale blue of the sky where they will be illegible (see right).

Filming static titles

Static titles are those in which the lettering is stuck to a background in a fixed position. The camera then simply films the board. The best way to shoot these titles is with a titling stand (see right) or a professional animation stand. If you want to avoid the expense of buying a stand it is quite easy to build one, using the instructions given on p. 198. However, if you feel that this is beyond you, there are two alternative ways to shoot static titles.

With a *horizontal titling set-up*, the easiest way is to pin the title-board onto a wall and to shoot using a camera on a tripod with a cable release. The board could also be supported on a wooden frame. With a *vertical titling set-up*, lay the title-board on the floor, between the tripod legs. For shooting, angle the camera down onto the title.

The lighting for all titling set-ups must be even, so use two cross-lit floodlights and set them at 45° to the title-board. The camera meter is designed to give an accurate reading from an average, mid-gray subject so a very white or dark title background will "fool" it. Instead, take a reading from an 18 per cent gray card (see p. 90), lock the aperture into the position indicated by the card and film in the normal way.

Backgrounds
Whatever the color or texture of the background there must be sufficient contrast between it and the lettering you use. A plain black typeface was chosen to stand out against the plain background.

Contrast
Never place light lettering against a light background or it will be illegible. When the lettering was placed on the sky it was illegible; the dark lettering shows up much better.

Pattern and relief
The brick wall was used to form a textured background. Black lettering, with a white outline was used to give relief against the lake background.

Correct   Incorrect

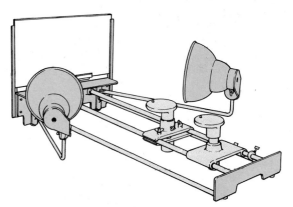

Static titles
This universal titling stand can be used with all cameras up to 16 mm. It can be used both horizontally and vertically and the camera's distance from the title-board can be adjusted.

Filming rolling films

In *Rolling* titles the lettering appears from the bottom of the screen and moves upwards until it disappears at the top. Roller drums are available as accessories for titling stands; they can also be made quite easily. Cover a large can with black satin or velvet and support it on a wooden frame in such a way that the drum can be revolved. Stick the lettering directly onto the black material and frame the drum so it fills the picture area.

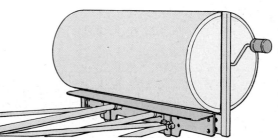

Rolling titles
Stick the lettering onto the surface of the drum and frame the title so that it fills the picture area. Revolve the drum slowly as you shoot. The last credit can either roll out of sight or can be faded (see p. 186).

Special Effects Titling

Echo effects are produced by zooming in on a title, back-winding and zooming in again, starting a couple of frames further on. Place the title slightly above or below center as you look through the camera. Stick tape around the lens and mark off about 40 equal lines (see p. 202); shoot one frame per mark. At the end of the first exposure shoot a few more seconds of the title, cap the lens and backwind to the start of the shot. Shoot a couple of frames with the lens cap still on. For the second exposure change the title's color using a colored gel. Shoot this exposure in exactly the same way as the first. To begin the third exposure advance the film two frames again (this will make it four frames further on than the start of the first exposure); change title color and continue.

The glowing effect is produced by gradually over-exposing parts of the title. Cover the title, apart from the part that you want to glow, with a neutral density filter (see p. 94). When the exposure rate is based on the filtered areas the uncovered areas will be over-exposed.

Superimposed titles

Specially-constructed boxes can be bought to produce superimposed titles. A transparency is projected onto a screen in the side of the box. This image is reflected by a partially silvered mirror, set at 45° to the camera which is positioned in front of the box. The camera views both the reflected image of the transparency and the titles, which it sees *through* the mirror. The same effect can be produced without this special box, using a glass or mirror shot (see p. 194).

If your camera can be rewound or if you have a backwinder, it is quite easy to fade up a white-on-black title at any stage in the film. You will, however, need a frame counter so that you can rewind accurately to the start of the first image. Begin by filming a black background for ten seconds, then fade up a white caption. Hold this for five seconds and then fade it out. Rewind the reel, film the live-action background, and then continue as normal. Shoot plenty of the background as extra security after rewinding as some margin for error will be needed.

Animated titles

Titles using animated drawings or objects are a novel alternative to the ones produced by in-camera effects. A single animated drawing conveys the title in a strong image and is often more effective than a long, written title. To make the letters appear to assemble themselves into the title, gradually arrange the letters and shoot single frames at each move. Use the animation techniques and equipment described on p. 196.

Action titles

These titles do not need special equipment and probably provide the most fluent way of beginning or ending a film. This is because the title is shot as a continuous part of the movie. For example, you could film a child writing the title in the sand on a beach. Shoot the rest of the film and then end with the sea washing the title away. Always try to make the end title in the same style as the main title to unify the whole movie.

Echo titles
These multicolored titles "zoom" towards the camera followed by visual echoes of themselves and can easily be produced if your camera has a backwind facility. They are a very dramatic and professional way of beginning a movie and the technique is simple to master.

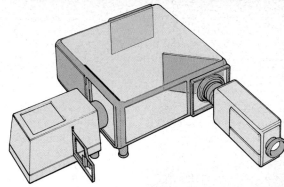

Superimposed titles
Superimposing titling machines, as their name implies, allow you to use 35 mm transparencies and movies as backgrounds for your titles. They usually include a facility for producing rolling titles.

Animated titles
The circular shapes were placed randomly on the titling board. They were gradually moved into position and a single frame shot. This procedure was followed until the whole title was formed.

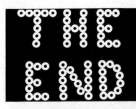

Action titles
These titles add a very personal touch to your movie. Like all titles they should reflect the subject matter of the movie.

PROCESSING
AND
EDITING

"The basic fact was true, and remains true to this day, that the juxtaposition of two shots by splicing them together, resembles not so much a simple sum of one shot plus another shot as it does a *creation*"

Sergei Eisenstein

Processing the Film

It is important to send your film off to be processed as soon as possible after exposing it. Exposed film tends to suffer from a rapid color shift, especially in hot conditions. With negative film, there is some possibility of correcting the color balance during printing (since all printing machines contain adjustable filter packs which can be used to make alterations to the color cast on certain parts of the film, see p. 229). But with reversal film – which carries a positive image and is designed to be projected in its original form – there is unfortunately no remedy at all.

Except in the USA super 8 film is usually sold with the processing included in the purchase price. In this case, you simply slip the exposed cartridge into a special envelope and send it off to the manufacturer. If processing is not pre-paid, you may send your film to a commercial laboratory to be processed. Laboratories vary in price and give very different results. The type of chemicals used by a particular laboratory, the temperature of the solutions and the length of the development time will all affect the quality of the processing – especially in the case of color film. Grain, for example, varies in direct proportion to processing time and temperature. It is therefore a good idea to experiment by sending films to different labs and then to go to the best – which may well be the manufacturers themselves.

One type of filmstock, Ektachrome SM 7244 (which is available in the 200 ft (61 m) super 8 sound cartridges) can be processed in a special Kodak Supermatic (SM) processor. These expensive machines are designed for small commercial labs, TV stations or film schools – in other words, for institutions where the turnover is high enough or the need for quick processing great enough to justify the price. The entire procedure of the Supermatic is automated and does not require any specialized knowledge. The processed film emerges dry in just over ten minutes.

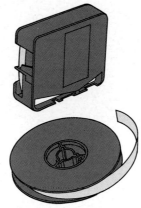

Super 8 processing
Most 50 ft (15 m) super 8 cartridges are processed by the manufacturer. In the laboratory, the film is removed from the cartridge, spliced onto a master roll comprising many separate 50 ft lengths, and fed through the processing machine in one go. Afterwards, the individual films are cut off the master roll and returned on 50 ft (15 m) plastic spools.

What happens during processing

There are different processes for different types of film. Although the principle is similar, the procedure for color film is very different from the much simpler method used for black and white film. Similarly, while *reversal* film produces a positive image which looks like the original scene, negative film produces a *negative* image in "complementary" colors; a positive print must be made from it before it can be viewed (see p. 52).

The way in which the light-sensitive silver halides within the layers of film are transformed into colored dyes is explained on p. 51. The colors produced depend on whether the film is reversal or negative stock. In either case, it is the chemical developer which converts the invisible, latent image recorded on the film into a visible image. In color processing, which can comprise up to twenty different stages, the temperature of the chemicals and the length of time for which they act on the film is absolutely critical. The processing machines are expensive, large-scale and highly automated.

Forced development

It is possible to ask the laboratory to extend the development of some films. This technique is known as *forced development* or *push processing*. The result is to increase the film's effective speed by one or even two stops. This means that a film shot in conditions where there was not enough light for a proper exposure can be "forced" during processing to increase the film's sensitivity to light and to produce a correctly exposed image. However, forced development is accompanied by an alarming increase in grain and contrast, and it should only be used as a last resort. Some films cannot be pushed at all – Kodachrome, for example – and, in general, forced development is not recommended for negative filmstocks, since the allowance for underexposure is better made at the printing stage.

Home processing

It is possible to obtain do-it-yourself processing kits for movie film. These usually consist of a plastic tank containing a circular reel or "snail". After the film has been exposed, it is removed from the cartridge and threaded carefully onto the reel. *This operation must be carried out in complete darkness* or the film will be fogged. The chemicals for processing – which are mixed in very precise quantities – are then poured into the tank. They must be at exactly the right temperature and must remain in the tank for the correct period of time, especially for color films.

The advantages of home processing are these: as long as the film does not include processing in the purchase price, developing it yourself will be cheaper; it will also be quicker; and, finally, it allows you to achieve special effects such as push processing, "solarization", or color-toning of black and white film. However, the process is complex and can be unreliable. In most cases, it makes sense to have your film processed professionally.

Home processing kit
This developing tank can be used for processing 8 mm, 16 mm or 35 mm films in various combinations. It has a series of circular plastic reels or "snails" which hold the film and which are adjustable to accommodate the different gauges. The film must be wound onto the reels in complete darkness. The developing solutions are poured into the light-tight tank through the funnel-shaped hole in the center of the lid.

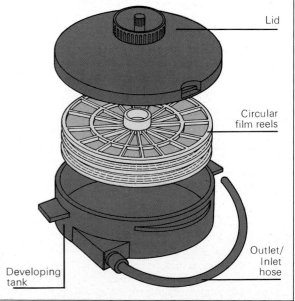

Lid

Circular film reels

Outlet/Inlet hose

Developing tank

Original or Workprint?

When you send off your film to the laboratory to be processed, you will have to decide whether you want a duplicate print of the film to use for editing, or whether you want to risk editing the original. Of course, in the case of negative film, you will need some sort of print in order to view the material at all.

Editing the original film

The great majority of filmmakers in 8 mm edit their films in the original. This means that it is the actual camera footage sent back from the lab which is cut and spliced. The great advantage of this method over working on a duplicate print is that the film is never finally "finished". You can go on changing your mind about cutting points, splicing in new material or re-editing sequences for as long as you like. The big disadvantage of editing the original film is that you have to be scrupulously careful that it is kept clean and undamaged. Film is scratched very easily indeed, and enormous care must be taken to protect the film from dust and damage.

Checklist of film care

Cleanliness is absolutely vital when editing – especially for super 8, where the frame enlargement is very great.
● Keep the cutting room clean. Avoid carpeted rooms.
● Do not drop the film on the floor. Hang it up carefully.
● Do not touch the film without wearing cotton gloves, and always hold the film by the edges.
● Never tighten the film on its spool by pulling it from one end – this will scratch the base.
● Project the film as little as possible. Use the viewer for editing, but do not wind the film back and forth more than necessary. Be very careful when threading the film into the projector or viewer. Always use a properly trimmed film leader on the head of the film.
● If the film gets dusty, clean it with a special fluid or send it to a laboratory cleaning service.

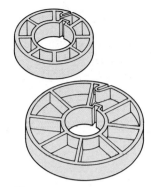

16 mm processing
In the 16 mm format, the processed film or workprint is usually returned from the lab on a plastic core. These can be used with "split reels" in the cutting room.

Film cleaning
Film can be cleaned by passing it very gently through a soft anti-static cloth moistened with film cleaner. If the cloth collects dust, turn it over to a clean part at once.

Editing a workprint

The purpose of having a *workprint* – or *cutting copy* as it is sometimes known – is to give you an expendable vehicle for your experiments in editing. A workprint is a duplicate copy of the original camera film and can be ordered from the lab when the film is sent off for processing. It is a direct, ungraded contact print from the master, and is used solely for editing. Because it is only a copy, not the original itself, the workprint can be cut and spliced more intensively, with a certain disregard for its physical condition. When the editing is completely finished, the workprint is matched to the original master, which is cut shot-by-shot so that it is exactly the same. This process is known as "conforming" or "neg cutting" (see p. 228), even if you are dealing with reversal film. It is possible to have it done by a lab which specializes in the work. Conforming is made much easier if the master and the workprint both have "edge numbers" along the side of the film (see below). Once it has been cut to match the edited workprint, the original may, if it is reversal film, be screened; or, if it is negative, a proper graded print may be made (see p. 229). Both should be in pristine condition.

Workprints are fairly expensive and if you want to keep your costs down you should ask yourself whether you really need one. A workprint should be seriously considered if you ever intend to make any prints from the original (which must be in perfect condition), if you intend to carry out intensive editing, or if you ever envisage wanting to extend a shot after having cut it. Once you have "put the scissors" into a shot, the cut will be noticeable should you ever want to splice it together again. Indeed, if you have used a cement splice, a frame will have been lost in the middle of the shot. A workprint allows room for second thoughts, since the original itself is not touched. Workprints are therefore standard practice at all professional and semi-professional levels.

Edge numbers

In 16 mm and 35 mm, "latent" numbers are printed onto the filmstock during manufacture. Known as *edge numbers* or *key numbers*, they are revealed during processing and appear along the edge of the film at intervals of every twenty or forty frames. The conforming or neg cutting process is therefore a simple matter of matching the numbers on the edges of the workprint to those on the original (see p. 228).

Super 8 does not have latent edge numbers. But it is possible, before editing, to get some labs to print a number sequence onto both the workprint and the original at corresponding frames throughout their length. This process is called *rubber numbering*. If you are editing double system sound, it is a good idea to have the reel of fullcoat magnetic film containing the sound track numbered in the same way. Before rubber numbering, you must attach matching leaders, with corresponding "sync marks", onto the original, the workprint *and* the mag film (see p. 240) to guarantee that the numbers are correctly positioned.

Super 8 rubber numbers Rubber numbers are always added after processing. On super 8 they sometimes spill into the frame.

16 mm edge numbers In the case of 16 mm, the film usually has latent edge numbers which are revealed during processing. It is also possible to have the film rubber numbered.

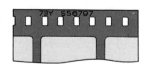

35 mm edge numbers Almost all types of 35 mm negative and duplicating filmstock have standard latent edge numbers printed onto the film at intervals of 1 ft (30 cm).

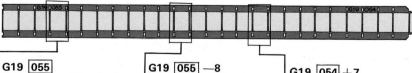

G19 055
You can pinpoint a single frame by boxing the edge numbers which appear opposite the frame in question.

G19 055 —8
For an intermediate frame, box the nearest edge number and count up towards the *head*. Indicate as a *minus* number.

G19 054 +7
Alternatively, count the number of frames from the nearest edge number towards the *tail*, and use a *plus* sign.

Why Edit?

Why should you bother to edit your films? What is the point of intercutting different shots? Why not simply project the film as you shot it? After all, many great directors have preferred long, uninterrupted takes to fussy intercutting, and Hitchcock's movie, *Rope*, does not contain a single cut. The answer is that they had at their disposal enormous resources and a highly sophisticated technique: a successful long take is very difficult to execute – since every segment must be interesting.

If you are making movies for the first time, you will realize as soon as you screen your first few reels of film why editing is necessary and why it is the single most important thing you can do to improve your movies. Editing gives you the chance to rectify the inevitable errors of shooting and to create a new order from the raw material. Editing is perhaps the most satisfying part of all

filmmaking. In the quiet of your cutting room, running the film through your viewer and selecting one exact frame to combine with another quite different but complementary image gives you your first opportunity to weigh one aspect of the material in relation to the other footage you have shot. You can now juxtapose images, intercut different angles of the same scene, begin to build up complex sequences, and establish the pace and mood you want. You may perhaps have visualized such juxtapositions, but only now can they be made to *work* as one combined image.

On the other hand, never cut just for the sake of it. Never overcut or lose confidence in your shot too early when editing. Trust your subject to hold on the screen, and when shooting try to vary the angles for a sound dramatic purpose rather than for reasons of safety.

Editing procedure
The flow chart below explains how to go about editing your movies. It introduces the stages in the editing procedure which are outlined in more detail in the following pages. It also assumes that you have shot footage without sound: if you are planning to edit sound movies or to add sound to your finished film, turn to p. 232.

To operate the chart, begin at the top and answer "yes" or "no" to each question in turn.

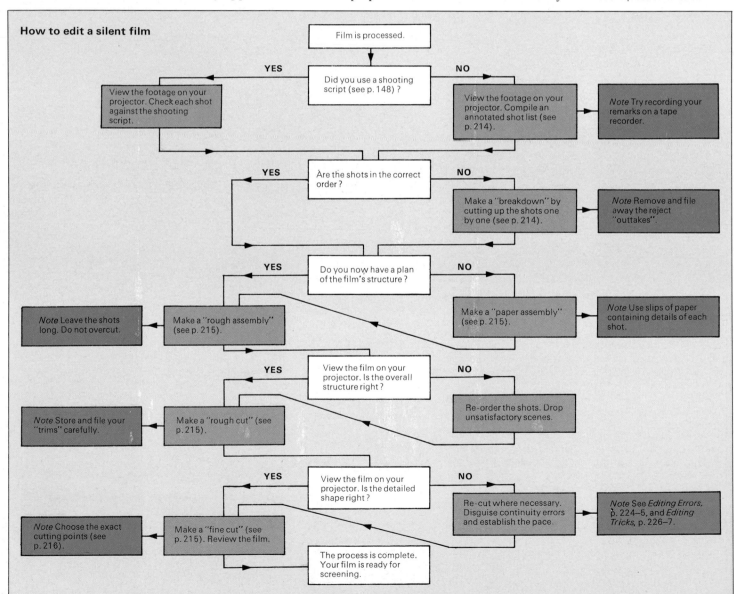

How to edit a silent film

Film is processed.

YES ← Did you use a shooting script (see p. 148)? → **NO**

View the footage on your projector. Check each shot against the shooting script.

View the footage on your projector. Compile an annotated shot list (see p. 214).

Note Try recording your remarks on a tape recorder.

YES ← Are the shots in the correct order? → **NO**

Make a "breakdown" by cutting up the shots one by one (see p. 214).

Note Remove and file away the reject "outtakes".

YES ← Do you now have a plan of the film's structure? → **NO**

Make a "paper assembly" (see p. 215).

Note Use slips of paper containing details of each shot.

Note Leave the shots long. Do not overcut.

Make a "rough assembly" (see p. 215).

YES ← View the film on your projector. Is the overall structure right? → **NO**

Re-order the shots. Drop unsatisfactory scenes.

Note Store and file your "trims" carefully.

Make a "rough cut" (see p. 215).

YES ← View the film on your projector. Is the detailed shape right? → **NO**

Re-cut where necessary. Disguise continuity errors and establish the pace.

Note See *Editing Errors*, p. 224–5, and *Editing Tricks*, p. 226–7.

Note Choose the exact cutting points (see p. 216).

Make a "fine cut" (see p. 215). Review the film.

The process is complete. Your film is ready for screening.

Editing Equipment

The equipment illustrated on this page is what you would require for editing silent movies. The additions that you would need if you wanted to move on to sound editing are discussed in the next chapter (see p. 232).

The most important piece of equipment is the *viewer*, which is used for looking at the film. The viewer contains a small bulb which shines through the film and throws the image onto a built-in rear-projection screen. The film is supported on either side of the viewer by *rewind arms* which allow you to run it to and fro during editing. On some viewers, the rewinds may be motorized.

In order to cut the film and to join one shot to another accurately and to join one shot to another accurately and invisibly, you will need a *splicer*. This may be of the type which welds the pieces of film together using cement, or the sort which sticks the film together using tape (see p. 212–13).

It is essential, especially when editing original camera film, that your cutting room is clean and dustfree. It is a good idea to wear thin cotton editing gloves to prevent grease from your skin getting onto the film. You should keep beside you a blower brush, a soft, lintless cloth and some liquid film cleaner so that you can clean the film after editing and before projection.

Other accessories you may need are these: a grease pencil (chinagraph marker) for marking cutting points; a magnifying glass; a pair of scissors for cutting the film without using the splicer; spare 50 ft (15 m), 200 ft (61 m) and 400 ft (122 m) reels and boxes; a rack with pegs to hang up shots; a film sorting box; plenty of film leader; a black fiber-tip marker for writing on the leader; a notebook for logging shots; a stopwatch; and some footage/time conversion tables.

1	Film spools
2	Film leader
3	Silent viewer
4	Film cleaner
5	Sound head
6	Frame counter
7	Sound fader
8	Tape splicer
9	Cement splicer
10	Notebook
11	Pens and markers
12	Scissors
13	Magnifier
14	Stopwatch
15	Editing gloves
16	Soft cloth
17	Cleaning fluid
18	Blower brush

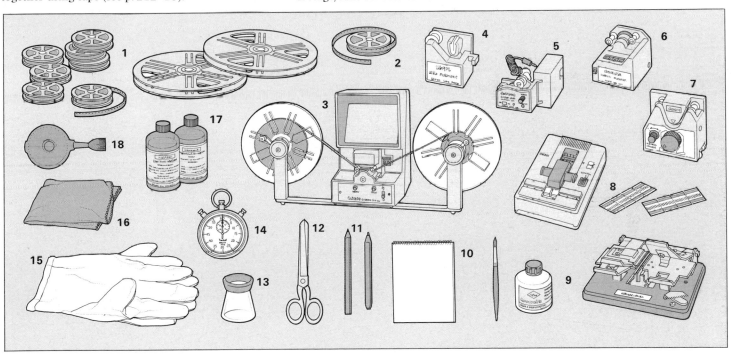

Choosing a viewer

Super 8 viewers vary greatly in quality and in price. If you are thinking of buying one, look for the following points. Is the viewer sturdy and well-built? Will it take at least 400 ft (122 m) of super 8 film? Is the image bright and sharp enough for use in a lighted room? Can the framing and focus be adjusted? If the viewer is motorized, does it have a variable speed? Can the film be moved to and fro one frame at a time? How does the viewer mark the cutting point on the film? Will the viewer accept an accessory sound head for single system editing? Does the emulsion on the film face up or down? (If you want to use the viewer with a "synchronizer" for double system editing or if you want to project the film during editing, the emulsion should face downwards.)

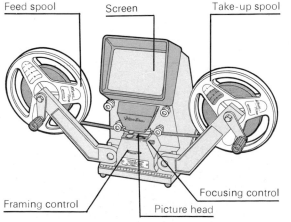

Feed spool   Screen   Take-up spool

Framing control   Picture head   Focusing control

How the viewer works
In most viewers, a small quartz bulb shines light down through the film. The image is picked up by a rotating 16-sided optical glass polygon which projects it, via a series of angled mirrors, onto the viewer's ground glass screen. some super 8 viewers are now motorized and have playback and recording heads linked to a built-in speaker. They can therefore be used for dubbing as well as editing.

Splicing the Film

Splicing is the technique of joining two lengths of film together – either during editing or to repair a broken strip of film. There are two kinds of splicers (although each has many variations) – the *tape* and the *cement* splicer. Both work very well, and each has its advantages. Tape splicers are more flexible for editing since, if you change your mind about a cut, the tape can be peeled off easily and the shot can be extended without the loss of a frame. Cement splicers are always used when a film is to be contact printed, or whenever any optical process is involved, since tape slices tend to show up as a white line under these conditions. Cement splicers *cannot* be used with polyester-based film such as Fuji's single 8 stocks.

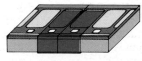

Tape splice

Tape splices

In tape splicing the two strips of film are buit-joined, not overlapped. It is therefore important that they are cut and joined accurately if the film is to pass through the projector smoothly. The two principal varieties of tape splicer are the presstape patch and the roll type.

Presstape splices

These splicers are only available in 8 mm formats. They use an individual perforated *patch* that wraps around the film but leaves the magnetic stripe uncovered so that the sound is uninterrupted.

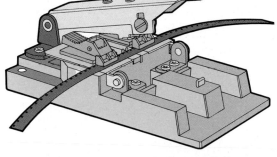

Presstape splicer
The Wurker S8 Duoplay was the first presstape splicer which left both the sound stripe and the balance stripe uncovered. The patch covers the whole film on the emulsion side but lies *between* the stripes on the base side. This means that the film can still be used for duo-track or stereo sound which records on both stripes (see p. 237).

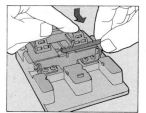 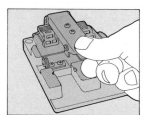  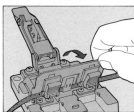 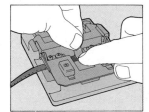

1 Place film glossy side down on metal pins; end should protrude by at least one frame. Depress and move right film clamp over.

2 Bring knife lever swiftly down and cut film without Applying force. Remove trimmings and repeat for left.

3 Place splicing patch, red end up on plastic pins. Hold rear half while pulling front half toward you. Press patch down.

4 Swing pivoting plate, still holding film, forward. Press firmly on splicing point, especially on cut ends and perforations.

5 Pull front end of patch over to wrap around film. Press firmly. Swing back plate, remove film and press between plates.

Roll-tape splices

These splicers use a *roll* of thin transparent tape rather than patches. The tape is sometimes perforated, sometimes not. The splicer holds the strips of film in perfect registration while you press the tape firmly onto the film. It then trims the edges automatically. The tape wraps around both sides of the film, but in most cases leaves the sound stripe uncovered. The tape usually covers two frames of the film, and if the splice is to be invisible on projection there must be no dirt or air bubbles trapped underneath the tape. Roll-tape splicers are preferable for editing fullcoat magnetic film.

Roll-tape splicer
This Ciro splicer uses a roll of special transparent tape to join the film. The machine automatically punches holes in the tape which match exactly the film's own perforations. The tape leaves the main sound stripe uncovered but does, unfortunately, wrap over the balance stripe.

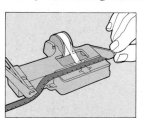 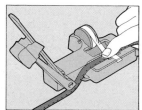  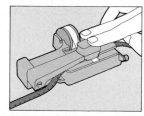 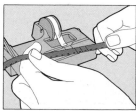

1 Before making a splice trim the ends of the film. Place film on pins and depress cutting knife to make a clean edge.

2 Place both film ends on registration pins, ends butting. Position the transparent splicing tape on the film.

3 Lower the pressure plate over the film and hold it in place with your finger. Make sure the film does not move off the pins.

4 Lower the lever so that it perforates the film splice. It will also cut the transparent splicing tape leaving an excess.

5 Raise lever and fold excess tape under film so that it adheres to film back and completes the invisible frame-line splice.

Cement splices

In cement splicing a liquid film cement is used to dissolve the base of one piece of film sufficiently to weld it to the base of an other piece. Film cement does not work on the emulsion layer, which must be scraped from one of the two ends to make the splice. Good cement splices are more permanent than tape.

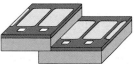

Cement splice

Cement splicer
The splicer shown left can be used for 8 mm or 16 mm film. It has guillotine blades for trimming the ends of the film and a built-in rasp for scraping away a small area of the emulsion layer. For a good splice, you must apply fresh cement in just the right quantity: follow the manufacturers' instructions.

Beveled-edge splicers

Most of the cheaper cement splicers make "film-on-film" splices, which means that the two ends of film are stacked on top of one another. Beveled-edge splicers scrape both pieces of film at a 45° angle and are better for sound-striped film.

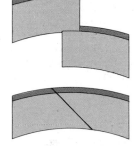
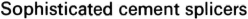

Film-on-film splice
A straight overlap splice like this will cause a sound drop-out.

Beveled splice
A 45° splice will not produce a sound drop-out.

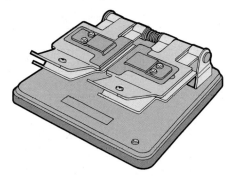

1 Lift and separate plates, keeping bottom right-hand side down. Place film on registration pins, emulsion side up.

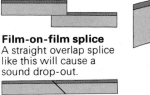

2 Press down the upper right-hand plate firmly to secure film. To cut film end, bring down the bottom left-hand plate.

3 Raise the right-hand plates with the film still inside. Remove the trimmings. Get ready to cut the left film section.

Sophisticated cement splicers

Good cement splicers must be precision-made and are therefore likely to be more expensive than tape splicers (although the film cement is much cheaper than rolls of tape or patches). Some splicers have a *motorized* cutting wheel for grinding away the emulsion layer automatically. Others, called *hot* splicers, are heated to speed up the drying time of the film cement.

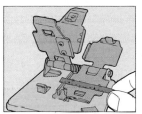

4 Place the film to be joined with the emulsion surface up on the left-hand plate. Lower the top plate to secure firmly.

5 Cut the film by pressing down with the two right-hand plates held firmly together. After cutting, raise these plates again.

6 Lift up the attached rasp and rub the film's cut edge lightly until the coating is removed. Wipe off dust with a brush.

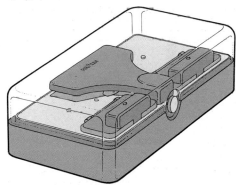

Power splicer (above)
The Braun FK 1 has a motorized scraper head which bevels the edges of the film.

Hot splicer (below)
This Maier-Hancock splicer has an electric element which heats up the cement to speed up drying.

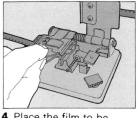

7 Remove detachable rasp and rub it lightly against right-hand cut edge until surface gloss disappears. Dust edge.

8 To join the films, apply liquid cement to the left-hand cut edge until the surface becomes moist. Do not apply too much.

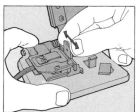

9 Press down right-hand plates with film inside. The cement will dry in about 30 seconds. Lift upper plates to remove film.

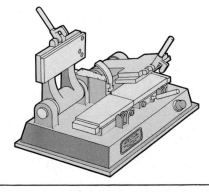

Cutting Room Technique

The unedited reels of film that come back from the processing laboratory are known professionally as *rushes* or *dailies*. The first thing to do, before you can begin to edit, is to view the rushes and break the film down into an orderly arrangement of component parts. If you used a shooting script at the time of filming, with each separate "take" properly "slated" (see p. 148), all this will be simpler. If not, use the opportunity of your first viewing to make a detailed *shot list*.

Viewing the rushes

If you have had a workprint made of your original footage, use that. Put the camera original away somewhere safe until the editing is completed. If your film is on several separate 50 ft (15 m) spools, it is a good idea to transfer it all onto one 400 ft (122 m) reel by tape splicing the ends together. Now thread the film onto your projector and view the footage. Assign a number to each shot as it appears, with a brief description of what it contains and short comments on its quality and duration. Try to jot down as much as you can. The information is certain to be useful later when you are trying to locate the shot you want or remember what a particular take was like.

It may be necessary to project the film in bursts, one shot at a time, for critical viewing and to give yourself enough time to make notes. You could try recording your remarks on a tape recorder as you go along; this will reduce wear and tear on the film, since you will not have to keep stopping and starting the projector. Look for good focus, framing, exposure, steadiness and pace. Check that the footage is completely free of filmstock faults, hairs, softness, lens flare, dirt and jerkiness. All these faults and virtues will be difficult to spot if you are only using a small-screen viewer.

Breakdown and logging

When you have finished projecting the film and you have made an annotated shot list, rewind the film and set it up on your viewer. You are now ready to break down the footage into separate shots. As you wind the film through the viewer, cut off each shot (or group of related shots). It is at this point that you can throw out some of the worst material – for example, footage that is over-exposed, scratched or out of focus. The rejected shots are known as "outtakes" or "n.g. takes". You can either splice them all together on a reel or file them in a can in some corner of the room. But resist the temptation to throw them away until after the editing is complete.

The selected shots can be filed in a variety of ways – on reels, in cans, on a row of pins, or in the "eggbox" system of grid boxes. But it is vital that you know where each shot is when you want it – so each one should be filed under the number it was given when you compiled the shot list. Number either the reel or peg, or write the shot number on the base side of the film with a grease pencil.

If the film has "edge numbers" or "rubber numbers" (see p. 209) these should be recorded alongside the shot numbers. This process is known as *logging*. Remember, of course, that if the film has been rubber numbered, these will not be the same as the latent edge numbers.

Shot 1	Pan across beach. Wobbly final hold (possibly OK for titles) 15 sec. Take 2: Ditto. Better.
Shot 2	Crab. Close-up. Good. 5 sec.
Shot 3	Zoom into B.C.U. of small girl. Out of focus. Hair in gate. No good.
Shot 4	L.S. surf. Good. 10 sec.
Shot 5	M.S. Reaction shot of father. 4 sec. (no edit needed between 4 and 5?)
Shot 6	Same as 4, but horizon slanted. No good.

Shot list (left)
When you view your film for the first time, write down details of each separate shot. It is a good idea to use a system of filing cards, since these can also be used to make a "paper assembly" when you are planning the structure of the film.

Logging sheet (below)
A "logging sheet" is a convenient way of noting down shot details. It contains slate and take numbers, edge and rubber numbers (if the film has them) and possibly a brief description.

Roll No.	Slate No.	Take No.	Edge Nos.	Rubber Nos.	Action	Dialogue	Remarks
6	41	1	J-34765-99	BB 5826-43	L.S. Robert	—	N.G. (hair)
	41	2	J-34801-25	BB 5844-58	L.S. Robert	—	N.G. (soft)
	41	3	J-34829-64	BB 5859-76	L.S. Robert	—	O.K.
	42	1	J-34868-83	BB 5877-84	M.S. Anne	Sync.	O.K.
	43	1	J-34884-906	BB 5885-96	Cutaway	—	O.K.
	44	1	J-34906-15	BB 5897-904	C.U. Robert	Sync	N.G. (false start)
	44	2	J-34917-28	BB 5905-11	C.U. Robert	—	O.K.
7	45	1	X-61972-94	BB 5912-23	Ext. house	—	O.K.
	46	1	X-61995-204	BB 5924-33	Trees in wind	—	O.K.

Viewing the film
Run the film from left to right through the viewer and locate the first shot as indicated on the shot list.

Marking the cuts
Mark the in-point of the first shot with a grease pencil. Allow plenty of leeway, and do not overcut.

Cutting the film
Wind the film forward a few frames and cut out the shot using a sharp pair of scissors or a film splicer.

Numbering the shots
Mark the number of the shot on the film. Use a grease pencil and do not write on the emulsion (matt) side.

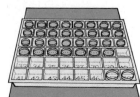

Storing the shots
Plastic trays are available with numbered compartments for storing shots – the numbers should correspond to the shot list.

Hanging up the shots
Alternatively, the shots can be hung up over a clean editing bin. Each shot has a numbered clip or peg.

The rough assembly

If you were working to some form of shooting script when filming, you can simply assemble the shots according to this outline – although naturally your plans will probably have been modified by events during the shooting. The shots should be left very long. Do not trim them down or intercut intensively at this stage. The aim is simply to establish the overall shape of the film, *not* to cut for action, effect or pace.

If your film does not have a pre-planned structure, you have a wide range of courses open to you. One of the best ways of arriving at a rough assembly is to jot down each element (which may be one shot, a group of shots, or just an idea for a sequence) onto a separate piece of paper. Each slip will carry the shot number or numbers to which it refers. If you used filing cards for your original shot breakdown, these will be suitable. The slips or cards can then be laid out on the table or the floor and moved around until you feel that they are beginning to make sense in terms of the film's structure. You can then put together the shots in this order.

It is customary to assemble the film from the top (or "head"), working from left to right on the viewer. Begin by fixing an empty 400 ft (122 m) spool on the right-hand rewind arm. Attach a generous length of plain film leader. Now take the first shot from the pin or box where it is filed and splice the head of the shot to the tail of the film leader. Continue in this way until all the shots are spliced together, in the correct order, on the one spool.

Do not make the common mistake of overcutting at this early stage. Leave all fine cutting until you are sure that the shape of the film is right. It is in fact quite rare for the structure of the first rough assembly to be retained through to the final cut, and you should not be dismayed if your first effort feels wrong when you project it. Try again, and remember that creative editing can do wonders with the most unpromising material. You are now ready to start the real job of editing the film – which many consider to be the most exciting and the most satisfying part of all moviemaking.

The rough cut

When you view the rough assembly on your projector, you will begin to see how the editing of the film may develop. You might decide that one or two shots are too long or that some could be dropped altogether.

The film is taken off the projector and threaded back onto the viewer. It is here, in producing what is called a *rough cut* from the rough assembly, that the real editing takes place: sequences are built up, continuity is established, and the cutaways and intercutting are developed.

As before, resist the temptation to overcut, especially if you are working on the original film. Also, avoid repeatedly viewing small sequences on your projector. Apart from the time and the wear, you will be unable to judge the effect, pace and indeed relevance of any sequence until you see it in the context of the rest of the film. Go on until you have finished the rough cut, and then review the whole thing in one screening.

The fine cut

The process of making a *fine cut* is the last part of the editing stage. The rough cut is deliberately "loose" – which means that the cuts between one shot and the next are still very flexible. You must now decide exactly how long each shot is to last and at exactly which frame the cut is to be made. It is here that the final delicate adjustments are made to the pace, rhythm and tension of the film. Fine cutting, in other words, is the reducing of the film to its final form.

Trims

The bits of film left over from the beginning and end of each shot that you have used are called *trims*. They must be filed and stored carefully. A "useless" trim can provide an invaluable cutaway, or it may be needed to extend the shot itself if you change your mind about a cut. If they are not numbered, trims should be identified clearly in grease pencil or by your filing system, and in double system editing they should be accompanied by their sound, with appropriate sync marks on each trim.

Marking a cutting point

Marking the film at the point where you decide to make a cut is usually done on the base (shiny) side with a white or yellow grease pencil. You should never mark the emulsion (dull) side of the film, and you should try to avoid marking the frame area designed to be left as part of the shot. Although grease pencil marks can be wiped off, they tend to leave small traces on the film. If you wish to be quite certain that the frame area is unspoiled, adopt a consistent policy of always marking a frame, say, three frames away from the point where you want to cut.

Most viewers allow you enough space to use a grease pencil with the film still in place, but many also have a device for automatically marking the cutting point. They cut a tiny notch on the very edge of the perf side of the film. Avoid viewers which actually damage the frame they are marking.

Marking the film (right)
You can mark the film with a grease pencil on most viewers, although in some cases the lamphouse must be raised first.

Identifying the cutting point (below)
The vertical line is the cutting point. The horizontal line indicates the footage to be discarded.

Automatic frame marking (above)
Some viewers mark the cutting point by making a tiny notch in the frame immediately to the right of it.

Where and When to Cut

Editing is largely a matter of experimentation. There are no hard-and-fast rules dictating what you must and must not do. However, just as there are certain useful principles of shooting (discussed in *The Elements of Film*, p. 54–86), so there are certain principles of editing which will help you put together coherent sequences. The two most important – cutting for continuity and cutting for the visual action – are explained opposite.

Films are not always cut for visual reasons. The sound may be more important than the action – especially in music or conversation, for example. And at other times the best cutting points for each medium may conflict. But, in general, the image on film is paramount. You will find that a very powerful image always tends to have more effect than a crucial piece of commentary. It is therefore the action that you should consider first.

Why cut?

When viewing your unedited footage, the first thing to ask yourself is whether a cut is needed at all. Even though you may have filmed an action from different angles, or if you have shot cutaways and reaction shots, you must now decide whether they will strengthen or weaken the main action. Does the master shot stand up on its own? Are the angles and information given by the other shots sufficiently different to enhance the scene, or will they merely complicate the action without strengthening it? Never cut just for the sake of it, or just because you happen to have covered a scene from more than one camera position. This is particularly true when you are filming a sustained performance or a delicate study of character, where the pauses and imperfections can be more telling than a polished and edited version.

Choosing a cutting point

Let us suppose that you have filmed a man walking up to a car door, opening it and getting in. You have shot the scene from three angles to give yourself maximum flexibility. Your plan is to cut from the long shot to the mid shot as he reaches the car, and to the close-up as he grasps the handle. Some of the problems and variations inherent in this scheme are shown opposite.

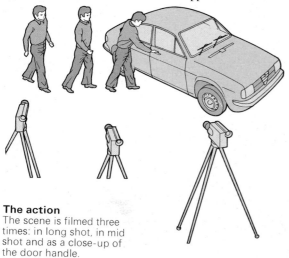

The action
The scene is filmed three times: in long shot, in mid shot and as a close-up of the door handle.

L.S. 1   M.S. 1   C.U. 1

L.S. 2   M.S. 2   C.U. 2

L.S. 3   M.S. 3   C.U. 3

L.S. 4   M.S. 4   C.U. 4

L.S. 5   M.S. 5   C.U. 5

L.S. 6   M.S. 6   C.U. 6

L.S. 7   M.S. 7   C.U. 7

Cutting for continuity

When you choose a cutting point for the transition between the long shot and the mid shot, you *must* maintain continuity. In other words, the man must have the same leg extended in both shots and his position relative to the car must be correct. You must watch the movement very carefully and match the action exactly so that when you cut the two shots together they flow smoothly from one to the other. The two things to avoid are the *jump cut* and *double action*.

If you make a cut which omits part of the action, this is known as a jump cut. It may be a small mis-match (in which case the man may appear to "skip"), or it may be a large one (in which case he will suddenly "jump" from one position to another). If you make a cut which repeats part of the action, this is known as double action.

Double action
Cutting from L.S. 3 to M.S. 1 will produce a double action. The action will be repeated and the man will appear to approach the car twice. The illusion of continuity will therefore be destroyed.

Matching cuts
Cutting from L.S. 4 to M.S. 4 will result in a well-matched, "continuous" shot. The man is picked up in the same position and at the same pace. The transition is smooth and uninterrupted.

L.S. 4   M.S. 4

Jump cut
Cutting from L.S. 2 to M.S. 4 will produce a "jump cut". The man will appear to "jump" suddenly from the end of the car to the side of the door.

L.S. 2   M.S. 4

L.S. 3   M.S. 1   M.S. 2   M.S. 3

Cutting for visual action

Try to choose a cutting point from the mid shot to the close-up just as the man makes the first suggestion of a move towards the door handle – that is, just as he *begins* to extend his arm. It is a general rule that *an action cut is best placed a fraction after the beginning of a movement.* The cut is then visibly motivated, and the action will carry the viewer's eye effortlessly over any breaks or flaws in the continuity. If the cut comes half-way through the action (for instance, just *after* the man's hand reaches the door handle), the cut will tend to be slack.

There are other possibilities within this whole sequence, of course. If you wanted to compress the scene, you could cut directly from the long shot to the close-up, leaving the door handle alone in the frame for a second or so before the man's hand came into the shot.

Cutting on the action
If you cut from M.S. 6 to C.U. 6 just after the man has started to move, the action in the close-up will pick up on the action in the mid shot and the movement will appear to be continuous.

M.S. 6   C.U. 6

Cutting in mid-action
If you cut after the action has begun, say from M.S. 7 to C.U. 7, there will not be such a strong visual movement to carry over the change of camera angle.

M.S. 7   C.U. 7

Compressing time
It is possible to manipulate the action so that it still makes sense visually and yet "real time" is compressed on the screen. L.S. 1 establishes that the man is walking towards the car. You can then cut to the door handle (as a "buffer shot") just before the man's hand grasps it.

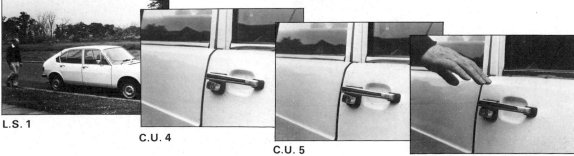

L.S. 1   C.U. 4   C.U. 5   C.U. 6

Shot Length

So far we have dealt only with cutting between shots of the same scene. However, not all action cuts are concerned with intercutting different camera angles of the same event. In any form of documentary film – from the family movie upwards – you will often be cutting together shots from different times and places that you have linked purely thematically. Each single shot will have its own rhythm, and probably a continuous series of separate actions throughout its length. The task is therefore to find a good "in-point" and also a satisfactory "out-point" in each case.

There are generally quite a number of possible ins and outs in any shot. Set the film up on the viewer, run it through a few times and look for some decisive action, such as the sweeping gesture of a hand or the departure of a person from the edge of the frame, to carry your eye into the new shot or out of an old one. Mark up the in-point (see p. 215), and then run the shot through the viewer – at the correct speed – until you feel you have located the exact moment where the shot should end. Mark it, and, before making the cut, consider it in relation to the shot that is to follow: very often, a right-to-left movement out of one shot which is effective in isolation can look wrong if the shot that follows is in the opposite direction. (Note that this is not a matter of continuity – since in this case the shots are of different subjects – but a question of visual effect.) If all looks well, make the cut, splice on the next shot, and assess the combined effect of the shots in conjunction. Avoid the temptation to keep viewing the film on your projector.

Choosing an in- and out-point
In this example, the movement of the girl across the frame is allowed to dictate the length of the shot.

1a In-point
Start the shot as the girl enters the frame.

1b Mid-scene

1c Mid-scene

1d Mid-scene

1e Out-point
End the shot as the girl leaves the frame.

Cutting static shots

Finding a moment of decisive action may be one way of deciding on a cutting point, but it is not the sole criterion for the length of a shot. Even more important is the length of time that the shot can "hold" on the screen. This will depend partly on the overall rhythm of the sequence (see p. 220–21). Judging the duration of a shot is particularly difficult if you are editing a series of static takes or cutaways. First, since nothing is actually "happening" in a static shot, it gives you no assistance in the way of action towards making your decision. Second, unless you are using a motorized viewer, the tendency is to wind the film through at the rate you want rather than at the correct film speed. You can control this to some extent by using a table of running times (see p. 274) to convert footage into screen-time. But the best thing to do is to cut the shot long at the rough assembly stage and then trim it down in the rough cut, after you have viewed the whole sequence at the correct speed on your projector.

Remember that the more information you are compressing into a single static shot, the longer it must be held. If the shot has been seen before, it can be quite short; but if it is a surprise, or packed with detail, it may need to be held longer on the screen. There is always a danger that as you edit you become over-familiar with the footage, and consequently cut the shots too short.

Shot duration
These two shots of a formal garden can be used to illustrate the difference between the various static shots. The close-up of a single flower (left) is a much "simpler" image than the wide-angle, long shot (right). You may find, therefore, that it will not need to be held on the screen for so long in order for the audience to assimilate it.

Assembling Shots

Establishing geography

There is a convention in movie photography that each new location or time-span in any film is introduced by an *establishing shot*. This is generally a fairly wide-angle, long or mid shot which shows the audience the relative position of the people or things that are seen in the subsequent shots. It tells the audience where the action is happening, which way the camera is facing in relation to the scene, and perhaps also that some time has elapsed since the previous scene. This convention therefore has a solid practical basis: it establishes the scene and then allows you to cut in closer – although in a long sequence it will probably be necessary to return to the wider shot from time to time. However, the formula can be varied for a particular effect. For example, it is a classic technique for building suspense to open with a series of mysterious and unexplained close-ups which are only made clear by a final wide-angle establishing shot.

The problems of "crossing the line" have already been explained in an earlier chapter (see p. 74), and it is crucial that the guidelines you used while shooting should be carried through in the editing of the film. Continuity of direction must be maintained when you cut shots together or the audience will become confused about what is happening where.

Matching and contrasting shots

When putting together shots, you will find that the succession of images you choose will dictate the "feel" of the sequence. For example, it is possible to improve the flow of a sequence, and in some way to suggest a harmonious connection between quite different objects, if there is a similarity between the neighbouring shots. This similarity may be one of composition, or even of color. On the other hand, if the composition is contradictory, or if the colors clash, the effect is of drama and contrast. This fact can be a valuable tool in the establishment of pace and atmosphere.

Just as the "look" of consecutive shots should be considered, so you should also be aware of the effect of joining together too many moving or static shots. The relation of movement to stillness in movie photography is a delicate one, and it has a great effect on the final result. At one extreme, the action might take place in front of a single, static camera; at the other, the camera may be continually zooming, panning and tracking in a restless, frenetic fashion. The chances are that you will want an effect somewhere in between. Unless you are aiming at a restless mood, avoid following one zoom or pan with another. Space out the moving shots – especially if they are in the same direction – with static shots, and in any case let the movements come to halt on a "holding shot" before cutting them.

Finally, bear in mind the different effects which can be created by varying the shot size and angle (see *Choosing Right Shot*, p. 60, and *Editing Errors*, p. 224). A large change from, say, a long shot to a big close-up is likely to look very dramatic on the screen. If this is the effect you want to achieve, it can be used very tellingly. But if it is unplanned it may appear clumsy and inappropriate, and may disrupt the flow of the sequence.

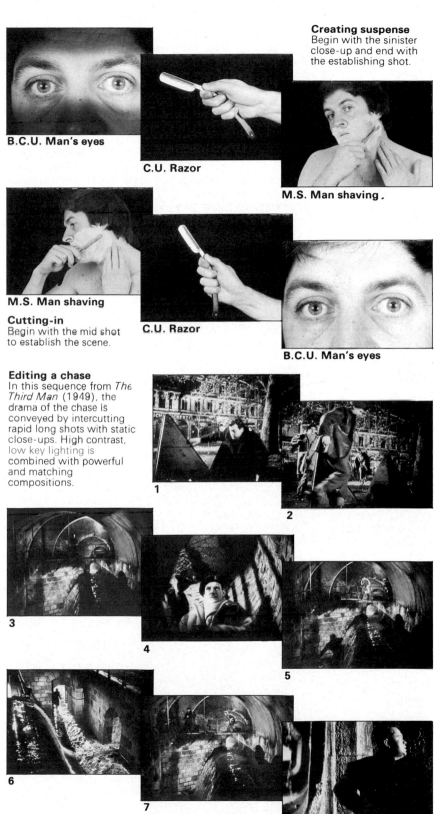

B.C.U. Man's eyes

C.U. Razor

M.S. Man shaving

Creating suspense
Begin with the sinister close-up and end with the establishing shot.

M.S. Man shaving

Cutting-in
Begin with the mid shot to establish the scene.

C.U. Razor

B.C.U. Man's eyes

Editing a chase
In this sequence from *The Third Man* (1949), the drama of the chase is conveyed by intercutting rapid long shots with static close-ups. High contrast, low key lighting is combined with powerful and matching compositions.

1

2

3

4

5

6

7

8

Building a Sequence

When you begin to assemble your shots, you should remember that the *rhythm* of a sequence is determined by the duration and frequency of the shots – and also by the amount of movement within each shot. Try to develop the habit of looking at your sequences, not just from the point of view of the developing action, but also with an eye for the pace and rhythm. The principal point to remember is that fast intercutting does not on its own produce either tension or excitement. What matters is the *variation* of cutting-tempo, not its average speed between two points. A slow build-up, followed by a rapid explosion of fast, strong single shots is far more dramatic than a monotonous and unmotivated fast-cutting sequence. If a sequence has to be fast, then the length of the shots can still be varied by including one longer shot

which derives its pace not from its brevity but from the speed of the action contained within the shot.

By contrast, you may be aiming for a mood of slow, dreamy contentment. In this case, you would tend to cut the shots at a rather regular pace – so that the variations in composition, duration and the frequency of the shots are just sufficient to maintain interest but not so great as to disturb the smooth flow of the images.

To build suspense, some form of compromise between the two rhythms can be used; for example, a series of slow long shots, followed by one or two very quick jolts, then another few long shots, and a few really violent jolts. The way to gauge the pace of a sequence is ideally on a motorized viewer, but, with practice, it is quite possible to use a manual viewer.

Action cutting

In this sequence, which comes from Joseph Losey's film, *The Servant* (1963), the cutting points are determined primarily by the action. Tony (James Fox) and Barratt (Dirk Bogarde) are engaged in a bizarre and sinister game with a tennis ball. However, the "game" turns

nasty, and the latent aggression between the two men explodes. In a series of short, fast cuts of mounting speed and power, the scene comes to a climax. Each shot begins and ends with a fast motion on the screen – in other words. all the cuts are action cuts.

Barratt: "Take your ball"

1 ⏱ 47 sec Long shot

2 ⏱ 24.5 sec Mid shot

Opening shots
The cut from shot 1 to shot 2 is from a long shot to a mid shot – the camera is still high. Barratt bends around to retrieve the ball. The cut to the close-up (shot 3) is made on the visual action – just as his head *begins* to turn.

3a ⏱ 1.5 sec Close-up Barratt

3b Barratt throws ball at Tony

Tony: "Take it yourself"

Subjective shot of Tony
The cut from shot 3 to shot 4 is made just as Barratt throws the ball back to him. It is the movement of the ball itself which dictates the cutting pace. During shot 4 Tony picks up the ball and hurls it violently back at Barratt.

4a ⏱ 2 sec Tony picks up ball

4b Tony throws ball at Barratt

4c Ball approaches

4d Ball hits camera

Barratt is hit
Because shot 4 is a subjective shot from Barratt's point of view, the ball comes directly at the camera. The cut to shot 5 is made a split-second before the ball, which virtually fills the frame, actually hits the camera lens. We see the impact in a cut back to the same camera position as for shot 3.

5a ⏱ 1.5 sec Close-up of ball hitting Barratt

5b Ball bounces off

5c Barratt recoils

5d He turns away

Thematic editing

The shots that build up a sequence may also be selected for reasons that have nothing to do with the requirements of clear action. They may be designed for purely symbolic effect, as in the famous opening sequence to *Citizen Kane* (1941). The whole film proceeds in a series of flashbacks and opens with the death of Kane. After a slow track up to his insane Gothic castle, we find ourselves in his death chamber. In a series of dissolves, snow is mysteriously superimposed on the interior, then a snowy cabin appears, revealed as a glass "snowstorm". Kane whispers "Rosebud", drops the snowstorm, and dies. It is revealed at the end of the film that "Rosebud" was the name of Kane's boyhood sled, and that the cabin was a childhood memory.

1 ⏱ **8 sec Kane in bed in front of window**

1a   Snow drifts across screen. Dissolve.

Kane's death bed
The sequence opens with a shot of an enormous window through which the dawn light is beginning to shine. In front of the window, in a huge bed, lies the dying Kane. Just as we decipher the image, however, it blurs, and the screen fills with snow. This is of course an optical effect. The scene eventually dissolves to shot 2.

Snow-covered house
The scene with the dying Kane dissolves into this extraordinary shot of a snow-covered house in front of which there are mysterious, shadowy figures. The snow still drifts across the screen and at first there is no sense of scale. There is a subtle dissolve to shot 3.

2 ⏱ **6 sec B.C.U. of "snowstorm"**

The glass globe
The dissolve from shot 2 to shot 3 reveals that the tiny house and figures are contained inside a water-filled glass globe, a "snowstorm". The camera tracks out and we see that the globe is lying in Kane's outstretched hand – though at this stage we have not seen Kane. In fact we do not see his eyes at all.

3 ⏱ **2 sec Kane's hand holding globe**

Kane: "Rosebud"

4 ⏱ **2 sec Kane's lips**

5 ⏱ **3.5 sec The globe falls**

The globe breaks
There is a shock cut to an extreme close-up of Kane's lips. The lips move, and he hoarsely whispers the word "Rosebud". In a new shot (actually a reverse cut from shot 3), the globe falls out of his hand. It is picked up in a 1 second low-angle shot, rolling towards the camera. It bounces down the stairs and smashes on the floor.

6 ⏱ **1 sec The globe rolls down steps**

6a The globe smashes

The nurse
Following the explosion of the glass globe, there is a cut to a distorted view of the bedroom door. It opens and a nurse enters. There is a cut to the same scene in long shot, seen through the curved glass of the smashed globe. She walks across to the bed and covers the face. Kane is dead. Fade to black.

7 ⏱ **1 sec Bedroom door opens**

7a Nurse enters

8 ⏱ **6.5 sec Nurse comes forward**

Symbolic Editing

All the guidelines included in the previous pages are merely ways to produce a smooth narrative. You can equally well decide to aim for a film that works on a symbolic level, bypassing the logical demands of narrative. In this kind of film you are not setting out to reproduce a recognizable version of ordinary reality, but creating a new and purely cinematic reality from a precisely controled succession of images. In fact, of course, all films do this to some extent, but the process can be carried to great lengths. It is seen at its most extreme in a large number of modern experimental films which have no narrative structure, no time-scale and no pretence of continuity. Ironically, this is, in a sense, the logical end to the great Russian tradition of silent film making: "editing is the creative force of filmic reality, and . . . nature provides only the raw material from which it works" (V. I. Pudovkin, 1929). Symbolic editing is in fact a technique of pure visual imagery, and as such it is well suited to the amateur·silent filmmaker who wishes to experiment with film in its most free and expressive form.

There is still no better illustration of the technique of symbolic editing than the early Russian cinema, since the tradition did not survive the impact of sound and the birth of the Talkies in the 1930s. In Pudovkin's case, the dramatic situation was still dominant. In the sequence on this page, which is taken from his film *Mother* (1926), he juxtaposes images in a purely cinematic way to produce a poetic evocation of a prisoner's joy at his forthcoming release. "I tried to affect the spectators not by the psychological performance of an actor, but by plastic synthesis through editing . . . The problem was the expression of his joy".

"Mother" (1926)
From the first subjective shot as the prisoner reads of his impending release, Pudovkin begins to build up the imagery of joy. We have already been told that "outside it is spring", and throughout the whole film the image of a frozen river melting has been used to express political liberation. Shot 4 in fact contains no less than five separate shots of rushing water cut together within 64 frames.

1 ⏱ 14.5 sec The letter

2 ⏱ 1.5 sec B.C.U. Hero's eyes

3 ⏱ 1.5 sec Hero in cell

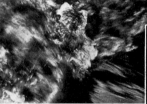

4 ⏱ 2.5 sec Water

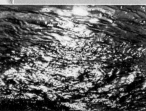

5 ⏱ 1 sec Hero's hand

The power of imagery
As the sequence builds up, shots of rushing water and a laughing child are rapidly and lengthily intercut with the hero sitting in his cell, and close-ups of his hand gripping the chair and of his beating heart. The crescendo of shots is at last resolved in shot 12, as the hero too is seen laughing with joy. The sequence ends with a fade to black.

6 ⏱ 2 sec Heart beating

7 ⏱ 2.5 sec Sunlight on water

8 ⏱ 2 sec Laughing child

9 ⏱ 1.5 sec Water

10 ⏱ 1.5 sec Laughing child

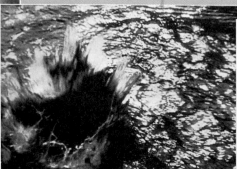

11 ⏱ 2 sec Water

12 ⏱ 4 sec Hero laughing. Fade-out

Editing for shock effect

Eisenstein, even in his early film, *Battleship Potemkin* (1925) was developing theories of intellectual symbolism to the point where, at times, the narrative was almost completely abandoned. The battleship "Potemkin" has mutinied against Tsarist rule, and has sailed out to meet the main body of the Russian fleet. There is a good deal of uncertainty as to whether the fleet will join her or sink her. The anxiety of the sailors builds up throughout the sequence until at last it is clear that the rest of the fleet has joined the mutiny. Eisenstein believed, with Pudovkin, that a film should proceed by a series of *shocks*. Each shot should add a new element to the drama. He despised the technique of master shot plus inserts and cut-ins. In Eisenstein's case, each composition derived its power from the contrast with the shots on either side.

"Will they open fire?"
Four rapid and dramatically contrasted shots lead up to another massive close-up of the gun barrel. Shots 8 to 12 build up the tension still further by strongly contrasting compositions of the battleship, the gun-loaders, the shells, and finally a sailor's face breaking into a delighted grin (which prefaces the caption "Brothers!").

1 ⏱ 3.5 sec "Potemkin"

"Battleship Potemkin" (1925)
The sequence opens with a shot of "Potemkin", in the hands of the revolutionaries sailing out to the fleet.

2 ⏱ 0.5 sec B.C.U. of gun barrel

Rapid intercutting
A sequence of seven shots of guns, gunmouths and preparations to fire culminate in the big close-up of the gun barrel.

3 ⏱ 1.5 sec Anxious sailor. Fade-out

4 ⏱ 1 sec B.C.U. of sailor

5 ⏱ 1 sec Sailor's hand on firing lanyard of gun

6 ⏱ 1.5 sec B.C.U. of gun barrel

7 ⏱ 1 sec Sailor

8 ⏱ 2.5 sec The battleship "Potemkin"

9 ⏱ 1 sec Sailors holding shells

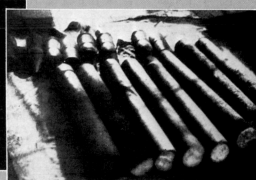

10 ⏱ 1 sec Pile of shells

11 ⏱ 1.5 sec Sailors training a gun

12 ⏱ 2 sec Sailor breaks into smile

13 ⏱ 0.5 sec Sailor cheers

The culmination
After the avalanche of rapid close-ups, the tension is released, and we pass from the big close-up of the sailor's face to this giant, liberating top-shot of the bow of the boat, as the cheering sailors rush to the rails.

Throughout, the sequence derives its force by contrast: contrasting angles, shot sizes, subjects, speed and composition.

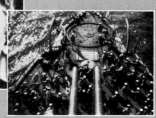

14 ⏱ 2 sec "Potemkin"

Editing Errors

The shots on these two pages are designed to illustrate some of the most common errors that are made when editing. Together, they combine to form a kind of "Chamber of Horrors" of mistakes that you should try to avoid when you edit your own movies. Some of them will be glaringly obvious to almost any audience; others may be noticed only by other filmmakers. But it is good practice to edit your movies as carefully as you can, to cut together your shots as smoothly as possible and to build up sequences that "read" logically.

Reverse cut
In between these two separate shots of a girl roller-skating, the camera has accidently crossed the line. In the first shot, the girl is moving from left to right; in the second shot, she has inexplicably changed direction. For guidance on how to cross the line successfully, see p. 74.

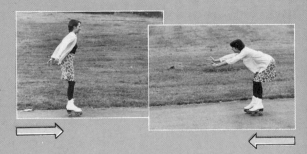

Jump cut
A jump cut is any cut which appears to "jump" badly on the screen. In the example here, the camera stopped filming and then started again after the man had moved to a different position.

1   2   3   4   Jump cut

Double action
When editing together shots of the same action filmed from different camera angles, take care to choose exactly the right cutting point (see p. 216–7). In the example here, the in-point for the close-up has been made too early; as a result, shot 4 repeats shot 2.

1   2   3   4   Double action

Change of camera angle

Any change in camera angle should be great enough to mark a distinct change in shot but not so great as to be shocking or disrupting to the audience.

Long shot

Long shot

Too small a change of angle (left)
These shots are too similar. The cut will appear slack on the screen.

Too small a change of image size (right)
The difference between these two shots is too slight for a good cut.

Too great a change of angle (left)
These two shots are so different that geography becomes confused.

Too great a change of image size (right)
The statue is so small in the long shot that the cut-in to the close-up is unrecognizable.

Very long shot

Long shot

Change of image size

Any change of image size should be great enough to make a noticeable difference but not so great as to interrupt the mood or flow of a sequence.

Mid shot

Medium close-up

Long shot

Big close-up

Incompatible eyelines

When shooting a scene containing more than one person, you must strive to maintain a clear sense of geography. The audience will only be absolutely certain where everyone is in relation to everybody else when they are all in the shot together. Therefore, as soon as you cut in to close-ups, you should see that your subjects look and speak in the right direction — that is, towards the point outside the shot in which the other characters are thought to be located (see p. 61).

Mis-matched eyelines
If you are filming a conversation by intercutting between single close-ups, take care that your subjects are facing in the right direction. Although the two girls in these shots are talking to one another, the camera angles make them appear to be back-to-back.

Inappropriate cutaways

A cutaway is a shot inserted into a sequence to show something other than the main action. It is often used to disguise a bad continuity cut or to introduce another aspect of a scene — a flashback, a subjective reaction or parallel action, for example. Obviously, the cutaway should appear to be related to the action. It should also —

unless it is your intention to do otherwise — match the mood of the sequence. It is pointless trying to enrich a scene by introducing cutaways which disrupt the pace, interrupt the flow, confuse the action, or which are plainly inappropriate. Be ruthless, and judge each shot in relation to the ones that surround it.

1 Master shot

2 Master shot

3 Cutaway

4 Master shot

Mis-matched cutaways
When inserting a cutaway into the main action, take care to match the mood of the overall sequence. The atmosphere of the picnic in the shots on the left has been disrupted by the cutaway of one of the girls frowning.

Continuity

Errors of continuity are probably the most common of all editing mistakes. The very nature of editing — the joining together of different shots, often filmed at different times and in different places, in order to create a convincing impression of real events — means that a film editor will always be faced with continuity problems. Many of the most serious and most obvious mistakes can only be

prevented at the time of filming (see p. 86), so take a careful note of all the details of each shot — either mentally, or on paper with an instant-picture camera. But bear in mind that when you join any two shots together continuity must be maintained, not only in appearance (dress, color, weather, etc.), but also in action, pace, and sound

Handbag

Different handbag

Burnt-down candle

New candle

Continuity errors
This series of shots illustrates some of the most commonly made continuity errors. If you are filming more than one take of the same scene, or two consecutive scenes in which the same subject appears, it is all too easy to overlook consistency between small details such as clothing, lighting, furniture or time of day. In these shots, the girl appears with different handbags, with the clock showing different times, with a new and a burnt-down candle, and with and without earrings.

11:45

12:10

Earring

No earring

Editing Tricks

Cutaways

The cutaway, a shot of something outside the flow of the main action, is one of the principle tools of all film editing (see p. 81). It can be used to introduce variety and an added dimension to a sequence; it can be used to divert the audience's attention away from continuity errors; to disguise unintentional jump cuts; or to conceal the fact that real time has been compressed on the screen. Thus, two shots which will not cut together can be linked by inserting a cutaway lifted from somewhere else. The cutaway itself need not be filmed at the same time.

1a

2c

1b

2a

2b

1c

1d

Inserting a cutaway
In this sequence a shot from a series of crowd reactions has been inserted into the main action.

2d

2e

Jump cutting

In the case of a cutaway, you can manipulate screen time by *inserting* extra footage into a sequence. But this is also possible by *removing* footage. For instance, if an interview contains a zoom-in from a mid shot to a close-up, the zoom itself can be removed, giving a straight cut from the mid shot to the close-up. The eyeline and expression should, however, match in both shots. This is one reason why interviews, on TV for example, usually contain several different shot sizes.

Jump cuts used to manipulate screen time in this way should not be confused with accidental jump cuts (see p. 224). If you take care to maintain continuity, then the cut will appear smooth; if you do not, then there will be an ugly and glaring jump on the screen.

1a

1e

Cheating the action
This sequence of a man shearing a sheep was shot as a long, slow zoom-in. You can "cheat the action" and compress screen-time by removing part of the footage in the middle of the zoom.

1b

1c

1d

The jump cut
In the example shown here, the middle three shots (1b to 1d) have been edited out. The sequence now cuts directly from the mid shot (1a) to the close-up (1e).

Dissolves

If it proves impossible to avoid a jump cut or a bad continuity cut, you can always resort to a fast dissolve (see p. 83). This softens the cut sufficiently to cover the break in continuity. Unfortunately, however, it is an optical effect which can usually be added only during the printing process in the laboratory.

A cut covered with a four-frame dissolve
This rather abrupt cut between a mid shot of the clown laughing and a close-up of him looking sad has been softened by a quick dissolve. It is possible to produce these effects in most cameras, but a four-frame dissolve of this kind would usually be added in the laboratory. See page 228 for how to indicate a dissolve to the lab.

Strong action-cuts

If you are faced with a scene filmed from two positions on opposite sides of the "line" (see p. 74), it may be possible to join the two shots together despite the fact that you will have made a "reverse cut". If you choose your cutting point carefully so that it coincides with some dramatic action, then the momentum of the action itself will carry the audience over the reverse cut and the apparent break in continuity will almost certainly pass unnoticed on the screen.

The reverse cut
Here, the mid shot of a man about to deliver a karate blow has been filmed from one side of the "line". The close-up of his hand has been shot from the opposite side.

The cut covered by a strong action
In order to cut the two shots together without too glaring a break in continuity, choose your cutting point just as the man's hand reaches the brick. The downward movement will cover the cut.

Buffer shots

An alternative answer to the problem of disguising a reverse cut is to use what is sometimes known as a "buffer shot" (see p. 75). If you begin with a shot in which your subject is seen walking in one direction, and you then wanted to follow it with another shot in which he or she is walking in the opposite direction, you might well be able to avoid the break in continuity by using a buffer shot. Typically, the second shot would begin with

the camera focused on some portion of the scene which did not reveal the main action. It might then zoom out or pan across to reveal the reverse action. Provided the action is clearly the same as before the cut (though in a new screen-direction), the buffer shot will blunt the force of the reverse cut by distracting the audience's attention from the break in continuity. The buffer shot acts as a "neutral" image.

The buffer shot
In the first shot, the boy is walking through the frame from left to right; in the second, he is walking from right to left. The change of direction was disguised by cutting to a close-up of the sign post (the "buffer shot"), then zooming out just before the boy walks into the frame.

Cutting the Master Copy

If you have been editing your original camera footage, you will by now have a film that is suitable for immediate projection. But if you have been editing a "workprint" (see p. 209), the original must be cut to match it. This process is generally known as *conforming* or *neg cutting*. It is a laborious and fiddly job, and, if you have any doubts about your capacity to do it accurately, you should send the film to a professional neg-cutting laboratory.

In 16 mm, neg cutting is done by matching up the "edge numbers" or "rubber numbers" (see p. 209) on the original and on the workprint. Neg cutting footage without these numbers (a technique known as *eye-matching*) is virtually impossible.

There are two methods of neg cutting. The first, known as *single-roll cutting*, means that you end up with one single roll of cut original which matches, shot-for-shot, the workprint. It is suitable whether the original is in reversal or negative form. However, when a print is made from negative film on a single roll, there is a tendency for the splices to "flash" slightly – that is, to show up as white lines. Also, if the original film is cut onto a single roll, there is no way that "dissolves" (see p. 187) can be incorporated in the printing process. For this reason, it is common practice professionally to make up the original on two rolls – *double-roll cutting*. Both methods require similar techniques. In all cases the object is to produce a precise match, frame-for-frame, between the original and the workprint.

Single-roll neg cutting

You will need a two-gang synchronizer (see p. 239) with rewind arms on either side, a cement splicer, a pair of cotton gloves and an absolutely clean editing bench. The best method is probably to break down the procedure into two steps. Since this involves handling the original film only once there is less risk of damaging it.

Begin by putting up the workprint on the synchronizer and go through from the top writing down the edge numbers at the in and out-point of each shot, *accurate to the frame*, so that you have a complete log of the film. Next, rearrange the shot list into a numerical order, so that the edge numbers are in the sequence which you will find when you work through the roll of original. Now thread up the original on the editing bench, remove

Double-roll neg cutting

Prints made from a single roll of original film tend to have visible splice marks. To avoid this, the master copy can be cut onto two separate but parallel rolls – this is known as *checkerboard* or *A and B rolling*. Each successive shot is on an alternative roll, and the portion of the other roll opposite a shot is filled with opaque black spacing to match. In printing, the original is passed through the printer one roll at a time, and the print is thus exposed

Marking up the workprint

If you are going to have your master copy cut by a professional neg-cutting service, you will need to know how to mark up your workprint so that the neg cutters will know what effects you want. There is a conventional way of indicating instructions with grease pencil on the shiny (base) side of the film. The most common are illustrated below.

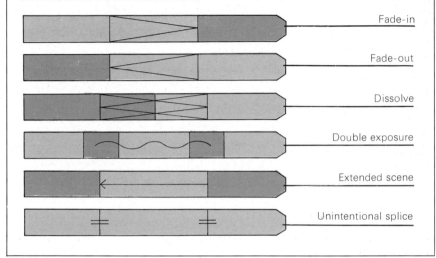

Fade-in

Fade-out

Dissolve

Double exposure

Extended scene

Unintentional splice

each shot you require in turn by referring to the log, and hang them up on numbered pegs (see p. 214). If the shot you are cutting out does not butt directly onto another piece of film you need, take out a generous leeway on either side – this should safeguard against cutting too little of a shot from the original. When all the shots have been removed from the master copy, wind the workprint back to the beginning, put it up on the back gang of the synchronizer, and begin to assemble the original on the front gang – taking the shots one by one from their numbered pegs, and using cement splices to join them together. At this point, you must check the exact sync between every frame of the original and the workprint as the two lengths of film move through the synchronizer.

twice. The black spacing in the A roll leaves gaps of unexposed film which are then exposed when the B roll is passed through the printer on the second pass.

A and B rolling also has the advantage of allowing smooth dissolves to be produced during the printing by overlapping the tail of one shot over the head of another. The printer automatically fades out the first shot on the A roll and fades in the second shot on the B roll.

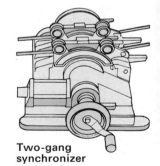

Two-gang synchronizer

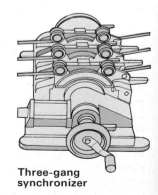

Three-gang synchronizer

A and B rolling

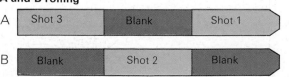

Producing a dissolve

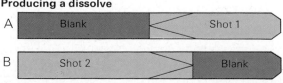

Making a Print of Your Film

There are many occasions on which you may need a duplicate print of your film. You may, first of all, want a workprint; you may then want a print to project so that the valuable original is not endangered; you may want extra copies to distribute; you may wish to correct errors of exposure; or you may even wish to blow up the film from one gauge to another, or to reduce it to a smaller format for easier projection. In all these cases a specialized lab will make the print for you according to your own specifications. There are two basic kinds of printing machines in use for making duplicate prints. The contact printer and the optical printer.

Contact printers
In a contact printer, the original film and the raw print-stock run, emulsion to emulsion, past a slit of light. The light shines through the original and exposes the print-stock accordingly. The gauge of the two filmstocks must of course be the same. Most modern contact printers run continuously and at high speed – and the intensity and (sometimes) the color balance of the lights can be varied from scene to scene to correct the appearance of the print. This is known as *grading* or *timing* (see right). All prints made on a contact printer must be projected with the emulsion *away* from the lens, whereas the original film carries the emulsion *towards* the lens. Contact printing is the most common method of making prints of a film.

Optical printers
In an optical printer, the original film and the raw print-stock are not in physical contact. Instead, the original is photographed through a series of lenses and the image is recorded on the print-stock. This method allows all kinds of possibilities. Unlike contact printing, the gauges need not be the same – so blow-ups and reductions of the original can be made. Optical printing can also be used to introduce a wide variety of optical effects – such as wipes (see p. 83), superimpositions (see p. 187), traveling mattes (see p. 186), freeze-frames, titles or zooms that were not on the original footage. On many machines, the instructions for these special effects are fed into the printer by means of a punched tape. Optical printing is, however, much more expensive than contact printing.

Liquid gate printing
Many optical printers now offer a *wet gate* or *liquid gate* technique, which is very effective in minimizing scratches and dirt – especially in the smaller gauges where the high degree of magnification often causes problems in this respect. In both cases, a transparent fluid is introduced at the point of printing. It coats the original film and "fills in" any defects. The liquid has the same refractive index as the film base, so light passes through it as if there were no scratches at all. In wet gate printing the fluid evaporates after passing through the gate; in liquid gate printing, the fluid, in larger quantities, flows continuously over the surface of the film and is siphoned off after the gate. Both processes are now readily available in all the gauges, although they are more expensive than the normal printing techniques.

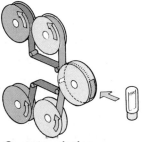

Contact printing
Light shines through the original and exposes the copy. The two stocks are sandwiched together.

Optical printing
Light shines through the original and exposes the copy through an optical lens arrangement.

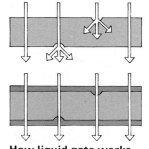

How liquid gate works
Fluid penetrates the scratches in the film so that the light is transmitted straight through.

Controlling print quality
It is axiomatic in all filmmaking that the film you project should be a duplicate copy and that you should store the original somewhere safe where it will not be damaged. Unfortunately, each stage of duplication leads to a drop in quality. The grain will increase, the contrast will build up, and the definition will deteriorate. The smaller the gauge, the more noticeable this will be.

If you intend to make prints from your camera original, the following points will help to minimize the loss of quality. Take the greatest care over exposure at the shooting stage. Use the slowest, finest grain film that you can. Avoid subjects with a high degree of contrast – since this will be exaggerated in the printing. Do not multiply the generations of copies that are to be made. Make certain that the print-stock you have selected is ideally matched to your original filmstock and to the nature of your subject. If you have a contrasty original, use a low contrast print-stock; if you have a low contrast original, boost the contrast by using a normal print-stock.

Grading and timing the print
Workprints are "ungraded", which means that they are printed with a uniform exposure and no attempt is made to compensate for any defects in the original. This is known as a *one-light print*, and is relatively cheap.

However, when you come to make your *release print* (or *show print*), you may want the shots to be given individual treatment. This is known as *grading* or *timing*. The original is put onto an electronic analyzer which assesses the density of each shot. A punched tape is then coded with the estimated ideal exposure for that shot. Many printers will also accept a different color filtration for each shot to correct uneven color balance.

Adding sound to the print
There are two types of sound track on film: magnetic and optical (see p. 110). Both can be placed on the print by the lab.

Magnetic sound is the norm in super 8 work. Optical sound in 8 mm is of relatively poor quality. The lab will usually transfer your sound track onto the magnetic stripe for you. For prints made on an optical printer, this presents no problem; but in the case of contact prints, the emulsion is on the side of the film which passes over the projector's sound heads – and unfortunately the sound stripe cannot be laid directly onto emulsion. Therefore, the lab must print onto stock specially pre-striped on the emulsion side.

Optical sound is more common at the printing stage in the larger formats. The sound is transferred onto the side of the print at the same time as the print is made.

The Film Laboratory

Specialist laboratories now offer super 8 and 16 mm filmmakers a wide variety of services. The range of facilities varies from lab to lab; but their availability and standards are higher in the USA than anywhere else.

One advantage of taking your film to a specialist lab to be processed is that you can instruct them to "force" the development in order to increase the film speed (see p. 208). They will also provide you with a contact workprint if you want one (see p. 209).

Many filmmakers who shoot double system sound movies get the lab to transfer their sound track from tape to fullcoat magnetic film and also to add a sound stripe to the original film (see p. 233).

Most labs offer a copying service enabling you to have duplicate prints made of your film. It is worth checking whether their machines have "liquid gates" (see p. 229). It is at this stage that you can order special optical effects such as dissolves, freeze-frames or mattes (see p. 228).

There is an increasing trend now for labs to offer a service for transferring super 8 film to video cassette (see p. 264) – either for video editing, for the addition of special video effects or simply for projection on a video player. After transfer from super 8 to videotape, the quality of the image is virtually indistinguishable from that of material originally shot on 16 mm film.

The problem that plagues all small gauge filmmakers is guaranteeing that the film is kept clean and undamaged. Because of the high magnification, the smallest specks of dirt or scratches are always visible on the screen. Several treatments are available which claim to protect the film. The methods vary, but they include lubricating, waxing and hardening the emulsion layers to guarantee smooth, steady projection, to reduce brittleness and to prevent scratching. You should check with your lab for specific details. On top of this, many labs will clean your film (using an ultrasonic process that removes most oil marks and fingerprints) or repair and recondition damaged or scratched footage.

Do's and don'ts with the lab

Dealing with the laboratory should not present any problems if you follow the guidelines given below. Above all, remember that the lab cannot perform the impossible: all printing and optical processes lead to a small loss in quality – and the smaller the gauge the more noticeable this will be.

- Make certain that the lab knows exactly what you want. Discuss your requirements with them and write orders clearly and accurately.
- Check whether they will accept tape splices and be wary of mixing different filmstocks on the same reel.
- Keep the original film absolutely clean, and do not attempt to duplicate a poor original.
- Keep the number of print-generations to an absolute minimum for good quality.
- Never intercut reversal original with a contact print, since the emulsions are on different sides of the film and will be defocused as a result.

Transferring from one gauge to another

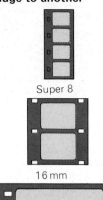

Super 8

16 mm

35 mm

Blow-ups and reductions

By using the optical printer (see p. 229), the lab can print from one gauge to another with the greatest ease. As a result, 70 mm epics can now be seen on in-flight movies in super 8 versions, and super 8 can be blown up for screening in movie theaters. Alternatively, you may have some footage in one gauge which you want to incorporate in a movie of another gauge.

In all these cases, you may choose one of three paths: you can go directly, in the form of a reversal print, or you can take the opportunity of producing an intermediate master, which will be either negative or positive. These are known as *internegatives* and *interpositives*, and they are special process-stocks. They can be used for all future prints – leaving the original untouched.

The charts below give some idea of the quality you could expect. The principles are the same whatever the gauge and whether you are printing blow-ups or reductions. But remember that there is no negative in super 8 and that the 35 mm "widescreen" or Cinema-Scope projection format is not the same as that of either 16 mm or super 8.

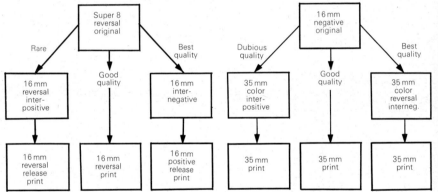

Optical blow-up from super 8 to 16 mm   **Optical blow-up from 16 to 35 mm**

Making multiple prints

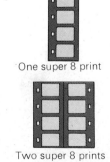

One super 8 print

Two super 8 prints

Four super 8 prints

Multiple prints

There are a number of ways of getting multiple prints of your films. Many methods involve making an "internegative" of the original which is then used to make all subsequent prints. If the internegative is of a larger gauge than the original, this will help to prevent loss of quality. For example, the best way to reproduce super 8 originals is to go through a 16 mm internegative. You will then find that subsequent super 8 reduction-prints will not have lost much in quality compared to the original. The advantage of all this is that the original camera film remains untouched, however many prints are made from the internegative. The disadvantage is the expense which the extra step incurs.

Another possibility for multiple printing is to print several parallel strips of the film onto a larger gauge. The larger gauge – which is perforated as for the smaller gauge, naturally – is then split to provide either two or four prints. For instance, two super 8 prints can be made side by side on a long roll of double super 8 film. In the same way, four super 8 prints can be made side by side on a roll of specially perforated 35 mm film.

EDITING SOUND

"The skilful use of sound does not only entail the addition of the most effective sound track to a previously conceived picture. It implies that the picture must be conceived, not independently, but in terms of possible sound associations" *Karel Reisz*

Editing Sound

Sound on film falls into two main categories: *synchronized sound* and *added sound*. Synchronized sound is sound recorded at the time of filming. It may be recorded either in the camera on the film itself (single system) or on a separate sound recorder (double system). Striped synchronized sound film is usually edited single system, which means that the image and sound cannot be moved independently of each other. The film is edited, sound and all, just as it comes back from the laboratory. Double system is edited as two separate lengths of film – pictures on one and sound on the other. This system allows much more freedom in the cutting room, since sound and pictures are not in a fixed relation to each other and can therefore be overlapped.

Added sound is any sound added to the film that is not synchronized: this includes music, commentary, wildtrack and effects recorded at the time of filming or

afterwards. The inclusion of added sound is essentially a dubbing procedure whether on tape, cassette, fullcoat magnetic film or magnetic sound stripe, and is discussed more fully on pages 244–8.

The difference between editing silent film and sound film is vast. The moment you have sync sound, the images are linked into an inexorable progression, which may be difficult to alter in the cutting room. Synchronized sound must be edited in conjunction with the pictures and, in many cases, will dictate the cutting. The price you pay for the greater realism provided by sync sound is a loss of flexibility at the editing stage, especially if you are working with single system striped film. On the positive side, you do not have to use elaborate symbols or captions to convey the essential facts of the narrative. If the sync sound is informative, even a commentary can be dispensed with.

Editing procedure
The flow chart below explains how to go about editing your sound movie. The actual processes and techniques are discussed in more detail in the following pages – whether you have a shot single system or double system sound, and whether you want to dub added sound to the film later. To use the chart, begin at the top and answer each question in turn.

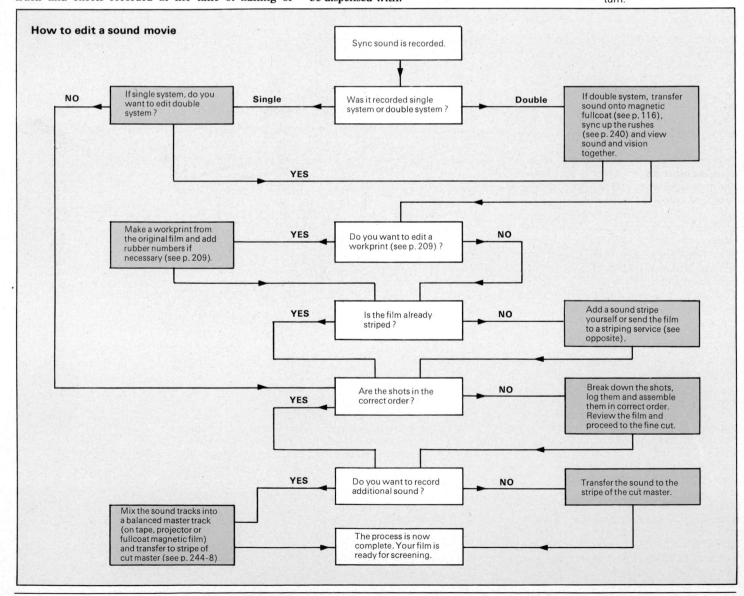

How to edit a sound movie

Sync sound is recorded.

Was it recorded single system or double system?

Single — If single system, do you want to edit double system? — **NO**

Double — If double system, transfer sound onto magnetic fullcoat (see p. 116), sync up the rushes (see p. 240) and view sound and vision together.

YES

YES — Make a workprint from the original film and add rubber numbers if necessary (see p. 209). — Do you want to edit a workprint (see p. 209)? — **NO**

YES — Is the film already striped? — **NO** — Add a sound stripe yourself or send the film to a striping service (see opposite).

YES — Are the shots in the correct order? — **NO** — Break down the shots, log them and assemble them in correct order. Review the film and proceed to the fine cut.

YES — Do you want to record additional sound? — **NO** — Transfer the sound to the stripe of the cut master.

Mix the sound tracks into a balanced master track (on tape, projector or fullcoat magnetic film) and transfer to stripe of cut master (see p. 244-8).

The process is now complete. Your film is ready for screening.

Striping the Film

Striping is the process of applying a blank magnetic sound track to a silent film. There are two ways of achieving this – either by sending the film out to a film laboratory (and risking it to the postal service) or by buying a film striping machine and adding the sound stripe yourself at home.

The stripe can be applied either as a paste or as a laminated strip and there are a variety of do-it-yourself kits for this purpose. All home-striping machines, though, use the laminated system and not all of them include the provision for adding a balance stripe to the film. The omission of the balance stripe will prove to be a drawback to users of twin track or stereo projectors (see p. 247), as the additional sound track is vital for stereo recording and playback. It also acts as a way of evening out film thickness and prevents it from overbalancing.

Some filmstock manufacturers now offer pre-striped film in silent super 8 cartridges. This allows you to add a sound track to your film after processing without having to add the stripe itself. However, this type of film is only available from Agfa and Fuji at present; it is unfortunately not yet marketed by Kodak.

Striping can be carried out after the film has been edited, but the splices tend to cause serious "hiccups" in the sound track unless beveled joins have been made (see p. 213). It is therefore a good idea to add the sound stripe before the silent footage has been edited. However, worthwhile economies can be made in both the workprinting and the striping processes by making a rough, preliminary edit of the material beforehand. Just eliminating the obviously unusable shots will not harm the original film or restrict any subsequent editing. Splices, however, should be kept to the very minimum at this stage to avoid sound "drop out".

How home striping works

If you want to add a sound stripe to your silent films yourself, it is probably best not to go for the cheapest home-striping machine. The demands placed on the machine are quite severe and call for a precision piece of equipment; the machine must be able to adhere a narrow strip of magnetic recording medium (0.8 mm wide) along one edge of the film. Striping machines able to add a balance stripe as well must lay a strip of recording tape of the same composition as the main stripe but a mere 0.45 mm wide accurately and securely along the other edge. Some striping machines are able to apply the main track and balance track simultaneously. To achieve this end, the amount of cement applied either to the film or the magnetic stripe itself must be precisely controled: too much cement and it will spread into the image area; too little cement and the stripe will peel off, taking your sound track with it. Also, the machine has to be designed so that the film is pulled through the guides and rollers evenly, without placing unnecessary strain on the film's sprocket holes. Finally, enough time must be allowed for the cement solution to dry before the film is wound onto the take-up spool.

Some types of striping machines first cut a shallow rut in the side of the film and then lay the stripe inside it. This removes the need for a balance stripe, which is designed to keep the film flat on the reel. But owners of twin track and stereo projectors will still want the balance stripe to record on.

Striping machines come either as completely independent units or as units that operate in conjunction with an ordinary projector. The film is first laced up through the striper and then through the projector. Once the film and striping material are correctly positioned, the projector is switched on and the process is then automatic. It is important to make certain that the projector and striper are correctly aligned and that the recommended distance between the two machines is maintained throughout the process to allow the cement time to dry before the film is taken up onto the spool. If the magnetic stripe is not in exactly the right place, it will "wander" off the projector's sound head; if it has not dried correctly, it will peel off.

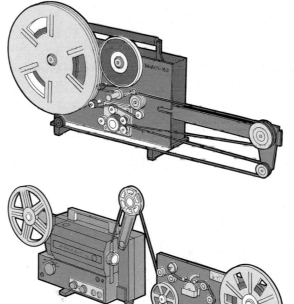

Magnetone Model 101
This home-striping unit is based on Magnetone's professional laboratory version, and is a precisely engineered, trouble-free piece of equipment. Rubber caps on the film spindles are used to determine the tension of the film passing through the striper, and they need to be adjusted each time you stripe a new film.

Projector/striper
Some do-it-yourself striping machines must be linked up to the projector. The distance between the two machines and their alignment is critical if the stripe is to be applied accurately.

The striped workprint

The normal workprint or cutting copy is a contact print, and it differs from the original film in that the emulsion faces towards the projector bulb, not away from it. The stripe, which in nearly all laboratory processes must be applied to the base side of the film, will therefore face the wrong way for the projector's sound head. To overcome this, the print may be made on pre-striped film *through* the base of the original. This will give poor definition, but at least the geometry of the workprint and the original will be the same. Overall, it is perhaps best to work on the original.

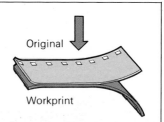

Original

Workprint

Pre-striped workprints
A striped contact workprint is made by shining light through the *base* of the original.

Editing Single System Sound

Single system sound editing has a lot to recommend it – you are dealing with a first-generation, original sound recording of high quality; you can never lose sync by accident; and you can easily dub additional sound over silent or unwanted sections of the pictures on most modern sound projectors. What is more, single system is both fast and relatively cheap.

The major disadvantage when it comes to editing super 8 single system is the 18-frame separation of sound and pictures brought about by the distance between sound head and exposure gate of the camera. (In 16 mm the separation is 28 frames.) In practice, this means that the first second or so of every sequence will be silent because the corresponding sound is 18 frames further on. Also, the final 18 frames of sound of every sequence will have no corresponding pictures. In the cutting room, if the first 18 frames are not cut every scene will start silently. While the second's silence can very occasionally be used as part of the dramatic content of the scene, usually the second of silence at the front, and the second of extra sound at the end of each shot, must simply be patiently endured.

Make allowances for editing

The key to successful stripe editing is a correct camera technique (see p. 115). When shooting sound that is to be edited later, allow at least one full second after starting the camera before the first important word or noise. Also, at the end of the shot leave the camera running for a second after the end of speech. This will allow you "to get the scissors in" to the pause.

Example 1

The 18-frame advanced position of the sound head means that the first second of every scene will be without sound. Likewise, the final second of sound will have no corresponding pictures. If the film is not to be edited this presents no problems because as *Scene 1* is being projected, the 18-frame advanced position of the projector's sound head is reproducing the corresponding sound (*Sound 1*).

Example 2

Shooting film in this way creates editing problems: the first second of *Scene 1* is mute; if you later decide to cut *Scene 1* where *Sound 1* ends you will remove the first 18 frames of *Scene 2*. If you cut for all the pictures of *Scene 2*, you will remove the final second of sound from *Scene 1*.

Example 3

For editing purposes, this is the best way to shoot single system sound. Before starting a scene, turn the camera on and expose 1 second (18 frames) of film prior to the action commencing. This 18 frames can later be cut so that sound and pictures start together. Leaving the camera running for 1 second (18 frames) after the last sound you want has been recorded, allows you to cut the last 18 frames without removing the first 18 frames of *Scene 2*. Shooting in this way allows *Scene 1* and *Scene 2* to be physically separated and repositioned because sound and pictures do not overlap between scenes.

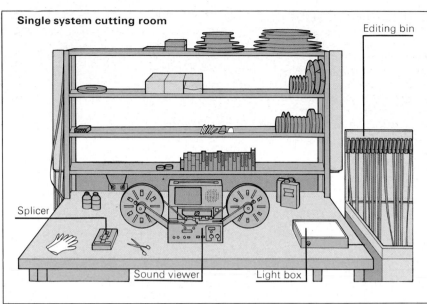

Single system cutting room

Editing bin

Splicer

Sound viewer   Light box

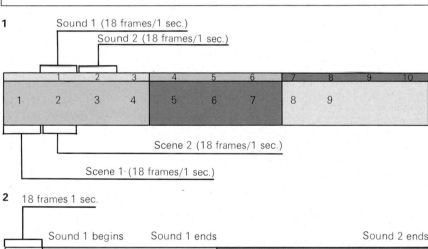

1

Sound 1 (18 frames/1 sec.)

Sound 2 (18 frames/1 sec.)

Scene 2 (18 frames/1 sec.)

Scene 1 (18 frames/1 sec.)

2   18 frames 1 sec.

Sound 1 begins   Sound 1 ends   Sound 2 ends

Scene 2

Scene 1   18 frames 1 sec.

3   1 sec. pause

1 sec. pause

1 sec. pause

1 sec. pause

Scene 1   Scene 2

18 frames   18 frames   18 frames   18 frames

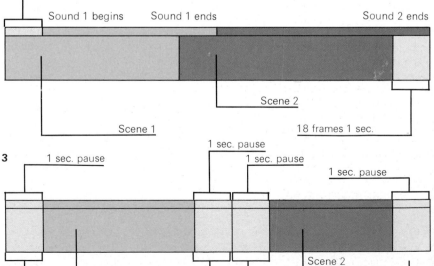

Equipment for single system

Before you take up the scissors and make the first cut, you will need some device that allows you to see the film as it will be projected and at the same time hear the recorded sound track. For really accurate single system sound editing you will need a *viewer*, either with an integral *sound head* or a silent viewer capable of accepting an *accessory sound head* and some means of amplifying and monitoring the sound signal transmitted by the sound head.

The sound viewer

Viewers, or editors, with integral sound heads are readily available – and there are many different models to choose from. A standard viewer consists of a mirror, screen, short focal length lens, lamp, prism shutter, gate and sprocket wheels. As the film is threaded through the gate, teeth in the sprocket wheel engage sprocket holes in the film. As the film is advanced through the gate, a sprocket wheel turns the prism shutter. The film is illuminated by a low-wattage lamp and the image is picked up by the lens, which projects it onto a mirror. The mirror then reflects the image onto the rear of the viewing screen. The image as seen on the other side is quite dim and cannot be seen properly in bright lighting unless the screen is recessed or shaded.

If you already own a silent viewer check to see if it will accept a sound head accessory as this will save you the expense of buying a completely new unit. The accessory sound head clips onto the right-hand side of the machine, 18 frames from the gate, and the sound is either fed to headphones or to a *squawk box* (a speaker and amplifier unit). Unless the viewer is motorized, some practice is needed to wind the film smoothly enough, and at the correct speed, for the sound track to be intelligible. But once you begin to handle the cut stripe film you will soon master the "feel" of the sound/vision discrepancy, which can be a little daunting at first. The gap between sound and vision is there in front of you, yet as you wind the film and monitor the sound track they appear simultaneous.

Monitoring the sound track

Ready made squawk boxes can be purchased from most large photographic retailers and consist of an amplifier unit, which picks up the signal from the sound head of the viewer, and a speaker or headphones, which allow you to monitor the sound. A good quality squawk box will make the time spent listening to the sound track much more pleasant and permit critical monitoring.

But a purpose-built squawk box is not essential, because many tape recorders will take the lead from the sound head and reproduce the sound through their own amplifier and speakers. This facility is standard on the Super 8 Sound recorder, but any recorder can be modified. Your domestic hi-fi amplifier can also be used, and all you have to do is plug the lead from the sound head into an appropriate input. If in doubt about which input to use, it is best to consult a hi-fi specialist. Remember to take along the wiring diagram which accompanies your particular amplifier.

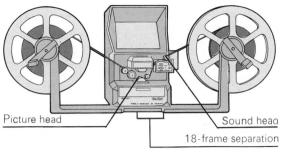

Picture head   Sound head

18-frame separation

Silent viewers
Accessory sound heads can be fitted to some silent viewers in order to monitor the sound track. These clip onto the right of the machine, 18 frames (3 in.) away from the picture gate. In this way the sound/vision separation is maintained.

Goko RM-5000
This sound viewer is a constant-speed, motorized model. Sound is reproduced through a speaker positioned next to the screen.

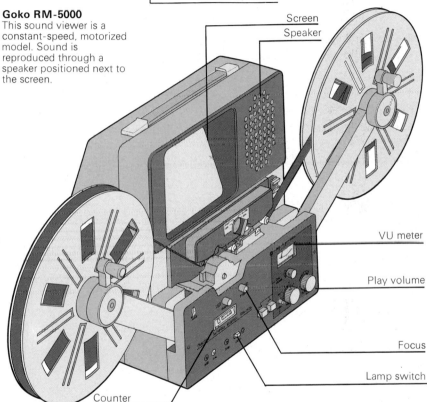

Screen
Speaker
VU meter
Play volume
Focus
Lamp switch
Counter

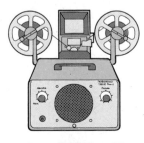

Squawk box (left)
Commercial squawk boxes can be used to monitor the signal sent from the sound head.

Tape recorder (right)
The built-in amplifier and speaker of your tape recorder can be used as an alternative.

Domestic hi-fi (left)
The signal sent from the sound head can also be channelled through your domestic hi-fi amplifier and speaker.

Headphones (right)
It is possible to do away with the speaker by using a set of headphones.

Editing Single System Sound

When editing single system you will inevitably be largely governed by the sound track. Because of the 18-frame displacement, any cut you make in the film will also cut the sound for the picture 18 frames behind.

After loading the film onto the spools and fitting them onto the rewinds, wind down the film until the first sound you want to keep in the shot hits the sound head. Rock the film to and fro until you are positive that you have located the exact spot where the sound starts, then pull it back a few frames (so as not to clip the first syllable) and mark the frame *at the sound head* with a wax pencil. Now check, *by winding back 18 frames*, that the picture opposite the frame you have marked in sound is usable. One problem you might find is that it contains the end of the previous shot, or it might show your subject's head turning before he or she speaks. If all is well, make the cut.

At the tail of a shot wind down to the end of the last word or sound, but this time mark the frame *at the viewing point*. Check again, *by winding forward 18 frames*, that the sound which falls against your cutting point does not contain any unwanted information. If you are unlucky it might contain the beginning of a new sentence, or even "Cut!"

From this it can be seen that the 18 frames of wasted film at the beginning and end of every shot is not a luxury but a necessity for smooth single system editing.

However, this does not make for particularly exciting cutting, and for this reason it is best to avoid intensive or ambitious editing with single system film. Go for longer takes and do as much editing in the camera as you can (see p. 115). What single system editing does best is to reorganize your film between shots. Cutting within a shot is best left to silent film or sound film shot on double system, where there is complete separation between the sound and picture films.

Counting frame displacement

To save yourself the bother of counting the 18-frame displacement between sound and pictures each time (and there is always the possibility that you might count incorrectly), cut a piece of leader to the 18-frame length and tape it to your editing table. When you next want to locate the 18-frame displacement, simply compare your footage to the pre-cut length of leader.

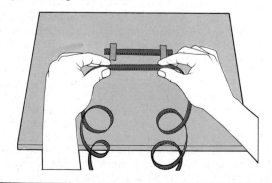

Direction of film travel

Head

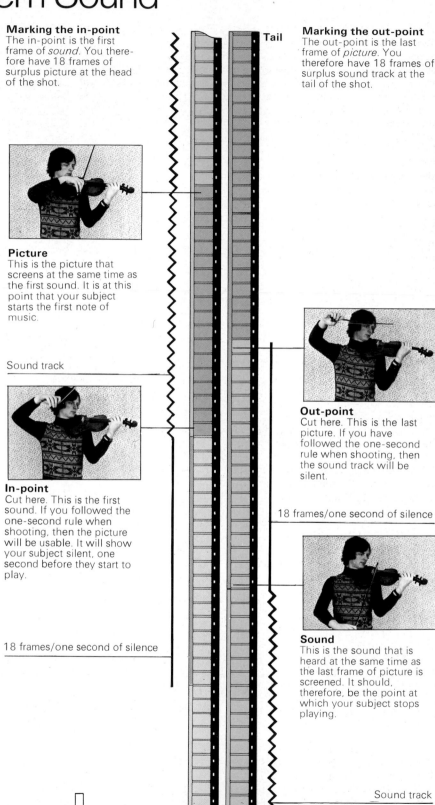

Marking the in-point
The in-point is the first frame of *sound*. You therefore have 18 frames of surplus picture at the head of the shot.

Picture
This is the picture that screens at the same time as the first sound. It is at this point that your subject starts the first note of music.

Sound track

In-point
Cut here. This is the first sound. If you followed the one-second rule when shooting, then the picture will be usable. It will show your subject silent, one second before they start to play.

18 frames/one second of silence

Tail

Marking the out-point
The out-point is the last frame of *picture*. You therefore have 18 frames of surplus sound track at the tail of the shot.

Out-point
Cut here. This is the last picture. If you have followed the one-second rule when shooting, then the sound track will be silent.

18 frames/one second of silence

Sound
This is the sound that is heard at the same time as the last frame of picture is screened. It should, therefore, be the point at which your subject stops playing.

Sound track

Avoiding sound drop out

To avoid sound drop out when editing single system, use either a bevel-edge cement splicer or, better still, a tape splicer (see p. 212–13). The tape splicer must be one that leaves the main sound track uncovered, and if you are planning to use a twin track or stereo projector you must use the type of tape splicer that leaves *both* tracks uncovered. If you are intercutting silent and sound footage, have the silent footage striped *before* editing. Better still, shoot the silent footage with a sound cartridge on a sound camera, or with pre-striped film in a silent camera. Then the difference in thickness between sound tracks will be minimized, resulting in little sound drop out on the joins (see p. 213).

Using wildtrack

If, for example, you have shot someone talking with music playing in the background (a band, for instance), and have stopped the camera a few times in order to get a variety of different camera angles, a problem might arise in editing. Foreseeing problems, you also decided to record a "wildtrack". In the cutting room you decide to combine these different camera angles by using "cutaways" to the band playing, which were shot at a slightly later time. Because of the time differential, "jumps" on the sound between the spoken words and the cutaways are bound to occur.

To solve this type of problem, and make the sound transition smooth and logical, you need to use a wildtrack, recorded either on a cassette or reel-to-reel recorder. After the film has been edited and the cutaways have been inserted, you can transfer the sound from the recorder onto the magnetic sound stripe corresponding to the cutaways, using the sound-on-sound facility on your projector. On some projectors, sound-on-sound is known as a "trick" sound control.

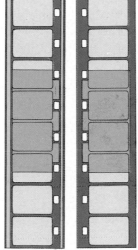

Splicing sound film
Owners of twin track or stereo projectors will want to use a tape splicer that leaves both the main sound stripe and the balance stripe uncovered, as illustrated above. In this way, the tape will not interfere with the sound reproduction.

Displacement recorder

To by-pass the problem of the 18-frame separation of sound and picture, it is possible to use a displacement recorder. This device is used to relocate the recorded sound in *level sync* (exactly opposite its related image). With the single system film in level sync, cutting for the sound is the same as cutting for the image, and cutting for the image is the same as cutting for the sound. After editing, the film and its sound stripe are once again passed through the displacement recorder and the sound track is returned to its correct position, 18 frames ahead of the pictures, ready for projection.

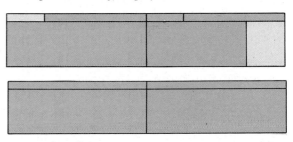

Editing in level sync
The first diagram above shows the normal 18-frame advance position of sound. The second shows sound in level sync.

Tape synchronizer

If you do not have access to a displacement recorder, a tape synchronizer can be used. The sound from the stripe is transferred in sync to perforated tape, and the tape is then transferred again back to the stripe with an 18-frame delay so that the film can be edited in level sync. After editing it is re-transferred to perforated tape, and then, at last, back onto the film stripe in the correct sync position. This system involves five generations of sound transfer and results in a substantial loss of sound quality.

Shooting single/editing double

By far the best solution to the problems of editing single system sound film is to transfer the sound track from the magnetic sound stripe onto magnetic fullcoat film. Once this has been done the sound and film can be edited *double system*, and with greatly increased flexibility (see p. 238–41). With a length of magnetic film (the sound track) exactly the same as that of the film containing the images, cuts can be made without regard to the 18-frame displacement between sound and pictures. After editing and mixing, the sound can be transferred back onto the stripe of the picture film at the dubbing stage in its correct sync position, 18 frames ahead of the picture, ready for projection. As with any re-recording of the original sound, this system does result in some loss of quality, but this is more than made up for by the freedom in editing. This system only involves two generations of sound. It is possible to use an equalizer at the transfer stage to correct any tonal imbalance such as hum or hiss. The advantage of making corrections at this stage is that subsequent dubbing operations will be simplified. During the second transfer (back from magnetic fullcoat into the film's sound stripe), music and effects can be combined with the original sync sound.

Editing a dialogue

In this example we are assuming that a dialogue has been filmed consisting of individual close-ups of two people speaking. In editing you decide to intercut shots of A talking with B replying. Knowing full well that the first second of each shot will be without sound, because of the 18-frame discrepancy between sound and pictures, the problem can be resolved if B appears to be listening to what A is saying for at least one full second before B starts saying his or her lines. Nothing in the attitude of B must reveal the fact that for the first second of his or her reaction in shot there are, in fact, no words being spoken. In this way, when the shot of A speaking is cut at the end of the sound, and spliced to the front of the next shot of B, the last second of A speaking will coincide with the first second of B in shot. This is a much better alternative than having a second's pause between the last word spoken by A and the first word of B's reply. The illustration on the right shows how your film should appear after editing. Note that the 18 frames of sound overlap the cuts in the conversation.

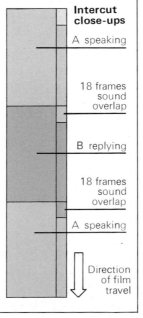

Intercut close-ups

A speaking

18 frames sound overlap

B replying

18 frames sound overlap

A speaking

Direction of film travel

Editing Double System Sound

Double system sound editing is any editing arrangement in which the pictures and the sound are edited separately, rather than together – as in single system where the sound is on the sound stripe running down the length of the film (see p. 230–33). In practice, the sound and the pictures are edited in parallel, so that "sync" (a simultaneous sound and action) can be maintained throughout a sequence. In other words, when the picture is cut, the sound is cut in exactly the same place and at the same time. It is this aspect of double system (the physical separation of sound and pictures) that gives it so much flexibility. Although, right through from the original shooting and recording, it is more expensive and requires more equipment than single system, double system is growing in popularity among enthusiasts who intend to edit extensively.

The most common method of maintaining sync when editing double system is to record the sound on a roll of magnetic fullcoat film, which is sprocketed to give frame-for-frame correspondence with the picture film. The physical dimensions and time durations of sound and pictures are therefore a perfect match and may be cut and moved with complete freedom. Unless the original sound was recorded on a portable fullcoat recorder, it will need to be resolved (transferred onto magnetic fullcoat) from tape before editing can start.

Another method of maintaining sync in double system is to use *perforated tape*, and is very popular in the United Kingdom. Its popularity is due to its cheapness and because any domestic tape recorder (once modified) can be used instead of a special fullcoat recorder. In all cases, the sync pulse recorded alongside the original sound track is converted into a one-frame advance (I/F) for the recorder to produce a sound recording in frame-for-frame sync with the pictures in just the same way as for a fullcoat recorder. With perforated tape the recording systems are of two types: those that use tape of a different "pitch" from super 8 film sprockets (and here the film dimensions and tape dimensions are quite different); and the newer type, which uses tape of the same sprocket pitch as super 8. The latter is obviously preferable, as the tape can be measured directly against the film during editing, and both can be put on a *sync block* without any differential. However, in both these systems the tape is $\frac{1}{4}$ in. (6 mm) wide and cannot be interchanged with film on a normal *synchronizer*. Perforated tape remains the only viable system for standard 8 because there is no fullcoat equivalent.

The workprint

To overcome the problem of the film being scratched or badly cut, a workprint (or "cutting copy") can be produced by a film laboratory. The workprint is a cheap copy of the original on which all editing is carried out: it can be continuously projected and cut until you are completely satisfied that all the cuts are in the right place, and it does not matter how many times it is dropped, scratched or abused. Once the workprint is right, the original footage is taken out of storage and edited so that it conforms, frame-for-frame, to the workprint (see p. 209).

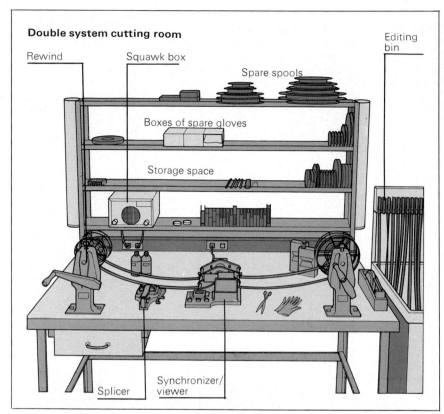

Double system cutting room

Rewind
Squawk box
Spare spools
Editing bin
Boxes of spare gloves
Storage space
Splicer
Synchronizer/viewer

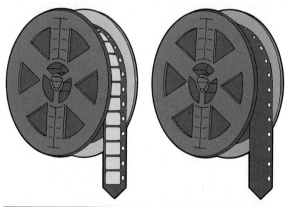

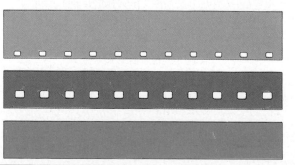

Film and fullcoat
The fact that the sound track and the picture film are totally separate is the big advantage double system editing has over single system. Once sound has been transferred onto fullcoat, there is an exact frame-for-frame match between sound and vision. Once the two are locked into the sync block, sync can be maintained throughout the editing process.

Perforated tape
Some perforated tapes use a sprocket "pitch" that differs from super 8.

Super 8
The different dimensions of super 8 and perforated tape create problems during editing.

Perforated tape
Perforated tapes using the same sprocket pitch as super 8 are preferable.

$\frac{1}{4}$ in. (6 mm) tape
This recording medium has the same dimensions as perforated tape.

Equipment for double system

The basic double system editing table should include a viewer, sync block, rewinds, a sound reader and a "squawk box". Some systems have motors to advance both pictures and sound films at variable speeds.

The synchronizer viewer

The only really essential piece of equipment for double system sound editing is a *synchronizer/viewer* or "pic-sync". The pic-sync can read the sound track and show the picture on its own integral screen. It may have two, three or four sprocketed wheels ("gangs") into which the rolls of film and magnetic fullcoat are "locked" to maintain sync. The gate of the viewer is usually in line with the sound heads. A typical synchronizer has the film at the front and the sound tracks on the rear gangs. The arms above the respective film channels may be released so that the relative positions of the tracks and film can be adjusted before being locked back into some new configuration. In this way, one channel of film may have up to three channels of sound running in parallel to it – one sync track, one music track and one effects or commentary track, for example. The sound from the tracks can be monitored either singly or together. The most usual arrangement, however, is that at the editing stage you use just one picture track and one sound track, which might be your original sync, or a music track or a pre-recorded commentary. After editing is complete, the different sounds are split into separate rolls, mixed and dubbed onto a final master track (see p. 248).

Horizontal editing machines

Horizontal or "flatbed" editing tables can also be used. The different name comes from the fact that the reels are positioned horizontally and not on their edge, or vertically. These are very common in both 35 mm and 16 mm editing. They are also available in super 8, but are still fairly expensive. With the horizontal editing table the fullcoat and film take-ups are motorized, and both forward and reverse functions work at fast and normal speeds. The film can be driven through the machine as slow as one frame per second or as fast as 180 frames per second while still maintaining sync, and all tracks can be individually switched in and out of sync with each other. Horizontal tables are referred to by the number of plates they hold: a four-plate machine can handle one picture track and one sound track; a six-plate machine, two sound tracks and one picture track, or any combination. These machines can be hired or you will use them if you rent a cutting room.

Rewinds

Double system vertical editors/viewers do not come with built-in rewinds as do most single system models. Instead, the arms are mounted on the bench either side of the synchronizer. The rewinds must be large enough to take the additional reels needed in double system and sometimes incorporate a braking system that allows you to adjust the tension on the reels, so lessening the chance of film spilling off.

Synchronizer/viewer
Synchronizers can be linked to a viewer so that sound and vision can be cut in a line across the block.

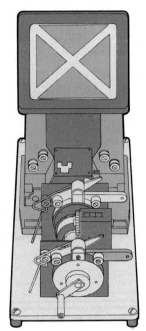

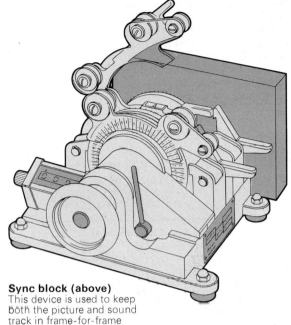

Sync block (above)
This device is used to keep both the picture and sound track in frame-for-frame sync during viewing and editing.

Super 8 editor (above)
These horizontal "flatbed" editors are relatively new to super 8 and represent a great saving in time spent editing sound and pictures.

16 mm editor (right)
Larger versions can handle one picture and three sound tracks.

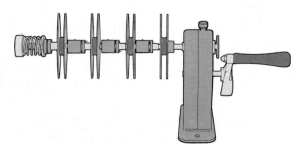

Rewinds
Double system rewinds need to be larger than their single system equivalents. This is so that they can carry both the spools of picture film and several different reels of magnetic fullcoat for editing the different sound tracks.

Editing Double System Sound

In double system editing the sound and pictures are physically quite separate but run in parallel. Whether you are making a parallel cut in sound and vision, or overlaying one sound over an unrelated image, you will always need some reference points on both sound and vision to maintain sync as both are run through the synchronizer/viewer.

Before you start to edit, however, the recorded sound must be transferred to fullcoat or "resolved".

Resolving

All the methods of resolving share one common feature: there must be a reference pulse on the tape that can be monitored by the resolver so that its speed can be varied to produce *frame-for-frame sync*. Resolving may be done professionally as a laboratory service or, in super 8, at home. In super 8 the sound recorded on a cassette or tape recorder is fed into a magnetic fullcoat recorder. The recorder monitors the sync pulse, either digital or pilot-tone (see p. 117), recorded alongside the sound track, and alters its speed to produce a recording on magnetic film that is a frame-for-frame match.

Other methods of resolving involve the use of a modified sound projector loaded with fullcoat magnetic film and linked, via a sync cable, to a tape or cassette recorder. For single system users who wish to edit double system, the sound on the striped film can be transferred via a sound projector onto magnetic fullcoat, either on a fullcoat recorder or on another modified projector.

"Synching up the rushes"

After the sound has been transferred to magnetic fullcoat, the picture and the sound must be put into sync for viewing and editing. This process is known as "synching up the rushes" (for an explanation of the term "rushes" see p. 209).

Sync can be established if you have used a *common start mark* when filming (see p. 118). Place the picture and sound film in their respective channels in the synchronizer. If you have used a clapper board as a common start mark, run the sound film over the sound head of the synchronizer until you hear the verbal announcement of the shot followed by a "clack" as the two elements of the board come together. At the very first frame of the clack's sound, use a wax pencil to make a sync mark (usually three vertical lines). Next, wind the picture film only through the synchronizer until you find the shot of the clapper board being closed for that shot, and place a sync mark (a cross inside two vertical lines) on the exact frame of the board being closed. The sound and pictures may now be locked into sync on the synchronizer. In this way all the sync shots on the roll of fullcoat can be assembled and run in parallel with the pictures. You will need to use appropriate lengths of *spacing* in the sound track to cover the portions of film for which there is no sync sound. After you have viewed the film in sync, the rolls of sound and pictures can be sent away to be rubber numbered (see p. 209). The next step is to break down the two rolls into their component shots (each of which has sync marks at the head) and store them carefully for editing.

Resolving
Resolving is the process of transferring sound recorded on stripe or, more commonly, on tape (either cassette or reel-to-reel) to magnetic fullcoat film. The illustration above shows one method: the fullcoat recorder is re-recording the sound track using a sync pulse as a reference to produce frame-for-frame sync.

Common start marks
Although not absolutely vital, common start marks make the task of "synching up the rushes" much easier. The point where the clapper sections come together and its corresponding noise on the sound track make a convenient reference point from which sound and vision can be matched in editing. Without this aid, you will have to rely on a simultaneous sound and action cropping up in each shot – a door closing, for example.

Sync marks
Traditionally, a cross inside two vertical lines (right) is used to mark in vision the point where the clapper board sections come together. Three vertical lines (right) are used to mark in sound the frame where the corresponding sound is heard. Long horizontal lines either side of these marks make finding them easier when running the film quickly through the synchronizer/viewer. All marks should be made with a wax pencil.

Assembling the film

The film is assembled from left to right across the synchronizer/viewer, with the edited rolls growing on the reels on the right-hand rewind arm. You should aim to do your cutting on the left of the synchronizer so that the cut you have just completed has to pass through the synchronizer and can be checked for sync before it is wound onto the take-up reels on the right. If you are just joining up one sync shot after another there will be no difficulty in maintaining sync, but this would be very dull and rules out the most interesting possibilities of double system editing.

Splicing fullcoat

When splicing fullcoat use a diagonal cut to prevent dropout. This is not normally possible with super 8 joiners. For a good join, mark a line on the frames to be spliced. When the two are put together, the line should be complete.

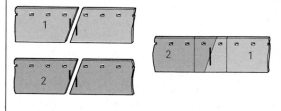

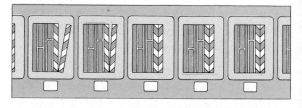

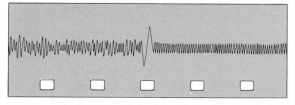

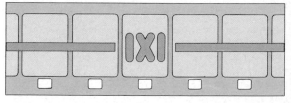

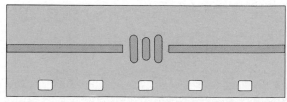

Intercutting sync and silent

If your film consists entirely of sync shots you will have no trouble in matching sound and vision. However, if you wish to use silent shots, and you do not want to "overlay" sync sound, you should use silent white spacing in the sound track to cover the sections of mute footage. This will guarantee that the total length of sound and vision remains the same and that sync is maintained on either side of the mute sections of film. In dubbing (see p. 244–8), the "hole" left by the inclusion of the white spacing will not be wasted as it can be filled with music or effects.

Overlaying sound

Overlaying sound is one of the typical problems that occur in double system editing. The example here shows how to insert a silent cutaway into a sync sequence. The cutaway could be of a reaction shot cut into a sync "master" shot of a person speaking.

The first step is to run the sound and vision of the master shot from left to right through the synchronizer until you find the point where you want to start the cutaway. Mark both the sound and vision in parallel.

Wind both the tracks back through the synchronizer and cut the out-point of the master shot on the picture film at the point marked (this leaves a "tail trim" of the master on the left-hand rewind arm).

Unclip the master shot from the synchronizer (you will not lose sync because the cutting point has been marked on the sound track). Now thread up the reaction cutaway, select a satisfactory in-point and mark this on the cutaway.

Insert the cutaway by joining it to the out-point of the master shot. The in-point must lie opposite the first cutting point marked on the sound track when both are locked into the synchronizer.

Now, run the joined-up cutaway through the synchronizer to its out-point and mark both sound and vision. Next, wind back to the beginning of the cutaway and place the tail trim of the master on the third gang of the synchronizer, so that its head lies opposite the original cut. Wind down to your chosen out-point (as marked on the sound and cutaway), mark the tail trim of the master in parallel, wind back slightly and cut it.

Next, join the master trail trim onto the out-point of the cutaway. It is now on the front gang of the synchronizer and will run in sync.

Store the trims on either side of the cutaway and the length of film you have cut out of the master shot in case you change your mind later.

In essence, what you have done by following this procedure is to have removed a length of film from the master shot and replaced it with another length of film (the cutaway). To ensure that sync is maintained on both ends of the cutaway, the length of the film removed from the master shot must be identical to the length of the cutaway. In this way, the relationship between sound and pictures is not disturbed and the overall length of sound track and picture film remains equal. With practice, this basic method can be developed to cover a wide variety of similar situations.

Using white spacing
Sync sound depends on a frame-for-frame correspondence between the sound track and the picture film. In the example on the right, a length of silent footage has been inserted into the picture film. To maintain sync, an identical length of silent white spacing has to be inserted into the sound track.

How to overlay sound with a silent cutaway

1 Wind down sound and vision until you find the point to start the cutaway. Mark both sound and vision in parallel.

2 Wind back and cut the master shot in vision at the point marked. Unclip the master shot from the synchronizer.

3 With the reaction cutaway in the synchronizer, select a satisfactory in-point on the cutaway and mark it in both sound and vision.

4 Insert the cutaway by joining it to the master shot. The in-point must lie opposite the first cutting point marked on the sound track.

5 Run the cutaway through to its out-point and mark sound and vision. Place tail trim on third gang so its head lies opposite original cut. Wind down to out-point of cutaway, mark tail trim in parallel, wind back and cut.

6 The final step is to join the tail trim of the master shot onto the out-point of the cutaway in the front gang of the synchronizer. This is done to the left of the synchronizer.

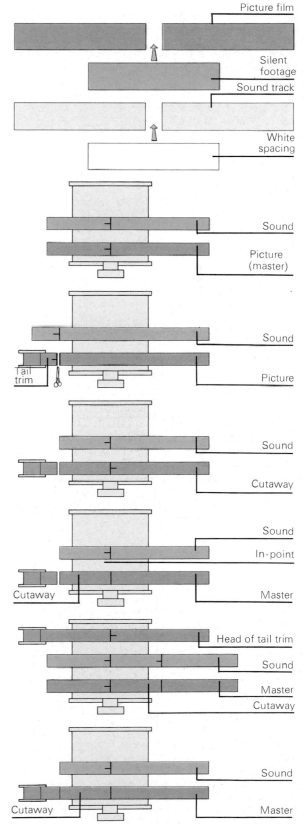

Picture film

Silent footage

Sound track

White spacing

Sound

Picture (master)

Sound

Tail trim

Picture

Sound

Cutaway

Sound

In-point

Cutaway

Master

Head of tail trim

Sound

Master

Cutaway

Sound

Cutaway

Master

Editing to Music

Editing to music is quite different to adding music to a film that has already been edited. Music that is simply added to an existing edited film can be used to add atmosphere and sometimes, if you are lucky and have chosen the musical accompaniment with care, the tempo may actually match that of the film. But, to be sure that a musical sequence is tightly integrated with the action, you should aim to cut the film with the sound running in parallel. In other words, *the music, even more than the pictures, should dictate the way the film is cut.* Double system is the only practicable system of editing in this way since you need the physical separation between sound and pictures.

The first step in editing to music is to choose the piece of music you wish to use with the film. Nearly all recorded music is protected by copyright law, which varies from country to country, but if the film you have made is only intended to be shown to family and friends and not a paying audience you are very unlikely to come up against any copyright problems.

Choosing the cutting point

Let us assume that you have a two-minute sequence of music that you have chosen to evoke a particular setting and mood. For example, you might decide to cut a sequence about a bullfight to a piece of Spanish music. Having selected the music (and cleared the copyright, if necessary) it must be recorded and transferred to magnetic fullcoat, which is then laced up on the pic-sync. Wind the sound track over the sound head and mark (with a wax pencil on the shiny side of the fullcoat) the parts of the music that you feel call for a cut. Remember that this is not the same as just marking up the beats on the music, as it can become monotonous if the film is cut dead on the beat, frame after frame. Instead, build up your climax through the cumulative variations of pace and not through repetitive rhythms. Next, sort out the shots you feel will fit the musical sequence and join them up in a rough approximation to the cutting points you have already indicated on the sound track. Then run sound and vision together and adjust the two until their cumulative effect is satisfying. Be prepared to make many changes, perhaps drastic ones before it is right.

Rapid cutting

When editing to hard rock music or a very fast effects track, you can accelerate the cutting from shot to shot, down to four – or even (for almost subliminal effects) two – frame cuts. When cutting to fast music it is not always a good idea to cut exactly on the beat; a parallel cut, where the pictures and music or effects are cut in exactly the same place, can sometimes appear slow. To create the impression of fast-moving action, you could try moving the entire edited musical sequence slightly out of parallel sync, so that the picture leads the sound by one or even two frames. For some reason, in a fast sequence the eye often perceives this as more synchronous than the the exact parallel cut and, as a result, the editing looks more snappy, It is certainly worth trying if, after all your efforts, the sequence feels sluggish.

How to backlay

1 With both the shot of the bullfight in progress and the sound track on the synchronizer make a mark on the sound track where the shot ends in vision.

2 Next, wind the sound track forward to the point where the musical climax is over the sound head. The picture film will detach from the synchronizer, but this does not matter if you have marked the sync point. Now place the new shot, with the death of the bull, in the synchronizer and move the picture around until the climaxes correspond.

3 After the two are precisely aligned, lock them together and wind them back until the out-point of the previous shot (as marked on the sound track) is opposite the center of the synchronizer. Mark the new shot exactly opposite that point. This is now the in-point for your new shot. Make the cut in the new shot to the right of the synchronizer and join the shots together.

Backlaying of sound and pictures

This editing technique is known as "backlaying" because it is often the case that you need to cut sound according to some synchronous event at the end, rather than at the beginning, of the shot. This type of situation is particularly true when editing to music, as the end of a piece of music often has a climax that may call for a correspondingly strong visual image.

In the example used previously of the bullfight, you might want the shot that shows the death of the bull to coincide with a crash of music at the end of the sound track you have decided to use. Let us assume that the end of the previous shot (showing the bullfight in progress) has already been decided, and that your problem now is to choose where to join the new shot so that the crash of music and the demise of the bull coincide. You will find that actually editing the film in the cutting room is easier than it sounds when described here in words, and if the technique used below is followed carefully, music and pictures will be in sync.

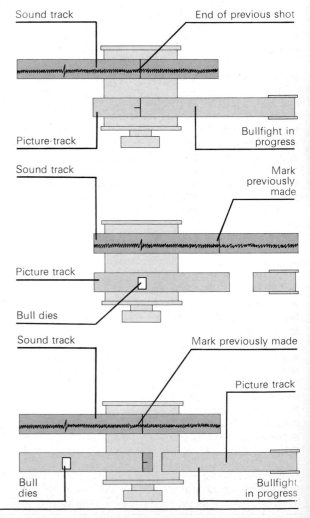

Sound track — End of previous shot

Picture-track — Bullfight in progress

Sound track — Mark previously made

Picture track

Bull dies

Sound track — Mark previously made

Picture track

Bull dies — Bullfight in progress

Editing to Speech

There is one major problem when editing a film to match· a pre-recorded commentary – when should you cut to the object or event being referred to? First, you should rarely cut to it after the end of the word in question, and certainly not after the whole sentence used to describe it. A better alternative is to cut to an illustration of what is being described just as the relevant word begins, *or slightly before it*. This should not, however, be repeated too often or an impression of overliteralness may be created. The timing is similar to the technique used when dubbing commentary onto a pre-cut sequence, though here the priorities are reversed – the sound is the master, and the vision cut to match. The only problems that are likely to arise involve moving shots, which have a fixed beginning and end. Try to adopt a flexible and varied approach to visual illustration of a commentary so that the audience is kept informed, sometimes surprised and never kept waiting for a point to be made. Avoid the temptation to overdo the commentary; where possible, let the images speak for themselves.

Overlapping dialogue

When you are intercutting between two or more people who are engaged in conversation, the obvious thing to do is to cut to each person as they begin to speak. This was, in fact, the way the early filmmakers used to edit dialogues. However, it will soon become clear that very often the most compelling shot will not be of the person speaking but rather the reaction shot of the listener.

When you are shooting and editing with double system film, it is easy to overlap one person's voice over a reaction shot of the listener, and this can be extended into all, or part of, the reply. This technique will give a more subtle switching from character to character, which you could not hope to achieve with simple shot-for-shot editing. You can manipulate not only shot size but also the pace and therefore the relative importance accorded to each participant in the dialogue.

In the example used here, a man is talking to a woman. He suspects she has been out with someone else, and is clearly jealous. As the dialogue progresses, his suspicion hardens into certainty, just as the woman's evasion turns into outright resentment. The cutting of this could perfectly well follow the pattern of speech, but the reactions would then be lost. Instead, a pattern such as the one suggested on the right might be adopted. We begin with one straight line from each of the participants involved in the conversation.

Then, after "Is your phone out of order?" we cut to the woman to catch the first ripple of apprehension before the man says "I phoned twice". Similarly, we cut back to the man after she says "I suppose it must be", so as to record his visible disbelief, and back to her once more as the word "Ritz" gives the game away for good. This is, of course, only one of the many possible ways of editing the sequence, and much would depend on the action – a vigorous hand movement, for instance, might well provide a better cutting point than the dialogue.

When editing an interview, you should always favor the subject, reserving your reaction shots for key moments or for cutaways to be used in editing.

Where to cut

When cutting a film to match a pre-recorded commentary, make certain that you listen carefully to the words *before* making the cut. The example on the right shows both the wrong and the right way to make a cut. Although the example may seem obvious, a cutting mistake like this could destroy the atmosphere you are trying to create as the audience dissolves into laughter.

Correct

The children went to the zoo and admired the camels

Incorrect

Man:	"Did you enjoy the evening?"	
Woman:	"I didn't go out."	
Man:	"Is your phone out of order?"	"I phoned twice . . ."
Woman:	"I suppose it must be."	"I must have it checked."
Man:	". . . and I could have sworn I saw you coming out of the Ritz." "I must have been mistaken."	
Woman:	"Yes you must."	

Man: "Did you enjoy the evening?"

Woman: "I didn't go out."

Man: "Is your phone out of order?"

Man: I phoned twice . . ."

Woman: "I suppose it must be."

Woman: "I must have it checked." **Man:** ". . . and I could have sworn I saw you coming out of the Ritz."

Man: "I must have been mistaken." **Woman:** "Yes, you must."

Added and Dubbed Sound

If you use a silent camera, at some stage you will probably want to add sound to your films. At its simplest, the sound may be a musical background, which only bears a thematic relation to the film. Alternatively, you can reinforce the film with effects, commentary and, if recorded, sync sound to produce a very sophisticated end-product, even if using fairly simple equipment. The methods and techniques of adding and dubbing sound are varied and in the following pages we will be looking at only some of them, ranging from the most simple of all possible techniques to the technique used in professional filmmaking.

The two simplest and most commonly used forms of added sound are music and commentary.

Adding a commentary

Commentary may be added, either with or without music, to any film that you find does not tell its story by purely visual means, or where sync sound needs some further explanation. At its crudest, a commentary for a very short film can be recorded and played "wild" as an accompaniment (see opposite), or the recorder and projector can be linked to a tape synchronizer for more accurate alignment of sound and images.

In a commentary, your role is to guide the audience into your film; you are subtly placing your own personality between the film and the audience, which is why so many filmmakers prefer to write and read their own scripts.

Writing a commentary

The fundamental problem when writing a commentary to accompany a film is that the information you give should add to the film without duplicating what is already on the screen. The writing should not, in general, be too jokey or too solemn, because after two or three showings you may well regret the intrusive style. It is best not to combine the moment of maximum verbal information with the strongest visual images as they tend to compete for the viewer's attention. Both are weakened as a result. It is most important, when writing a commentary, to time the delivery of the words so that those which are crucial to the new shot are spoken *as the new shot begins*. To illustrate this point, we can use a simple example. You may have used two different locations in your film – a woodland setting and a coastal area. When writing the commentary to cover the transition between these locations, you should aim to hit the word "sea" just as the shot cuts from one scene to the other (see right).

This particular example may seem pretty obvious, but if carelessness of this kind is carried across the whole film the effect on the audience can be one of unease; they will be jarred every time the spoken word and picture clash. If the commentary is well presented, the audience will absorb the information without being aware of it.

The commentary should be written and recorded so that key words in each sentence hit the cuts or events precisely as the relevant piece of film is projected. In this way, *the sound will appear to motivate the cut*, not the other way round.

Choosing the music

By far the most common form of added sound is music. For a private film that you have no intention of exhibiting in public, you can choose from the vast range of recorded classical and popular disks or cassettes. Alternatively, you can make a choice from the various, but somewhat anonymous, "mood music" recordings.

The best solution of all to finding a musical accompaniment to your film is a piece that is specially composed. If, for instance, you have a friend who can improvise on the guitar or piano, let him or her view the film a few times until it is familiar. Then, when they are confident, record the improvisation onto either synchronized tape or directly onto the film's sound stripe.

Recording a commentary

The quality of any voice is not easily changed, so you should be honest with yourself when deciding if your voice is the best available. Set up the microphone a few feet away, check for the sound level, make the recording and then play it back to check the result. You should aim for a cool, conversational delivery with neither histrionics nor flatness. The method you use to match sound to picture will vary according to which of the main dubbing systems are in use. In any case, make sure the timing is satisfactory; otherwise you will have to re-record. Finally, if you are recording with the projector running, beware of intrusive motor noise. If possible, set up the projector and recorder in different rooms.

"... after so many days in the forest we began to long for the sea (cut) ..."

Correct

"... the sea occupied our thoughts during those days in the forest (cut) ..."

Incorrect

Silent Projector and Tape Recorder

Unsynchronized tape

This technique involves simply running an unsynchronized tape recorded sound track at the same time as you project the film, and is perfectly adequate to provide a music or atmosphere track; but you should not expect to adapt this technique to reflect the transitions from one scene to another in a long film. This is because the unsynchronized speeds of the projector and the tape recorder will cause the pictures and the music to start to drift apart almost as soon as the two machines are started. The effect will always tend to be cumulative – the longer the film, the more noticeable the discrepancy between sound and vison, especially in close-ups.

However, if you just want to run a piece of music over your film with the hope that it will be approximately right, then you must make corresponding *start marks* on both the tape and film leaders so that the two can at least be started together. The start marks could be a scratched white frame on a black film leader and a corresponding white dot on the base (shiny) side of the tape; or you could simply use the junction between the leader and the tape (or film) as the reference point in both cases. Whichever method you adopt, the start marks must be set against the sound head and the projector gate and the two started simultaneously: *some form of common-start procedure is used in all dubbing systems*. In more sophisticated set-ups, the tape or fullcoat recorders are triggered automatically as the first frame goes through the projector gate.

Locating the in-point

Not all music will run from the beginning of a film. It may be wanted half-way through, for instance. To find an appropriate moment to start the music, note the time between the start mark and the first frame you want covered by sound. This can be done with a stop watch or, if your recorder has a footage counter, by zeroing it at the start mark and noting the elapsed footage. Stop the recorder at the selected point and turn the projector off. This is now the point where you want the first sound. Set up the recorder in the record mode, using the pause button for an instant, click-free recording, and pre-monitor the music. If recording from a disk, place the needle so that it is just short of the piece of music you want to record, then start the recorder and record player together and you should obtain a clean recording from the first bar. Except at the very beginning of a film, you will often want to *fade-up* the recording level from zero.

Locating the end-point

If you want a fading of sound (or the ending of sound) to be recorded on the tape, the end-point should be determined at the same time as the in-point – by stop watch or footage counter. When you arrive at the allotted point in the music, simply lower the recording level on the recorder. Unless the film is very short, a closely synchronized "hard" ending is not practicable using "wild" (unsynchronized) recorders and projectors. For a predictable effect a *tape synchronizer* is needed.

Synchronized tape

This technique involves linking a projector and tape recorder with a *synchronizer* to govern the speeds of their motors. The term "synchronizer" is usually applied to the sprocketed synchronizer block used in double system editing (see p. 239); but this should not be confused with a *tape synchronizer*, which is a device used to lock together a tape recorder and projector during editing and viewing. Tape synchronizers can be either mechanical or electronic units and they either adjust the speed of the recorder to match that of the projector, or (more likely and more satisfactorily) they adjust the speed of the projector to match that of the recorder. Some use belts, others use cables or purely electronic pulses to do the job. It should be noted, however, that perfect frame-for-frame sync will only be achieved if you are using some form of pulse-tape or sprocketed-tape arrangement (see p. 238). With ordinary tape there will still be a tendency to drift out of sync.

Using the tape synchronizer

The mode of operation when using a tape synchronizer in all cases is that the tape and film must be aligned against their respective start marks before recording, transfer or playback is attempted, and the two machines must be well warmed up before being started simultaneously. From then on they can be run together, locked in sync, and a complex sound track can be constructed on tape. The synchronizer can also be used to transfer the sound track onto the film stripe.

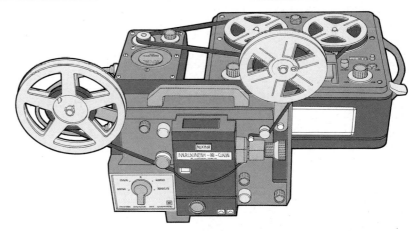

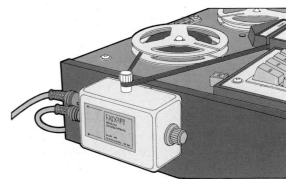

Tape synchronizer
Because the motor governing the speed of the tape recorder and the motor governing the speed of the projector are not the same, sound and pictures will not remain in sync unless a tape synchronizer is used (above). Smaller tape synchronizers can be used that attach to the side of the tape recorder itself.

Building a Composite Sound Track

This process involves the blending together of different sound tracks – for example, a music track, a commentary track and an effects track – into one composite master track. In its final form, the master track will be made up of these individual sounds, the relative volume of each adjusted so that the music fades out, for example, as the commentary begins, and fades in again when the commentary comes to an end.

To construct this composite sound track, your only real requirement is a stereo or four-track tape recorder, which can run at least two tracks in a given direction with independent recording and playback of each track. The ideal type of recorder should be fitted with three heads: a recording head, a playback head and an erase head. This arrangement has the flexibility of allowing you to monitor the sound you have just recorded while the actual process of recording continues. Finally, it is a great asset if your recorder can superimpose sound from one track onto an existing recording on another track. This ability is known as "sound-on-sound super-imposition". The same facility on a sound projector is sometimes referred to as a "trick" control.

A machine with the above specification will allow you to record music on one track and commentary on the other (see p. 244). The tape recorder can then be synchronized with a silent projector so that as the film is being screened the two sound tracks are played together to give the effect of a mixed, composite sound track. The volume should need no further adjusting and the relative balance should be satisfactory. It is fair to say that this technique requires some perseverance before the results are just as you want them.

Making a pilot track

The idea of a pilot track is to record a verbal guide onto one of the tracks of the tape (via a tape synchronizer). This guide can then be used to cue in your dubbed sound and link it to the images. Using a tape synchronizer in this way to lock in sync two parallel tracks, a music and commentary track can be constructed.

To record a pilot track, place the film in the projector and the tape in the recorder, both aligned against their start marks. Link them via the tape synchronizer. Set up a microphone to record onto one of the tracks available, and start the machines together. Then, using a rapping device, a heavy pen against the table, for example, record a sound that will mark the first frame of film and then the point where each new scene begins. Follow each "rap" with a description of the scene. In sections requiring complicated effects or music changes, the pilot track will be detailed, but probably less so in other places. Continue in this way until the end and then disconnect the synchronizer and projector.

Rewind the tape and zero the counter when you hear the first "rap". This equates to the first frame of film. Mark the tape at this point. Then work through the tape compiling a *cue sheet* (see p. 248), which will indicate every significant sound cue in the film *as indicated by the recorder's footage counter*. From this cue sheet you can see where music, commentary or effects are to be added, based on the shot list you have compiled.

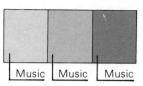

Hard fade
This is how you could arrange three musical passages with hard fade-overs between.

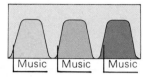

Soft fade
This representation shows how to arrange a soft fade-in and fade-out between musical passages.

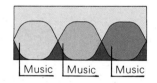

Sound dissolve
A very effective dissolve can be created by overlapping the fade-in and fade-out.

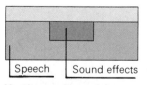

Hard superimposition
This illustration shows how a commentary track might be overlaid with taped sound effects.

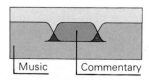

Fade superimposition
This shows how you can fade-over a commentary.

Balancing the sound tracks

The process of *balancing* involves adjusting the volume of the respective sound tracks so that they are in the correct relation to each other throughout the film. In other words, the music, for example, can be made to dip before every piece of commentary and rise again afterwards.

You are now ready to record music on one track and commentary on the other, for example. After balancing, they will be replayed to give the effect of a mixed track.

One of the simplest ways of balancing two tracks is to play the tape on your recorder as you screen the film and manually adjust the "balance" control on your amplifier so that one track is faded up as the other is faded down, and vice versa. This system is, however, very hit-and-miss and you will, of course, have to repeat the process each time you screen the film.

Alternatively, you can adjust the recording level of the sound at the time of recording the music, commentary or effects. For example, record the commentary first, using the taps and cue sheet for precise alignment. Rewind the tape to the beginning and reset the footage counter. Go through the first music section, noting the ins and outs of the commentary. These will be the points during which the music must be muted when you come to record it. Start up the first music cue and slowly (if you want a fade-in) bring the input level up to the pre-determined level for a good recording. When you get to the point where the commentary is about to begin, fade the music well down. At the end of the commentary section, fade the music up again, and so on.

If you wish, a comparable technique may be used where the lines of commentary are prerecorded on a cassette recorder or another tape recorder. Then, only when the lines of commentary are just the way you want them, the recording can be played into the composite, single-track tape on cue just after the music has been faded well down. The added advantage with this method is that the volume of the commentary can be pre-determined and no further mixing should be necessary.

Another method of balancing the relative strength of the two sound sources is through the "sound-on-sound" or "multiplay" facility available on most of the better quality recorders. After the first recordings have been made, music on one track and commentary on another, the recorder is switched to "sound-on-sound" to combine them in the correct proportions. What in fact happens is that the music track (the first track laid down) is half erased during the portions of commentary. The commentary is then transferred from one track to the other (or superimposed), on top of the music track. This is the same as the "trick" facility control found on sound projectors, and is very convenient for building up multiple tracks.

However, there are, drawbacks with this particular method, and they apply equally to the "trick" facility on projectors. All these systems rely on the partial erase of the music track (the lower track), and you should be aware that the erase head of the recorder affects the high frequencies much more than the low frequencies. The result is that the music running under the commentary is, in fact, distorted.

Dubbing on a Sound Projector

This is the process of adding a sound track onto the film on a magnetic stripe sound projector. You can either dub sound onto silent film that has been striped (see p. 233) or onto sound film that already carries a single system sync track. Your basic requirement is a projector with microphone and line inputs, with manual and automatic control of recording levels, a footage counter for accurate cueing of sound inputs and, as a luxury, a sound-on-sound or trick control. A number of the better projectors also include a device which allows you to preprogram the abruptness or shallowness of a fade. It is possible to build up a composite track on tape first (see left) and then transfer the whole thing, already balanced, onto the film stripe.

Timing the end of film music

You may want the end of your film to coincide with the end of the chosen music, but since tape recorders do not run backwards at playing speeds, the end of the music cannot be backlaid in the same way as it can on fullcoat magnetic film (see p. 242). The procedure with tape is to run the film in the projector to the last frame and stop it. Run the tape to the last bar of music and stop it also, without changing the location of the tape from right to left, reverse the reels. Now start the tape and projector simultaneously, with the projector running in reverse and the tape running forward in its playback mode. (The music will be running backwards on the other track.) When you reach the point a few feet beyond the in-point for the music, stop the two machines exactly together. Reverse the reels on the tape recorder and you are ready to transfer the music onto the film stripe.

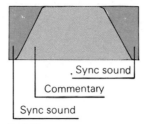

Dubbing a commentary
Added sound can be faded in or out on top of original sound. In this case, a commentary has replaced a section of the original sync sound.

How to cue and dub sound

When dubbing directly onto the magnetic stripe using a sound projector, the cue for your recorded sound will not be taken from a pilot track recorded on tape but from the film footage counter on the projector itself. (This assumes that you are not building up a composite track on tape in the first instance.) Each sound cue will need to be logged as the film is projected, and the various sound sources prepared. The usual procedure is to record the music first, either live or from disk, with the appropriate fades between music sections. The commentary is then recorded on top of the music using the "trick" superimposition device. There are, however, drawbacks with this system of dubbing sound.

First, if you are recording over the top of the original sync sound and make a mistake, the original is ruined. To safeguard against this, it is best to take the precaution of making a recording of the whole of the sync track on tape or, better still, on magnetic fullcoat film before attempting to dub on top of it.

Second, it is easy to "fluff" a line of commentary while recording it, and this again will ruin a composite track. The solution here is to prerecord the commentary sections on either a tape or cassette recorder and then to play in the sections of commentary onto stripe one at a time. This has the added advantage that there will be no projector noise to spoil the recording.

For precise instructions on how to carry out these procedures, read the instruction manual that accompanies your particular machine – they do vary considerably in operation. All the problems noted here can be avoided by using a twin track or stereo projector.

Twin track and stereo projectors

These types of projectors are only available in super 8 and they represent an important extension of the sound possibilities for the filmmaker. They use the tiny balance stripe on the side of the film (see p. 112) to record a second sound channel.

With twin track machines, the two tracks may be replayed or recorded separately or in "duo", which is to say in mono combination. This process has become known as "duoplay"

Stereo machines are constructed with two separate amplifiers and can record or play back both tracks at once with complete separation. In the case of a dialogue across the screen, for example, the distinction between the two sound sources will be apparent as they come from four different reproduction systems and through different speakers.

Both types of projectors can replay from one track and record on the other, which allows very complex tracks to be built up using the superimposition control. If these facilities are combined with preprogramming of recording, automatic gain control and single-frame advance, the possibilities are extensive. What is more, the sound quality of stereo reproduction is remarkably good despite the fact that the balance stripe is so narrow (0.45 mm).

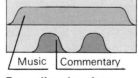

Recording duoplay
Using duoplay, music and commentary are both recorded at full level.

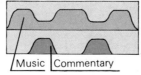

Playing back duoplay
On playback, the music track will fade down each time the commentary track starts.

How to use both tracks

One possible way of approaching the problem of dubbing sound directly onto the magnetic stripe might be this: in order to preserve the original sync sound on the main track you could do all your dubbing of music, commentary or effects on the balance track, and replay the combination in the "duoplay" mode.

Alternatively, you could first lay the music then commentary on the balance track and transfer them across to the main track only when you are certain they are in the correct position. This would leave the balance track free for the addition of further sound. The important point to remember is that it is to your advantage to use both tracks to the full when building up a composite sound track.

Remember that, if you are using the "trick" control to lay a sound track with more than two layers, the superimposition degrades the quality of the sound on the lower track. Therefore, if you want to make certain that the original sync track is fully protected, lift it onto the balance stripe complete and dub it back onto the main track *on top* of the other sounds after they have been compiled. After dubbing, the balance track can be used again for the addition of any other sound source the film might need.

Double System Dubbing

If you have been editing the sound track on fullcoat magnetic film, you will by now have several different tracks of sound that you will want to mix together into one master track. The master can then be transferred onto the film stripe or projected as it is through an interlocked fullcoat recorder at the same time as the film is being screened. If you have three tracks of sound – for example, sync sound, music and commentary – each should have a leader that contains the title of the production, the type of sound track it is and a one-frame "bleep tone" at a standard, preselected point before the first frame of film or sound. The idea of the bleep tone or "sync plop" as it is sometimes called, is that when the tracks are run together through the mixer, all three "plops" or "bleeps" should be heard absolutely simultaneously. If one track has drifted out of sync it will be immediately clear from the uneven bleep tones. A bleep tone can be quite easily made by recording a long whistle on fullcoat, then chopping it into single frames, and then splicing the tone into the fullcoat and film leaders at exactly the same point.

With the tracks already split into their various component parts, you will now be working through them from the head of the synchronizer to make certain that there is enough sound overlap at each end of the track sections to give you room to mix between them. You will also want to produce a *dubbing chart* or *cue sheet* to help during the mix (see right). The cue sheet is prepared only after the film has been viewed in its final form and sound requirements exactly determined.

Using four fullcoat recorders
This technique involves the use of four interlocked fullcoat recorders – three for playing back the separate sound tracks and one for recording the composite master track. If you wish to dub the sound while viewing the pictures, a projector can be run as well, linked by a photo-start device that starts the recorders in sync with the first flash of light from the projector. This facility is more likely to be rented than bought by an individual. It is a fast and efficient method of dubbing and all sound is first generation, but the tracks cannot be rolled backwards in sync. Therefore you have to go through the dub in one sweep – if you make a mistake you will have to go back to the top and start again. The recorders are set up so that the output from each machine is connected to the input of the mixer. The output of the mixer unit is connected, in turn, to the input of the fullcoat recorder operating in the record mode.

Using a four-track recorder
For this method only one fullcoat recorder is needed. You will also need a four-track tape recorder. The fullcoat recorder transfers the first sync track to track one of the tape, while simultaneously laying down a reference pulse onto tape-track two. Then, tracks one and two are transferred to tracks three and four of the tape using the reference pulse already on the tape to lock the two machines in sync. Now all three tracks can be run in sync for the final mix, with the fullcoat recorder acting as the interlocked recording machine.

The cue sheet
The cue sheet should show the footage at which each new sound is needed (although there should be a sound overlap in front of and beyond this point). The footages will be determined either on the synchronizer or recorder used for the dub. Here we have assumed that three tracks are being used, but the sync sections could be split up so that each is balanced separately. With this chart the mixer can see the precise in- and out-points for each scene and the last words of each section of commentary.

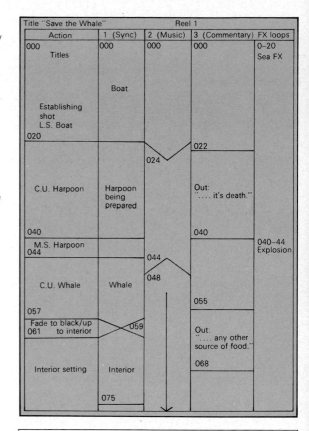

Title "Save the Whale"		Reel 1		
Action	1 (Sync)	2 (Music)	3 (Commentary)	FX loops
000 Titles	000	000	000	0–20 Sea FX
Establishing shot L.S. Boat	Boat			
020			022	
		024		
C.U. Harpoon	Harpoon being prepared		Out: "…. it's death."	
040			040	
M.S. Harpoon 044	044			040–44 Explosion
		048		
C.U. Whale	Whale		055	
057				
Fade to black/up 061 to interior		059	Out: "…. any other source of food."	
			068	
Interior setting	Interior			
075				

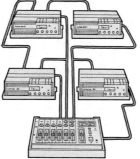

Fullcoat sync mix
The arrangement of fullcoat recorders and mixer shown above will give excellent results. All four fullcoat machines run in sync. One might carry original sync sound, one might carry music, and one commentary. All three can then be dubbed via the mixer onto the fourth machine.

Rock and roll dubbing
With this method of dubbing, the various rolls of fullcoat track can be moved both forward and backward while locked in sync, and the recording can be interrupted and picked up at any point during the dub. This means that you do not have to complete the dub in one hectic burst. The film is projected throughout the dub via a sync-locked projector, and each sound track is on a separate playback machine. The film footage is constantly displayed on a large read-out under the screen, and this is referred to during the dub as a cue for the sound mixer.

The usual procedure for rock and roll dubbing is to mix the music-and-effects track first, which includes any sync sound, and then to record any commentary on another track. In the final mix, the music-and-effects track and the commentary track are combined and balanced. Each channel of the inputs has its own equalizer, and echo facilities can be used selectively to balance voice and music that need to match a prerecorded sound (see p. 126). With rock and roll dubbing, you can complete a very small section, rock the tracks back, then continue forward into the next section, picking up the recording as soon as you are certain that the tracks are running at the correct speed.

PROJECTING
THE
MOVIE

"Depth and movement alike come to us in the motion-picture world not as hard facts but as a mixture of fact and symbol" *Hugo Munsterberg*

Projectors

Silent super 8 projectors

Super and single 8 film have the same dimensions and can be run on the same projector, but standard 8 mm cannot. For this reason dual-gauge projectors are made, capable of projecting all three types of film. They are usually sprocketless, roller-feed projectors and the conversion for the different types of format only requires moving a lever. The standard shooting and projecting speed for silent super 8 is 18 fps. Some silent projectors are capable of running at slower speeds, and also of projecting single frames (in these cases the light is often dimmed automatically to prevent the film from burning). The aperture of the lens has a direct effect on the brightness of the image; the wider it is, the brighter the image. A cheap projector usually has a modest lens aperture of f1.6; a middle range, around f1.4; and an expensive one might even be as large as f1.0.

In most cases, the trimmed film leader is threaded into the entrance guide and the machine automatically picks it up, takes it through the gate and onto the take-up spool. It is useful to have a projector with a removable side cover so that you can take out the film in the middle of the movie without having to run on to the end. Choose a projector with an easily accessible gate. This not only makes it easier to remove the film if it should get stuck, but gives easier access for cleaning. Choose a machine which runs quietly and has a steady image.

Sound super 8 projectors

Almost all super 8 sound projectors are equipped with a magnetic rather than an optical sound system (see p. 110). With striped film, they are capable of playing and recording on either the main track alone, or on the main and the balance tracks, and this can be done in "duoplay" or in stereo (see p. 112). The smooth movement of the film over the sound heads must be separated from the intermittent movement of the film through the gate. This is done using the same 18 frame delay loop that is found in the camera's mechanism. A capstan, linked to a flywheel for added smoothness, drives the film across the sound heads and this governs the film transport mechanism. All sound super 8 projectors operate at both 24 fps and 18 fps, and many have a single frame facility.

Most sound projectors have a sound-on-sound facility where the replay head "doubles" as a recording head. This superimposing device is sometimes known as a *trick* facility. The track is partially erased and another sound track is superimposed on it. Another increasingly common feature is the program control which allows for pre-programmed fades, dissolves and superimpositions. On some models you can select the exact frame at which the fade is to begin along with the degree of abruptness of the fade. This is especially useful if you intend to mix your sound on the projector. In some cases the pre-programmed record setting can be linked to the remote-start control of the in-put tape recorder. All projectors incorporate an auxiliary line in-put for a microphone, and some have a line out-put too. This is very important if you plan to use an external speaker, or if you plan complex track-transfers from stripe to tape.

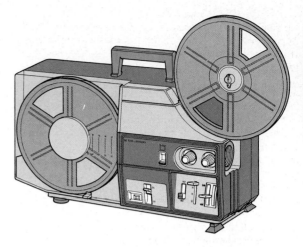

Bell and Howell 1481
This is a multi-format silent projector capable of showing super 8, single 8 and standard 8 mm movies. It has an automatic threading guide and a variable running speed of 18, 9, 6 or 3 fps. It is capable of forward and reverse motion and has a fast rewind system.

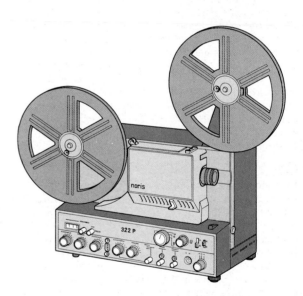

Norisound 322
This sound projector is capable of showing single and super 8 mm movies, and it runs at 18 and 24 fps. It has a programmable control and a variable sound dissolve. There is also a public address facility to use during projection.

Bolex 521
This projector is capable of showing all single or double perforated 16 mm movies whether they are silent, magnetic or optical sound. It has running speeds of 18 and 24 fps as well as single-frame projection. There is also a choice between a 2 or 3 bladed shutter. Apart from being able to record on the magnetic stripe of the film the projector has facilities for direct mixing and superimposition.

16 mm projectors

No silent 16 mm projectors are made, and most sound 16 mm projectors only have optical sound reproduction. However, some also offer magnetic playback (with or without a recording facility). Another type of projector has the facility for a parallel playback of a separate roll of fullcoat magnetic film. This is known as a "sepmag" or "double band" projector.

The basic principles are the same as in super 8, but 16 mm projectors are considerably heavier and more expensive. Automatic threading is available on some machines, but does not seem to have been brought to the state of perfection that exists in super 8. In fact, the whole approach of 16 mm projection equipment is more manual than automatic, and the more sophisticated magnetic dubbing facilities of super 8 are not found in 16 mm. All are designed to run at 24 or 25 fps. Silent films are best shown on 16 mm projectors which match their original running speeds of 18 or 16 fps. However, unless the projector has a three-bladed shutter (an alternative to the usual two-bladed one), the image will tend to flicker at these speeds. Most modern 16 mm projectors can run at slower speeds without the problem of overheating. This is because of the lower wattage lamps used and also because of the separate cooling motor which ventilates the gate area.

Each frame of 16 mm is four times as large as a single frame of super 8. This means that there is four times as great an area through which the light can pass, and the image is steadier, sharper and brighter.

Cartridge projectors

In some projection systems the film is inserted into a cartridge, after which it need never be touched again. The main advantages of this system are that the film will not be damaged by excessive handling, and that the cartridges are easy to store. The cartridge is dropped into the projector in much the same way as a tape cassette. The projectors thread automatically and the majority are capable of a variety of speeds. Some now have a pull-out mini-screen which allows you to watch your movie in daylight. There is, however, no standardization between rival cartridges. Your projector will not accept cartridges produced for another machine.

Rear projection projectors

These projectors provide another alternative to conventional projection for super and single 8 movies. They are about the size of a portable TV set and unlike standard projection systems do not require a separate screen. The screen is incorporated into the "box" of the projector. Because they use rear projection methods the image is very bright and the movie can be viewed in daylight. Apart from the main viewing screen there is a facility for projecting the image in the conventional way in a darkened room, by swiveling a built-in mirror to deflect the image. The film threads automatically, from standard feed spools and like most projectors, has rapid forward and reverse motion. The system offers a number of running speeds, including the ability to freeze the image on a single frame.

Bauer TR200 Retrosound
This projector is capable of showing single and super 8 movies on its rear projection screen. It threads automatically and has running speeds of 18 and 24 fps. The projector has magnetic sound recording and playback and a fast rewind system.

Bauer Micro Computer T610
This projector is capable of showing single and super 8 movies. It threads automatically and has a duo-play facility. This allows twin-track sound mixing during playback. It is also capable of automatic fades.

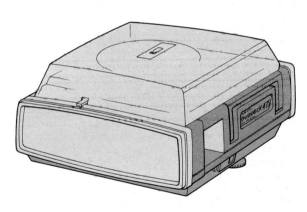

Kodak Moviedeck
This projector is capable of showing super and single 8 movies. It threads automatically and has a variety of running speeds. Movies can be projected in the conventional way as well as on the "mini-screen" which can be pulled out for viewing.

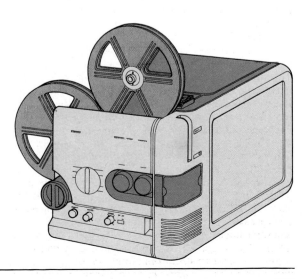

How the Projector Works

A *projector* illuminates, enlarges and displays your film. It is as integral a part of your moviemaking as your camera, and you should give it just as much thought. The projector that you buy should be of the same quality as the rest of your movie equipment. A cheap projector should not be used to show movies made with an expensive camera (and vice versa). The inferior lens on the cheap projector will blur the sharp images produced by the expensive camera and therefore ruin the effort and energy put into the movie.

There is a wide range of projectors on the market and you should take as much care choosing this part of your movie system as you would with the camera itself. Do you want a sound or silent projector? Sound projectors are capable of projecting silent movies so think of your future needs even if you are only using a silent camera at the moment. The advantage of sound projectors is that they can be used for recording commentaries or music (see p. 247) and they can also be used to transfer sound onto fullcoat or quarter inch tape (see p. 116). Most projectors have variable speed settings so that the movie can be projected at either 18 or 24 fps. They may also have the facility for projecting single frames (this should be done with care because of the risk of burning the film as it is held in front of the lamp). A number of projectors have a "sprocketless drive" system. The film is transported by rubber rollers instead of sprockets and one great advantage is the fast inpath rewind. This means that the film can be wound backwards or forwards without any danger of tearing the film.

The projector must be kept in good working order with regular cleaning. Remove the projector housing and clean all the parts that come into contact with the film using spirit and some cotton wrapped around an orange stick. Be careful never to touch any metal surface, especially the pressure plate, with a metal or even a wooden object. The slightest scratch on the plate will permanently damage any film you project.

Super 8 projector
This cutaway illustration of a super 8 projector is based on the Elmo ST 800. It is a stereo machine, with sound-on-sound facility, and is shown here with an f1.3 15 to 25 mm lens.

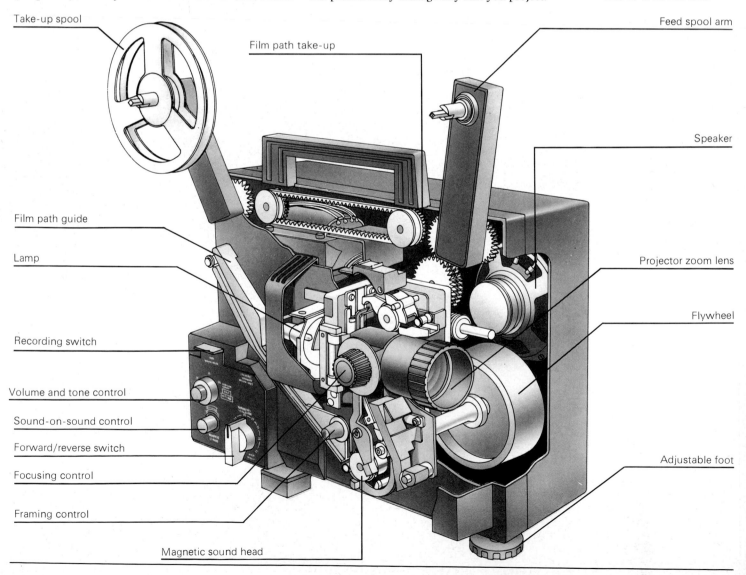

Take-up spool

Film path take-up

Feed spool arm

Film path guide

Speaker

Lamp

Projector zoom lens

Recording switch

Flywheel

Volume and tone control

Sound-on-sound control

Forward/reverse switch

Focusing control

Framing control

Adjustable foot

Magnetic sound head

How it works

The full spool of film is held on an arm or *feed spool*, away from the body of the projector. The film is then threaded along a path through the *gate* and out onto an empty *take-up spool*. The film transport mechanism usually includes sprocket wheels above and below the gate. A pull-down *claw* engages the perforations on the film and pulls it down through the gate, frame by frame. When the frame is in position the film stops briefly and the shutter opens to allow light from the projector lamp to shine onto it. The image is projected onto the screen and the film moves on. In other words, the projector shutter opens and closes on the frame just like the camera shutter except that the one in the projector has a circular shutter with three cut-outs (*a triple shutter*). As each frame stops in the gate, the shutter moves through 360° and exposes the image three times. The triple shutter decreases the duration of each flashed image from 1/40th to 1/120th second and eliminates flickering.

The film is transported by an *intermittent movement*. To prevent the image jumping on the screen each frame has to be held in exactly the same position in the gate as the preceding one. A framing device masks the surrounding image so only the frame area appears.

The optical system

The projector's lamp, situated behind the film, shines through the film which is held against the gate by the pressure plate and the beam is focused onto the screen by the lens. There are three basic types of lamp in use: tungsten, low-voltage quartz, and arc. Tungsten lamps are now rather old-fashioned. They are large, give off considerable heat, and require a condenser between themselves and the film. For this reason they have generally been replaced by the smaller, low-voltage quartz types. These lamps require a transformer, which is built into the projector, and they run at either 8 or 12 volts. They range from 50 to 150 watts in output and are supplied with an integral dichroic reflector. This eliminates the need for a condenser and also the reduces the amount of heat given off. Arc lamps give a purer, whiter light than any tungsten source, as well as greater brilliance, but they are rarely used in super 8. In the larger gauges the most common form is the Xenon arc, and in movie theaters large carbon arcs are used.

The brightness of the image on the screen is determined by three factors besides the light output of the lamp: the aperture of the lens, the size of the projected image and the reflectivity of the screen. Some super 8 projectors now have f1.0 lenses and this greatly increases the brightness in the smaller format. Zoom lenses are now common, although their optical quality is not always as high as the old fixed focal-length lenses. They are used because the image size can be adjusted without moving the projector. Remember that it is the final size of the projected image that determines brightness, not the distance between the projector and the screen.

Shutter system
The projector, far right, has three blades while the camera, near right, has only the half-moon shutter blade – usually with a cut-out segment of 165°. This means that, in the projector, each frame is shown three times instead of once. Because of this, movies shown at 18 fps are effectively shown at 54 fps. This guarantees a flicker-free image on the screen.

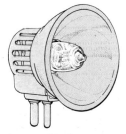

Low-voltage quartz lamp
This 250 watt tungsten-halogen lamp with its built-in reflector is typical of those in modern super 8 projectors.

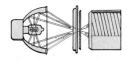

Modern lamp
The condenser is incorporated into the lamp bulb.

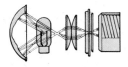

Old fashioned lamp
This lamp requires a separate condenser and reflector.

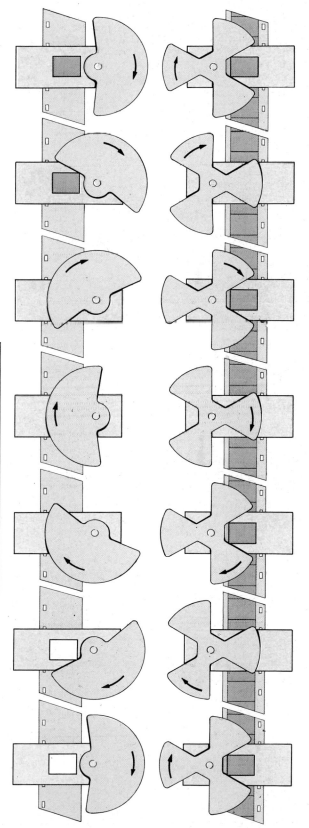

Screens and Screening

The two main things to consider when buying a projection screen are its size in relation to your projection area, and its surface. A simple guide to size is that the last row of your audience should be no further away from the screen than six times its projected width. Thus, if you plan to set up the screen about 15 ft (4.6 m) away from the projector, the minimum screen size you want is 30 in. by 30 in. (76 cm by 76 cm).

The purpose of a screen is to reflect light from the projector back to the audience. Different types of screen distribute light in different ways, according to how they are made. Some reflect most of the light in a narrow cone, while others reflect it over a wide angle. The zone in which the projected image still appears bright is known as the *angle of reflectivity*. The wider the angle of reflectivity, the less bright the image will be. The four main types of screen have varying reflectivity.

Matte screens
A matte screen has a plain, white surface and can be canvas, white-painted hardboard, a sheet, or even a white wall. It has a wide angle of reflectivity, so the movie can be seen equally well from a wide range of angles. Because the screen has low reflectivity the brightness of the image is not very good in comparison with other screen types. However, the image brightness is constant over the whole projection area and the color representation is better than from any other surface.

Lenticular screens
A lenticular screen has a patterned cloth surface which reflects the light like a mirror or lens. In some lenticular screens the cloth surface is coated with aluminum paint which is embossed with a pattern. It frequently looks like corduroy, with the ribs running vertically down its surface. Lenticular screens amplify the amount of reflected light, almost doubling the image brightness. Some metallic screens are four times as bright as matte screens because of their narrow angle of reflectivity.

Beaded screens
A beaded screen has clear glass chips embedded into its white cloth surface. It reflects an extremely bright image. The angle of reflectivity is small, but partly because of this narrow viewing area the image produced is four times as bright as that on a matte screen. However, the brightness falls off very rapidly beyond an angle of 5° from the projection line, and at 25° from it the image is unsatisfactorily dull. These screens are ideal for long, narrow rooms.

High-gain screens
Rigid screens like Kodak's Ektalite have a concave surface of specially processed aluminum foil pressed together in sheets. They are highly reflective, and produce an image twelve times brighter than that of a matte screen. They have an angle of reflection of about 30°, but nothing can be seen beyond this. The image is so bright that it can be viewed satisfactorily in daylight. However, the screen is limited in size to 48 in. by 48 in. (122 cm by 122 cm).

Screen buying guide

Screen surface					
Screen surface	Matte	Beaded	Metallic lenticular	Non-metallic lenticular	High-gain
Best viewing area	Unlimited	10°	25°	35°	30°
Brightness compared to matte screen	—	Up to 4 times	2–4 times	2 times	12 times
Can be wall or ceiling hung	Yes	Yes	with added tension	with added tension	On rigid support
Room Illumination	Quite dark	Completely dark	Partially dark	Partially dark	Light

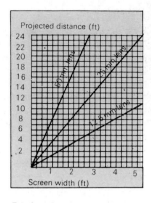

Projection distance
A 25 mm lens will fill a 2 ft screen at a distance of 12 ft.

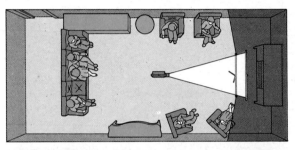

Matte screens
These are ideal for wide rooms and large audiences. Although they are less brilliant than other forms they are uniformly bright, so everyone sees the image at the same brightness. The room has to be darkened.

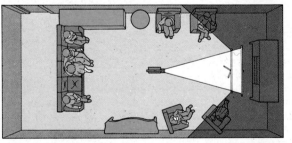

Lenticular screens
These screens are ideal for wide, undarkened rooms and large audiences. They are even better in darkened rooms. Although the viewing angle is quite wide, the illustration shows that the two people sitting nearest the screen will not be able to see properly.

Beaded screens
These screens are best suited to narrow rooms with small audiences, or to projectors with poor light output. The room has to be darkened completely for the images to be seen. There will be a slight loss in contrast.

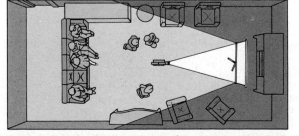

High-gain screens
These screens are best suited to narrow rooms with small audiences. They can be used to project movies without having to darken the room and the image is about twelve times as bright as a matte screen. Unlike other screens they are not collapsible.

Screening

First decide how you want your audience to be seated. The easiest way to do this is to set up your screen and projector according to the image size you want (see far left). Then project the movie and move around to check the projected film: how near can you comfortably sit to the screen? How near can you sit to the projector without its noise disturbing you? How far from the projection axis can you sit before the image becomes too dim? And, finally, how near to the projection axis can you go before you cast a shadow onto the screen? This may seem laborious, but remember that you will only have to "map out" your seating arrangements once in this way. Having taken the trouble to find the best positions, you can put your chairs straight into position when the time comes.

If you know in advance when you are going to be showing your movies, have all of your equipment set up before the audience arrives. Keep your projector reasonably high off the ground (custom-made stands are available, although tables will do). Set up your screen. Apart from the high-gain Ektalite which cannot be folded, screens fall into two categories – those which stand on tripod legs and are braced from behind, and those which hang from a wall. Your screen should have a wide black border to give the image an even sharper appearance. Adjust the projector's zoom until you have the picture in the right place.

Speakers

If you have a sound projector with an external speaker, place the speaker as close as possible to the screen. Do not put the speaker too near to the corner of the room or the bass notes will tend to be accentuated. If you are projecting in stereo you will need two speakers, but they should not be more than 6 ft to 8 ft (1.85 m to 2.75 m) apart, on either side of the screen. Unless you are passing the projector-output through an additional amplifier you should use high-efficiency speakers of low impedence (8 ohms at most, and preferably 4 ohms). Home hi-fi speakers generally require quite heavy loading to give their best results and even, in some cases, to be audible at all. The amplifiers in most projectors are nominally rated at 10 or 12 watts per channel. Test the sound level before projection begins.

Threading the projector

The majority of 8 mm projectors are threaded automatically. To be sure that the film feeds through correctly you should trim the end of the leader before you place it into the threading guide. Many projectors have a built-in trimmer. Push about $1\frac{1}{2}$ in. (3 cm) of the leader into the opening so that the edge of the slot runs between two perforation holes on super and single 8. On standard 8 align the cutting edge to cut through the hole. The leader should be free from any creases and be curled slightly clockwise. Although automatic threading devices save the filmmaker time, they do tend to damage film. For this reason, always allow for about 65 in. (1.60 m) of film leader – if the threading is to go wrong it is better for it to happen to the leader than to the film.

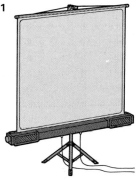

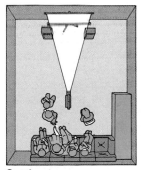

Setting up
The best position for speakers is on either side of the screen. Before threading the film, trim the leader using the projector's trimmer.

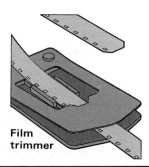

Film trimmer

Types of screen
Apart from the various types of screen surface, there are different ways of supporting the screen. Choose whether you want a portable or fixed screen, whether you want a motor control for unrolling it, or a screen with built-in sound speakers. Many high-gain screens have only a small black border but it is possible to paint in the border with matt black paint.

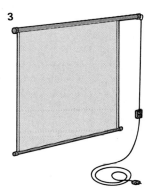

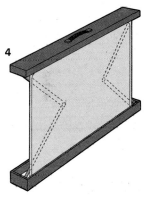

1 Collapsible stereo screen

2 Stand model with tripod

3 Motorized wall screen

4 Collapsible boxed screen

Projection checklist

To guarantee that your movie show runs smoothly there are a number of points that you should remember:

- Plan out your show and set up your equipment before the audience arrives.
- Before you load your movie make sure that the projector gate is clean – the smallest speck of dust will damage your film.
- Clean your films regularly (see p. 209).
- Have plenty of leader on the beginning of your film spool.
- Thread the film and run it through to check on sound levels (the sound will change slightly when the audience comes in).
- Always keep a light by you so that you do not have to turn up the main lights in emergencies.
- Keep a spare projector lamp
- Keep a tape splicer for mending broken film.
- If a hair appears in the gate while you are projecting, do not remove it with your fingers. Leave it until the next splice comes along to dislodge it, or use an air-brush.
- Never rewind during the show – use the feed spool from one movie as the take-up spool for the other.
- Alternatively, use a non-rewind spool like the Gepe system where, using an adaptor, the film is fed into the projector from the spool core.

Widescreen Techniques

The term widescreen is used to describe a variety of techniques used to change the aspect ratio of the standard film format. In 1927 Henri Chrétien introduced his "squeeze" lens which he called the Hypergonar. The lens became known as the anamorphic lens and it changed the standard format of 1.33:1 to 2.66:1, by altering the width of the projected image in relation to its height. The competition of television spurred the cinema to revive the widescreen process in the fifties. Cinerama (a three projector process) was followed by a variety of anamorphic systems including CinemaScope, Cineavision and Panavision.

Anamorphics

The most common way to produce widescreen effects is to use a lens, both on the camera and on the projector. This lens is known as an *anamorphic* or *A-lens*. It is a cylindrical concave lens and, because its axis of curvature is vertical, it only acts as a wide-angle attachment on the horizontal plane. In other words, the image is squeezed horizontally but the vertical axis is untouched. The subject is shot with the lens attached to the camera; this produces a "squeezed" image on the film. The anamorphic lens is then transferred to the projector where it unsqueezes the image as the movie is projected. Anamorphic lenses, producing varying amounts of "squeeze", are available for super, single and standard 8 mm film and 16 mm. In super 8, you may find that there is some "vignetting" at the corners at certain focal lengths and apertures, but their improved design now guarantees that you can shoot at most focal lengths and use the zoom on the camera.

CinemaScope

CinemaScope is the trade name given to the most widely known anamorphic technique in the commercial cinema. It had an original aspect ratio of 2.55:1, but with the addition of four magnetic sound tracks, this is now reduced to 2.35:1. CinemaScope lens attachments can be used on super 8 cameras, but the results are more successful when it is used in the larger gauges. Widescreen also has a considerable effect on composition and cutting. First it is possible to include several elements of a story in one shot, rather than two, so that intercutting is reduced. Secondly, horizontal and vertical rather than diagonal compositions dominate widescreen photography. Finally, close-ups are more difficult to frame, since a face is round, not oblong.

Mattes

Widescreen effects can be produced using the existing lens in the projector. Because the widescreen image is not optically compressed, as in other techniques, this process is often referred to as the *flat process*. It is produced by masking off the projector aperture with a specially designed *matte* so that the top and bottom of the standard frame are effectively cut off. This gives an image with an aspect ratio which varies between 1.65:1 and 1.85:1. The difficulty with this system lies in the shooting – what area is masked off? Viewfinders marked with "safe action areas" are therefore available.

Widescreen techniques
A variety of techniques exist which change the standard Academy format of 1.33:1. The image area can either be masked off to give an aspect ratio of 1.85:1, which is frequently done in feature movies, or an anamorphic lens can be used. This is the method used to produce CinemaScope, which has an aspect ratio of 2.35:1.

Academy 1.33:1
Widescreen 1.85:1
CinemaScope 2.35:1

Anamorphic photography
An anamorphic lens or lens attachment is attached to the camera prior to shooting. This "squeezes" an image of the scene onto the 1.33:1 format of the film. When the lens is attached to the projector the image is unsqueezed and screened in its correct proportions – with a 2.35:1 ratio.

Unsqueezed image

Squeezed image

CinemaScope (below)
This picture is the projected result of a movie shot with an anamorphic lens. The proportions and shape of the original scene are ideally suited to the widescreen technique.

Mattes
In this widescreen technique, which is common in the professional movie industry, the aspect ratio is changed from 1.33:1 to 1.85:1 by masking off the top and bottom of the image. No extra lens is needed. This shot is from Claude Chabrol's *Le Boucher*.

TECHNICAL REFERENCE

"Although the motion-picture medium more than any other calls for the imaginative mind, more than any other, too, it calls for the practical mind" *Eric Elliott*

Maintaining the Equipment

To guarantee that your movie equipment works properly and does not break down during shooting or projection, you must keep it well maintained. This means checking the camera, sound recorder and projector for any possible faults and also regularly cleaning them. Certain parts of the equipment can easily be looked after by the filmmaker. These include those which only need to be dusted or cleaned – such as the aperture plate or sound heads. It is important to keep the equipment dust-free, because the super 8 frame is so small that even the smallest amount of dust will detract from the projected image. The equipment should also be overhauled periodically by a professional, as directed in the owner's manual. This may mean sending it to a specialist shop or back to the manufacturer.

The camera lens

This is the most expensive part of your camera and you should take care to keep it dust-free by cleaning it before you set off filming. If possible, remove the camera lens and then use a blower brush or compressed air to get rid of any dust. Pay special attention to the lens rim where it joins with the glass because it is here that dust will accumulate. If the blower cannot dislodge the dirt, use a cotton swab or an orange stick tipped with cotton. Remove any spots on the lens glass by very gently wiping them with a special lens cleaning tissue, with a lens cleaning fluid, or lens foam. Never use eyeglass cleaning tissues because they remove the anti-flare coating of the lens. Clean the viewfinder and reflex shutters in the same way. During filming you may choose to protect the lens with a skylight or ultraviolet filter; always cover the lens with a lens cap when you have finished filming.

The camera interior

The inside of the camera should be cleaned as regularly as the lens. Apart from the dust, the mechanism inside the camera can become clogged with dried lubricating oil and deposits of film emulsion. You will need a long hair brush, a blower brush and a soft cloth. Open up the camera and use either the brush or the blower brush to remove all the dust from the *film path*.

In some cameras the *aperture* and *pressure plates* can be removed or opened up for cleaning. If you are removing the plates, make sure that the pulldown claw and registration pin are fully withdrawn, or they may cause damage. Always check your owner's manual for specific instructions. The kind of dirt that accumulates in these parts is emulsion and it must be removed regularly to prevent its scratching the film (usually every couple of rolls of film). If the blower brush does not remove it, use a cotton swab or an orange stick tipped with cotton dipped in a specially-formulated solvent. Never touch the gate with a metal or hard wooden probe.

The *sprockets* and the *film travel rollers* should also be cleaned of any emulsion that builds up on them. Certain areas may be inaccessible for cleaning, but a blower brush and swab can be used on those which you can reach. Wipe over the cleaned parts with a soft cloth but take care that no thread or lint is left behind.

The camera should be carried and stored in a container of some sort so that it is protected from dust, dirt and knocks. The most convenient cases are the soft plastic or leather shoulder bags; the strongest are the aluminum ones. Put the lens cap on the camera before you put it in its case and take great care when you are shooting in a sandy or dusty place. If you are filming on the beach, never put the camera down on the sand unless it is well wrapped up (for example, in a towel). If the air is very dusty keep the camera in a plastic bag, and if it is wet wrap it up in a towel. Avoid any extremes of temperature – for example, never leave your camera on the sunny window ledge or back seat of your car. When shooting in snowy or very cold conditions, keep the camera mechanism warm with a sound barney (see p. 113).

Cleaning the lens
First remove dust from the lens surface with a blower brush, hair brush or compressed air. Then take a special lens cleaning tissue with some cleaning fluid or foam and gently remove any specks of dirt from the lens surface. Never clean the lens unless absolutely necessary and never grind dirt in.

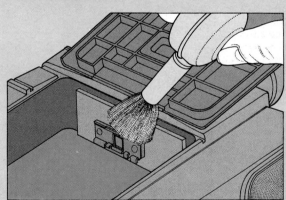

Cleaning film aperture
Before you load the camera check that the aperture is dust and lint-free. Lay the camera on its side so that any particles removed will not fall into the rear of the lens. Remove dust with a soft brush or blower brush, and emulsion with a cotton-tipped orange stick.

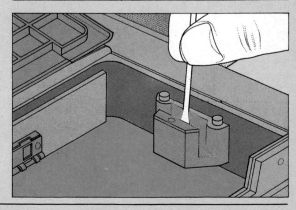

Cleaning the sound head
The magnetic sound recording head on sound cameras should be cleaned occasionally. It is not usually dust which causes a problem here, but the residue of sound track material. Use a cotton-tipped orange stick, dipped in alcohol, but take care when you touch the metal.

Projectors

To guarantee that the movie can be projected without the film being scratched or the equipment breaking down, the projector should be as well maintained as the camera. Get into the routine of cleaning the projector before you show the movie. On some projectors the gate area either swings out from the main body, or can be removed entirely – this allows for even greater access. Use a blower brush on all the moving pieces and parts which touch the film paying particular attention to the film gate. Any stubborn pieces of emulsion should be eased off with a cotton swab or an orange stick covered with cotton. Never use a sharp object as this will permanently damage the film path and therefore any piece of film which passes over it.

Filmstocks

All filmstock is perishable and the only way to make sure that it produces the results it is designed for is to store it correctly, both before and after exposure. All filmstock is packaged in an ideal way for storing – that is in plastic and foil – and it carries an expiry date, after which the color will start to deteriorate. Store color negative stock for up to six months in temperatures no higher than 50°F (10°C). Any longer than six months and the stock should be kept in a refrigerator at around 32°F (0°C), or below. Allow the film to warm up for an hour before loading it in the camera.

Once the film has been removed from its protective casing it will deteriorate rapidly. For this reason you should not leave unexposed film in the camera longer than you have to, nor should you expose the camera and film to heat and humidity. Keep them in the shade where the air can circulate around them.

Exposed film deteriorates much more rapidly than raw stock. Therefore, as soon as the film is exposed it should be sent off for processing. If you are shooting a large amount of film put each exposed cassette or magazine back into its protective package and tape it shut. Place the packages into a plastic bag which can be sealed shut. It is also a good idea to put a dessicant, such as silica gel, in the bag as well to absorb any moisture.

Sound recorders

On single system cameras, the magnetic sound recording head must be cleaned regularly to remove any deposit left by the striped film as it passes. The soft oxide sticks to the capstan shaft and roller, and unless it is removed the sound will not be recorded properly. Take the film cartridge out and leave the film door open. Lock the camera so that it runs continuously. Soak the cotton tip of a swab in spirit and then clean the capstan roller and shaft as they move.

The tape recorder used in double system recording should also be cleaned regularly – check the specific instructions in the manual. Clean the sound head with spirit, or run a special cleaning tape through the recorder. De-magnetize the sound head from time to time, using a special de-magnetizer (see p. 115). Make certain that the de-magnetizer has a protective plastic sleeve so that none of the metal will be scratched.

Cleaning the gate
Most projector lenses either swing out from the main body of the machine or can be completely removed. Gently clean the gate area with a brush and the lens with a blower brush or compressed air. For really severe dirt on the lens clean the front and rear elements with special lens cleaning fluid and a lens cloth. Clean all parts which come into contact with the film itself to get rid of emulsion pieces.

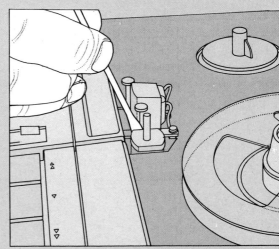

Cleaning the film (above)
Specially designed cloths are available for cleaning the film. The film is slowly wound through the folded cloth. Always let the fluid dry before moving the film further onto the take-up reel.

Cleaning the recording head
Use either commercial head cleaner or alcohol with cotton-tipped orange sticks, to clean the recording head. Also clean the tape, guides, capstans and pinchrollers.

Fault Finding Guide

Locating faults in the camera

Symptom	Fault	Remedy
Camera motor will not run.	The batteries have not been inserted correctly, or they are flat. The connecting power cable or plug is defective. The motor has been damaged. The spring motor has not been properly wound. The temperature is too low.	● Check the batteries regularly and replace if necessary. Recharge them if NiCads are used. ● Check the cable for any breaks and the connectors for damaged pins, then repair them if necessary. ● Send the camera to a specialist repair shop. ● Wind up the camera motor or, if necessary, replace the broken winding device or spring. ● Check that the camera runs in normal temperatures.
Film is not being taken up.	The film has run out. The take-up mechanism has broken, or keeps slipping. The roll film has not slotted properly into the take-up "core".	● Check to see whether the film cartridge has finished (super 8), turn the film spool over (standard 8), or insert a fresh spool of film (16 mm). ● Check the film transport mechanism. ● Open the magazine in a dark room or changing bag and insert the end of the film into the core.
Film tears.	The film has not been threaded correctly.	● Check the tension of the upper and lower loops of the film; if still in doubt check your manual.
Camera runs too slowly.	The battery charge is too low. The camera mechanism's lubrication is too cold.	● Check the battery charge. ● Use winter lubrication and keep camera warm.
Camera runs too fast.	The voltage in the power source is too high. The rheostat is faulty.	● Adjust the voltage to one suitable for the camera. ● Send the camera to a specialist shop for repair.
Low sound or no sound.	The camera has been loaded with a silent film cartridge. The microphone has been connected wrongly. The microphone is not close enough to the sound source.	● Reload with the appropriate film cartridge. ● Check that the microphone is picking up a signal. ● Reposition the microphone.
Camera too noisy.	The pressure plate is not properly adjusted. The camera is poorly lubricated. The shutter is running off center.	● Check the registration pins and claw to see if they are marking the film. ● Check the manual's "correct lubrication guide". ● Send the camera for specialist repair.

Locating faults in the projector

Symptom	Fault	Remedy
Film will not thread.	The first few inches of film are crimped. There is not enough splice-free film at the beginning of the film. There is an obstruction in the film path.	● Cut off the crimped film and rethread. ● Splice about 65 in. (1.6 m) of film leader to the front of your film. ● Remove the top or side of the projector; check and clean the film path.
No image on the screen although film runs.	The projector lamp does not light.	● Check that the light bulb is inserted correctly. ● If light still does not come on, change the bulb.
Poor quality picture.	The lens and/or the film gate are dirty.	● Remove the lens when possible and clean it. ● Clean the gate of any dust, pieces of film or splices.
Film starts jumping.	The film has been badly spliced. The film perforations are torn.	● Remake the splice. Make sure the ends are even, then re-splice them with splicing tape or cement. ● Remove the section with the tears and re-splice.
Film stops suddenly; a hole burns in the caught frame.	The film has been badly spliced or the perforations have been damaged.	● Turn off the projector and follow the film path until you find what is causing the obstruction. ● Remove the film. Cut out the damaged frame and then re-splice the film together. ● Check for damaged perforations – re-splice. ● Check the fuse on the projector.
No sound recorded.	The projector was not set on the recording mode. There was broken film lodged in the sound head.	● Re-record the sound with the projector correctly set. ● Check that the film you are using has a sound stripe. ● Clean the sound head with a swab and spirit.
Sound only patchily recorded.	The sound stripe has been damaged, worn away or covered up.	● Examine the magnetic stripe. If a tape splice has been stuck over it, the sound track will not be picked up by the projector's sound head. Remove the tape and re-splice correctly – using the proper tape or a cement join. (See Splicing the Film, p. 212). ● Re-stripe the film (see p. 233).

Locating faults on the film

Symptom	Fault	Remedy
Film completely black.	The film has not been exposed at all.	● Check that you remove the lens cap before shooting. ● Check that the camera is running correctly and that the film is moving through the gate. ● Check that roll-film (standard 8 mm and 16 mm) has been properly loaded.
Film completely clear.	The film has been exposed to bright white light and as a result has been fogged.	● Load and unload the camera in subdued light or in a changing bag. ● Hold rolls of film so that they cannot unravel. ● If you think that there is a light leak in your camera, have it checked by a repair shop.
Pictures too dark.	The film has been under-exposed. There was not enough light available at the time of exposure or the aperture was too small.	● Open the aperture to give the correct exposure. ● Check that the correct film speed has been set. ● Check that the camera's built-in light meter is functioning properly. ● Use some form of additional artificial lighting.
Pictures too light.	The film has been over-exposed. Too much light was allowed onto the film at the time of exposure.	● Stop down the aperture to give the correct exposure. ● Check that the correct film speed has been set. ● Check that the camera's built-in light meter is functioning properly.
Pictures unsharp.	The camera lens was incorrectly focused.	● Use the camera's viewfinder to focus accurately, or measure the subject-to-camera distance. Focusing is critical at long focal lengths and wide apertures.
Pictures foggy and unclear.	Dirt or moisture on the lens or filter.	● Clean the surface of the lens or filter with a soft, lint-free cloth. Always check for dirt or moisture.
Streaks of yellow–orange on the edges of the picture.	Light has accidently leaked onto the edges of the film and caused slight fogging.	● Do not load the camera in bright light. ● Do not allow the film to become loose on its spool during loading and unloading. ● If the fault persists, get a repair shop to check the camera for light leaks.
Frame line dirty.	Dirt or dust in the camera or projector gate.	● Dirt, dust or some other foreign body in the camera or projector aperture is known as "hair in the gate". If you adjust the framing device on the projector and the hairs move up and down with the frame-bar the dust is in the projector. Clean the gates carefully.
Black flecks on the picture.	Dust particles on the film show up on the screen as black flecks moving rapidly across the picture.	● Remove dust and dirt from the film by using special film cleaning fluid and a soft, lint-free cloth.
Vertical lines on the picture.	Scratches on the film show up as continuous vertical lines when projected. They are caused by dirt in the camera or projector gate, or by processing faults. On negative film, white lines are on the original; black lines, on the print.	● Clean the camera and projector regularly. ● If the scratches persist, have the camera checked. ● Laboratories can sometimes polish out scratches.
Pictures unsteady and jerky.	Camera shake.	● Hold the camera as steady as you can (see p. 56). ● Use a tripod whenever possible. ● Remember that projection exaggerates every slightest camera movement.
Pictures "jumping" and blurring vertically.	The film is "out of registration": it is not being held stationary in the gate. The camera may be too cold.	● Check the camera and projector loading. ● If the film "chatters" in the projector it may help to treat it with movie film lubricating fluid. ● In very cold conditions, run the camera for a few minutes before loading the film so that it warms up.
Picture has overall blue color cast.	Tungsten (indoor) film has been used without a color correction filter. Haze in the landscape has been recorded as blue.	● Use an "85" daylight conversion filter on the camera when shooting outdoors (see p. 92). ● Use an ultra-violet filter on the camera (see p. 93).
Picture has overall yellow color cast.	Daylight film has been used in artificial light without a color conversion filter.	● Use an "80B" tungsten conversion filter on the camera when shooting indoor scenes (see p. 92).
Picture has washed-out green or red color cast.	Old film, exposed and/or processed after expiry date. The film has been stored badly in hot and humid conditions.	● Expose and process your film as soon as possible. ● All film should be stored in a cool, dry place – preferably below 50°F (10°C). A household refrigerator is ideal. Never leave film on the back shelf of a car.
Light areas of picture too washed out, dark areas too dark.	The lighting at the time of exposure was too contrasty.	● Reduce the contrast by adjusting the lights so that you have a balanced set-up (see p. 102). ● Outdoors, use a reflector to "bounce" light into the dark areas of your subject (see p. 108).

Polavision

The Polavision system, introduced by Polaroid in 1977, is the world's first instant movie set-up. It consists of a camera, a film cartridge called a *phototape cassette* and a *player* for projecting and developing the film. The camera, loaded with the cassette, is used in the normal way. The exposed cassette is then slotted into the player which acts as a "black box" for the 90 seconds it takes for the cassette to be processed. The film is never removed from the cassette and projection takes place in the player. When the film reaches the end, it is automatically rewound by the machine and the cassette pops up ready to be stored or used again.

However, because the film cannot be edited, other than in-camera, the system is perhaps best used to shoot single incidents. In the future Polaroid say that it will be possible to edit Polavision. They also plan to introduce a single system sound camera that records on $\frac{1}{4}$ in. tape.

The camera

The compact and lightweight body of the Polavision camera is similar in shape to the Fuji single 8 camera (see p. 35). The camera's 1/40th second shutter opens and closes at 18 fps to photograph each frame singly and produce a series of still images (the film itself has a super 8 format). After each exposure the claw hooks into one of the perforations along the side of the phototape and pulls the next frame to be exposed into the gate. The power for the camera comes from four alkaline batteries which are located in the handgrip.

The camera has an eight element f1.8 lens with a zoom ratio of 2:1. The lens zooms from 12.5 to 25 mm but can only be operated manually using a lever on the side of the lens barrel. There are two focusing ranges: "near" which covers 6 ft to 25 ft (2 m to 5 m) and "far" which covers 25 ft to infinity (5 m and over). There is a reflex, or through-the-lens, viewfinder which means that there are no problems with parallax when you frame your shots (see p. 48). There is a ± 3 diopter eyepiece which can be adjusted to suit your own eyesight (see p. 44). As you look through the viewfinder, a red light flashes when you start to film and then again six seconds before the end of the cassette. The light is activated when a small cut-out in the phototape passes a pressure switch at the gate as the film moves from the feed spool to the take-up spool. When you have completely run out of film the red light stays on.

The exposure system is automatically controled by an "electric eye" positioned above the lens. Light entering the electric eye falls on a CdS photocell (see p. 49) and the voltage generated by this controls the scissor-like movement of the aperture blades. The aperture ranges from f1.8 to f22 and is selected by the exposure control. As a lever on the back of the handgrip of the camera is squeezed, the electric eye is activated and the correct aperture set. When the lens is at minimum or maximum aperture an indicator appears in the viewfinder. The phototape cassette is balanced for a color temperature of 3,400° K for filming in artificial lights. The camera therefore has a type 85 conversion filter for filming in daylight. There is a socket on the top of the camera to hold a "Twi-light" bulb which acts as a "movie light".

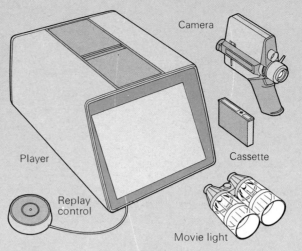

Camera

Player

Replay control

Cassette

Movie light

Polavision system
This system consists of a slim, light camera into which the unique phototape cassette slides. The camera operates like a normal super 8 camera. The cassette is both developed and projected in the player which is like a portable television set. The exposed film is slotted into the top of the player and this activates the developing process. The chemicals for this are contained in a sealed pod which breaks when the cassette is depressed.

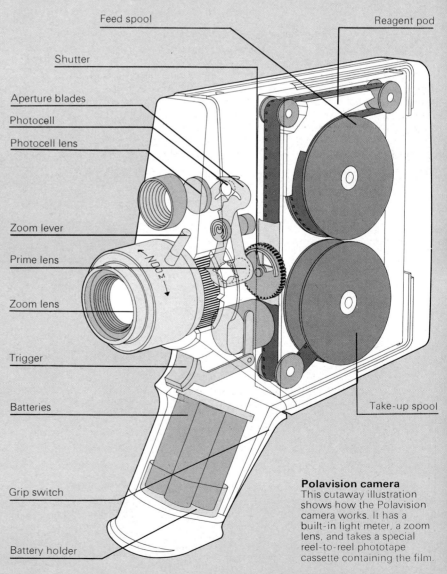

Feed spool

Reagent pod

Shutter

Aperture blades

Photocell

Photocell lens

Zoom lever

Prime lens

Zoom lens

Trigger

Batteries

Take-up spool

Grip switch

Battery holder

Polavision camera
This cutaway illustration shows how the Polavision camera works. It has a built-in light meter, a zoom lens, and takes a special reel-to-reel phototape cassette containing the film.

Filming

The Polavision phototape cassette allows for 2 minutes 35 seconds filming time. Like the Fuji single 8 cartridge, it has reel-to-reel rather than coaxial design and simply slots into the side of the camera. The camera does not have provision for direct sound recording, but the filmstock has a magnetic sound stripe down one side. This means that you can add narration or music without sending the film back to the lab to be "striped". The film cannot at present be edited in the conventional way so it has to be edited in-camera. Because you will have no opportunity to pick and choose your shots at the editing stage you must plan exactly what you want to show before you start shooting. This may mean preparing a shooting script, with the order of the scenes and the times for shooting them. Choose the focal range setting on the lens, frame your subject and press the lever on the back of the handle. This automatically sets the exposure. The first four seconds take up the leader of the film and then the red light comes on to show the start of shooting time. Remember that because of the short zoom range you may have to move around more than usual to get a varied range of shots.

The camera movie light

If you want to film indoors and there is insufficient light you should attach the special "Twi-light" unit. This is a twin-bulbed design which attaches to the top of the camera. It is battery operated, but the cord attaches neatly to the bottom of the camera so that it does not get in the way of the lens. The unit is very light, but its working range is short: it only lights up an area up to 9 ft (2.75 m) from the lens.

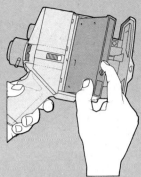

Loading the cassette
With the lens facing you slot the cassette into the camera, aligning the arrows and colors correctly.

Processing and projection

The Polavision player automatically processes and projects the exposed film cassette within 90 seconds. After projection the player rewinds and then ejects the cassette, ready to be played again.

Drop the exposed cassette of film into the slot on top of the player and push down. The player immediately begins to rewind the film and as it does so a small amount of processing reagent is spread on the film through a precisely-placed nozzle. It penetrates the multi-layers of the film and so processes them. By the time the film has been rewound the first part of the film is ready to be projected.

The player acts as a rear projector and the film can be viewed in relative brightness. The reason for rear projection is that the film is very opaque. Light is projected from a 100 watt lamp with a Fresnel lens onto the prism in the cassette side. The light is then deflected down through the film (which is in the form of a positive transparency) to the projection lens. The light between the film and the lens is interrupted by the shutter. The image is then bounced off an angled mirror onto the viewing screen. The player runs at a speed of 18 fps. The image is sharp and the colors saturated and bright, but the picture does tend to be grainy and contrasty. An instant replay button allows the user to select and play any part of the cassette.

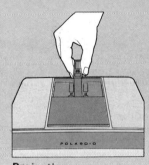

Projection
Push the exposed cassette into the player.

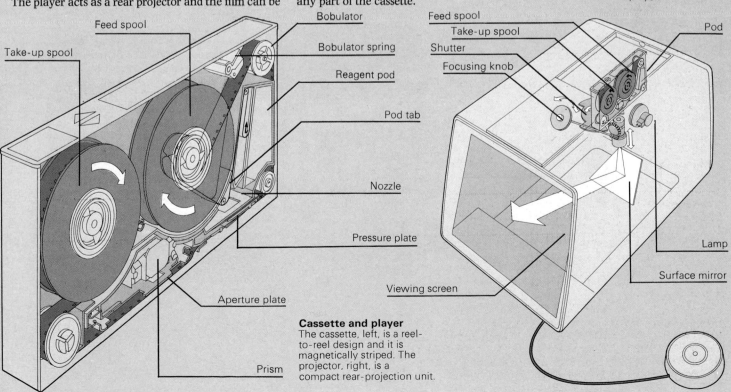

Feed spool

Take-up spool

Bobulator

Bobulator spring

Reagent pod

Pod tab

Nozzle

Pressure plate

Aperture plate

Prism

Feed spool

Take-up spool

Shutter

Focusing knob

Pod

Lamp

Surface mirror

Viewing screen

Cassette and player
The cassette, left, is a reel-to-reel design and it is magnetically striped. The projector, right, is a compact rear-projection unit.

Video

Video is an umbrella term used to describe any form of electronically generated image. In practice, this means television and its associated processes. From its outset, the television industry had recognized the need for some type of program recording that permitted instant replay, and in 1927 Scotsman John Logie Baird utilized disk-cutting equipment to record pictures generated by his 30-line television scanner. Advances on Baird's technique substituted magnetic recording tape for the "shellac" disk, and gave rise to video in its basic form as it is recognized today. The new videoplayers, cameras and recorders for the domestic market have transformed a sophisticated, professional industry into an easily accessible area for today's amateurs. As the equipment becomes cheaper and more portable, its future will be assured.

How video works

A television picture consists of a large number of horizontal lines, each of which is composed of a series of dots. The more lines the screen contains, the greater the definition of the image produced. The number of lines varies from system to system: in the USA there are 525 lines; in Europe (except for France) there are 625 lines. The camera's electronics scan the focused image in much the same way you read a book, left to right and from top to bottom, and the scan occurs many times a second. Each point of the scan is encoded into a signal that records the brightness of that particular portion of the screen. In color television, the camera has three tubes, corresponding to the three primary colors – red, green and blue.

The videoplayer

The videoplayer is a machine of special interest to the amateur filmmaker, as it is designed to show super 8 film on an ordinary television receiver. It may also be used in conjunction with videotape recorders to produce a tape-transfer of a film original; in the world of commercial television this process is known as a *telecine chain*. This particular development opens up all kinds of possibilities. Apart from the advantage of being able to show super 8 film on television, it is also possible to make any number of tape copies of an original film for distribution. The costs of this process are very low and the quality of the duplicates is very high, perhaps better than duplicates made from the traditional reversal process. The economies are especially striking for longer lengths of film.

Certain Kodak videoplayer models will accept either rolls of film or cartridges. The film needs no threading and does not run on sprockets. Instead, it runs continuously past a scanning system, which is of the *flying spot* type. With this system, a spot of light, generated by a cathode ray tube, flies to and fro across each frame of film as it passes, and then the transmitted signal is encoded as the output. The frames are "sensed" electronically not mechanically, and the videoplayer will accept original films that have been shot at various different speeds – either at 18 fps (the usual frame-rate for silent super 8 movies) or at 24 fps (the usual running speed for super 8 sound movies).

The video system
Modern video systems, such as the one illustrated below, can be adapted to a wide range of recording mediums.

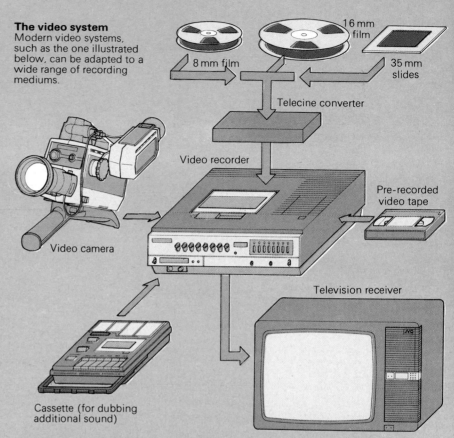

16 mm film

8 mm film

35 mm slides

Telecine converter

Video recorder

Pre-recorded video tape

Video camera

Television receiver

Cassette (for dubbing additional sound)

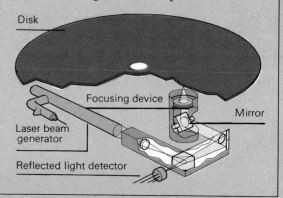

Film videoplayer
The Kodak videoplayer (above) is able to play super 8 color or black and white film, either silent or magnetic stripe stock. The videoplayer plugs into any television's antenna socket and, once connected, it will transmit either the Kodak Supermatic cassette or any super 8 reel of film. This videoplayer can also be connected to a closed-circuit system and transmit to as many receivers as there are in the system.

Video disk

There are certain advantages in using a video disk instead of tape – any part of the recording can be found quickly without having to run through the whole tape; also, the disk can be "played" in slow motion. The way in which most of us have seen the application of this feature of the disk is during a sports program as the "instant replay". The disk recorder features variable slow motion in both forward and reverse as well as normal speed replay and freeze-frame control. The disk's disadvantage is its short recording time – about half an hour's recording is the best at present.

Disk

Focusing device

Mirror

Laser beam generator

Reflected light detector

Videorecorders and recording

All video recording is made on tape, although the video disk (which can only be used for playback) has an undoubted future as a distribution medium. The problem with video recording is that a vast amount of information has to be crammed into every second of tape, and an ordinary $\frac{1}{4}$ in. (6 mm) tape at $7\frac{1}{2}$ ips, for example, could not begin to handle that quantity of information. In professional recording a 2 in. (5 cm) tape is used and this flows past the tape heads at $7\frac{1}{2}$ or 15 ips. To obtain the equivalent of the necessary tape speed, the recorder has four recording heads placed on a rotating drum, and these rotate at very high speed at right-angles to the tape's motion. Thus, the information is striped diagonally across the tape as it flows past the heads.

There are a number of smaller-gauge versions of this machine, which are all, unfortunately, incompatible with each other. They include Sony's Betamax, Philip's VCR and JVC's VHS systems. All use cassettes and all use the *helical scan* system. In this system, the recording tape is shaped into a helix as it travels round a rotating drum, which contains a number of recording and playback heads. The tape runs diagonally across the horizontally rotating heads.

Videorecorders can be used with a portable camera to produce cheap electronic movies. The cost of portable color cameras is still high, but on the other hand the cost of the recording medium is low: one hour of super 8 filmstock is the same price as twenty hours of videotape. Another advantage of videotape is that, like magnetic tape, it is re-usable time after time.

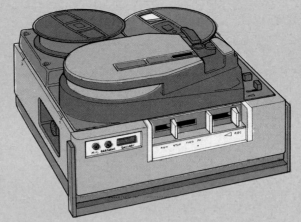

Videorecorders
The Sony videorecorder (left) is a two-head, helical scanning unit. The videorecorder picks up the signal transmitted by the camera and records sound and vision on tape. The tape can be replayed on a monitor or, for instant reference, on the electronic viewfinder of the camera itself. The diagram (below left) shows a typical helical scan videorecorder layout.

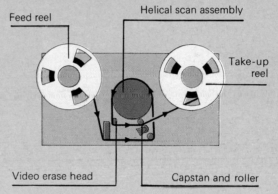

Feed reel — Helical scan assembly — Take-up reel

Video erase head — Capstan and roller

Track positioning
In a helical scanning recorder using 2 in. (5 cm) tape, the information is recorded as in the diagram above.

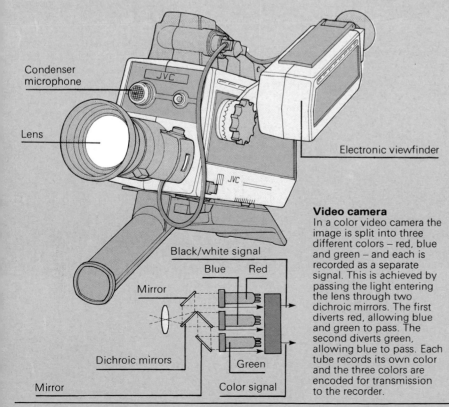

Condenser microphone

Lens

Electronic viewfinder

Black/white signal

Blue   Red

Mirror

Dichroic mirrors

Green

Mirror   Color signal

Video camera
In a color video camera the image is split into three different colors – red, blue and green – and each is recorded as a separate signal. This is achieved by passing the light entering the lens through two dichroic mirrors. The first diverts red, allowing blue and green to pass. The second diverts green, allowing blue to pass. Each tube records its own color and the three colors are encoded for transmission to the recorder.

Limitations of video

If all this sounds too good to be true, it is! Apart from the initial expense of the equipment, and the incompatibility of the different systems, there is one major disadvantage with home video movies – they cannot be edited without the use of a second recorder. Therefore, video movies are only to be recommended for long takes or, at best, for the kind of in-camera editing that you would apply to single system super 8 (see p. 115). Taking the limitations which this places on you into account, it is just as well that the tape is so inexpensive. In the commercial video world, the editing equipment may well take up a whole room.

However, with microprocessors and advanced circuitry it is already possible to computerize editing to a single frame; and the new tape coatings, such as the pure metal coatings coming onto the market, are bound to transform the recording systems. It is even possible that the very expensive recording heads will become obsolete. If this happens, prices will be drastically reduced and super 8 home movies will be seriously threatened. But until that time, it is probably best to regard video as a recording medium parallel to, but not yet as a replacement for, photographic emulsion.

Camera Specifications

The chart below and on the next three pages covers a wide range of super 8 cameras currently available. All of the cameras listed there have power zoom lenses; and their range and the maximum lens aperture are indicated beneath the model number. Most motor-driven zooms work at only a fast and slow speed but some have continuously variable zoom speeds.

Many zoom lenses are capable of macro focusing, useful for extreme close-ups or for slide copying (see p. 178). Very fast lenses and shutters are found on XL cameras which can film in low light conditions. In most cases, the zoom lens is an integral part of the camera's construction, and only a few super 8 cameras have the facility of accepting interchangeable lenses.

Most of the cameras listed have reflex, through-the-lens viewing. Where they do not, as with some XL cameras, focusing is achieved through the use of a separate rangefinder.

All the listed cameras have built-in metering systems, most of which are fully automatic and usually through the lens. Many of them have a manual facility for overriding the automatic metering or for compensating for backlit subjects. In all cases, the automatic metering system is cross-coupled to the different running speeds so that adjustment is automatically achieved. The running speeds vary from 1 frame per minute for time-lapse photography, through 18 and 24 fps, the normal frame-rate, to 70 fps for slow motion.

The two most common in-camera effects are fades (in and out) and dissolves. Single-frame capacity has to be supported by an intervalometer if time-lapse photography exceeding one frame per minute is needed. A further refinement on several super 8 cameras is the presence of a PC socket on the camera. It not only permits the use of electronic flash for single-frame exposures but it also serves as the connection for double system sound filming.

Super 8 sound cameras

All double system cameras must contain provision for a sync signal. This is usually the PC socket mentioned above. They should also all be able to run at either 18 or 24 fps, although many of them have only one running speed – 18 fps. Single system sound cameras all have an integral recording amplifier. They should permit monitoring of the sound during filming.

Single 8 system

Fuji make the only single 8 cameras, for use with their single 8 cartridges. Except for the fact that they are designed only to take single 8 film, Fuji cameras are identical in facilities to super 8 cameras; and on their most advanced models offer more features than most, such as interchangeable lenses, a very bright viewfinder and a variable shutter.

Super 8 and Single 8 Camera Guide

Group headers (left to right): FPS Speeds | Lens features | Exposure meter | Viewing system | Shutter system | Sound features

Camera types	FPS Speeds	Accepts interchangeable	Power zoom	Macro	Direct non-reflex	Automatic TTL	Manual override	Thru lens/Manual	Warning signals	Direct non-reflex	Reflex	Low light XL	Fades or dissolves	Timer and/or intervalometer	Single-frame facility	PC contact for flash or double system sync	Single system sound	Audio monitor	Sound dissolves or fades
BAUER																			
C14XL 9-36mm f1.7 lens	18		□			●		○			□	▲			□	silent camera			
C104 9-36mm f1.8 lens	18·36		□	▲		●	□	○			□	▲			□	silent camera			
C107XL 7-48mm f1.2 lens	9·18·36		□	▲		●	□	○			□	▲	○	●	□	silent camera			
C108 7.5-60mm f1.8 lens	9·18·36		□	▲		●	□	○			□	▲	○	●	□	silent camera			
S204XL 9-36mm f1.7 lens	18·24		□			●		○			□	▲			□		○	●	
S207XL 17-45mm f1.2 lens	18·24		□	▲		●	□	○			□	▲	○	●	□		○	●	□
S209XL 6-51mm f1.2 lens	18·24		□	▲		●	□	○			□	▲	○	●	□		○	●	□
S715XL Microcomputer 6-90mm f1.4	9·18·24		□	▲		●	□	○			□	▲	○	●	□		○	●	□
A508 7.5-60mm f1.8 lens	12·18·24·54		□	▲		●	□	○			□		○	●	□	▲	○		
A512 6-70mm f1.8 lens	12·18·24·54		□	▲		●	□	○			□		○	●	□	▲	○		
BEAULIEU																			
40082M4 6-70mm f1.4 lens	1·80	●	□	▲		●	□	○			□	▲	○		□	silent camera			
1008XL 7-45mm f1.2 lens	9·18·24·36		□			●	□	○			□	▲	○		□			●	□
5008MS 6-70mm f1.4 lens	8·18·24·45	●	□	▲		●	□	○			□		○		□	▲	○	●	□

Super 8 and Single 8 Camera Guide

Camera types	FPS Speeds	Lens features				Exposure meter				Viewing system			Shutter system				Sound features		
		Accepts interchangeable	Power zoom	Macro	Direct non-reflex	Automatic TTL	Manual override	Thru lens/Manual	Warning signals	Direct non-reflex	Reflex	Low light XL	Fades or dissolves	Timer and/or intervalometer	Single-frame facility	PC contact for flash or double system sync	Single system sound	Audio monitor	Sound dissolves or fades
BELL & HOWELL																			
2123XL 8.5-24mm f1.2 lens	18		□			●	□		○	□	▲				□		silent camera		
2143XL 8.5-24mm f1.2 lens	18		□			●	□		○	□	▲	○			□		silent camera		
2146XL 8.5-24mm f1.2 lens	18·56		□	▲		●	□		○	□	▲	○			□		silent camera		
1238XL 7.5-60mm f1.8 lens	18·24·56		□	▲		●	□		○	□	▲	○					○	●	□
1237XL 7-45mm f1.2 lens	18·24·36		□	▲		●	□		○	□	▲	○			□		○	●	□
BOLEX																			
625 9-25mm f1.1 lens	9·18		□		○					□	▲						silent camera		
680M 7-56mm f1.8 lens	9·18·54		□	▲		●	□		○	□		○	●		□		silent camera		
551XL 8-40mm f1.2 lens	18·24		□	▲	○	●	□			□	▲	○	●		□		○	●	□
581 7.5-60mm f1.7 lens	18·24		□	▲			□			□		○	●		□		○	●	□
5122 6-72mm f1.8 lens	18·24·36		□	▲		●	□		○	□		○	●		□		○		□
660 7-42mm f1.8 lens	9·18·45		□	▲		●	□		○	□	▲	○			□	▲		○	
564XL Autofocus Sound 8-48mm f1.2 lens	18·24·36	□				●	□		○	□	▲	○	●			▲	○	●	□
BRAUN NIZO																			
148M 8-48mm f1.8 lens	9·18·24·36		□	▲		●	□			□		○	●				silent camera		
156M 7-56mm f8 lens	9·18·24·36		□	▲		●	□			□		○	●				silent camera		
481M 8-48mm f1.8 lens	18·24·56		□	▲		●	□			□		○	●		□		silent camera		
561 7-56mm f1.8 lens	18·24·56		□	▲		●	□			□		○	●		□		silent camera		
801 7-80mm f1.8 lens	18·24·56		□	▲		●	□		○	□							silent camera		
3048 8-48mm f1.8 lens	18·24	□				●	□		○	□	▲	○			□	▲	○	●	
3056 7-56mm f1.4 lens	9·16⅔·18·24·25·36	□				●	□		○	□	▲	○	●		□	▲	○	●	
4056 7-56mm f1.4 lens	9·16⅔·18·24·25·54	□				●	□		○	□	▲	○	●		□	▲	○	●	
4080 7-80mm f1.4 lens	9·16⅔·18·24·25·54					●	□		○	□	▲	○	●		□	▲	○	●	
CANON																			
310XL 8.5-25mm f1. lens	18		□	▲	○					□	▲				□		silent camera		
514XL 9-45mm f1.4 lens	9·18		□			●	□			□	▲			●			silent camera		
512XLE 9.5-47mm f1.2 lens	9·18·36		□	▲		●	□		○	□	▲	○			□		silent camera		
814XLE 7.5-60mm f1.4 lens	18·24·40		□			●	□		○	□		○			□		silent camera		
312XLS 8.5-25.5mm f1.2 lens	18		□	▲	○				○	□	▲						○	●	
514XLS 9-45mm f1.4 lens	18·24		□	▲		●	□			□	▲	○			□		○		□
1014XLS 6.5-65mm f1.4 lens	9·18·24·36		□	▲		●	□		○	□	▲	○		●	□	▲	○	●	□
CHINON																			
753XL 8.5-25.5mm f1.7 lens	18		□	▲		●	□			□	▲						silent camera		
555XL 8-40mm f1.2 lens	9·18·36		□	▲		●	□			□	▲	○		●	□		silent camera		
60AFXL 8-48mm f1.2 lens	18		□	▲	○		□		○		▲						○	●	□
60SMXL 8-48mm f1.2 lens	18		□	▲		●			○		▲			●			○	●	□
60SMRXL 8-48mm f1.2 lens	18·24·36		□	▲		●	□			□	▲	○		●	□	▲	○	●	□

Super 8 and Single 8 Camera Guide

Camera types	FPS Speeds	Accepts interchangeable	Power zoom	Macro	Direct non-reflex	Automatic TTL	Manual override	Thru lens/Manual	Warning signals	Direct non-reflex	Reflex	Low light XL	Fades or dissolves	Timer and/or intervalometer	Single-frame facility	PC contact for flash or double system sync.	Single system sound	Audio monitor	Sound dissolves or fades
CHINON																			
80SMR 7.5-60 mm f1.7 lens	18·24·36		□	▲		●	□				□	▲	○	●	□	▲	○	●	□
2008XL 7-56mm·f1.4 lens*	18·24·25·36		□	▲		●	□		○		□	▲	○	●	□	▲	○	●	
Pacific 12SMR 6-72mm f1.8 lens	18·24·36		□			●	□		○		□		○	●	□	▲	○	●	□
COSINA																			
XL204M 9-36mm f1.2 lens*	18·24		□	▲		●	□		○		□	▲					○	●	
XL206M 7.5-45mm f1.8 lens*	18·24		□	▲		●	□		○		□	▲					○	●	
ELMO																			
350SL 9-27mm f1.2 lens	18		□	▲		●	□		○		□	▲					○	●	
1012SXL 7.5-75mm f1.2 lens	18·24		□	▲		●	□				□	▲	○		□	▲	○	●	□
612SXL 8.5-51mm f1.2 lens	18		□	▲		●	□				□	▲					○	●	□
3000AF 9-27mm f1.2 lens	18·24		□	▲		●	□				□	▲	○		□		○	●	□
EUMIG																			
830XL 7.5-22mm f1.2 lens	9·18·24·45		□		○		□		○			▲	○	●	□		silent camera		
860PMA 8-48mm f1.8 lens	9·18·24·45		□			●	□		○		□		○	●	□		silent camera		
880PMA 7-56mm f1.8 lens	9·18·24·45		□			●	□		○		□		○	●	□		silent camera		
31XLS 8.5-24mm f1.3 lens	18·24		□	▲		●	□		○		□		○				○	●	□
FUJICA																			
P2 11-25mm f1.8 lens	18					●			○		□						silent camera		
ZC1000 7.5-75mm f1.8 lens	12·18·24·36·72	●	□	▲				▲	○		□		○		□		silent camera		
ZXM300 9.7-26mm f1.2 lens	18			▲		●					□	▲					○	●	
ZXM500 7.5-36mm f1.3 lens	18		□	▲		●	□		○		□	▲	○				○	●	□
ZXM800 8-64mm f1.8 lens	18		□	▲		●	□		○		□	▲	○				○	●	□
KODAK																			
250 9-21mm f1.2 lens	18		□		○		□				□						○	●	
260 9-21mm f1.2 lens	18		□		○		□				□						○	●	
MINOLTA																			
XL401 8.5-34mm f1.2 lens	18		□	▲		●	□		○		□	▲	○	●	□		silent camera		
XL601 7.5-45mm f1.7 lens	18		□	▲		●	□		○		□	▲	○	●	□		silent camera		
XL225 10.5-26mm f1.2 lens	18		□			●			○		□	▲					○	●	
XL440 8.5-34mm f1.2 lens	18		□	▲		●			○		□	▲					○	●	
XL660 7.5-45mm f1.2 lens	18		□	▲		●			○		□	▲	○				○	●	□
NIKON																			
R8 7.5-60mm f1.8 lens	18·24·54		□	▲		●	□		○			▲	○		□		silent camera		
R10 7-70mm f1.4 lens	18·24·54		□	▲		●	□		○			▲	○		□		silent camera		

*Takes 200ft cartridge

Super 8 and Single 8 Camera Guide

Camera types	FPS Speeds	Lens features			Exposure meter					Viewing system			Shutter system			Sound features			
		Accepts interchangeable	Power zoom	Macro	Direct non-reflex	Automatic TTL	Manual override	Thru lens/Manual	Warning signals	Direct non-reflex	Reflex	Low light XL	Fades or dissolves	Timer and/or intervalometer	Single-frame facility	PC contact for flash or double system sync.	Single system sound	Audio monitor	Sound dissolves or fades
ROLLEI																			
XL8 7-56mm f1.4 lens	18·24·48		□	▲		●	□			□	▲	○			□		*silent camera*		
SANKYO																			
ES88XL 7.5-60mm f1.8 lens	18·24·36		□	▲		●	□		○	□	▲	○					*silent camera*		
ES44XL 8.5-34mm f1.2 lens	9·18·36		□	▲		●	□		○	□	▲						*silent camera*		
EM30XL 10-30mm f1.2 lens	18		□	▲		●	□		○	□	▲				□		*silent camera*		
EM60XL 7.5-45mm f1.2 lens	18·24·36		□	▲		●	□		○	□	▲	○			□	●	*silent camera*		
XL320 10-30mm f1.2 lens	18		□	▲		●			○	□	▲	○			□		○	●	
XL620 7.5-45mm f1.2 lens	18·24·36		□	▲		●			○	□	▲	○	●		□	▲	○	●	□
XL61200 7.5-45mm f1.2 lens*	18·24		□	▲		●	□			□	▲	○					○	●	□
XL800S 7.5-60mm f1.8 lens	18·24		□	▲		●	□		○	□	▲	○					○	●	□
YASHICA																			
50XLII AF50 Autofocus 8-40mm f1.2 lens	18		□	▲		●	□		○	□	▲							○	

*Takes 200ft cartridge

Choosing a 16 mm camera

16 mm cameras are larger, heavier and more expensive than super 8. If you are thinking of buying a camera, it would be worth your while to explore the possibilities of obtaining a used, second-hand model or hiring the equipment you need; there are plenty of camera rental companies around who will probably have the most up-to-date cameras and all the accessories.

When choosing a 16 mm camera, bear some of the following things in mind. How portable is the camera? Will you have to sacrifice ease of operation for quality? How much film will the camera carry? Will it accept 200 ft (61 m) or 400 ft (122 m) magazines? Does it have a built-in spring-wound or electric motor? What kind of power supply does it require? Does it have the lens or lenses you will need? Are they interchangeable? And if so, which of the four most common lens mounts does the camera have – a bayonet, C-mount, regular Arri or bayonet Arri?

The smallest and lightest cameras are, of course, the simplest and the ones with the least facilities. The Bolex H16 (see p. 38) or the Bell and Howell DR 70, for example, do not have reflex viewfinders and have only spring-wound motors.

More sophisticated 16 mm cameras have reflex viewfinders, electric motors with rechargeable batteries and automatic light metering systems – for example, the Beaulieu R16 (see p. 38), the Bolex H16 EL (see p. 129) or the Canon Scoopic (see p. 35). The most expensive cameras – such as those made by Arriflex, Eclair or Aaton – are self-blimped for very high quality sound filming. They are of superbly robust construction and accept every conceivable accessory such as 1,200 ft (370 m) magazines and video viewfinders.

Shooting sound films on 16 mm falls into two categories: single system and double system. For single system, it is possible to obtain sound-striped 16 mm filmstocks, and there are a few cameras which will record sound-on-film. These include the Canon Sound Scoopic, a version of the Arriflex 16BL, the Beaulieu News 16 and the Paillard Bolex 16 Pro. They are used chiefly for newsreel and documentary work, where fast processing and editing is essential.

For double system filming, you should check whether the camera can be locked to crystal sync or whether you will need a cable to link it to the recorder (see p. 117). You should also investigate whether the camera is quiet enough to use when recording sync sound at close quarters; many are not, and you may need a sound barney or blimp to reduce the camera noise. Some of the best, and the most expensive, 16 mm cameras are the sound-proofed, double system models – for example, the Arriflex 16BL and 16SR (see p. 38), The Eclair ACL and 16 NPR and the Aaton 7.

Projector Specifications

Almost all filmmakers today use either super 8 or single 8, and all super 8 projectors will show either. However, some, which are dual gauge, are capable of showing standard 8 films as well.

A bright, sharp picture is essential and the larger the lens aperture, the greater the brilliance of any given image size. An f1.0 lens is much brighter than an f1.6. Many projectors have zoom lenses which make the positioning of the projector easier for achieving the proper image size on the screen – although inexpensive zooms may throw an unsharp picture.

Each of the projectors listed in the chart below is auto-threading, and many of them also contain controls for framing adjustment. Many machines are capable of reverse projection and stop motion. There should be some facility for removing the film part way through.

The normal silent projection speed for super 8 is 18 fps. Sound projectors may also be run at 24 fps, which will give higher fidelity because of the greater speed over the sound head.

8 mm sound projectors

Most of the 8 mm projectors currently being manufactured are for showing sound movies. They use the narrow magnetic stripe running down the side of the film to play and record a sound track. Some machines also have a sync facility which allows you to play a sound track on a tape recorder in sync with the film.

An increasing number of projectors have a facility for superimposing one sound over another – voice over music, for example. Twin-tracking or duoplay permits sound recording on both the sound stripe and the small "balance" stripe. In the same way, a few machines now allow for stereo recording and playback.

16 mm projectors

Most sound models have optical reproduction, although more and more are now able to play back magnetic sound tracks. In most cases, the capacity of the reels is 2,000 ft (600 m). Many machines take interchangeable lenses (such as anamorphics for widescreen movies),

Super 8 and Single 8 Projector guide

Projector types	Reel Capacity	Fps Speeds	Self threading take up	Freeze Frame	Reverse Projection	Framing Control	Dual format Super 8/Standard 8	Rear projection unit	Bulb Size	Sound record facility	Connection for external amplification	Superimposition ("trick")	Auto recording level control	Optical Sound play	Magnetic sound play/record	Stereo unit or duo-plug	Auto fade control
BAUER																	
T21 16.5-30mm f1.5 lens	400ft 120m	8·12·16·24	●		▲	○	●		75W	Silent projector							
T49 16.5-30mm f1.3 lens	400ft 120m	6·18·18·24	●		▲	○	●		100W	Silent projector							
TR100 16.5-30mm f1.3 lens	600ft 180m	18·24	●		▲			□	100W	▲	○	●	□		○		
T82 16.5-30mm f1.3 lens	400ft 120m	18·24	●	□	▲		●		100W	Silent projector							
T171 16.5-30mm f1.5 lens	600ft 180m	18·24	●		▲				100W	▲		●	□		○		
T192 16.5-30mm f1.3 lens	600ft 180m	18·24	●		▲		●		100W	▲		●	□		○	●	
T502 15.5-28mm f1.2 lens	800ft 240m	18·24	●	□	▲				150W	▲	○	●	□		○	●	□
T610 15.5-28mm f1.2 lens	800ft 240m	18·24	●	□	▲	○			150W	▲	○	●	□		○	●	□
TR300 16.5-30mm f1.3 lens	600ft 180m	18·24	●	□	▲			□	100W	▲	○	●	□		○		□
BEAULIEU																	
708EL 11-30mm f1.1 lens	2300ft 700m	18·24	●		▲	○			150W	▲	○	●	□		○		
BELL AND HOWELL																	
1462 16.5-30mm f1.3 lens	400ft 120m	3·6·9·18	●	□	▲	○		□	75W	Silent projector							
1481 16.5-30mm f1.3 lens	400ft 120m	3·6·9·18	●	□	▲	○		□	100W	Silent projector							
1776 20-32mm f1.5 lens	600ft 180m	18·24	●	□	▲	○			100W	▲	○	●	□		○		□
DCR 15-25mm f1.4 lens	600ft 180m	18·24	●		▲	○			100W	▲		●	□		○		
DCM 15-25mm f1.3 lens	600ft 180m	18·24	●		▲	○			100W	▲	○	●	□		○		□
BOLEX																	
18-3TC 15-30mm f1.3 lens	400ft 120m	3·6·9·12·18	●	□	▲	○	●		100W	Silent projector							
102 MTC 7-25mm f1.3 lens	400ft 120m	3·6·9·12·18	●	□	▲		●	□	100W	Silent projector							
SP8E 15-30mm f1.3 lens	600ft 180m	18·24	●		▲				100W	▲	○		□		○		
SM80 12.5-25mm f1.2 lens	800ft 240m	18·24	●		▲	○			100W	▲	○	●	□		○		□

Projector types	Reel Capacity	Fps Speeds	Self threading take up	Freeze Frame	Reverse Projection	Framing Control	Dual format Super 8/Standard 8	Rear projection unit	Bulb Size	Sound record facility	Connection for external amplification	Superimposition ("trick")	Auto recording level control	Optical Sound play	Magnetic sound play/record	Stereo unit or duo-plug	Auto fade control
BOLEX																	
Sound 715 14-30mm f1.3 lens	600ft 180m	18·24	●		▲	○		□	100W	▲	○	●	□		○	●	□
BRAUN																	
1000 Visacustic 14.5-26mm f1.1 lens	600ft 180m	16⅔·18·24·25	●	□	▲	○			150W	▲	○	●	□		○	●	□
CHINON																	
DS 300 15-30mm f1.3 lens	600ft 180m	18·24	●		▲			□	100W	▲		●			○		
7000 15-30mm f1.3 lens	600ft 180m	18·24	●		▲				100W	▲		●	□		○		
9500 15-30mm f1.3 lens	600ft 180m	18·24	●		▲	○			150W	▲		●			○	●	
SS 1200 15-30mm f1.0 lens	1200ft 360m	18·24	●		▲				150W	▲		●			○	●	□
ELMO																	
K 100 SM 15-25mm f1.3 lens	400ft 120m	14·24	●	□	▲	○	●	□	100W	*Silent projector*							
GS 800 15-25mm f1.3 lens	800ft 240m	18·24	●					□	100W	▲	○	●	□	▲	○	●	□
GS 1200 12.5-25mm f1.1 lens	600ft 180m	18·24	●		▲		●		150W	▲		●		▲	○		
ST 600 15-25mm f1.3 lens	600ft 180m	18·24	●		▲			□	100W	▲	○		□		○	●	
EUMIG																	
610D 15-30mm f1.3 lens	400ft 120m	3·6·9·12·18	●	□	▲	○	●		100W	*Silent projector*							
R2000 D 7mm f1.3 lens	400ft 120m	3·6·9·12·18	●	□	▲	○	●	□	100W						○		
S912 SP 14-30mm f1.3 lens	600ft 180m	18·24	●	□	▲				100W	▲	○	●	□				
RS3000 HQS SP 13.6mm f1.3 lens	600ft 180m	18·24	●	□	▲				100W	▲	○		□		○		
824 Sonomatic HQS D 12.5-25mm f1.2 lens	600ft 180m	18·24	●	□	▲	○	●		100W	▲	○	●	□		○		
FUJICA																	
M36 15-25mm f1.3 lens	400ft 120m	18·24	●		▲				100W	*Silent projector*							
SH8 15-25mm f1.3 lens	600ft 180m	18·24	●		▲				100W	▲		●	□				
SH9 15-25mm f1.3 lens	600ft 180m	18·24	●		▲				100W	▲		●			▲		
HEURTIER																	
P942 12-30mm f1.3 lens	400ft 120m	18·24	●		▲	○			100W							●	
Duovox 15-30mm f1.3 lens	600ft 180m	18·24	●		▲	○			100W	▲	○		□	▲			
Stereovox 12-30mm f1.3 lens	600ft 180m	18·24	●		▲	○			100W	▲	○		□	▲		●	
IMAC																	
300 18-30mm f1.3 lens	400ft 120m	14·18	●	□	▲		●		100W	*Silent projector*							
Bi-sonix 16.5-30mm f1.3 lens	400ft 120m	18·24	●		▲				100W	*Silent projector*							
NORIS																	
Norimat D Special 16.5-30mm f1.3 lens	600ft 180m	18·24	●	□	▲	○	●		100W	*Silent projector*							
322 16.5-30mm f1.2 lens	600ft 180m	18·24	●	□		○			100W	▲	○		□	▲	○	●	
342 15.5-28mm f1.2 lens	600ft 180m	18·24	●	□		○			100W	▲	○		□	▲	○	●	
SANKYO																	
501 15-25mm f1.4 lens	600ft 180m	18·24	●		▲				100W	▲	○		□	▲		●	
700 15-25mm f1.4 lens	600ft 180m	18·24	●		▲				100W	▲	○		□	▲		●	
800 15-30mm f1.0 lens	600ft 180m	18·24	●		▲				100W	▲	○		□	▲		●	□
TACNON																	
606 16.5-30mm f1.3 lens	600ft 180m	18·24	●						100W	▲		●	□		○		
707 20-32mm f1.5 lens	600ft 180m	18·24	●						100W	▲		●	□				
808 15.5-30mm f1.2 lens	600ft 180m	18·24	●		▲				100W	▲		●	□		○	●	

Filmstock Specifications

A wide variety of filmstocks are available to the amateur filmmaker, and on these pages we describe some of the most common. The list is not meant to be definitive, as many "house brands" are not mentioned, but it does cover all the representative types.

Many of the super 8 filmstocks are also available in 16 mm form. The general description and exposure information are the same for both gauges. All super 8 film is reversal (it gives a "positive" image); no negative stocks are available.

Choosing a filmstock depends on the conditions in which it will be used. In general, you should go for the film which gives you the best color rendition and projection quality for your shooting conditions. Also consider sharpness, graininess, contrast and resolution (see p. 52). All super 8 cameras have a built-in "85" daylight filter which is slotted into the light path when shooting outdoors (see p. 92). When in place, this cuts down the amount of light actually reaching the film. In other words, it cuts down the effective film speed. Therefore, all super 8 film is quoted as having two film speeds (or "exposure indexes") – one for daylight, and one for artificial light (when the filter has been removed).

In difficult lighting conditions you may need a "faster" film than usual. Super 8 color film is now available with an exposure index of 160 ASA, and Fuji make a single 8 color film with a speed of 200 ASA. Used in modern XL cameras, these filmstocks allow shooting in almost any situation (see *Low Light Filming*, p. 95).

If you want to shoot single system sound movies, you will want "striped" sound film (see p. 112). If you only have a silent camera but you want to add sound to your silent movie at a later stage, you can either stripe your film after it has been processed (see p. 233) or use sound film in a silent cartridge (several manufacturers now offer their sound film in this form – Fuji and Agfa).

Black and white super 8 film is still available in many countries, although it can be very difficult to obtain. Apart from the great pleasure of filming in black and white, the film can be home-processed and is cheaper than color (see p. 208). Black and white film is readily available in 16 mm, in standard 8 and double super 8.

One of the great advantages of super 8 over standard 8 and 16 mm is that the cartridge-loading design enables you to exchange films in mid-reel. Only a few frames of film will be fogged when you open the camera, and these can be easily removed during editing. This means that you can change from one type of filmstock to another while you are shooting. It is therefore easy to experiment with different filmstocks and to make simple tests for the purposes of comparison. To be absolutely certain that you will always have the correct filmstock, it is a good idea to carry three types of film with you when filming – say, a slow fine-grain film, a fast daylight/artificial light film, and a "mixed" light (Type G) film.

Two other factors to bear in mind are film cost and availability of processing. Buying in bulk from a discount house can be much less expensive than your neighborhood shop, and, if you choose a filmstock other than Kodachrome, a variety of independent laboratories may be available to process it.

Super 8 and single 8

Kodachrome 40
This is a fine-grain, sharp color film of moderate speed with a wide exposure latitude and good color balance. It produces good flesh tones and vivid reds. It is balanced for 3,400°K (Type A) and has an exposure index of 40 ASA without a filter and 25 ASA with the built-in "85" filter when shooting in daylight. It is available in a silent and sound-striped version. The sound film also comes in 200 ft (61 m) cartridges.

Ektachrome 40
A sharp, fine-grain film similar to Kodachrome 40, it is balanced for 3,400°K (Type A) and is exposed at 40 ASA under tungsten lighting conditions and at 25 ASA with the filter in place in daylight. It is not yet available in a sound version.

Ektachrome 160
A high speed color film which is grainier, less sharp and more contrasty than Kodachrome 40. It is intended for use in low lighting conditions such as indoors or outdoors at night. It is balanced for 3,400°K (Type A) and is exposed at 160 ASA without a filter in artificial light and at 100 ASA in daylight. It can be pushed to 320 ASA or even 640 ASA by a laboratory. It is available in silent and sound versions.

Ektachrome 160 (Type G)
A tolerant high speed color film designed for shooting without the camera's built-in filter in varied existing light conditions, such as daylight, tungsten light, fluorescent light or candlelight. It is particularly suitable for mixed lighting where both daylight and artificial light are used (see p. 107). It has an exposure index of 160 ASA for all types of illumination, and does not at present come in a sound version.

Ektachrome EF
A moderately fast color film useful in difficult exterior and interior lighting conditions. It is balanced for 3,200°K (Type B) and is exposed at 125 ASA in tungsten illumination and at 80 ASA in daylight. It is available in silent and sound versions, including a 200 ft (61 m) cartridge.

Ektachrome SM
A fast color film with fair grain and reasonable color rendition it is useful for shooting in low light conditions without supplementary lighting. It is balanced for 3,200°K (Type B) and is exposed at 160 ASA in tungsten illumination and at 100 ASA in daylight conditions.

3M Color Movie Film
This stock is similar to Fujichrome in that the emulsion is coated onto a polyester base. Although it is thinner than acetate super 8 film, it comes in the usual 50 ft (15 m) cartridge. The film is made by an Italian company and is sometimes known as *Ferrania* or *Dynachrome*. It is less fine-grained than Kodachrome and is rated at 40 ASA in tungsten light and 25 ASA in daylight conditions.

Agfachrome Super 8
A general-purpose, fine-grained and sharp color film similar to Kodachrome 40. It is exposed at 40 ASA for artificial light and at 25 ASA with the filter in daylight.

Agfachrome Super 8 Plus
Same as above; although it comes in a silent cartridge, it is sound striped so that a sound track can be added after processing and played on a sound projector.

Agfachrome Super 8 Sound
Same as above; but it comes in the slightly larger 50 ft (15 m) sound cartridge.

Fujichrome R25
This is a single 8 filmstock for use in Fuji single 8 cameras. It is a slow color film balanced for daylight and used without the built-in filter. It gives good color fidelity, resolution and grain structure. It is exposed at 25 ASA and is available in silent and sound versions.

Fujichrome RT200
This is also a single 8 filmstock. It is the fastest super 8 color film and has comparatively fine grain with acceptable resolution. It is balanced for 3,400°K (Type A) and is exposed at 200 ASA in tungsten light or at 125 ASA in daylight with the filter.

Kodak Plus-X
A slow, fine-grain black and white reversal film used as a general-purpose filmstock under good light conditions. It is exposed at 40 ASA in tungsten and 50 ASA in daylight.

Kodak Tri-X
A fast black and white reversal film with relatively low graininess. Slightly more contrasty than Kodak Plus-X, it is designed for filming under low light conditions. It is exposed at 160 ASA in artificial light and 200 ASA in daylight.

Kodak 4-X
A very fast, grainy black and white reversal film used in extreme low light situations. It is exposed at 320 ASA in tungsten lighting and at 400 ASA in daylight.

16 mm and standard 8

Kodachrome 25
A color film balanced for daylight, this stock gives superb definition and color reproduction, has a wide exposure latitude and very fine grain. Exposed at 25 ASA in daylight and 8 ASA with a filter in artificial light, it is available in 16 mm and standard 8.

Eastman Color Negative 7247
This is the standard filmstock for all 16 mm negative shooting. It has very high resolution and tolerance. Balanced for tungsten, it is rated at 100 ASA in artificial light and at 64 ASA in daylight.

Ektachrome Commercial ECO 7252
A color reversal film rated at 16 ASA in daylight (with a filter) and at 25 ASA in artificial light. This low contrast film is used to produce high quality reversal prints.

Gevachrome 700

Made by Agfa-Gevaert, this is a general-purpose color reversal film with an exposure index of 80 ASA in tungsten light and 40 ASA in daylight. It comes in a variety of forms, including pre-striped.

Gevachrome 710

A general-purpose color reversal film similar to Kodachrome, with a speed of 125 ASA in tungsten light and 64 ASA in daylight. It also comes striped, and can be pushed three stops to 1,000 ASA.

Gevachrome 720

Similar to the above in uses and forms except that it is balanced for daylight and rated at 125 ASA. It is therefore not recommended for shooting in artificial light.

Gevacolor 682

A new filmstock from Agfa, this color negative film is compatible with Kodak's and can be intercut with it. It is rated at 100 ASA in tungsten light and 64 ASA in daylight.

Eastman Double-X

A high speed black and white negative film exposed at 200 ASA in tungsten light and 250 ASA in daylight. It is good for shooting in adverse lighting conditions.

Eastman 4-X

An even faster black and white negative film exposed at 400 ASA in tungsten light and 500 ASA in daylight. It is recommended for general work under difficult lighting conditions.

Gevapan 166

A general-purpose black and white negative film with a film speed of 64 ASA in tungsten light and 80 ASA in daylight.

Gevapan 195

A fast black and white negative film with a film speed of 200 ASA in tungsten light and 250 ASA in daylight.

Notes for charts

1 In the case of daylight exposure indexes for tungsten balanced film stocks, account has been taken – where appropriate – of the light loss due to the presence of the camera's built-in "85" daylight filter.

2 This and similar films are sold under several other names by independent suppliers.

3 In the case of exposure indexes, account has been taken – where appropriate – of the light loss due to the presence of a color conversion filter.

4 High contrast film used for titles.

Super 8 and single 8 filmstocks

Color films	Exposure index[1] Day-light	Exposure index[1] Tung-sten	50 ft silent	50 ft striped silent	50 ft sound	200 ft silent	200 ft sound
Kodachrome 40	25	40	●		●		●
Ektachrome 40	25	40	●				
Ektachrome 160	100	160	●		●		
Ektachrome 160 (Type G)	160	160	●				
*Ektachrome EF	80	125	●		●	●	●
Ektachrome SM	100	160	●		●	●	●
3M²	25	40	●				
3M (Type G)²	160	160	●				
Agfachrome Super 8	25	40	●				
Agfachrome Super 8 Plus	25	40		●			
Agfachrome Super 8 Sound	25	40			●		
Fujichrome R25	25	—	●	●	●		
Fujichrome RT200	125	200	●	●	●		
Black and white films							
*Kodak Plus-X	50	40	●				
*Kodak Tri-X	200	160	●				
*Kodak 4-X	400	320	●				
*ESO-S Super Panchro	50	40	●				
*ESO-S De-luxe Sepia	50	—	●				
*ESO-S High speed Sepia	200	—	●				

*Only available in the USA.

16 mm and standard 8 mm filmstocks

Color films	Color balance Day-light	Color balance Tung-sten	Exposure index[3] Day-light	Exposure index[3] Tung-sten	16 mm	Standard 8
Kodachrome 25	●		25	8	●	●
Kodachrome 40		A	25	40	●	●
*Ektachrome EF		B	80	125	●	
*Ektachrome EF	●		160	40	●	
Eastman Color Negative 7247		B	64	100	●	
Ektachrome Commercial ECO		B	16	25	●	●
Gevachrome 700		●	40	80	●	
Gevachrome 710		●	64	125	●	
Gevachrome 720	●		125	—	●	
Gevacolor 682		●	64	100	●	
Black and white films	Reversal	Negative				
Kodak Plus-X	●		50	40	●	●
Kodak Tri-X	●		200	160	●	●
*Kodak 4-X	●		400	320	●	●
*Kodak Recordak⁴			4	4	●	
Eastman Double-X		●	250	200	●	
Eastman Plus-X		●	80	64	●	
Eastman 4-X		●	500	400	●	
Gevapan 166		●	80	64	●	
Gevapan 195		●	250	200	●	
*ESO-S Economy Plus⁴			3	3	●	
*ESO-S De-luxe Sepia			50	—	●	●
*ESO-S High Speed Sepia			200	—	●	●

*Only available in the USA.

Charts and Tables

Film running times

The tables below enable you to convert the length of your super 8, standard 8 or 16 mm film into the time that it will last on the screen. The first table is for converting footage into screen time; the second is for converting screen time into footage. The tables are useful during editing to estimate running time if you are working on a synchronizer or viewer with a footage counter. They are also useful when comparing the relative footages of different gauges – when considering laboratory blow-ups or reductions, for example.

Metrication guide
Use the center column in the charts below and read off either side to convert metric measurements.

Film Format	Super 8		Standard 8		16 mm	
Projection speed in frames per second	18	24	18	24	18	24
Inches per second	3.0	4.0	2.7	3.6	5.4	7.2
Film length and screen time	min. sec.	min. sec.	min. sec.	min. sec.	min. sec.	min. sec.
feet 50	3 20	2 30	3 42	2 47	1 51	1 23
100	6 40	5 0	7 24	5 33	3 42	2 47
150	10 0	7 30	11 7	8 20	5 33	4 10
200	13 20	10 20	14 49	11 7	7 24	5 33
300	20 0	15 0	22 13	16 40	11 7	8 20
400	26 40	20 0	29 38	22 13	14 49	11 7
500	33 20	25 0	37 2	27 47	18 31	13 53
600	40 0	30 0	44 27	33 20	22 13	16 40
700	46 40	35 0	51 51	38 53	25 56	19 27
800	53 20	40 0	59 16	44 27	29 38	22 13
900	60 0	45 0	66 40	50 0	33 20	25 0
1,000	66 40	50 0	74 4	55 33	37 2	27 47
1,100	73 20	55 0	81 29	61 7	40 44	30 33
1,200	80 0	60 0	88 53	66 40	44 27	33 20

Film format	Super 8 (72 frames per foot)		Standard 8 (80 frames per foot)		16 mm (40 frames per foot)	
Projection speed in frames per second	18	24	18	24	18	24
Running time and film length	Feet + frames	Feet + frames	Feet + frames	Feet + frames	Feet + frames	Feet + frames
seconds 1	0 18	0 24	0 18	0 24	0 18	0 24
2	0 36	0 36	0 36	0 48	1 8	0 24
3	0 54	1 0	0 54	0 72	1 14	1 32
4	1 0	1 24	1 0	1 16	1 32	2 16
5	1 18	1 48	1 10	1 40	2 10	3 0
6	1 36	2 0	1 28	1 64	2 28	3 24
7	1 54	2 24	1 46	2 8	3 6	4 8
8	2 0	2 48	1 64	2 32	3 24	4 32
9	2 18	3 0	2 2	2 56	4 2	5 16
10	2 36	3 24	2 20	3 0	4 20	6 0
20	5 0	6 48	4 40	6 0	9 0	12 0
30	7 36	10 0	6 60	9 0	13 20	18 0
40	10 0	13 24	9 0	12 0	18 0	24 0
50	12 36	16 48	11 20	15 0	22 20	30 0
minutes 1	15 0	20 0	13 40	18 0	27 0	36 0
2	30 0	40 0	27 0	36 0	54 0	72 0
3	45 0	60 0	40 40	54 0	81 0	108 0
4	60 0	80 0	54 0	72 0	108 0	144 0
5	75 0	100 0	67 40	90 0	135 0	180 0
6	90 0	120 0	81 0	108 0	162 0	252 0
7	105 0	140 0	94 40	126 0	189 0	252 0
8	120 0	160 0	108 0	144 0	216 0	288 0
9	135 0	180 0	121 40	162 0	243 0	324 0
10	150 0	200 0	135 0	180 0	270 0	360 0

mm		in.
25	1	1/32
50	2	1/16
75	3	1/8
100	4	5/32
125	5	3/16
150	6	1/4
180	7	9/32
205	8	5/16
230	9	11/32
255	10	3/8

cm		in.
2.5	1	3/8
5	2	3/4
7.5	3	11/4
10	4	13/4
12	5	2
15	6	23/8
17	7	23/4
20	8	33/16
22	9	31/2
25	10	4
50	20	8
76	30	12
101	40	16
127	50	20
152	60	24
177	70	28
203	80	31
228	90	35
254	100	39

m		ft
0.3	1	3.2
0.6	2	6.5
0.9	3	10
1.2	4	13
1.5	5	16
1.8	6	20
2.1	7	23
2.4	8	26
2.7	9	30
3.0	10	33
6.1	20	66
9.1	30	98
12.2	40	131
15.2	50	164
18.2	60	197
21.3	70	230
24.4	80	262
27.4	90	295
30.5	100	328

Lens angles-of-view

The angle-of-view of a lens varies in direct proportion to its focal length. It also varies according to the film format: a given focal length has a narrower angle-of-view on super 8 than it does on 16 mm. The table (right) gives figures for the most common lenses.

Depth of field

Depth of field fluctuates according to four variables: the focal length of the lens, the aperture, the distance at which the lens is focused, and the film format. Depth of field is not visible if you have a non-reflex or beam-splitter viewfinder, so use of the tables is essential.

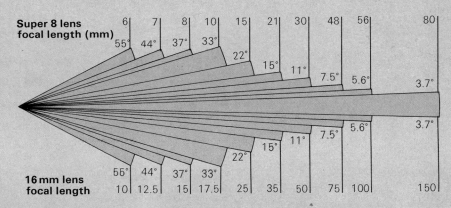

Super 8 depth of field tables

Focal length of the lens	Lens focus (feet)	f1.8 Near	f1.8 Far	f5.6 Near	f5.6 Far	f11 Near	f11 Far	f22 Near	f22 Far
6 mm	∞	3 ft 11 in.	∞	1 ft 5 in.	∞	11 in.	∞	7 in.	∞
	10	3 ft 0 in.	∞	1 ft 4 in.	∞	10 in.	∞	7 in.	∞
	5	2 ft 5 in.	∞	1 ft 3 in.	∞	10 in.	∞	7 in.	∞
12 mm	∞	13 ft 4 in.	∞	4 ft 5 in.	∞	2 ft 4 in.	∞	1 ft 3 in.	∞
	10	6 ft 0 in.	∞	3 ft 3 in.	∞	2 ft 0 in.	∞	1 ft 2 in.	∞
	5	3 ft 10 in.	7 ft 3 in.	2 ft 7 in.	∞	1 ft 10 in.	∞	1 ft 2 in.	∞
34 mm	∞	105 ft 0 in.	∞	33 ft 7 in.	∞	16 ft 11 in.	∞	8 ft 4 in.	∞
	10	9 ft 2 in.	11 ft 0 in.	7 ft 9 in.	14 ft 0 in.	6 ft 4 in.	22 ft 6 in.	4 ft 7 in.	∞
	5	4 ft 9 in.	5 ft 3 in.	4 ft 4 in.	6 ft 10 in.	3 ft 11 in.	6 ft 11 in.	3 ft 2 in.	10 ft 9 in.
48 mm	∞	209 ft 0 in.	∞	66 ft 11 in.	∞	33 ft 10 in.	∞	16 ft 8 in.	∞
	10	9 ft 6 in.	10 ft 6 in.	8 ft 8 in.	11 ft 9 in.	7 ft 8 in.	14 ft 10 in.	6 ft 3 in.	23 ft 0 in.
	5	4 ft 11 in.	5 ft 2 in.	4 ft 8 in.	5 ft 5 in.	4 ft 4 in.	5 ft 10 in.	3 ft 9 in.	7 ft 0 in.
66 mm	∞	372 ft 0 in.	∞	119 ft 0 in.	∞	60 ft 3 in.	∞	29 ft 8 in.	∞
	10	9 ft 9 in.	10 ft 3 in.	9 ft 2 in.	10 ft 11 in.	8 ft 6 in.	12 ft 0 in.	7 ft 5 in.	4 ft 11 in.
	5	4 ft 11 in.	5 ft 1 in.	4 ft 9 in.	5 ft 3 in.	4 ft 7 in.	5 ft 6 in.	4 ft 2 in.	6 ft 1 in.

16 mm depth of field tables

Focal length of the lens	Lens focus (feet)	f1.8 Near	f1.8 Far	f5.6 Near	f5.6 Far	f11 Near	f11 Far	f22 Near	f22 Far
10 mm	∞	5 ft 2 in.	∞	2 ft 2 in.	∞	1 ft 2 in.	∞	7 in.	∞
	10	3 ft 11 in.	∞	1 ft 11 in.	∞	1 ft 1 in.	∞	7 in.	∞
	5	2 ft 1 in.	5 ft 6 in.	1 ft 4 in.	∞	ft 10 in.	∞	6 in.	∞
25 mm	∞	30 ft 0 in.	∞	15 ft 0 in.	∞	7 ft 9 in.	∞	4 ft 0 in.	∞
	10	8 ft 0 in.	13 ft 3 in.	6 ft 0 in.	29 ft 0 in.	4 ft 3 in.	∞	2 ft 9 in.	∞
	5	4 ft 5 in.	5 ft 8 in.	3 ft 9 in.	7 ft 7 in.	3 ft 0 in.	14 ft 10 in.	2 ft 2½ in.	∞
50 mm	∞	120 ft 0 in.	∞	60 ft 0 in.	∞	30 ft 0 in.	∞	15 ft 0 in.	∞
	10	9 ft 0 in.	10 ft 8 in.	8 ft 6 in.	12 ft 0 in.	7 ft 6 in.	15 ft 0 in.	6 ft 0 in.	30 ft 0 in.
	5	4 ft 10 in.	5 ft 2 in.	4 ft 7 in.	5 ft 5 in.	4 ft 4 in.	6 ft 0 in.	3 ft 9 in.	7 ft 5 in.
75 mm	∞	300 ft 0 in.	∞	65 ft 0 in.	∞	35 ft 0 in.	∞	25 ft 0 in.	∞
	10	9 ft 9 in.	10 ft 3 in.	9 ft 0 in.	11 ft 2 in.	8 ft 9 in.	11 ft 9 in.	7 ft 9 in.	14 ft 2 in.
	5	4 ft 11 in.	5 ft 1 in.	4 ft 9 in.	5 ft 3 in.	4 ft 8 in.	5 ft 5 in.	4 ft 4 in.	5 ft 10 in.
100 mm	∞	500 ft 0 in.	∞	200 ft 0 in.	∞	120 ft 0 in.	∞	85 ft 0 in.	60 ft 0 in.
	10	9 ft 10 in.	10 ft 2 in.	9 ft 10 in.	10 ft 2 in.	9 ft 3 in.	10 ft 11 in.	4 ft 10 in.	5 ft 2 in.
	5	5 ft 0 in.	5 ft 0 in.	4 ft 11 in.	5 ft 1 in.	4 ft 10 in.	5 ft 2 in.	4 ft 8 in.	5 ft 5 in.

Glossary

A

A and B rolling Cutting room technique in which the original film is cut to match the edited workprint. Successive shots are distributed between two rolls, alternating with black leader to make them up to equal length. The two rolls are used to make a print which is free from splice marks and to produce printed optical effects such as dissolves.

Academy aperture Standard frame size of 35 mm film. It has a format of 1.33:1.

Active filter A sound system which allows one section of the frequency range to be raised or lowered in volume.

Acoustic The environment that surrounds and affects any given sound, particularly when making a recording.

Acutance The sharpness of the boundary between dark and light areas of the image produced on the film.

Additive principle Creation of other colors of light within the spectrum by combining the primary colors – red, blue and green.

Aerial image The image formed in space by some viewfinders. A cross helps the eye to focus on the plane where the image should appear.

AGC Automatic gain control.

A-lens Anamorphic lens.

"A" mount One form of bayonet-fitting mount for lenses.

Amplifier Electrical circuit which increases the power of a signal without affecting its quality.

Anamorphic lens Cylindrical lens which compresses a wide horizontal angle-of-view into the standard frame. A similar lens on the projector re-forms the image onto a wide screen.

Angle of reflectivity The widest angle from which a bright image can be seen on a projection screen.

Angle-of-view A measure of the proportion of the subject and its surroundings which can be included in the image. This depends on both the focal length of the lens and the gauge of the film: a shorter focal length or wider film gives a greater angle-of-view.

Aperture Opening which controls the amount of light transmitted by a lens. Its size can be varied to control the amount of light passing into the camera.

Aperture plate Metal plate in the camera or projector which has a rectangular hole through which the film is exposed or projected. It governs the format of the film.

ASA American Standards Association. This denotes a numerical system which expresses the sensitivity to light of each type of filmstock. The higher the ASA number, the "faster" (more sensitive) the film.

Aspect ratio The ratio of width to height of the film frame or projected image.

Assembly First stage in editing in which the shots are arranged in the basic sequence decided by the editor.

Autofocus Automatic focusing system.

Automatic gain control Facility on most sound recorders which automatically maintains a steady level of sound input.

"A" wind Single perf 16 mm film in which, when the emulsion faces inwards and the film unwinds clockwise, the perforations face towards you.

B

Background light Artificial light used to give a lighter background behind the principal subject.

Backlaying Editing technique in which the end rather than the start of a shot is synchronized with a particular moment on an independently recorded soundtrack.

Back light Light placed behind and slightly to one side of the principal subject in order to produce highlights which "lift" the figure from its background.

Back projection Method of projecting a photographic image onto a translucent screen so that it is viewed from the side opposite to the projector. This is especially useful for effects such as faking a moving background.

Balance stripe Stripe of magnetic material laid on the film along the opposite edge from the stripe on which the soundtrack is recorded. It guarantees that the film is the same thickness at both edges so that it winds evenly onto the reel, and it can also be used to record half of a stereo sound track.

Balancing Adjusting the relative volume of the different components of the soundtrack to give a balanced composition to each part of the film.

Barndoors Metal screens fitted in front of a lamp. They can be opened or closed to give selected areas of the subject extra illumination.

Barney Foam rubber soundproofing fitted over the camera body to minimize the noise of the motor.

Base The fabric of film, on top of which the emulsion is laid. It takes the form of a thin flexible strip of cellulose acetate or polyester, and, except for supporting the emulsion, plays no part in forming the image.

Beaded screen Projection screen which has a white fabric surface embedded with a multitude of tiny glass spheres.

Beamsplitter A split glass block which diverts a portion of light to either a viewfinder or a light meter while allowing the remainder to pass onto the film.

Behind the lens (BTL) Any viewfinder or metering system which views through the taking lens itself. cf. "through the lens" (TTL).

Bellows Folding sleeve inserted between the lens and the body of the camera to lengthen the distance between the lens and the film plane, usually used for close-up filming.

Benchwork Filming on an animation stand or with a rostrum camera.

Beveled-edge splicer Cement splicer which pares the ends of the pieces of film at an angle so that they can overlap without an increase in thickness at the join.

Bleep tone A device whereby, as the camera starts, one frame of film is flashed and a bleep is placed on the sound track. No slate is then needed.

Blimp Heavy metal case which fits around the camera to absorb the noise produced by the motor.

Blue Lamp filter used to bring artificial light to the color temperature of daylight. May be gelatin or dichroic glass.

Boom Pole used to suspend a microphone over the sound source but out of sight of the camera.

Bounced light Light which is not cast directly on the subject but reflected off a white surface such as a wall or ceiling.

Brute High intensity 225-amp carbon arc lamp.

BTL Behind the lens metering.

Buffer shot Shot inserted between two others to disguise a break in continuity, or, occasionally, a shot which itself begins or ends in such a way as to disguise a jump-cut.

"B" wind The most common form of single perf 16 mm film in which the sprocket holes face away from you when the film is wound clockwise; the emulsion faces inwards.

C

Cable release Remote control mechanism for operating the camera shutter.

Camera original The film itself, whether negative or positive, on which the original exposure was made.

Cardioid microphone Microphone which is more responsive to sound sources which are in front of it than to those behind or to the side. The pattern of response is heart-shaped.

Cartridge Container in which film or tape is packaged, so that the camera or recording system is simpler to load and operate. Film cartridges contain feed and take-up reels which engage with the camera mechanism, and carry notches which lock into the automatic exposure system to make the correct setting for the appropriate film speed.

Cassette Container for film or magnetic tape similar to a cartridge in function. Some cassettes for projectors contain a loop of film which can be displayed continuously.

CdS Cadmium di-Sulfide, a compound used in light-sensitive cells. The electrical resistance varies in inverse proportion to the light received.

Cel Transparent sheet of cellulose acetate used for animation drawings.

Cement splice Join between two lengths of film in which their ends are overlapped and welded together by a liquid cement.

Central microprism A focusing system which produces a shimmering image in the center of the viewfinder. When the image clears, the subject is in focus.

Center-weighted metering Through-the-lens metering system which reads the amount of light received by the whole frame but is biased towards the central portion.

Changing bag Light-tight black fabric bag used for handling film without risk of inadvertent exposure to light.

Checkerboard rolling A version of A and B rolling.

Chinagraph Grease pencil which can be used for marking the base (shiny) side of film or fullcoat.

Cinema Scope The trade name of a widescreen process used by 20th-Century Fox having a ratio of 2.35:1.

Clapper board Hinged wooden board which is clapped together in camera at the start of each shot. It carries a visual identification of the shot and establishes a common reference point so that sound and vision can be coordinated for editing.

Claw Operated by the camera or projector motor in time with the shutter, the claw moves the film into position and holds it absolutely still in the gate while the shutter opens.

Close-up Shot which concentrates on one detail such as a face.

C mount Screw-in mount for lenses.

Color compensation, see color correction.

Color conversion Use of a filter over the lens which converts the color temperature of the existing light and allows daylight film to be used in artificial light or tungsten film in daylight.

Color correction Use of a lens filter which makes up for slight differences between the color temperature of the light source and that for which the film is balanced.

Color temperature A scale in degrees Kelvin (°K) which measures the color balance of light. Artificial lighting, for example, contains less blue than daylight and has a lower color temperature.

Complementary colors The colors which combine with each of the primaries to produce white light. They are cyan, magenta and yellow, for red, green and blue respectively.

Compressor Recording device used to narrow the range of volume of sound without producing noticeable distortion.

Condenser Arrangement of lenses which focuses light into a parallel beam.

Conforming Process of matching an original film to an edited workprint. The original is cut shot by shot and spliced up so that it is identical with the final edition of the workprint or cutting-copy.

Contact printing The most common method of producing a copy of a film. The original and the copying film are placed with their emulsion sides together and run past a slit of light which exposes the copy through the original.

Continuity Correspondence in details such as props, costume, lighting, sound level and direction of movement across the screen between successive shots of the same piece of action.

Contrast The range of brightness from highlight to shadow in a given subject or image.

Contrast gradient The extent to which a film reproduces the range of brightness in the subject. A film with a high contrast gradient exaggerates shadows and highlights. The contrast gradient is expressed as a Gamma.

Contre-jour Shooting into the light.

Cookie, see Cukaloris.

Cooling filter Filter which reduces the proportion of red in the light entering the camera.

Crane shot Shot during which the camera is raised or lowered vertically.

Crystal sync Sophisticated system based on two vibrating piezo-electric crystals, one in the camera and one in the sound recorder, which are used to keep sound and vision perfectly synchronized without a connecting cable.

Cue sheet List referred to when mixing the master sound track. It is drawn up by viewing the final edited version of the film and noting the footages at which each new sound should be introduced.

Cukaloris Studio accessory fitted on the front of a lamp and used to project mottled shadows onto a background.

Cut Transition from one shot to another which results from splicing the two together.

Cutaway Shot of something not covered by the master shot, but in some way relevant to the main action.

Cutting copy, see Workprint.

Cutting height Level at which the human figure is conventionally cut by the frame without giving a displeasing composition.

Cycle In animation, a phase of action which is repeated.

D

Dailies, see Rushes.

Day-for-night Technique of under-exposing film shot in daylight to give an impression of night time.

Daylight film Film which is balanced to give an accurate rendition of colors as they appear when seen in natural light.

Dead acoustic Environment with very low reverberations, in which sound is absorbed and "deadened" by surfaces such as carpets.

Depth of field The range of distances within which the subject is in acceptably sharp focus. It is increased by tightening the aperture or by shortening the focal length of the lens.

Diagram The device in the lens which allows the aperture to be varied.

Dichroic glass filter Filter used to raise the color temperature of a lamp to that of daylight.

Dichroic rangefinder A device which produces different colored overlapping images in the viewfinder. When the images coincide, the subject is in focus.

Diffraction lens Special effect lens which produces rainbow-colored highlights.

Diffusion filter Filter placed over the lens to give a soft-focus effect.

Digital counter Accessory-on most sound recorders which "clocks up" the length of tape that has been played. If it is always set to zero at the start of a tape, the numbers can be used as reference points for the different sounds that have been recorded. They are also found on many sound projectors.

Digital sync System used to keep sound and vision perfectly synchronized. A signal is sent from the camera to the sound recorder each time one frame is exposed. This is recorded alongside the sound track. The signal can subsequently be used to synchronize a tape or fullcoat recorder to the film.

DIN Deutsche Industrie Norm. The German system of rating a film's sensitivity to light, sometimes used in place of ASA.

Diopter Unit of measurement for the light-bending power of lenses. The diopter value of a lens, multiplied by its focal length in meters, equals one.

Diopter lens Magnifying lens used in close-up photography. It is placed in front of the taking lens and the power is rated in diopters.

Direct metering System in which the intensity of the light is measured by a light-sensitive cell placed alongside the lens.

Direct viewfinder System in which the camera operator views the subject not through the lens but from a position parallel to it.

Displacement recorder Device used in editing single system sound films. It transfers the recorded sound 18 frames backwards on the magnetic stripe so that it is brought exactly level with the corresponding picture. After editing, the standard 18-frame separation is restored so that sound and picture will be synchronized when projected.

Dissolve Double-exposure effect in which one image slowly appears as another fades out.

Dolby Noise-reduction system incorporated in many tape recorders to reduce the hiss inherent in the tape itself. Dolby recordings and recorders must be used in conjunction.

Dolly A wheeled platform on which the camera can be mounted for tracking shots.

Dope sheet Shooting script, for animation.

Double action A cut in which part of an action is repeated from another angle.

Double band projector Projector which can play a separate fullcoat magnetic sound track in parallel with the film. Also known as *sepmag.*

Double 8 Standard 8 mm film.

Double exposure Effect created by allowing light to pass onto the film on two separate occasions so that two images are superimposed.

Double-roll cutting Cutting room technique in which the original film is split onto two separate rolls for printmaking. This leads to a final print on which the original splices are not visible.

Double super 8 This film is 16 mm wide, and each half of the strip is perforated as for Super 8. After exposure – once in each direction – and development, the film is split down the middle in the same way as Standard 8 mm to produce two Super 8 rolls of film.

Double system Arrangement using a camera and a tape recorder to record the sound and picture separately. Some form of pulse is needed on the tape to keep the two synchronized.

Doubling-up Using a single drawing for more than one frame in animation.

Dropout Momentary losses of the sound in a recording caused by dust or imperfections in the tape.

Dubbing Combining several sound tracks, whether from tape or fullcoat, onto one final sound track, which may be on stripe, fullcoat, or tape.

Dual gauge projector Projector which can take super 8 or standard 8 film.

Duo-play Sound system in which two tracks may be recorded separately and "mixed" as they are played together during playback. This makes use of the balance stripe for the second track.

E

Echo chamber System for increasing the reverberative resonance of recorded sound. It may be mechanical or electronic.

Edge numbers Latent numbers printed along the edge of all filmstocks larger than super 8 during manufacture. They are revealed during processing and can then be used to identify each frame on the copies as well as the master film.

Editing Process in which the raw material of the film as originally shot is cut and rearranged to create a coherent and satisfying whole.

85 filter An orange color conversion filter which reduces daylight to the color temperature of tungsten lighting. It is a built-in feature of super 8 cameras, since most films in that format are balanced for tungsten light.

Emulsion The mixture of light-sensitive silver salts which is laid in a thin layer on a polyester or acetate base to form a film. It is the emulsion which records the image.

Equalization Process of filtering recorded sound in order to produce an improved balance between the range of frequencies.

Establishing shot Shot used to introduce a new location or time span. It is frequently a wide-angle.

Exposure The process of exposing film to light. The degree of exposure is a product of the time for which each frame is exposed and the aperture setting of the lens, but since in movie photography the time is not usually varied, the aperture stop alone is generally used to indicate the exposure.

Exposure index (E1) Measure of a film's speed or sensitivity to light, given in ASA or DIN units.

Exposure lock Device which overrides automatic metering by holding the aperture at a selected stop.

Extension tube Rigid metal tube inserted between the lens and the body of the camera in order to lengthen the distance from lens to film. It is used for close-up filming.

Eye light Lamp arranged to produce an attractive glitter in the subject's eyes.

Eyeline The direction in which a subject is looking relative to the camera. It involves consideration not only of left-to-right orientation but also of height.

F

Fade In-camera or laboratory effect in which the image slowly appears or disappears into darkness.

Feed spool Revolving spool from which the film is unwound as it is carried through the camera or projector.

Filler A light used to relieve the shadows cast by the principal light source.

Filming to Playback Procedure whereby a pre-recorded sound track is played back at a fixed speed and interlocked with the camera, while a performance is mimed. It is often used in musicals so that one long sound track can be split into many shots.

Film plane The point behind the lens at which the film is placed. This plane coincides with the plane at which the rays of light are brought into sharp focus.

Filter Disk of colored glass or gelatin which fits over the lens. It is used to cut down particular wavelengths in the light entering the camera or to create special effects.

Filter factor An indication of the amount of light that a filter absorbs, given in terms of the adjustment that must be made to the aperture in compensation.

Fine cut Final stage of editing in which the exact frame which starts and finishes each shot in the sequence is selected.

Fisheye lens Extreme wide-angle lens, giving a circular image.

Flare Light deflected from any bright highlight into a darker area of the frame. It may be caused by mechanical or optical defects, but usually it is generated by the sun shining onto the front element of the lens.

Flat process Method of producing a widescreen image by simply masking off the top and bottom of the projector aperture.

Flickers The visual sensation produced by rapidly alternating periods of light and dark which are not fast enough to allow the phenomenon of persistence of vision to create an impression of continuous illumination.

Flood Full diffusion. Also, a lamp with a parabolic reflector. This gives a broad parallel beam of light which is used for overall illumination. "Full flood" is the term used when a variable lamp is fully diffused.

Flutter A fault in the recorded sound producing a gurgling effect on speech, usually caused by unsteadiness in the sound recorder or reproducer.

f number Number which indicates the relative aperture of a lens at different diaphragm settings. It is calculated by dividing the focal lengths of the lens by the effective diameter of the diaphragm. As the aperture narrows, reducing the amount of light reaching the film, the f number increases.

Focal length The distance between the lens and the film plane when a very distant object is brought into focus. Different lenses are usually described by their focal lengths; a greater focal length will give a larger image of the same object.

Focusing Altering the distance between the lens and the film until a sharp image is obtained.

Focusing screen Viewfinder screen on which the image can be seen as the subject is brought into focus.

Fog filter Special effect filter which diffuses the image while retaining sharpness.

Fogging A fault caused by exposure of the film to light causing an unwanted detectable density in the image.

Following focus The technique of keeping a moving subject constantly in focus.

Forced development Laboratory technique which increases the effective film speed and produces a correctly exposed image from an under-exposed film. Best used on reversal film. ·

fps Frames per second. The speed at which the film moves through the camera or projector.

Frame The rectangular area of the film which is exposed each time the shutter opens. Its dimensions are determined by the shape and size of the camera aperture.

Frame bar Narrow strip of unexposed film between successive frames.

Frame-rate The speed at which the film is moved through the camera gate, given in fps (the number of frames exposed in each second).

Freeze-frame An effect in which the action is arrested. This may be produced by a projector facility or as an optical process during printing, where the same image is repeated for several frames.

French flag Opaque panel which is used to deflect direct light from the camera lens or to shade part of the action.

Frequency A measure applied to wave-motion, in units of cycles per seconds (Hertz). In sound, this indicates pitch (a low note has a low frequency).

Frequency response The ability of a recording system to record or reproduce the full range of sound frequencies.

Fresnel lens A stepped-surface condenser lens which, though thin and light, performs the same function as a thicker normal lens when attached to lights.

Front projection The usual method of projection, in which the image is reflected by a screen and viewed from the same side as the projector.

Fullcoat Perforated magnetic oxide film onto which the sound track may be recorded. The sprocket holes have the same pitch as those of the camera film and provide for frame-by-frame synchronization with the picture.

Full frame The traditional shape of picture in which the ratio of width to height is 1.33:1. It was originally devised by Edison and George Eastman for 35 mm silent movies.

G

Gaffer tape Very strong thick, wide adhesive tape used in rigging lighting equipment.

Gamma Contrast gradient.

Gang In a synchronizer, the sprocket wheel which carries each length of film.

Gate The part of the camera or projector in which each frame of the film is held while being exposed or projected.

Gauge Width of the film. For movie films, this is usually 8, 16 or 35 mm.

Gel Short for gelatin, the medium used on photographic materials as a means of suspending light sensitive halides.

Glass Shot Scene in which part of the set is created by a picture carried on a sheet of glass. The glass is placed between the camera and the rest of the set.

Grading Printing technique in which the exposure and color filtration of the copy is adjusted for each shot to compensate for defects in the original film. The operation is controled either electronically or by means of a punched tape.

Grain The "texture" of the image caused by the silver particles which constitute the emulsion of a film. Fast film is more grainy than slow film, and therefore the projected image will be less smooth, with poorer resolution of fine detail.

Ground glass This can be used for all or part of the viewfinder screen, giving a hazy image when the subject is out of focus.

Guide track Sound track recorded while filming to playback. It is used to match the mimed action to the master track.

Gun mike, see Shotgun microphone.

H

Halide Chemical term for a compound of any metal with fluorine, chlorine, bromine or iodine. The silver halides are light-sensitive and are used in the emulsion of all types of film.

Heads The recording head of a tape recorder converts the electrical impulses from the microphone into a varying magnetic field. This leaves a record on the tape by rearranging the metal oxide particles which coat the tape. When the tape is played, the playback head responds to the pattern on the tape and sends an electrical impulse via the amplifier to the loudspeakers. The erase head removes any previous recording on the tape.

Hide Construction used to camouflage the camera operator while filming wildlife.

High angle shot Shot from a camera placed above the subject and pointing down.

High-gain screen Rigid projection screen which has a concave aluminum surface. It is limited in size but produces an extremely bright image.

High key Lighting in which the overall level is bright. This kind of Hollywood "look" is also conventionally associated with glamorous backlighting.

Housing Watertight container in which the camera is placed for underwater filming.

Hyperfocal distance The distance between the camera and the nearest point of the subject which is sharp, when the lens is focused on infinity at any given aperture.

I

Impedance The total resistance of an electrical system, measured in Ohms. (Ω). Components such as microphones, tape-recorders and speakers must be matched in impedance to operate correctly together.

In-between In animated movement, this is a frame which makes the transition between successive key positions.

Infrared Rays that occur beyond the red end of the electro-magnetic spectrum and which are invisible to the human eye.

Incident meter Instrument for measuring the amount of light falling onto the subject.

In phase If stereo recordings are to be correctly reproduced, the two loudspeakers must be "in phase". In other words, each positive terminal on the speaker must be connected to a positive output on the amplifier.

In-point Frame selected during editing to be the beginning of a shot.

Insert Shot of a part of the scene covered by the master shot, sometimes taken from a different camera angle.

Integral tripack Color film composed of three layers of emulsion, each sensitive to a different primary color of light.

Internegative Negative film used in some printing processes. It is made as a negative copy of the master, and then used for the production of all further copies.

Interpositive Positive film used in a similar way to an internegative in some intermediate copying techniques.

Intervalometer Timer mechanism which causes single frames to be exposed at pre-set intervals.

Inverse square law This law of physics states that the intensity of light is inversely proportional to the square of the distance from its source. This means that at twice the distance from the source, the amount of light falling on an object will be quartered, while at three times the distance, only one ninth as much light will be received.

Ips Inches per second. The speed at which magnetic tape or film runs past a sound head.

Iris A special fade-in or fade-out effect in which the transition from one scene to another is achieved by an enlarging or diminishing oval.

J

Jump cut Cut in which a portion of the action is omitted, often by removing a section from a shot and rejoining the two remaining pieces. This may cause a jarring break in continuity, but can also be used as a technique for compressing time.

K

Kelvin Scale of basic temperature units used to describe color temperatures of light sources which are degrees centigrade measured from absolute zero or $-273°C$.

Keylight Main source of light for an interior shot.

Key number Another term for edge number.

Key position One of a series of basic positions into which a movement is broken down for animation.

L

Lap dissolve A special visual effect in which a second image gradually replaces the first image by increasing in amplitude or brightness.

Lavalier A term used for a microphone worn hung around the neck.

Leader Length of plain film or tape attached to the beginning of a reel of film.

L.E.D. Light emitting diode used in viewfinder.

Lens One or more pieces of precisely curved glass arranged in a tube to direct light rays from the subject into the camera. The rays are bent by the lens so that they converge on the film, forming a focused, inverted image.

Lenticular screen Projection screen which has a patterned cloth surface, sometimes coated with metallic paint.

Lighting ratio Ratio of the power of the keylight to that of the filler light.

Light meter Instrument which measures the amount of light emitted by the subject. The meter is calibrated to give the appropriate aperture for a given film speed and exposure time or frame-rate.

Line An imaginary line used as a reference for positioning the camera when taking different shots of the same scene. It may be the subject's eyeline or direction of movement or some other line of interest. Filming from the same side of the line preserves continuity.

Lip Sync The precise synchronization of lip movements and speech sounds.

Liquid gate printing An optical method of producing a copy of a film, in which a fluid flows continuously over the surface of the original. This helps to minimize scratches.

Live acoustic A resonant recording environment.

Locking-off A special effect technique whereby the camera is locked in position half way through a shot. After a period of time, the camera is restarted, for a trick effect.

Logging The procedure of listing the edge or rubber numbers of the film against the corresponding shots on the shot list.

Long shot Shot taken from a distance to include the overall scene.

Loop sensor A device in the camera which senses the size of the loop of film and adapts accordingly.

Looping A dubbing process which uses a continuous loop of magnetic film either as an effects track or for post synchronization.

Low angle shot Shot taken from a camera placed close to the ground and pointing upwards.

Low key Low-level, but possibly high contrast lighting which emphasizes dark tones and shadows, creating a dramatic or sinister atmosphere.

M

Macrophotography The technique of filming in extreme close-up to give a highly magnified image.

Magnetic film Magnetic fullcoat film, also known as "mag".

Magnetic sound The most common method of sound recording, in which magnetic variations are made on a tape or film coated with a magnetic substance. The recording head produces these variations by converting the electrical signal from the microphone into a fluctuating magnetic field. The playback head reverses the process: it monitors the tape signal and feeds the information to the amplifier.

Master shot Main shot of a scene, filmed continuously from one camera. Other shots of the scene may be cut in to the master shot during editing.

Matte An opaque piece of metal, card, or film which masks off part of the image in either a camera or printer.

Matte box Accessory which fits in front of the camera to provide both a sun-shade and a holder for filters and mattes.

Matte screen Projection screen, such as a painted board, which has a plain white surface.

Microphone Device which converts sound airwaves into mechanical, then electrical energy.

Mid shot Shot of part of a scene, from a sufficient distance to include most of the body of an actor or a group of people.

Mini-brute Set of small quartz lamps used together to provide powerful illumination.

Mirror shutter A variety of viewfinder system in which light is intermittently diverted to the eyepiece by a mirror in the shutter mechanism.

Mixer Part of a sound system which allows the signals from different inputs to be balanced in volume.

Montage A rapidly cut film sequence which produces a generalized visual effect even though it may be made up of dissolves or superimpositions.

MOS "Mit-out sound", i.e. silent, or mute shooting.

Movielight Small quartz light mounted on top of the camera.

Multi-screen A multiple-exposure technique in which a composite image is built up by masking off different parts of the frame each time the film is wound back and re-shot. It is also used to describe multi-projector displays.

Multi-track Professional recording system in which eight or even sixteen separate sound tracks may be recorded simultaneously. They are then mixed to produce a balance between the components of the sound or to add special effects.

N

Negative film Film which is processed to give an image in which the colors of the subject are replaced by their complementary colors. In the case of black and white film, dark and light are interchanged. To be viewed in the original tones, a positive print must be made from the negative.

Neutral density filter Gray filter which reduces the amount of light entering the camera without altering its color balance. Graduated neutral density filters have gray upper halves only, so that the sky may be darkened.

N.G. take Shot rejected during editing.

Ninelight Set of small quartz lights which provides powerful studio illumination.

Nodal point Theoretical optical center of a lens

Omnidirectional microphone Microphone which responds equally to sound received from all directions.

One-light print A copy of a film made at a single exposure.

Optical printing A sophisticated method of producing a copy of a film by photographing the original through a series of lenses. It allows a change in gauge to be made, and many special effects can be added.

Out of phase The condition in which two loudspeakers are wrongly connected to the amplifier so that their cones vibrate in opposite polarity. The stereo effect will be lost if the speakers are "out of phase" in this way.

Out-point Frame selected during editing to end a particular shot.

Outtake Shot rejected during editing.

Overall metering Built-in camera system which measures the light received by the whole frame area.

Overcrank To shoot the film at a speed faster than that at which it will be projected. This gives a slow-motion effect but reduces the exposure of each frame.

Over-exposure Allowing too much light onto each frame, giving a pale, washed-out effect.

Overrun To use a bulb at a power higher than its nominal wattage.

Pan To rotate the camera so that the field of view sweeps round in a horizontal panorama.

Pan head Mount which supports the camera on the tripod while allowing it to be panned and tilted smoothly.

PAR Quartz light with a built-in parabolic aluminized reflector.

Parabolic reflector Lamp fitting which produces a broad, parallel, directed beam.

Parallax Apparent change in position of an object when viewed from different points. With a direct viewfinder camera, this causes a discrepancy between the image

seen and that actually formed by the lens.

Parallel action Sequence intercut with the master shot. It is usually a simultaneous and related scene which does not occur in the same place as the main action. It may also be a flashback or an imagined future event.

Passive filter Part of a sound system which removes some of the low or high frequencies in a signal.

PC Proctor contact. A flash synchronizer switch on a camera.

Perf Perforation. "Double perf" film has sprocket holes down both edges, while "single perf" has them only on one side and leaves space down the other side for the sound track.

Personal mike A chest microphone worn by a speaker which leaves the hands free.

Perspective "Sense of depth" in a two-dimensional image created by the relative size, position and shape of the objects that appear.

Phase In animation, the section of action from one key position to the next.

Photoflood Lightbulb with standard screw fitting but very high power output and color temperature of either 3,200°K or 3,400°K.

Phototape cassette Cartridge film used in the instant movie Polavision system.

Pic-sync Device used in double system film editing which combines a viewer and synchronizer.

Pilot tone System which keeps sound and vision perfectly synchronized. A steady signal sent from the camera to the tape recorder is recorded alongside the sound track. The tone acts as a reference for subsequent transfer from tape to magnetic fullcoat.

Pilot track Verbal cues recorded on one track of a tape while watching the final edit of the film. This facilitates the recording on the other tracks of sounds chosen to accompany the images.

Pitch The distance between one sprocket hole and the next.

Platen Sheet of glass used in animation to hold down the layers of cels.

Polarizing filter Filter which cuts down glare and reflected light of a given polarity. It also reduces haze and darkens blue skies at 90° to the sun. The filter should be rotated and the effect gauged through the lens.

Polavision Instant movie system produced by Polaroid.

Post synchronization A process by which sound is synchronized to a pre-recorded picture.

Power zoom A zoom lens in which the change of focal length is motor-driven.

Pressure plate Metal plate which presses the film in place against the gate. In super 8 this is built into the plastic cassette.

Primary colors The three colors which can be combined additively to produce any other color on projection. For light (rather than pigments), these are blue, green and red.

Prime lens Lens with a fixed focal length.

Prism lens Special effect lens which gives a multiple image.

Prism shutter Variety of mirror shutter which uses a prism to deflect light to the viewfinder between exposures.

Proctor contact (PC) switch Switch which opens and closes once for every frame that passes through the camera gate. It is connected to a socket into which a flash unit or tape recorder may be plugged.

Pulling focus Changing focus to follow a moving subject.

Push processing Forced development.

Radio microphone Small portable film transmitter and receiver linked to a microphone.

Rangefinder An optical system which measures the distance from the camera to the subject.

Raw stock The original unexposed camera film before processing, editing or printing.

Reaction shot Shot of subjects' response to some part of the action, often filmed as a cutaway after the master shot.

Reflected light meter Device which uses a light-sensitive cell to measure the amount of light reflected by the subject.

Reflector Lamp fitting used to control and direct the light, or reflective sheet used to balance light levels in day-light shooting.

Reflector flood Photoflood with a silver coating on the inside of the bulb to form a built-in reflector.

Reflex viewfinder A system which diverts some of the light passing through the lens to the eyepiece, so that the image is identical to that received by the film, and can be viewed as it is brought into focus.

Refraction The bending of a ray of light at the point where it passes obliquely from one transparent medium to another.

Registration Degree of accuracy in the positioning of one frame after another as the film is run through the camera. The smallest variation will show as a jump or blur when the film is projected.

Registration pegbar Device which keeps cels accurately positioned for animated films.

Registration pin This pin, in some cameras, holds the film in place as each frame is exposed.

Release print Copy print of a film, which will be used for showing to an audience so that the original may be kept in safety.

Relief The degree to which texture is brought out in the form of shadows and high-lights. Hard, directional lighting produces high relief.

Resolution The degree to which fine detail in the image can be distinguished.

Resolving The process of transferring the sound track from tape or striped film to fullcoat magnetic film so that it matches frame-for-frame with the picture.

Resolving power The ability of a film to record fine detail. It is measured in terms of the number of vertical lines that can be recorded distinctly in 1 mm of film.

Reverb Short for reverberation (echo).

Reverberation plate Device which increases to a variable degree the reverberation of recorded sound.

Reversal film Film which produces a positive image after processing. In other words, it gives an image in which the colors coincide with those of the subject. It can be viewed directly, without making a print.

Reverse cut Editing cut in which the change of camera angle makes the subject appear to be moving in opposite directions at the end of the first shot and the beginning of the second.

Rewind arm Piece of editing equipment on which a reel of film may be mounted and rotated rapidly by hand or electric motor. It is usually geared.

Rim-lighting Rear-lighting which highlights the outlines of objects.

Rock-and-roll dubbing Method of sound mixing in which the separate reels of fullcoat magnetic film sound track can be moved forwards or back while locked in sync. Dubbing can be discontinuous.

Rostrum camera Camera mounted on adjustable columns so that it can be moved up and down over a horizontal board on which animation cels or titles are placed. The zoom is commonly interlocked with the column control.

Rough cut Stage in editing after the assembly in which the shots are more carefully arranged to establish the structure of the film.

Rubber numbering Laboratory process of printing a sequence of numbers along the edge of a film and its copies so that corresponding frames can be identified. Rubber numbers are added after the film has been processed but before editing begins.

Rumble or "hum" filter Sound filter which cuts out low frequencies.

Rushes Processed, unedited reels of film.

S

Safety film A film containing a plastic film base which is of low inflammability.

Saturated color Pure color which contains no ingredient of black or white.

Scene Part of a film consisting of an unbroken piece of action occurring in one location at one time.

Scenic projection Method of creating a set by projecting a filmed or photographed image behind the actors.

Scratch filter Sound filter which cuts out high frequencies.

Scrim Translucent wire screen placed in front of a lamp to cut down its brightness.

Segway A lap dissolve in sound.

Separation light Back light.

Sepmag projector Double band projector.

Set Arrangement of scenery, whether real or simulated, within which the filmed action takes place.

Shooting schedule Timetable prepared from the filmscript in which the scenes are arranged in appropriate groups for shooting, with details of location, actors and props required, and so on.

Shooting script Detailed list of shots in the order that they are to be filmed.

Shooting speed Frame-rate.

Shot Part of a film recorded in one continuous run of the camera.

Shotgun microphone Highly directional microphone which responds only faintly to sounds from more than 20° on either side of the direction in which it is pointed.

Shoulder pod Support for a camera, allowing it to be carried or braced against the shoulder.

Show print Release print.

Shutter The device lying between the film and the lens which controls the exposure time. Usually in the form of a rotating disk with a segment cut away, the shutter momentarily admits light to expose a single frame, then blocks it off while the film moves on to the next frame.

Single-roll cutting Cutting room technique which produces one roll of cut original to match exactly the final edited workprint.

Single system Camera which records the sound and the picture

simultaneously on film striped with magnetic iron oxide.

Single 8 Film similar to super 8, but packed in a different design of cartridge. The film has a polyester base which is stronger and thinner than the acetate used for super 8, but more difficult to splice. Single 8 films and cameras are manufactured only by Fuji. The cartridges are not coaxial.

16 mm The gauge of film used by television companies and many amateur and professional film-makers. It provides a cheaper alternative to 35mm, at the price of a reduction in picture quality.

Slash point A black and white contrast work print.

Slating Conventional procedure for identifying the start of a shot and establishing sound synchronization by using a clapper board.

Snoot Open-ended cone which fits in front of a lamp to give a narrow circle of light.

Softlight reflector Reflector fitting which includes a shield in front of the bulb so that a diffuse light is produced.

Solarization Reversal or partial reversal of the image by extreme over-exposure.

Sound-on-Sound superimposition (S.O.S.) Facility in some tape recorders and sound projectors for recording one sound on top of another while partially erasing the original. Also known as a "trick" facility.

Spacing Lengths of silent blank film used in double system editing to fill in sections of the sound track where there is no sync sound to match to the picture.

Speed (film) Measure of the sensitivity to light of the film, given in DIN or ASA units. A "fast" film reacts more rapidly and to less light than a "slow" film.

Speed (lens) The f number of the lens aperture when it is fully open. A "fast" lens is suitable for shooting in low-level lighting.

Spider Device which holds the legs of a tripod in fixed relative positions on a slippery floor.

Splice To join two separate lengths of film by taping or cementing their ends together.

Split-field diopter lens A close-up lens which has been sawn in two. The remaining half therefore operates only over half of the frame, usually the lower.

Split-image rangefinder This produces a split image of the subject in the viewfinder. When the two halves are lined up without a visible join, the subject is in focus.

Split-screen Technique in which the two halves of the frame are separately exposed, giving a split, composite picture when screened.

Spot meter This exposure meter gives an extremely accurate measurement of the light reflected by a very small area of the subject.

Spotlight Lamp designed to give a very powerful and narrow beam of hard light.

Spreader Device which holds tripod legs in fixed relative positions. Also known as a "Spider".

Sprocket Rotating toothed wheel which transports the film through the camera or projector. The teeth lock into holes perforated along the edge of the film.

Spun Short for spun fiber glass sheeting used to diffuse lighting.

Squawk box Unit combining a speaker or headphones and an amplifier. It is used for monitoring the sound track during editing of stripe or fullcoat magnetic film.

Squeeze lens, see Anamorphic lens.

Standard 8 16 mm film which is run twice through the camera in opposite directions, each time exposing half its width. When it is processed, the film is split down the middle and joined end to end to give a length of film 8 mm wide with sprocket holes down one side only.

Starburst lens Special effect lens which dramatizes highlights by creating star-shaped flares of light.

Stop Any of the range of fixed aperture settings. Opening the aperture by one stop allows twice the amount of light into the camera as the previous stop. The stops are in a logarithmic progression. Thus, the standard stops correspond to f numbers of 1.4, 2, 2.8, 4, 5.6, 8, 11, 16, 22 and so on.

Stop pull Technique of altering the aperture by hand during the course of a shot.

Storyboard An ordered collection of sketches representing consecutive shots as they are visualized by the filmmaker while planning the production.

Striping Process in which a magnetic oxide stripe is applied to the edge of the film, so that a sound track may be recorded later. The stripe may be in the form of either a thin paste or a laminated strip.

Strobing A visual interference between the frame-rate and any regular patterned object in motion. For instance, a fast pan across railings may appear jerky; or a spoked wheel may appear to run backwards.

Subjective track Tracking shot in which the camera moves in place of a character in the film and reveals what is supposed to be the scene through their eyes.

Subtractive principle The basis of the method of forming colored

light by using filters to remove specific components of white light, which is in fact a mixture of all colors.

Sungun Hand-held battery light.

Superimposition Effect in which film is exposed twice so that one image appears on top of another.

Super 8 8 mm wide film packaged in cartridges which are very easy to load into the camera. It has smaller sprocket holes than standard 8, giving a larger frame and hence a higher quality image when projected. Super 8 sound cartridges carry film which is coated with a thin band of magnetic iron oxide onto which the sound track is recorded.

Super 16 Film format which gives a larger than standard frame on 16 mm single perf film, by using the space normally reserved for a sound track.

Sync Synchronization, i.e. accurate correspondence between sound track and vision.

Sync cable Lead connecting camera and tape recorder. It carries the sync pulse from the camera in double system filming.

Synchronizer Device used in the cutting room for maintaining sync between various lengths of film or fullcoat. It consists of two or more sprocketed wheels mounted on a single revolving shaft so that as the films are wound, the correspondence between frames is maintained.

Sync plop One frame of sound placed at the beginning of a sound track to establish sync during the mix of multiple tracks.

Sync pulse Electrical signal sent from the camera to the tape recorder as part of a method for synchronizing sound and vision during double system filming.

T

Take-up spool Revolving core on which the reel of film is wound after passing through the camera or projector gate.

Tail trim Frames at the end of a shot which are left over after the shot has been edited into a cutting-copy.

Tape splice Join between two pieces of film in which they are butt-joined and held together by transparent adhesive tape.

Tape synchronizer Electrical or mechanical device used during editing and viewing to keep a tape recorder and projector locked together, adjusting the speed of one to match the other.

Telecine transfer The transfer of film onto video tape through a telecine chain.

Telephoto Lens with long focal length, giving a narrow angle-of-view.

Thirds rule Principle of composition which states that strong horizontal or vertical lines should cut the picture in thirds rather than in halves.

Three-shot Mid or long shot in which three people appear.

35 mm This was the gauge of the earliest movie films, but the expense of 35 mm film and equipment has restricted its use to the movie industry, where the highest quality image is required.

Through-the-lens A variety of meter in which some of the light passing through the lens is diverted to a light-sensitive cell. This measures the intensity of the light that will reach the film, and in some cameras controls the automatic adjustment of the aperture.

Tilt Pan in a vertical direction.

Time lapse Technique of exposing single frames at regular intervals so that the event filmed appears greatly speeded up when projected as normal.

Timing, see Grading.

Tracking Moving the camera horizontally across the ground while filming a shot.

Tram lines Vertical scratches which appear throughout the film caused by a faulty gate or processing operation.

Transmission stops T stops.

Traveling mattes Laboratory process for superimposing the action from one scene upon the background from another.

Treatment Written reinterpretation of a story, an idea or a theme in terms of film.

Trick control Projector facility which allows sound-on-sound superimposition.

Trims Pieces of film cut off from the head or tail of each shot during editing.

Triple shutter Circular shutter with three cut-out sections. This is used in 8 mm projectors so that each frame is shown three times. This eliminates flicker.

Tripod Adjustable three-legged stand on which the camera is held steady.

T stops A scale of aperture settings which takes into account the light lost as it passes through the various parts of the lens and thus reflects the true amount of light received by the film.

TTL Through-the-lens metering.

Tungsten Metal used for the filaments of light bulbs.

Tungsten film Film which is balanced to give an accurate rendition of colors as they appear when seen in tungsten lighting.

Turret A mount on the camera body which carries a group of interchangeable lens and which can be rotated for a rapid lens-change between shots.

Two-shot Shot in which two people appear.

Type A film Film balanced for shooting in tungsten light of a color temperature of 3,400°K.

Type B film Film balanced for shooting in tungsten lighting of a color temperature of 3,200°K.

Type G film Film suitable for shooting under mixed lighting conditions. It has reduced sensitivity to colors at both extremes of the spectrum.

U

Ultra-violet filter Filter designed to cut down ultra-violet light, which, while invisible to the human eye, produces a blue haze on film.

Undercrank To shoot the film at a speed slower than that at which it will be projected. This gives each frame a longer exposure, and gives a speeded-up effect on projection.

Under-exposure The effect of allowing too little light onto each frame, giving an excessively dark image.

Uprating Exposing and processing a film as though it had a higher speed than its nominal rating.

V

Variable shutter Shutter which allows exposure time to be altered without varying the aperture or frame-rate. This is done by varying the angle of the cutaway segment in the circular disk.

Videocassette The container in which small gauge videotape is both recorded and replayed. There are several standards.

Viewer Piece of equipment which is used for viewing the film during editing. The image is seen on a small rear-projection screen as the film is run through.

Viewfinder The optical system through which the subject is viewed by the camera operator.

Vignetting Fading of the image towards the corners of the frame. It is sometimes produced by an aberration or fault in the lens, but it can also be introduced as an optical special effect.

VU meter Instrument for monitoring sound level.

W

Warming filter Filter which reduces the proportion of blue in the light entering the camera.

Wet gate printing Optical printing method of producing a copy of a film. It is similar to liquid gate printing, but in this process the fluid covering the surface of the film evaporates rather than being siphoned off.

Whip pan Very rapid pan which completely blurs the subject and the background.

Wide-angle lens Lens with a short focal length which provides a wide angle-of-view.

Widescreen Any of a range of techniques used to produce a wider than normal screen image from a frame of standard dimensions.

Wildtrack Sound recording made at the time of filming but without a sync system linking it to the camera.

Wipe An effect in which one shot appears physically to displace another on the screen. It may be created as an optical laboratory effect or in the camera with mattes. Wipes may be vertical or horizontal.

Workprint Duplicate of the original film, used as a cutting copy for editing. Once the workprint is finalized the master original is then cut and spliced at the same points to make a perfect match.

X

XL Existing light. The term applies to cameras which can be used in poor lighting conditions. They have a fast lens and a shutter designed to give a longer than normal exposure time.

Z

Zoom-in Reducing the angle-of-view by increasing the focal length of a zoom lens during the course of a shot. The result is that the subject becomes larger in the frame.

Zooming ratio The ratio of the longest to the shortest available focal length of a zoom lens. For example, a 10 mm to 50 mm lens is said to have a zooming ratio of 5:10.

Zoom lens Lens of variable focal length. This means that an object can be held in focus while the angle-of-view and magnification of the image is varied during a shot.

Zoom-out Widening the angle-of-view by shortening the focal length of a zoom lens during the course of a shot. The result is that the subject becomes smaller in the frame.

Index

Acknowledgments

The author would like to state the obvious: this book is very much the product of a team, though the errors, such as they are, should be laid at my door alone. Thanks are gratefully offered, first, to the patient and tireless editors, designers, photographers and researchers whose names are to be found here and on p. 4. It is really they who have made this book.

I would also like to add to this heroic list Gavin Millar, whose practical and critical work in filmmaking has for many years been both a profound collaborative pleasure and something of an inspiration. I meanwhile hope that other valued colleagues will forgive me if I have singled out just one of many to whom I am indebted. The greatest pleasure of filmmaking, as of book-making, is the pleasure of collaboration.

Dorling Kindersley would like to give special thanks to Angela Murphy who undertook the daunting task of picture research for this book, to Nick Collins for his help in selecting and photographing frame enlargements for the sequences from the movies, to Vincent Oliver and Andrew de Lory for providing so many of the specially commissioned photographs, to Les Smith and Jim Robins for setting the standard of the illustrations and for working through the night on many occasions to produce them, and to Chloe Munro and Carin Vandrehle for their research.

Special thanks must also go to the following: Brian Castledine, Norman Carr, Gordon Thomson, Joel Finler, Yossi Bal, Sidney Smith, Lesley Gilbert, Sue Mennell, Verity Meldrum, Chris Petit and, for typesetting, all the staff of Filmtype Services, Scarborough.

The photographs in this book were taken by the following:
Aerofilms Ltd 180cl,cr,bl,br
Ardea 174t,c
Aspect 175;178tl,tr,cl,cr;179t,cl,cr,br
David Bruton 62btr;63tl;96cr;172tr;204t,cl,br
John Bulmer 185cbr
Amy Carroll 130cl;131tl,c,b;166ct;172br
J. Allan Cash 160bc,bl;174b
Brian Castledine 51;52c;60t;66t;91c;115;138–9;146c;
  185cl,cr;206c
David Cheshire 59br;62br;64bl;68tr;86br;91br;96cl;
  144–5;168t;169tl,bl;172tl;173tl,tr,ctl,ctr;180t;183tl;
  205c,br;244
Chusak 1;48tr;50cl;58t;59cr;91cr;96t;97tl,cl;127;164bl;
  182ctl,ctr,cbr,bl,br;183bl,br;184;185b;186b;187t,
  br;205t;249
Nick Collins 52b
Colorsport 160cbl,cbr
John Couzins 47br;58b;59bl;60b;61
Andrew de Lory 43br;44r;46r;50bl;53;59tr,cl;62t,c,bl;
  63tr,cl,bl,br;64tr,br;66cl,cr;68c,b;69;92tr;93tl,tr;96b;
  102;104ctr;108b;130 except cl;131tr,ctl,ctr;146
  except c;164ctl,ctr,cbr,br;165c,b;166br;167;168c,b;
  169tc,tr,ctl,ctr,cbr,br;172c;182tl,tr,cbl;183tr,ctl,ctr,
  cl,cr,cbl,cbr;185t;186c;187cr;188t,c;189c,t;192–3;
  224ct;243tl
Christopher Dorling 63tc;204cr,bl
The Ronald Grant Archive 17;18t,br;19t,br;22tr;23bl,br;
  27c
Chris Harvey 86t,c;162–3;224tr,btl,btr;225tr,c,btl
Peter Higgins 98
Mat Irvine "Small Space" Collection 190;191t,cr,b;195t
Carolyn Johns 136–7;170–71
Kingston-upon-Thames Museum 19br
The Kobal Collection 2–3;4;6;7;16;18bl,cr;20tr,c,br;
  23t;24ct,cb,b;25t;26;27t,b;28;29t,bl,btr;30b;31;
  95cb;104t;105ctl,ctr;156c,bl,br;157t,tr,cl,cr;164tr;
  165tl,tr
David Levin 166tr,cb
Fiona MacIntyre 179bl
Iain MacIntyre 169cbl;178b
Mansell Collection 21tl,tr,cr;25bl,br
C. S. Middleton 19bl;20bl;22c,b;24t
Ian O'Leary 108cr
Vincent Oliver 60cr;65;66br;67;70–71;72–3;74–5;76–7;
  78–9;80–81;82;83t,c;93b;94c;97bl;104br;105cbr;
  132–3;142–3;156t;161;164tl,cbl;166tl,bl;181;194t;
  196–7;206b;216–17;218;219t;224bl,br;225bl,btr,br;
  226–7;236;243tr,b
Lelio Orci 178b
Roger Perry 33cr;47tr;91t,cb;92cr,br;94t,b;95t,ct,b;
  97cr,br;134–5;188b;189b
Seaphot 176;177
Syndication International 160t,ctl,ctc,ctr,br
Malkolm Warrington 103;107;172bl;173tc,cb,bl,br

The movie sequences and frame enlargements in this book are reproduced by courtesy of the following organizations:
Artificial Eye Film Company
  10–11, 105t *The Red Desert* (Dir: Michelangelo
  Antonioni) 1964
  54–5 *Padre Padrone* (Dir: Paulo and Vittorio Taviani)
  1977
  150–51 *The Spider's Stratagem* (Dir: Bernardo
  Bertolucci) 1970
  256cb *The Red and the White* (Dir: Miklós Jancso)
  1969
Connoisseur Films
  12–13, 83b *A Bout de Souffle* (Dir: Jean-Luc Godard)
  1960
  84–5, 256b *Le Boucher* (Dir: Claude Chabrol) 1968
Contemporary Films
  29br *Shoot the Piano Player* (Dir: François Truffaut)
  1960
  201br *Heavy Traffic* (Dir: Ralph Bakshi) 1973
  222 *Mother* (Dir: V. Pudovkin) 1926
  223 *Battleship Potemkin* (Dir: Sergei Eisenstein) 1925
  256ct *Last Year at Marienbad* (Dir: Alain Resnais) 1961
EMI Elstree Studios
  87, 220 *The Servant* (Dir: Joseph Losey) 1963
  152–3, 219b *The Third Man* (Dir: Carol Reed) 1949
  154–5 *The Lady Killers* (Dir: Michael Balcon) 1955
  194b *Black Narcissus* (Dir: Michael Powell, Emeric
  Pressburger)1946
  201bl *Great* (Dir: Bob Godfrey) 1976
Gala Films
  33b, 256t *Jules et Jim* (Dir: François Truffaut) 1961
GPO Film Unit
  203r *Color Box* (Dir: Len Lye) 1935
Imperial War Museum
  27tl *Triumph of the Will* (Dir: Leni Riefenstahl) 1934
MGM
  30t *2001: A Space Odyssey* (Dir: Stanley Kubrick) 1968
Paramount Pictures
  191cl *War of the Worlds* (Dir: Byron Haskin) 1952
RKO General Pictures
  8–9, 104, 221 *Citizen Kane* (Dir: Orson Welles) 1941
Twentieth Century Fox
  14–15 *Walkabout* (Dir: Nicholas Roeg) 1972
  158–9 *The French Connection* (Dir: William Friedkin)
  1971
United Artists
  195b *Dr No* (Dir: Terence Young) 1962
  201t *Yellow Submarine* (Dir: George Dunning, Heinz
  Edelmann) 1968
Visual Programme Systems Ltd
  6b, 88–9 *Mahler* (Dir: Ken Russell) 1973
Walt Disney Productions
  200 *The Whalers* 1938

Key: t:top;c:center;b:bottom;l:left;r:right

Information, technical assistance and loan of equipment was kindly provided by:

Bell & Howell Ltd
Craven Instrument Co.
Norman Dunham of Arriflex
  Ltd
Mr Elworthy of J. J. Silber
  Ltd
Fred Haskell of Pelling and
  Cross Ltd
Nigel Hodgson of A. V.
  Distributors Ltd
Peter Maw of Bolex/Eumig
  (UK) Ltd
Mayfair Photographic
  Suppliers
Ken Oberg of Kodak Ltd
Photopia Ltd
David W. Samuelson of
  Samuelson Film Services
  Ltd
Sankyo Ltd

Illustrations and studio services by:

John Bishop
Gilchrist Studios
Hayward and Martin
Ron Pickless
Ros Pickless
Mark Richards
Jim Robins
Les Smith
Venner Artists

Photographic services by:

Negs
Paulo Colour
W. Photoprint

Typesetting by:

Filmtype Services Ltd
  (Scarborough)
Focus Typesetting
Art Repro

Lithographic reproduction by:

A. Mondadori (Verona)